Britain and the Mine, 1900–1915

Richard Dunley

Britain and the Mine, 1900–1915

Culture, Strategy and International Law

Richard Dunley
The National Archives
Kew, London, UK

ISBN 978-3-319-72819-3   ISBN 978-3-319-72820-9   (eBook)
https://doi.org/10.1007/978-3-319-72820-9

Library of Congress Control Number: 2018934854

© The Editor(s) (if applicable) and The Author(s) 2018
This work is subject to copyright. All rights are solely and exclusively licensed by the Publisher, whether the whole or part of the material is concerned, specifically the rights of translation, reprinting, reuse of illustrations, recitation, broadcasting, reproduction on microfilms or in any other physical way, and transmission or information storage and retrieval, electronic adaptation, computer software, or by similar or dissimilar methodology now known or hereafter developed.
The use of general descriptive names, registered names, trademarks, service marks, etc. in this publication does not imply, even in the absence of a specific statement, that such names are exempt from the relevant protective laws and regulations and therefore free for general use. The publisher, the authors and the editors are safe to assume that the advice and information in this book are believed to be true and accurate at the date of publication. Neither the publisher nor the authors or the editors give a warranty, express or implied, with respect to the material contained herein or for any errors or omissions that may have been made. The publisher remains neutral with regard to jurisdictional claims in published maps and institutional affiliations.

Cover credit: © ilbusca. Getty Images

Printed on acid-free paper

This Palgrave Macmillan imprint is published by the registered company Springer International Publishing AG part of Springer Nature
The registered company address is: Gewerbestrasse 11, 6330 Cham, Switzerland

To Bun and Andrea

Acknowledgements

This project has its origins in a short conversation that took place following a seminar at King's College, London in 2008. Since then it has grown out of all recognition, but at every stage this has only been possible due to the help and support of colleagues and friends. I would like to thank the Arts and Humanities Research Council for supporting my PhD research from which this book has developed.

I am indebted to the staff of the numerous archives, libraries and other institutions I have visited whilst conducting this research. Knowing the extreme pressures felt at present across this sector makes me all the more grateful for the many archivists and librarians who have gone out of their way to share their knowledge and expertise of the collections they hold. Special thanks must go to Andrew Choong and Jeremy Michell at the Brass Foundry in Woolwich, who are not only an invaluable mine of information, but also provided me with a near constant stream of mince pies no matter the time of year I visited.

I am grateful to my friends and colleagues at The National Archives for their insight and support, as I have sought to broaden out the project from my original doctoral research. Working surrounded by colleagues with such an extraordinary knowledge of the archival collections opens up many new avenues for research, and has led me to numerous discoveries I would never have made on my own. Particular thanks must go to James Cronan, Janet Dempsey, Juliette Desplat, George Hay and Laura Tompkins.

viii ACKNOWLEDGEMENTS

Throughout my time researching for and writing this book I have benefited from a supportive network of fellow researchers. The PhD and wider naval history community at King's College, London proved to be an essential group for discussing ideas, sharing experiences and bemoaning the 'struggles' of PhD life. I would particularly like to thank Andrew Breer, Stephen Cobb, Jennifer Daley, Marcus Faulkner and Catherine Scheybeler. Special mention must also go to Alan Anderson, a fellow traveller on this path. He has provided important feedback, ideas and more than occasional good humour over the course of a number of years, and I am very grateful. My PhD examiners, Matthew Seligmann and Jan Rüger, gave me extremely useful feedback, and Matthew has continued to prove a mine of information, especially on Admiralty records. I am grateful to Rear-Admiral James Goldrick and Brigadier Michael Clemmesen for their comments on the thesis, and to Palgrave's manuscript reviewers for their helpful remarks.

This book began life as a PhD project, and a special debt of gratitude is owed to Andrew Lambert, who not only was willing to take on a troublesome student with an obscure project, but has provided essential guidance and support ever since.

Finally I would like to thank my parents, and most especially Gwen, without whose support and forbearance this work would never have come to fruition.

Contents

1	Introduction	1
2	Mining in a Cultural Context	9
3	British Attitudes to Mining Before 1904	23
4	Mine Warfare in the Russo-Japanese War: The Royal Navy Perspective	45
5	The Russo-Japanese War: Outrage and Reaction	73
6	Mining and International Law: Britain and the Hague Conference	97
7	The Strategic Shift: The Origins of British Mine Warfare	131
8	Development and Institutionalisation: Offensive Mining 1906–1909	165
9	Strategic Flux and Technical Failure	193

x CONTENTS

10	The Test of Conflict	225
11	War, Law and Diplomacy	267
12	Conclusion	297
Archival Sources		305
Index		309

ABBREVIATIONS

ADNI   Assistant Director of Naval Intelligence
ADT   Assistant Director of Torpedoes
CID   Committee of Imperial Defence
COS   Chief of the Admiralty War Staff
DID   Director Intelligence Division (Admiralty War Staff)
DMO   Director of Military Operations
DNC   Director of Naval Construction
DNI   Director of Naval Intelligence
DNO   Director of Naval Ordnance
DOD   Director Operations Division (Admiralty War Staff)
EC   Electro-Contact (Mine)
EM   Electro-Mechanical (Mine)
FGDN   Arthur J. Mardar, ed., *Fear God and Dread Nought: The Correspondence of Admiral of the Fleet Lord Fisher of Kilverstone*
FRUS   *Foreign Relations of the United States*
LWOS   Low Water Ordinary Springs (Tide)
NID   Naval Intelligence Department
PP   Parliamentary Papers
RE   Royal Engineers
RMA   Royal Marine Artillery
RMLI   Royal Marine Light Infantry
SOS   Superintendent of Ordnance Stores

CHAPTER 1

Introduction

> Human conscience, gentlemen, could not tolerate the idea that a belligerent should be permitted to sow mines profusely in seas frequented by the world's merchant marines: but international law does not at present prohibit such acts, and it is to be feared that, long after the conclusion of peace, neutral vessels navigating the seas far from the scene of war will be exposed to terrible catastrophes.[1]

This statement, made on 27 June 1907 by Captain Charles Ottley to delegates at the Second Hague Peace Conference, was part of Britain's concerted effort to get the use of mines banned under international law. Ottley was a torpedo officer, who, twenty-three years previous, had invented the apparatus that allowed mines to be laid on a large scale in the open sea. Whilst serving as Director of Naval Intelligence, he developed war plans which relied upon the use of mines on a scale never previously envisaged. Yet, when in June 1907, he stood before the august gathering of diplomats and naval officers he, as far as we can tell sincerely, pressed for the weapon to be banned. In making this statement Ottley came to embody the highly contested position which the mine occupied in the outlook of the Royal Navy, and Britain more generally, in the decade before the First World War.

By the standards of the early twentieth century, the mine was not a complex piece of technology, nor was the basic concept a novel one. Yet this simple device posed a greater ideological challenge to the Royal Navy than any other item of technology. The reason for this was simple.

© The Author(s) 2018　　　　　　　　　　　　　　　　　　1
R. Dunley, *Britain and the Mine, 1900–1915,*
https://doi.org/10.1007/978-3-319-72820-9_1

The innate purpose of the weapon was mutual sea denial, the prevention of anyone from using a specific area of sea for any purpose. This stood in total contradiction to the idealised view of Britain's role as a maritime power, and the Royal Navy's self-appointed mission as guardian of the seas. Use of the seas for both commercial and military purposes was perceived to be a basic right, guaranteed under some sense of Pax Britannica. The mine represented the antithesis of this in material form. Not merely challenging Britain's right to exercise command of the sea, but denying it to all.

The problem for the Royal Navy came from the fact that the mine proved to be an extremely effective weapon in naval combat. Events in the Russo-Japanese War in particular removed any lingering doubts about the impact mines could have on war at sea. This juxtaposition of the weapon's obvious effectiveness with its objectionable intrinsic quality created a contested space in which the debates in the Royal Navy, the British government and the country at large took place. It is this space that is the focus of this study. In particular, it will examine the reactions of the British government to the mine in the separate spheres of strategy and international law, highlighting the problems and inconsistencies thrown up by the conflict between the technology and the specific national and organisational cultures which were dominant in this period.

The field of early twentieth-century naval history is an extremely active one, and within it considerable attention has been devoted to questions of technology. Despite this, the mine has barely featured in the historiography. In many respects this is surprising. The mine was one of the most important naval technologies of the First World War. It was used extensively by all sides, achieving dramatic results including the sinking of the super-dreadnought *Audacious*, and the death of Lord Kitchener. This was, however, only the tip of the iceberg. The real impact of mining came not in the sudden successes, but in the way it came to shape the very maritime environment in which the war at sea was fought. From the large mine barrages targeted at German U-boats to the swept channels routing merchant shipping around the British coasts, the mine slowly but dramatically altered the human geography of the sea, and so fundamentally changed the experiences of those using it. This had a profound influence on both the naval and maritime histories of the war but lacked the drama of the engagements between capital ships, or the novelty of the U-boat war. As such it has been virtually ignored within the historiography of the conflict. This book will address part of this lacuna in our understanding of the First World War, but it is not an operational or purely technical history. Instead it is focused on the asymmetric challenge posed by mines and the impact that had in terms of strategy and law. The most obvious result of this is that the book largely ignores the issue of mine clearance. The reason for this is simple: mine clearance, whilst technically very challenging, fitted easily into the accepted views of the role of the Royal Navy, and that of Britain more generally in the maritime sphere. Sweeping the seas clear of any threats or obstructions to British or neutral shipping was a role which the Royal Navy had played for many years and was an accepted part of its self-defined mission. Mine clearance could be directly assimilated into this outlook and as will be seen there were public calls for the Royal Navy to engage in mine-clearance operations during the Russo-Japanese War, in order to ensure the safety of neutral vessels. Although the Admiralty resisted these specific calls there was little argument that mine clearance would, and crucially, should be an important part of the Royal Navy's role in future. Thus the issue failed to open up the same type of contested space created by the debates over the use of mines as an offensive technology.

By exploring the issues surrounding offensive mining this study provides insight into a range of wider questions regarding British strategy, maritime culture and perceptions of international law. The debates which surrounded the use of mines throughout the period had their roots in a simple question: what type of war was it that Britain could or should fight? The cleavage between the idealised perceptions of the maritime world and naval combat, and the realities embodied by the mine, starkly revealed the debate which took place in the Royal Navy, and in Britain more widely, over attitudes towards warfare at this time. The questions over the use of mines were ones of balancing the rights of belligerents to conduct their wars as against those of neutrals to continue their activities in peace; gauging the importance of military necessity as against that of international law; and ultimately asking what limitations morality and civilisation placed on warfare. These themes fit directly into a much broader debate which had been conducted across Europe throughout the last quarter of the nineteenth century and continued into the twentieth. This debate saw regular attempts by both international lawyers and governments to limit warfare and codify the laws of war.[2] This project reached its apogee in the two peace conferences held at The Hague in 1899 and 1907 and arguably came to something of a conclusion in the middle of the First World War, as nineteenth-century attitudes towards warfare were submerged beneath a rising tide of belligerence. The questions raised by mines only formed one aspect of this debate, but the nature of the technology provoked extremely strong reactions, and consequently provides a rich seam of information on the broader issue. The debate over the nature of warfare is one of real historiographical importance, marking a watershed between nineteenth- and twentieth-century attitudes, and providing a crucial context for understanding British strategic policy.

The scope and range of this debate mean that it cannot be easily explored within the bounds of the usual historical sub-disciplines. Questions of international law, and the attitudes of politicians and diplomats, shaped the debate in equal measure with the more direct issues of naval strategy facing professional sailors. All of the protagonists operated within a distinct cultural context which was very different from the cultural landscape of twenty-first-century Britain. Furthermore, distinct organisational cultures, particularly that of the Royal Navy, shaped the attitudes of those taking decisions in this debate. Thus this study avowedly seeks to go beyond the usual disciplinary boundaries and explore the issue from a range of perspectives. It draws upon the literatures on naval policy, naval and maritime culture, and international law and demonstrates how interconnected these usually distinct topics actually were. This methodology is facilitated by the in-depth archival approach taken. The necessity of exploring the full range of reactions to technology has meant that the book draws upon a wealth of sources that have rarely been used in combination, or even at all, in order to present the most comprehensive picture possible.

Exploring the inconsistencies in British attitudes towards mining, and the wider debate on the nature of war, provides meaningful contributions to a number of significant and distinct historiographical debates. Historians of technology have long acknowledged the crucial role that culture plays in shaping technological change.[3] Many now argue that one can go further, and say that within large technically focused organisations, such as navies, there is a feedback loop through which the technology begins to impact on the organisational culture.[4] Naval historians have been slow to incorporate this thinking into their work, but there is a growing trend in this direction.[5] The new scholarship has helped shed light on the process of technological change within the Royal Navy, emphasising the role that culture played in shaping decision-making with regard to both strategy and technology.[6] Examining the issues surrounding mine warfare not only expands this work, but also provides a particularly powerful example. This is because the antithetical nature of the technology to traditional Royal Navy thinking forced the service to work through the assumptions and attitudes that lay behind its opposition. This, in turn, has made visible what is usually hidden to the historian, the attitudes and practices that were so universally accepted that they rarely needed to be set to paper.

The growing emphasis on the importance of culture within the work of historians looking at naval technology has been mirrored in that of historians of international law. In particular there has been a real focus on the attitudes of the German military towards international law, and a debate over the extent to which military culture shaped its response.[7] Recently Isabel Hull has made a strong case for German exceptionalism with regard to that country's military culture and attitudes towards international law.[8] There has been little work done specifically on British perceptions of international law, and where the issue has come to the fore, regarding maritime rights, there is no consensus among historians. The issue of mine warfare is a particularly useful one in shedding light on the British attitudes towards international law and assessing its relationship with military culture. The legal debate surrounding mine warfare was an issue of considerable importance to Britain both prior to and during the First World War. Despite the failure of British attempts to ban the use of mines at the 1907 Hague Conference, there remained widespread public and governmental concern about the subject up until the outbreak of war. From August 1914 through until the late spring of the following year, German use of mines was to provide the basis for British legal diplomacy. At the same time widespread use of mines was regularly discussed by the Royal Navy in prewar planning and was adopted by the Cabinet in October 1914. Thus the issue of mines provides an excellent insight into how the British government viewed international law in this period, highlighting where it perceived it to be useful, and under what circumstances it was willing to ignore it on the grounds of military necessity.

The examination of the role of the mine in British prewar strategy also provides insight into naval policy, particularly with regard to the blockade. Within contemporary debates the discussion of mining was invariably bound up in the contested issue of blockade. Indeed it is fair to say that the Royal Navy's engagement with the mine as a technology derived almost entirely from its potential for use in a blockade scenario, and the mine and the blockade were inextricably linked in the minds of contemporary naval officers. Debates over blockade were at the heart of discussion of British strategy throughout the prewar and wartime period. It was an essential feature of how Britain would prosecute any major war. It provided home defence and protected Britain's far-flung lines of communication. It acted as the country's primary offensive weapon in the form of economic warfare and facilitated potential combined operations. Its centrality to British strategy was undisputed, but technological and legal restrictions meant that its application was deeply problematic. This subject is one which has concerned military, diplomatic and legal historians for almost a century, and yet the mine barely features in any discussion of the subject.[9] By viewing the blockade question from the perspective of this crucial technology it is possible to gain new insight into the way these problems were conceptualised and how the Royal Navy and British government attempted to resolve them.

The outbreak of war saw these issues addressed with renewed urgency, and once again the mine came to be a crucial issue. One result of the conflict was the merging of the previously largely separate spheres of international law and naval strategy, and the inconsistencies between them that had marked prewar attitudes towards the technology were eventually unpicked. Throughout the first year of war the mine remained at the heart of British strategic thinking, and a focus on the technology makes clear how much continuity there was with prewar planning. By looking at a weapon with a unique role in strategic thinking about the blockade, it is possible to gain a very different perspective on the highly controversial issues around British naval policy. Furthermore, the contested legal position of the mine highlighted the remarkable symmetry between the British plans for using mines and the diplomatic offensive conducted against German mining. Both of these debates had at their heart the question of how war should be fought, and it was a gradual resolution to this question that saw mining fade from prominence as a contested issue from 1915 onwards. The mine would remain a crucial weapon in the arsenal of the Royal Navy, but it ceased to occupy a contested position in the minds of naval officers and their political masters.

NOTES

1. James Brown Scott, *The Proceedings of the Hague Peace Conferences: The Conference of 1907*, vol. 3 (New York: Oxford University Press, 1920), p. 524.
2. Geoffrey Best, *Humanity in Warfare: The Modern History of the International Law of Armed Conflicts* (London: Weidenfeld & Nicholson, 1980), pp. 128–215; Stephen Neff, *Justice Among Nations: A History of International Law* (Cambridge, MA: Harvard University Press, 2014), pp. 298–340.
3. Wiebe Bijker, Thomas Hughes, and Trevor Pinch, eds., *The Social Construction of Technological Systems: New Directions in the Sociology and History of Technology* (Cambridge, MA: MIT Press, 1989).
4. Thomas P. Hughes, 'Technological Momentum', in Merritt Roe Smith and Leo Marx, eds., *Does Technology Drive History: The Dilemma of Technological Determinism* (Cambridge, MA: MIT Press, 1994).
5. This gap is not quite as bad as has been recently suggested by Don Leggett, but there is still considerable adherence to the Heilbronerian school of technological determinism. See Don Leggett, *Shaping the Royal Navy: Technology, Authority and Naval Architecture, c. 1830–1906* (Manchester: MUP, 2015).
6. See for example Duncan Redford, 'Naval Culture and the Fleet Submarine, 1910–1917', in Don Leggett and Richard Dunn, eds., *Re-Inventing the Ship: Science, Technology and the Maritime World, 1800–1918* (Farnham: Ashgate, 2010).
7. Isabel Hull, *Absolute Destruction: Military Culture and the Practices of War in Imperial Germany* (Ithaca: Cornell University Press, 2005); Alan Kramer, *Dynamic of Destruction: Culture and Mass Killing in the First World War* (Oxford: Oxford University Press, 2008).
8. Isabel V. Hull, *A Scrap of Paper: Making and Breaking International Law During the Great War* (Ithaca: Cornell University Press, 2014).
9. For some of the more recent scholarship see: Greg Kennedy, ed., *Britain's War at Sea, 1914–1918: The War They Thought and the War They Fought* (London: Routledge, 2016); Nicholas Lambert, *Planning Armageddon: British Economic Warfare and the First World War* (Cambridge, MA: Harvard University Press, 2012); David Morgan-Owen, 'Cooked up in the Dinner Hour? Sir Arthur Wilson's War Plan, Reconsidered', *English Historical Review*, vol. CXXX, no. 545 (2015), pp. 885–888; and Matthew Seligmann, 'Failing to Prepare for the Great War? The Absence of Grand Strategy in British War Planning before 1914', *War in History* (2017), e-publication.

CHAPTER 2

Mining in a Cultural Context

'A Diabolical and Cowardly contrivance of the Enemy'; this was how Admiral Sir John Warren described a mine which killed an officer and ten seamen off the American coast in 1813.[1] This was one of the first times the Royal Navy encountered what could be called a modern naval mine, and it set the tone for the service's approach to the technology. By the time the Russians were deploying rudimentary mines in the Baltic, during the Crimean War, these devices were frequently derided as 'infernal machines' and were considered to be weapons of dubious morality. Throughout the second half of the nineteenth century the Royal Navy had relatively little contact with independent naval mines; this was partly a product of the limits of the technology, and partly because of the lack of major conflicts. This meant that mines of this type were rarely a priority for the service and barely featured in the broader popular consciousness. This changed dramatically from the middle of the first decade of the twentieth century, and mining would be an important issue strategically, politically and legally through into the First World War. The Royal Navy of this period took a pragmatic and progressive approach to technology, something that had served it well over the preceding decades. Evidence of this can clearly be seen in the development of mining from 1905 onwards. This is, however, only one strand of the story and to truly understand the reaction to mining it is necessary to look at the cultural milieu surrounding the issue.

Cultural norms form a vital framework for understanding the adoption and institutionalisation of any technology.[2] This is especially

© The Author(s) 2018
R. Dunley, *Britain and the Mine, 1900–1915*,
https://doi.org/10.1007/978-3-319-72820-9_2

applicable where the technology could be described as dissonant; that is, not conforming to the accepted structures and patterns of the host organisation or society.[3] British reaction to the emergence of mine warfare as a major issue from 1904 onwards was a case in point. General attitudes to mines were frequently shaped by British culture and perceptions of the maritime world, and this in turn had a discernable effect on British policy.[4] The more specific Royal Navy organisational culture had an even greater impact in shaping reactions to this challenging new technology. The history of mine warfare in Britain between 1905 and 1915 is arguably best understood in the context of the conflict between a deep-rooted suspicion of the technology, grounded in a very distinct culture, and a pragmatic realisation of the value of the weapon. To uncover the true nature of Britain's response to the mine it is therefore necessary to look at both British culture, in particular its strong maritime and imperial identity, and the Royal Navy's organisational culture, which developed from it.[5]

It is not my intention to get drawn into the complex debates over the terminology of cultures which have grown up since the subject came to the fore in the early 1980s, but it is useful for clarity to note what I mean. I am using the phrase organisational culture to denote the specific cultural environment found within the Royal Navy as distinct from any strategic or military culture which may have existed within the defence or policy community more generally.[6] By contrast I am using the simple, but vast phrase 'British culture', for want of a more specific term to refer to the attitudes and consciousness of the wider public sphere. At the time defence-related concerns formed a far larger influence on this than they would later in the twentieth century, but the concept remains too broad to be covered by terms such as strategic culture.

Britain in the second half of the nineteenth century viewed itself as primarily a maritime, imperial and trading nation. The sea was at the heart of the British imperial project. As the commentators Sir Charles Dilke and Spenser Wilkinson wrote in 1892 about the location and scope of the empire, 'it is as though the sea had been saturated with British influence, and deposited it along all the unprotected portion of its margin'.[7] Given this disposition it is unsurprising that the sea was the one thing that bound the British Empire together, facilitating defence, governance and trade. Beyond this it was central to the economic health of the country. Britain had comfortably the largest merchant marine, trading with virtually every port, and sailing every sea across the globe.

London was also the heart of the shipping, banking and maritime insurance industries, which served to further entrench British domination of global trade.[8] The ability to use the seas as highways for commerce was essential to the British imperial mission.

British connections with the sea extended even further; indeed the very notion of British identity in the late nineteenth century was inextricably linked with the sea.[9] Derived from a particular understanding of their history and racial and ethnic background Britons believed themselves to have a unique bond with the maritime world. The journalist, historian and travel writer, James Froude, argued that the sea was 'the natural home of Englishmen', a sentiment that was widely shared and put in its most blunt form by the future Prime Minister, Lord Salisbury, when he declared simply 'we are fish'.[10] In both cases the implication was that Britain did not simply use the seas; instead, it was where the essence of Britishness lay. Buttressing this notion was the belief that Britain had a predisposition, or perhaps even a right to exercise sovereignty over the world's oceans. Drawn out of a certain reading of the past it was felt that God, or Providence, had granted Britain this right and that she exercised it in keeping with the civilised liberal and moral traditions of the country.[11] In the eyes of many it was 'the function of the British Navy to police the sea in every region not under the territorial jurisdiction of a strong civilised power'.[12] This had, it was believed, been a great virtue for the rest of the world:

> The freedom of the seas is the proper name for a state of things which existed for two or three generations before the year 1914. It was a condition of law and order over all the navigable salt water, which covers three-quarters of the globe. Every ship of every nation could sail from any port in the world to any other port, unarmed, in perfect security, unconscious of any dangers except those of the wind, the waves, the rocks and the shoals.[13]

This position was not restricted to imperial writers; the International Law Committee, a body set up in 1918 by the British government and chaired by the Home Secretary, concluded that 'the record shows that seapower in her [Britain's] hands has been used in the defence of liberty, and, as in the present war, for the freedom of the world'.[14] This interpretation of Pax Britannica draws on a strong tradition in Britain which presented the navy and seaborne pursuits as essentially peaceable and saw British sovereignty of the seas as a carrier of 'freedom and liberty throughout the world'.[15]

Underwater weapons, and the mine in particular, represented, in material form, the antithesis of this view of the maritime world. As Sir Julian Corbett set out, in *Some Principles of Maritime Strategy*, command of the sea is not analogous to command of the land. There is no benefit in exercising that command except in the form of control of maritime communications, be they for trade, or military purposes.[16] When viewed from this perspective the mine appears a nihilist technology. It was not a tool with which another power could seek to exercise command of the sea; its fundamental mission was to deny that right to any party. For an empire which was bound together by maritime lines of communication any technology which was specifically designed to endanger those connections was clearly a direct challenge.

On a deeper level, underwater weapons also eroded some of Britain's cultural certainties regarding the sea and the nature of maritime power. The new technologies called into question the idea of sovereignty over the seas. In a 1901 *Punch* cartoon Neptune warns Britannia 'Look out my dear you are Mistress on the Sea, but there's a neighbour of yours that's trying to be Mistress under it'.[17] This was specifically referring to the French submarine construction programme, but mines fit into a very similar framework. Fundamentally mines and submarines were seen as alien objects intruding into a British space, and doing so in such a way as to make it virtually impossible to remove them. Underwater weapons also challenged the idea that naval power was somehow a peaceable agent of liberal values to be contrasted with the oppressive militarism of land power. This view largely stemmed from the simple fact that such weapons did not fit with British notions of naval power, but there was an element of truth in it. Mines and submarines could not be used for the sorts of policing, deterrence and power-project operations which Britain had employed to spread its values throughout the nineteenth century. Perhaps most objectionable of all of the mine's traits from a British perspective was its indiscriminate nature. It made no distinction between warship and passenger liner, belligerent and neutral. For an empire reliant in peace and war on the sea, this made it a particularly dangerous technology and this drove much of the British reaction in the first fifteen years of the twentieth century.

Britain's reaction to independent mines in the late nineteenth and early twentieth centuries was largely muted by a lack of awareness of the true nature of the technology and threat it posed. Instead the novel technology of the submarine came to be the focus of considerable attention. The submarine shared many of the same traits as the mine in terms of the challenge it posed British maritime culture, but its novelty and connections with popular culture meant that it was rapidly picked up by the press. The negative symbolism which was used to paint submarines as somehow unfair and piratical could have been applied just as easily to mines.[18] As will be seen this changed markedly following the widespread use of mine warfare in the Russo-Japanese War, and for the following decade British popular interaction with the mine was largely shaped by the cultural preconceptions of the audience. This in turn had a direct influence on the way the British government reacted to mining questions across a broad range of areas.

One of the first reactions of both the British government, and the British people more generally, was to turn to international law as a potential solution to this new threat. The decades prior to the First World War saw a growth in attempts to regulate warfare. Stephen Neff has described how the acceptance of war as a part of state interactions meant that European societies believed steps needed to be taken to limit its scope. The idea was 'that war would be fought with more than a trace of sporting ethos—on the basis of strictly even-handed rules agreed by both sides prior to the conflict, with low practices such as deception kept to a minimum'. It also meant that it was widely accepted that conflict should be professionalised and 'there was an ever greater insistence on the exclusion of civilians from the business of war—either as participants or as victims'.[19] The creation and understanding of international law is very heavily influenced by the culture of the society or societies engaged.[20] The way in which Britain came to view the mine as a technology meant that it was seen as one of the most obvious areas for an international legal agreement. From a British perspective it appeared to be a weapon of dubious morality, whose use ran contrary to the trend to codify the rules of war. Furthermore its impact on non-combatants and neutrals set it at odds with the desire to separate war from the rest of society. It was this interpretation of the technology which led to the claims of barbarism and lack of civilisation against the powers, particularly Germany, who resisted British attempts to get mines banned. This would continue into the First World War, when German minelaying was seen as some of the earliest evidence of the attitude of the 'terrible Hun'.

The development of mine warfare in Britain in the early twentieth century was shaped not only by the broad British cultural milieu, but also by a connected, but clear distinguishable Royal Navy organisational culture.[21] There has been considerable debate over differing ideas of organisational and strategic cultures within military organisations; however it is widely accepted that military services do have their own distinct cultures and that this influences decision-making.[22] We will, therefore, explore three areas which played an important part in shaping the service's response to mine warfare, these being notions of how war was to be fought, the concept of honour and chivalry and the primacy of the battlefleet as a cultural symbol.

Throughout the late Victorian and Edwardian era the Royal Navy had certain very clear ideas about how naval campaigns were to be fought. First among these was the primacy of the offensive. In common with many of the leading armies of the period the Royal Navy was culturally predetermined to favour the offensive for tactical, strategic and, above all, moral reasons. Captain W. H. Hall summed it up in a plan for a campaign against Russia produced in 1884, writing that '(a) *defensive* policy is ... utterly at variance with the traditions of the British Navy, whose role has always been that of *attack* and not *defence*.'[23] By 1902 the navy was willing to make an even clearer statement of principle, declaring in a paper for the Dominion governments that 'the primary object of the British Navy is not to defend anything, but to attack the fleets of the enemy, and, by defeating them, to afford protection to British Dominions, shipping, and commerce. This is the ultimate aim.'[24] An offensive policy designed to sweep the enemy from the oceans naturally fed into the wider British perception of sovereignty over the seas. For the Royal Navy in wartime this was to have a physical as well as a cultural dimension, with most officers accepting, in principle at least, Philip Colomb's adage that 'the frontier of our Empire is the enemy's coastline'.[25] Within this cultural framework, which prioritised attack over defence, there was a distinct sense of how a battle should be fought. At its heart was the old Nelsonian idea that 'no captain can do very wrong if he places his ship alongside that of an enemy' and the concept of the ship-on-ship duels that this would entail still had a clear resonance within the Royal Navy.[26] This drew in the notion of offensive spirit, but also incorporated a clear sense of honest combat between two adversaries.[27]

The mine did not fit into this sense of how the Royal Navy would prosecute a war. Although mines could be used offensively, they were innately a defensive and passive technology. It was very difficult to conceptualise how the Royal Navy could use mines in its stated mission to sweep the enemy's ships from the seas. This would require the use of active technologies which would allow the service to hunt down its foes wherever they may be and then destroy them in battle. The mine did not appear to fit any of these criteria. Furthermore the fundamental premise of a mine, to deny the use of the seas to all mariners, appeared entirely contrary to the purposes of the Royal Navy. The aim of the service was to ensure that the seas were safe for Britain and, it was argued, all other peaceable nations, to use in order to carry on their business. It seemed perverse for an organisation which set its own frontier on the enemy's coastline to then limit its freedom of action on the very seas it was seeking to command.

The sense of honour and chivalry which formed a key part of the culture of the Royal Navy officer corps at this time was also an important factor in shaping the response of the service to the mine. Honour had long been an essential part of Royal Navy culture, but it was reinforced in the later nineteenth century by a growing connection between the service and Britain's aristocratic elite.[28] The reclaiming and reinterpretation of the notion of chivalry, which was taking place at the same time, naturally fed into this dynamic.[29] The recapturing of a supposed golden age of morality and honour is highlighted in the symbolism used to describe the navy, most famously in Churchill's 'castles of steel' arrayed at Spithead.[30] The concept of honour was closely connected with the idea of honest and fair combat and the extension of this into the naval sphere reached its apogee in the plans drawn up by Vice-Admiral Lord Charles Beresford to attack the Russian fleet at the height of the Dogger Bank incident in 1904. Beresford informed the Admiralty in London that he only intended to use four of his eight battleships to fight the four Russian ships, declaring that 'it appeared to me that it would only be chivalrous under the circumstances'. Unsurprisingly, this decision was condemned by officials in the Admiralty, but gives a clear indication of how deep-rooted the concept of chivalry was in the service.[31] Indeed for some officers this sense of honour and fighting fair even led them to question the words of the Royal Navy's "earthly god" Nelson. In 1916 Reginald Tyrwhitt wrote to Rogers Keyes 'I echo your remarks about the Huns & their beastly 17" guns. "All the more honour if we beat them". I have always grudged Nelson's remark "only numbers can annihilate". He should have transposed "guts for numbers"!'[32]

Bound up in the notion of honour was a sense of moral purpose, which remained strong within the culture of the Royal Navy through into the First World War. The service had a very clear sense that it was a force for good in the world, spreading the freedom and liberal values on which Britain prided itself to the uncivilised world. This came in many forms, from the suppression of the slave trade to arbitration in local disputes, but it always combined a sense of comfortable superiority with that of honour and moral purpose.[33] In order to support this image of the Royal Navy, some of its greatest heroes were reconstructed to conform to the current ideals. As such Sir Francis Drake ceased to be the buccaneer of legend and was instead recast as a 'warrior-patriot' who sought to spread the 'civilising effect of British rule'.[34] The story of Nelson was similarly rewritten to emphasise his moral and human qualities. Nelson's famous Trafalgar prayer went: 'may humanity after victory be the predominant feature in the British fleet'. For the late Victorian navy this was a point of fundamental principle.

The Royal Navy's cultural preconceptions around honour and chivalry helped to shape its response to underwater weapons, and the mine in particular. The essence of mine warfare involved laying a form of ambush for one's enemy, and this type of *ruse de guerre* had a long and celebrated tradition in the service. Where mining was different was that it did not offer your opponent the opportunity to fight back. Instead of confronting them in a fair fight the vessel which laid the mines would then "run away". By the time any enemy vessel struck the mine there would be no one around for them to fight. This sense that those using mines were somehow cowardly conformed with similar ideas around submarines. As the naval writer Archibald Hurd put it 'the blue-jacket and his master, the naval officer, love an old-fashioned fight, and are apt to regard with disfavour all other modes of attack which are less open and direct'.[35] Mining was unquestionably the most objectionable of these underhand methods of conducting war, because of its indiscriminate nature. In the eyes of many within the service, to use such weapons would be to abandon humanity in search of victory.

The final factor which had a direct impact on attitudes towards the mine was the Royal Navy's cultural association with the battleship. British preeminence at sea throughout the nineteenth century was based upon the possession of a battle fleet superior to that of any other power, and this continued into the First World War. The battleship was the technology on which the service relied for its military position, but it was also culturally at the heart of the Royal Navy's identity. Service with the battle fleet, preferably on the flagship, was central to most successful naval careers and command of a new battleship or premier fleet were among the most desirable posts in the navy.[36] Those serving with the battle fleet, especially in the Mediterranean, viewed themselves as the elite naval force in the world's premier navy. There was a general acceptance that in any future conflict Britain would have to face the naval forces of its opponent in a decisive battle, and it was the battle fleet that would win this 'second Trafalgar'.[37] In a world heavily influenced by Mahanian ideas of sea power, this was the ultimate aim of any navy, and so the primacy of the fleet could not be questioned.

In an era of rapidly changing technology the newest battleships came to be obvious symbols of the power of the Royal Navy, with *Warrior* giving way to *Inflexible*, *Royal Sovereign* and ultimately *Dreadnought*.[38] These deep associations meant that weapons systems that presented an asymmetric challenge to the battle fleet were viewed with far more scepticism than those which could be assimilated within the current technological paradigm. The Royal Navy spent a huge amount of time and effort trying to fit the torpedo and later the submarine into the battlefleet mould, but the mine presented an even greater challenge.[39] For many within the Royal Navy the mine and the battleship were at different ends of the spectrum in terms of how power could be exerted at sea, and as such they were fundamentally incompatible. The Royal Navy was, and would remain a battleship navy and so had no need to waste time with more unconventional technologies like mines. The events of the Russo-Japanese War shook this belief, but it remained a clear strand within Royal Navy thinking regarding mines well into the First World War.

The Royal Navy's organisational culture clearly predisposed the service to look upon mines in a negative manner, and evidence of the impact of this can be found throughout the period. It must, however, be kept in mind that the navy still developed a strong mining service, planned at various stages to deploy mines and in the end did use the technology in the test of war. The service was even willing to break the limited legal restrictions which Britain did manage to place on mining. The reasoning behind this was simple: mines were cheap, effective and ultimately very useful to the Royal Navy. Isabel Hull and others have written extensively about the concept of military necessity in the context of the German armed forces in this period, and in particular how the German view of the concept and its relation with international law was the product of a specific German culture.[40] It is apparent that although the concept of military necessity can be applied across most military endeavours the attitude of the organisations involved towards it varies hugely, dependent largely on their culture. The Royal Navy's willingness to adopt and eventually deploy mines, in the face of internal cultural opposition and a restrictive legal framework, was rooted in the same culture that rejected mining in the first place. The service had a clear sense of how it wanted to win a future conflict, and ideally mines would not feature. Ultimately, however, important as humanity was within the service's view of how it should conduct itself, victory always had to come first.

The process through which technology is shaped, adopted and used is a very complex one, but at its heart are the social actors; the people, or groups of people, who develop and utilise that technology. In order to understand the technology it is, therefore essential to understand the people. The cultural norms both in British society and more narrowly in the Royal Navy formed the environment in which mining was introduced and discussed. This environment was, and would remain, broadly hostile to the development of mine warfare. The technology was adopted and institutionalised in spite of, rather than because of, its cultural surroundings. The Royal Navy was a pragmatic and realistic organisation and for this reason was willing to explore a new technology where it saw fit. In defining the nature of these parameters and formatting the considerable internal debate over their scope, culture provided a vital force in shaping British reaction to the mine well into the First World War.

NOTES

1. The National Archives (TNA), ADM 1/504, Warren to Croker, 22 July 1813, O.156/13, f. 26. I am grateful to B. J. Armstrong for pointing me to this reference.
2. Wiebe Bijker, Thomas P. Hughes, and Trevor Pinch, eds., *The Social Construction of Technological Systems: New Directions in the Sociology and History of Technology* (Cambridge, MA: MIT Press, 1989).
3. For the classic study of dissonant technology see Edward Constant II, *The Origins of the Turbojet Revolution* (Baltimore: The John Hopkins University Press, 1980).
4. The centrality of culture in understanding military history is now widely acknowledged. For seminal works establishing this see John Keegan,

The Face of Battle: A Study of Agincourt, Waterloo and the Somme (London: Penguin, 1978) and John A. Lynn, *Battle: A History of Combat and Culture* (Boulder, CO: Westview, 2003).

5. The subject is one which is increasingly the focus of historiographical attention, but the best point of entry remains Jan Rüger, *The Great Naval Game: Britain and Germany in the Age of Empire* (Cambridge: Cambridge University Press, 2007).

6. For an introduction to the concept of organisational culture see Elizabeth Kier, *Imagining War: French and British Military Doctrine Between the Wars* (Princeton: Princeton University Press, 1997).

7. Charles Dilke and Spenser Wilkinson, *Imperial Defence* (London: Macmillan & Co., 1892), p. 40.

8. P. J. Cain and A. G. Hopkins, *British Imperialism 1688–2000*, 2nd ed. (Cambridge: Cambridge University Press, 2002), pp. 158–160 and *passim*.

9. Glen O'Hara, *Britain and the Sea Since 1600* (Basingstoke: Palgrave, 2010).

10. James Anthony Froude, *Oceana, or, England and Her Colonies* (London: Longmans, Green & Co., 1886), p. 18; Miles Taylor, 'Introduction', in Miles Taylor, ed., *The Victorian Empire and Britain's Maritime World, 1837–1901: The Sea and Global History* (London: Palgrave Macmillan, 2013), p. 1.

11. Cynthia Behrman, *Victorian Myths of the Sea* (Athens, OH: Ohio University Press, 1977), pp. 26–34.

12. Spenser Wilkinson, *British Aspects of War and Peace* (London: Duckworth & Co., 1919), p. 18.

13. Spenser Wilkinson, *British Aspects of War and Peace* (London: Duckworth & Co., 1919), p. 9.

14. TNA, FO 372/1186, 'Freedom of the Seas', 12 December 1918, 206760/539/350.

15. John Leyland, *The Achievement of the British Navy in the World War* (London: Hodder & Stoughton, 1918).

16. Julian S. Corbett, *Some Principles of Maritime Strategy* (Uckfield, East Sussex: Naval & Military Press, 1911), pp. 78–80.

17. *Punch*, 23 January 1901; for a more detailed analysis of this cartoon see Duncan Redford, *The Submarine: A Cultural History from the Great War to Nuclear Combat* (London: I. B. Tauris, 2010).

18. Redford, *The Submarine*.

19. Stephen Neff, *War and the Law of Nations: A General History* (Cambridge: Cambridge University Press, 2005), pp. 189–190.

20. Geoffrey Best, *Humanity in Warfare: The Modern History of the International Law of Armed Conflicts* (London: Weidenfeld & Nicholson, 1980), pp. 128–147.

21. For a rare internal statement of these ideas see TNA, ADM 1/7114, 'Sovereignty of the Seas', 1 January 1892.
22. Lawrence Sondhaus, *Strategic Culture and Ways of War* (London: Routledge, 2006); Roger W. Barnett, *Navy Strategic Culture: Why the Navy Thinks Differently* (Annapolis: NPI, 2009).
23. TNA, ADM 231/5, Remarks on a Naval Campaign, W. H. Hall, 1884.
24. TNA, CAB 18/10, 'Papers Relating to a Conference Between the Secretary of State for the Colonies and the Prime Ministers of the Self-Governing Colonies; June to August 1902', Appendix IV 'Memorandum on Sea-Power and the Principles Involved in It'.
25. P. H. Colomb, 'Imperial Defence', in P. H. Colomb, ed., *Essays on Naval Defence* (London, 1896), p. 20.
26. Julian S. Corbett, *Fighting Instructions: 1530–1816* (London: NRS, 1905), p. 318.
27. For example see Beatty to his wife, 20 October 1914, in Brian Ranft, ed., The *Beatty Papers: Selections from the Private and Official Correspondence of Admiral of the Fleet Earl Beatty*, vol. I (London: NRS, 1989), pp. 144–146.
28. Robert L. Davison, *The Challenges of Command: The Royal Navy's Executive Branch Officers, 1880–1919* (Farnham: Ashgate, 2011).
29. Allen J. Frantzen, *Bloody Good: Chivalry, Sacrifice, and the Great War* (Chicago: University of Chicago Press, 2004); Stefan Goebel, *The Great War and Medieval Memory: War, Remembrance and Medievalism in Britain and Germany, 1914–1940* (Cambridge: Cambridge University Press, 2007).
30. Winston Churchill, *The World Crisis*, vol. 1 (London: Thornton Butterworth, 1923), p. 225; Redford, *The Submarine*, p. 59.
31. TNA, ADM 1/7725, Summary of Vice-Admiral's intended procedure on being ordered to act against the Russian Fleet, n.d. (November 1904), V289/04.
32. British Library (BL), Add Ms 82404, Tyrwhitt to Keyes, 9 March 1916.
33. John Oldfield, 'After Emancipation: Slavery, Freedom and the Victorian Empire', in Miles Taylor, ed., *The Victorian Empire and Britain's Maritime World, 1837–1901: The Sea and Global History* (London: Palgrave Macmillan, 2013), pp. 53–60; Geoffrey Lowis, *Fabulous Admirals and Some Naval Fragments* (London: Putnam, 1957), pp. 145–146.
34. Bruce Wathen, *Sir Francis Drake: The Construction of a Hero* (Cambridge: D. S. Brewer, 2009), pp. 139, 156.
35. Archibald Hurd, 'The Coming of the Submarine: The New British Boats', *The Nineteenth Century and After*, LI (1902), p. 222.
36. Andrew Gordon, *The Rules of the Game: Jutland and British Naval Command* (London: John Murray, 1996), pp. 295–314 and *passim*.

37. TNA, ADM 116/3093, *Naval Necessities II*, 'Floating Mines', Battenberg Memorandum, p. 168.
38. Andrew Lambert, 'The Power of a Name: Tradition, Technology and Transformation', and Jan Rüger, 'The Symbolic Value of the Dreadnought', in Robert J. Blyth, Andrew Lambert, and Jan Rüger, eds., *The Dreadnought and the Edwardian Age* (Farnham: Ashgate, 2011).
39. Richard Dunley, '"The Most Resistless and Revolutionary Weapon of Naval Warfare That Has Ever Been Introduced": The Royal Navy and the Whitehead Torpedo 1870–1890', in Michael LoCicero, Ross Mahoney, and Stuart Mitchell, eds., *A Military Transformed?: Adaptation and Innovation in the British Military, 1792–1945* (London: Helion, 2014); Duncan Redford, 'Naval Culture and the Fleet Submarine, 1910–1917', in Don Leggett and Richard Dunn, eds., *Re-inventing the Ship: Science, Technology and the Maritime World, 1800–1918* (Farnham: Ashgate, 2010).
40. Isabel V. Hull, '"Military Necessity" and the Laws of War in Imperial Germany', in Stathis Kalyvas, Ian Shapiro, and Tarek Masoud, eds., *Order, Conflict and Violence* (Cambridge: Cambridge University Press, 2008); Isabel V. Hull, *Absolute Destruction: Military Culture and the Practices of War in Imperial Germany* (Ithaca: Cornell University Press, 2005).

CHAPTER 3

British Attitudes to Mining Before 1904

In August 1884 Lieutenant Charles Ottley, a staff officer at the torpedo school HMS *Vernon*, developed a new apparatus to automatically moor a mine at the correct depth.[1] This device, together with similar equipment produced at around the same time by an Austrian officer named Lieutenant Pietruski, would revolutionise mine warfare. Until this point it had been necessary to take soundings of the location where you wanted to lay your mine and then adjust the length of the mooring cable between the mine and the sinker to ensure that the mine floated at the correct depth below the water. Ottley's ingenious mechanism ensured that this was no longer the case. Instead it relied on a simple set of floats and ratchets to ensure that a mine simply dropped over the side of a ship would automatically take the correct depth. Although no one at the time really recognised it, this development fundamentally changed the nature of the mine as a weapon. Suddenly what had been a littoral weapon that needed time and careful planning to lay out, became an oceanic weapon which could be laid quickly and on a large scale. It is reasonable to suggest that mine warfare, in the modern sense of that term, began in 1884 with the development of the automatic depth-taking mine sinker.

For almost twenty years prior to Ottley and Pietruski's inventions mining had formed an important part of naval warfare, and one which had been wholeheartedly embraced by the Royal Navy. This mining was very different from that which came to be so influential in the twentieth century. Focusing on the littoral regions, particularly around defended ports, it more closely resembled siege warfare than the oceanic

© The Author(s) 2018
R. Dunley, *Britain and the Mine, 1900–1915*,
https://doi.org/10.1007/978-3-319-72820-9_3

campaigns of ambush and attrition that marked out mining in the First and Second World Wars. Mines of this period can broadly be divided into two types, independent mines and controlled mines. Independent mines are those which would be most readily recognised today, and in their simplest form consisted of a buoyant shell that was filled with explosives and set to detonate on being struck by a ship. The crucial point with these weapons was that they were entirely self-contained and once laid would fire on contact with any ship, friend or foe. These were also occasionally referred to as blockade mines. In the period before the First World War there were two types of independent mine, distinguished by the design of firing pistol used to detonate the weapon. The most basic were mechanical mines, which, as the name implies used a simple mechanical device as a firing pistol, whilst an electro-mechanical mine relied upon some form of inbuilt battery to fire the charge.

Controlled mines, whilst technically similar to their independent cousins, were a very different type of weapon. Fundamentally, they consisted of a charge of explosives connected by cables to an electric battery on shore, where a human operator could ensure that they would only detonate when desired. In effect the human link meant that controlled mines were "intelligent weapons" and the location of the battery on shore meant that they could be safely removed when no longer necessary. These advantages were balanced against some major disadvantages: namely, that they could only be laid in waters visible from the shore, and were resource-intensive. Within this type there were two separate classes of mines: observation mines were large charges of explosive set on the bottom of a channel and which could only be detonated by an observer on shore. The second class were called electro-contact mines. These were like independent mines in that they would go off when struck by a ship, but they would only do so if they had been armed by those on shore, who had to connect a battery to their firing cable.

Controlled mines, first used during the Crimean War, came of age in the American Civil War, where they were deployed to great effect by both sides. For the next twenty years they would be the primary mining technology, and they became an essential part of any major coast defence scheme. The reasons for the success of the technology are obvious. Prior to the invention of the automatic depth-taking mine sinker, laying a minefield was a slow and labour-intensive process, and one which was invariably restricted to the coastal waters around major ports. In such areas the drawbacks of controlled mines were heavily outweighed by their advantages in terms of safety. The technology was adopted by all the major powers, including Britain, where the Royal Engineers (RE) provided detailed schemes as part of the army's defences of naval and commercial ports.

Far more surprisingly, the Royal Navy also embraced controlled mining technology, although it did so in a very specific way, determined by its strategic vision and organisational culture. In the 1870s and 1880s the Royal Navy's unchallenged position at sea led to it exploring offensive operations aimed at destroying enemy fleets in harbour and projecting power from the sea onto the land.[2] Within this broad strategic vision the organisation found it necessary to adopt and adapt controlled mining technologies.[3] In a war situation it was expected that the British fleet would blockade its enemy, most likely France, or Russia. In order to do this in the steam era an advanced base would be established near the main enemy harbour.[4] Controlled mines were to form a vital part of the protection of such a base, and for this reason standard mining equipment was developed. The basic designs were for a 500-lb observation mine, and a 72-lb, later increased to 76-lb, electro-contact mine.[5] Although the concept of independent mining was widely deprecated in the navy at this time, a modification was produced which would allow the electro-contact mines to be converted into electro-mechanical mines.[6]

An assault on an enemy's naval base protected by controlled mines presented a more difficult challenge and the Royal Navy adapted the technology in order to fit its offensive strategic vision. What the service required was a method of clearing a protected minefield to allow the British ironclads to destroy any fortifications and enter the harbour. To achieve this the Royal Navy developed a policy of countermining. This involved dropping a string of large explosive charges into the water and then detonating them electrically. This would either set off, or destroy any mines in that thin strip of water. This process would be repeated to clear a channel through a minefield.[7] It was difficult and dangerous work, especially considering it would have to be done in the face of enemy fire, but it was considered 'the most rapid and certain method of clearing a channel'.[8] Crucially, it was the only way to facilitate the Royal Navy's primary strategic policy of the time. Britain was the only power with a serious interest in coastal assault operations in this period and this, combined with the strong cultural attachment to the offensive, ensured that the Royal Navy's response to the challenge of controlled mining technology was unique.[9] As the Director of Naval Ordnance (DNO) declared in 1881 'the importance of countermining is not appreciated by foreign nations because they seek to perfect the defence. The role of the British fleet, however, would be to attack, and against submarine defence countermining presents more chance of success than any other method now known.'[10] Controlled mining became a key technology for the Royal Navy because it enabled the organisation to pursue its strategic vision, one which was rooted in its culture as much as it was in Britain's grand strategy.

The strategic context which fostered the Royal Navy's interest in controlled mining disappeared rapidly from around 1885. Britain's comfortable superiority at sea, which had characterised the mid-Victorian period, came under increasing pressure, largely due to heavy French and Russian investment in naval construction programmes. This naturally forced the Royal Navy to spend more time focusing on the potential threat at sea, and interest in power projection operations waned. At the same time developments in quick-firing artillery meant that the service no longer viewed mines as so important in defending an advanced base, whilst heavier breech-loading ordnance offered the opportunity of bombarding an enemy port from beyond any feasible controlled minefield. These factors combined to mean that the Royal Navy no longer viewed controlled mining as an essential technology in pursuing its key strategic goals. Although the Royal Navy continued to issue controlled mining equipment to its fleets and detailed exercises were commonplace through until 1905, the absence of a realistic wartime role meant that the technology became something of a backwater.

For roughly fifteen years, from 1870 onwards, mine warfare, in the form of controlled mining, was at the heart of how the Royal Navy intended to prosecute a major conflict. This weapons system was at the cutting edge both technologically and strategically, and attracted many of the best young officers in the navy to *Vernon*. It should be noted that the torpedo school was primarily interested in mining; the Whitehead was very much a secondary weapon, and one for which the navy was struggling to find a realistic strategic role.[11] The list of officers involved in the early development of mining or who qualified as torpedo lieutenants, passing through *Vernon* in the 1870s and 1880s, contains many of the names of those who would be influential in the development of the Edwardian navy. The torpedo school's first commander was John Fisher, whilst Arthur Wilson and William May were both on the teaching staff in its early years. The students who passed through the school in this time included many of those who would become the intellectual and technical elite of the prewar Royal Navy. Henry Jackson, Alexander Bethell, Frederick Hamilton, Charles Ottley, Doveton Sturdee, Edmond Slade, Charles Madden and Reginald Bacon are just a few of the more important figures who were intimately involved in mining and torpedo work at this time.[12]

I

The one aspect of mine warfare in which the Royal Navy showed little interest was independent mining. The rejection of these weapons dated back to the joint Admiralty and War Office Floating Obstructions Committee, which reported in 1868 that any British mining programme needed to be based on controlled, as opposed to independent mines. The committee carefully explained their rejection of independent mines, stating that 'once placed in position and ready for action they must be equally dangerous to friend and foe; and when their employment is no longer necessary, their removal cannot be accomplished without risk of accident'.[13] For an empire that viewed the seas as part of its domain this was simply not acceptable. The committee's views were endorsed by John Fisher, one of the service's foremost experts on underwater weapons, who felt that it was 'difficult to conceive of the circumstances anywhere' in which independent mines could 'be applied with advantage.'[14] Privately Fisher went even further, describing independent mines as 'the suicidal system'.[15]

This remained the official position of the Royal Navy throughout the 1870s and early 1880s, but the development of the automatic depth-taking apparatus led to a reopening of the subject. The navy realised that the invention of a means to quickly and easily lay mines opened up new possibilities in terms of where and when they could be utilised. The discussion of Ottley's invention in the *Vernon* Annual Report for 1884 suggested that '(a)nother most important operation which is rendered more possible by the introduction of automatically moored mines is ... a "Torpedo Blockade"'.[16] By this it meant an operation to mine the entrance to an enemy's harbour, something that had been effectively impossible with the previous technology. This offensive use of mining technology resonated both with the service's strategic outlook and with its broader culture. With this in mind the navy ordered a number of sets of Ottley mooring sinkers and began to experiment with independent mines.

Much of the impetus for this work came from the far side of the globe, where Ottley had recently been appointed as torpedo lieutenant on *Nelson*, the flagship on the Australia Station. He continued the experimental work which he had been carrying out on *Vernon*, and received considerable high-level support from the Commander-in-Chief, Rear-Admiral George Tryon. One aspect of this work was overseeing trials of a new design of mine, developed by a member of the Melbourne submarine mining corps, Captain Robert Joseph. Joseph had designed an independent mine which had a mechanical firing pistol, but, he claimed, could easily be armed or disarmed by connecting it to an electric battery. The idea appears to have been that the mine would have been laid whilst in 'safe' mode, could then be armed in situ when necessary, and then disarmed for safe retrieval. The service's reaction to this new design gives a good indication of the changing attitudes towards mining in the late 1880s. Ottley and Tryon both reported very favourably on the technology, suggesting that when combined with the new mooring sinker it fulfilled all of the requirements of a mechanical mine, as set out in the Torpedo Manual.[17] As such it could potentially replace the 72-lb service mine in its roles as both an electro-contact and an electro-mechanical mine. They did, however, conclude that 'one condition it does not fulfill, it could not readily be used to lock an enemy up in his harbour'.[18] The reason for this was that Joseph's mine would be laid whilst disarmed, and would then have to be armed by connecting it to a battery after it was in the water. This was not a practical proposition off an enemy's harbour. Until very recently the Royal Navy had not given much consideration to using independent mines in this way, but the development of the automatic mooring sinker together with new gunnery technology meant that this was no longer the case. When Ottley and Tryon's report on the Joseph mine reached London it was heavily critiqued by the First Naval Lord, Admiral Sir Arthur Hood. He wrote, regarding the unsuitability of the mine for use in a "torpedo blockade", that 'from a naval point of view this is a very important point, in which this torpedo is not satisfactory'. He concluded that 'I would observe that this mine is for defensive operations, and not for offensive, and therefore in my opinion is far more valuable to the department interested with defensive operations, viz. the War Office than to the naval service'.[19] This remark was undoubtedly partially inspired by a desire to get the War Office to pay the considerable sum Joseph was asking for a number of mines to be sent to Britain for trial. It does, however, highlight how the idea of independent mining gained currency in the Royal Navy in the period, and how this was intimately connected to the idea that mines were an offensive weapon. Despite further exhortations from both Ottley and Tryon, Joseph's mine never received a full trial, with neither the Admiralty nor the War Office willing to meet the inventor's financial demands.

By the late 1880s there was a clear awareness in the Admiralty that independent mining, particularly in the form of a "torpedo blockade", could form an important part of a future conflict. John Fisher suggested that such an operation was 'perhaps the most essential of all naval requirements as regards the use of mines'.[20] Fisher's remark was undoubtedly something of an exaggeration, but it does demonstrate the shift away from controlled mining and a new interest in independent mining as an offensive technology. Despite this, and continued experiments and exercises with electro-mechanical mines and the automatic depth-taking mooring sinker, little was done to take independent mining from a theoretical to a practical concept. This changed in 1890 when Vice-Admiral Sir Anthony Hoskins, the Commander-in-Chief, Mediterranean, wrote to the Admiralty recommending that the ships of his fleet be issued with a larger number of independent mines in place of their controlled mining equipment.[21] Hoskins' sudden interest in the subject appears to have stemmed from intelligence that the French were planning on using such mines on a large scale, but it was perhaps not a coincidence that Ottley had recently joined his flagship, *Victoria*.

The Admiralty clearly took Hoskins' report seriously and ordered that detailed experiments be carried out using the cruiser *Undaunted* under the command of Captain Lord Charles Beresford; the vessel was adapted to carry 18 electro-mechanical mines over her stern.[22] *Undaunted* carried out a number of experiments to simulate an operation to mine an enemy's harbour, culminating in a high-speed run conducted at night. Beresford considered the results to be 'extremely satisfactory'.[23] The remarks made on Beresford's report reveal that whilst some within the service viewed independent mines as offensive weapons which could fit into the Royal Navy's strategic vision, this was not universal. Rear-Admiral Lord Walter Kerr, second in command in the Mediterranean, led the critique, remarking that 'blocking up an enemy's port is a policy we should not provide for to any great extent' and that 'it is undesirable to crowd men of war with the necessary gear and mines'. Even Hoskins appeared to step back from some of his early enthusiasm, signalling his general agreement with Kerr, but added that he felt 'it desirable to have blockade mines on every station and with every squadron'. These positions were conflated by the DNO saying that the weapons were, 'on the whole desirable', but should be placed on special ships, probably paddlers.[24] The focus on paddle steamers was mainly driven by concerns that mines dropped over the stern could become entangled in the screws of a conventional vessel, something that would likely end in disaster. The manoeuvrability and shallow draft typical in paddlers would also have been a major benefit for the types of mining operations then under consideration. The Admiralty encouraged further experimentation with these weapons, asking both *Vernon* and the fleet in the Mediterranean for improvements in terms of the mine and the laying process.

Charles Ottley was once again at the forefront of these developments, supported by Tryon's appointment to replace Hoskins as Commander-in-Chief, Mediterranean.[25] In late 1891 Ottley ran a series of experiments with electro-mechanical mines, aiming to simulate laying a large minefield and test the mines' safety and reliability.[26] Whilst the experimental fittings for laying the mines worked admirably there were clear issues concerning safety and the Admiralty requested that Captain William Hall of *Vernon* write a report on the subject. Hall's report began by looking more broadly at the question of mining, and sought to separate the Royal Navy's existing use of electro-contact and observation mines, which he saw as defensive, from the proposed use of independent mines, which was characterised as being offensive.[27] This is particularly instructive in the light of comments Hall made in his introduction to the *Vernon* Annual Report of that year. He remarked upon 'the *temporary* nature of the mine defence required by a navy like ours, whose rôle has been, and always must be the offensive'. Hall went on to suggest that 'the occasions when our ships will require to protect themselves against enemies ships by means of a minefield will be rare' and that it was more likely that the Royal Navy would need to attack such a defended anchorage, referring to the continued interest in countermining.[28] Despite these remarks, Hall felt that electro-contact mines should continue to be carried by fighting ships for use in protecting any advanced anchorages and other defensive requirements. 'Offensive or "blockade" mines' by contrast would be 'required in large numbers and are to be laid by special steamers'. Hall set out the key requirements of an independent mine, arguing that it should contain its own means of ignition, be safe to handle and lay, be certain to act when wanted and become safe if it broke adrift from its moorings. The standard service mine fitted as an electro-mechanical mine did not meet these requirements and instead Hall recommended that the navy develop a simple mechanical mine in order that 'it can be fitted and used by persons not possessing any electrical knowledge'.[29] Important within this was the Admiralty's decision that it was no longer necessary for independent mines to be capable of being made safe so that they could later be raised. Up until this point the navy had always insisted on being able to recover all mines laid. Such a policy made sense when mines were only used in protecting harbours, but was wholly unrealistic for use in offensive mining. In 1892 the navy relaxed this requirement, something that facilitated a revision of independent mining materiel.[30]

As a result of Hall's report the Admiralty asked *Vernon* to develop an effective and safe blockade mine. In addition to the plan drawn up by the officers at the torpedo school three other designs were submitted for trial, including ones by Commander Ottley and Commander H. B. Jackson. After a comprehensive series of experiments it was decided that Jackson's design was the most suitable for the navy's requirements. It was a mechanical mine, containing 49-lbs of guncotton and using a spring-based inertia firing system. Intriguingly, the mines were tested for their ability to resist countermining, something that suggests the navy had failed to properly understand the implications of the development of effective independent mines.[31] In 1894 *Vernon* informed the Admiralty that it had successfully developed a mechanical blockade mine, and sought further guidance.

At this point the whole question of the suitability of independent mines was opened up again by a memorandum written by the Assistant Director of Torpedoes (ADT), William May. Critically, May challenged the notion that independent mines were offensive weapons, instead claiming that 'the blockade mine is essentially a defensive weapon to be used only by the weaker fleet'. He concluded that 'considering the cost of providing mines and the necessary vessels for laying them down; also the difficulties of putting them down close enough to an enemy's port to be an effective barrier to the egress of their ships, I consider it doubtful whether we should adopt this form of naval warfare'.[32] These views were supported by the DNO, Henry Kane, and the Controller, John Fisher.[33] This was not an uninformed decision; all three men had built their careers as torpedo specialists and understood both the technical and strategic aspects of the issue. Instead the sudden change in attitudes reflects the difficult position which mines occupied in the strategic outlook of the Royal Navy at this time. As a form of mutual sea denial, independent mines did not easily fit with the Mahanian concepts of sea power which were increasingly prevalent in the Royal Navy. Crucial within this was the shift in the perception of independent mining from being an offensive, to a defensive technology. The cultural attachment to the offensive within the Royal Navy was such that even though May envisaged the mines fulfilling the same role as that which Hall had discussed two years previous, the labelling of that role as defensive was enough to call into question its importance to the service.

The Director of Naval Intelligence (DNI), Cyprian Bridge, and Captain Gerard Noel developed a further point; that, according to Bridge, British adoption of such mines 'will tend to justify and encourage other nations in the indiscriminate use of scattered mechanical mines, from which we will suffer most'.[34] This notion that British adoption of a weapon would encourage other nations to use it was one frequently presented to discourage the use of underwater weapons. There does not appear to be evidence of British actions having any impact on the decisions made by other powers with relation to mines. The decision was taken by the First Naval Lord, Admiral Sir Frederick Richards, that it was 'not proposed to adopt blockade mines as a form of naval warfare and the experiments in *Vernon* may be discontinued'.[35]

The decision not to adopt independent mines in 1895 did not lead to an end to mining within the Royal Navy. The service maintained its traditional mining policy based around controlled mines and countermining. Fleet exercises with these weapons continued unabated, as they would until 1905. It is clear however that the subject was becoming something of a backwater. The strategic circumstances which had led to the development of the mining policy in the 1870s had disappeared. Heavy breech-loading artillery rendered controlled mines ineffective; the range of the guns was such that most harbours could be bombarded from outside of the minefield. The strategy of coastal assault, for which countermining had been developed, was no longer a primary focus for the service, which was increasingly preoccupied by the threat at sea. The development of effective automatic depth-taking apparatus meant mining could be undertaken on a far larger scale, limiting the feasibility of countermining. Within the torpedo service the Whitehead was seen as a more promising area of endeavour, with rapid developments both within the weapon and its delivery systems. Mining had ceased to be at the cutting edge of the navy's strategic outlook, and suffered accordingly.

II

The Royal Navy's attitude towards mining fitted into a broader scepticism towards underwater weapons, which was particularly apparent in the 1890s. This was brought into relief by the response to the proposals for the 1899 Hague Peace Conference.[36] The conference was called by the Tsar, who was keen to place some limits on the defence expenditure of the Great Powers, which had escalated rapidly over the previous decade. One of the ways in which the Russians hoped to achieve this was by restricting the adoption of new technologies.[37] Two such proposals directly pertained to the naval sphere, the first being that the Great Powers should not increase the calibre of ordnance, or power of explosives on new ships. The second proposed that signatories 'prohibit the use in naval warfare of submarine torpedo-boats or plungers, or other similar engines of destruction'.[38] The First Lord of the Admiralty, George Goschen, requested that the DNI, Reginald Custance, comment on the proposals.[39] Custance's remarks, which were to form the basis of the Admiralty's position for the conference, were generally marked by their scepticism towards both the intentions and the reality of the Russian proposals. He argued that any attempt to limit either naval expenditure or the development of naval technology would be contrary to British interests. The only place where this stance wavered was on the Russian proposal to ban submarines. The DNI acknowledged that '(a)s the submarine boat will use the same weapon as the above water torpedo boat and its crew will probably run just as much risk as the crew of the latter, it is not seen why the use of submarine boats is less humane than that of the Torpedo Boat.' This did not mean that Custance could not see the advantages of such a proposal to Britain:

> The submarine boat is the arm of the weaker navy. It would be in our interest to prohibit it, as well as mines and torpedoes of all kinds, because the efficiency of our blockades would be much increased. The fact is that the advantage which the superior Navy gained by the use of steam has been counterbalanced by what it has lost through the introduction of mines and torpedoes.[40]

These remarks did not make it into the official response from the Admiralty to the Foreign Office, in which the former gave its views on the Russian proposals. Instead the Admiralty rejected all restrictions on arms development which would 'favour the interests of savage nations and be against those of the more highly civilised'.[41] The British naval delegate at the conference, Vice-Admiral Sir John Fisher, did, however, pick up on Custance's strand of thought. When the restrictions on naval technology came to be discussed before the Second Sub-Commission of the First Commission of the Conference Fisher adopted somewhat contradictory positions. He argued that any restrictions on the size of naval ordnance or the power of explosives were 'out of the question'. Conversely, he fully supported the proposal to ban submarines, so long as the agreement was unanimous. Fisher's positions naturally owed more to British interests than any notion of what was either moral or practical. In the end the French and the Americans came out strongly in opposition of any ban on submarines, and even the Russians, who had first put forward the proposal, chose to reserve their opinion, something that provoked much amusement both at the conference and in the Admiralty in London.[42] The 1899 conference did not place any restrictions on submarines and did not even discuss limitations on mines or torpedoes, but the attitude of the Royal Navy towards the conference proposals does give a good indication of its views regarding underwater weapons. Although there was clear scepticism over the entire concept of arms control, few seem to have doubted that it would have been in Britain's favour for underwater weapons to be removed from the arsenals of the Great Powers entirely.

The failure of the conference to place any restrictions on the development of submarines, although not unexpected, placed additional focus on the question of how the Royal Navy was to respond to the challenge, and eventually led to a reopening of the entire subject of independent mining. The Admiralty had been tracking developments in France from 1898, with naval attachés H. B. Jackson and Douglas Gamble warning of the feasibility of the new submarines and the threat that they could pose. Fisher, who went straight from The Hague to take up command of the Mediterranean Fleet, took a strong interest in the issue. In particular he was concerned about the threat that submarines could pose to any blockade of Toulon and began investigating methods for destroying submarines. It was in relation to this that H. B. Jackson, newly appointed to command the torpedo depot ship *Vulcan*, suggested that 'the question of using blockade mines might with advantage be reopened'. He went on to emphasize that 'it is an offensive weapon and great importance is attached to its use by foreign European navies'. Jackson's fondness for independent mining is perhaps unsurprising, considering his long association with the subject.[43] Fisher picked up on the comment and in typically direct style sent a request to the Admiralty that '24 of the mines … may be sent out as soon as possible'.[44] He would have been well aware that this was in contravention of the decision taken in 1895 to abandon these weapons, to which he had wholeheartedly agreed. Fisher presumably believed that this direct approach would force the Board to reconsider the issue seriously and direct any negative comment about the original decision away from himself.

The Admiralty did not immediately acquiesce to Fisher's demand, but instead reopened the whole question of independent mining. Edmund Jeffreys, the DNO, reexamined the grounds on which the 1895 decision had been made, concluding that 'foreign nations especially France and Russia have not waited for our "justifying and encouraging them" but have adopted the system on, I believe an extensive scale'. Looking forward, Jeffreys argued that 'the submarine boat appears to be rapidly approaching a defined position as a new instrument of war' and 'the only practical way to stop these boats, or frighten them so much as to keep them at home, seems to be by blockade mines'.[45] Jeffreys' views were broadly supported by the Board, with concern being expressed at the revelation that all five of the major European powers had now adopted systems of blockade mining. The DNI Reginald Custance, however, represented a strong branch of thought within the navy when he stated that 'it can hardly be argued that the blockade mine is the only practical way to meet the submerged boat'.[46] He felt that merely scaring the submarines into remaining in harbour was an inappropriate course of action for an organisation built upon an offensive tradition. The Senior Naval Lord, Walter Kerr, appears to have broadly shared this sentiment. Whilst accepting the adoption of independent mines he insisted that they should not 'be carried in the ships beyond what is necessary for instruction.'[47] Experiments were restarted at *Vernon*; however there remained a healthy scepticism amongst many in the service, who viewed these weapons as a potential threat rather than an opportunity.

The Royal Navy developed a very pragmatic attitude to technology in this period, and where it did not have the skills or expertise itself, it sought to purchase them. Thus in early 1901 the Admiralty sent two of its best young officers, H. B. Jackson and Reginald Bacon, to Genoa to look at purchasing the 'Elia' mine, a design adopted by a number of European nations. Bacon and Jackson reported that the mine was a well designed and effective system, which fulfilled all the requirements that would be expected of a blockade mine. They went on, however to note that 'the Elia mine possesses no secret unknown to the staff of H.M.S. *Vernon* but what it does possess is certainty of action produced by years of experience and lengthy trials'. The report noted regarding the Elia's strengths that 'there is no doubt that these features might have been evolved in our own Service by this time had not the particular type of mine been discarded'. One can clearly sense Jackson's frustration as the mine adopted in 1894 was his own design, and one he believed to be at least equal to that now on sale.[48] In accordance with the report's proposal the navy did not purchase the rights to the Elia design, but instead *Vernon* was requested to develop a design 'as expeditiously as possible'. To aid this, an additional £5000 was made available.[49] Interestingly, Jackson and Bacon presented a clear picture in their report of the offensive potential of independent mining. They felt that mines of this type could be used with advantage to 'blockade an enemy, either in or out of his own ports' and additionally could be used as part of a blockade of a commercial port. Regarding both such operations they emphasised the importance of both speed and scale. They did, however, state that 'we do not consider that this class of mine is of any great value as a defence against submarine boats'.[50] The reasoning behind this statement is far from clear. It appears to entirely contradict Jackson's earlier arguments for reopening the case for independent mining. It is possible that Jackson was merely using the attention given to submarines at the time as a vehicle to get the Admiralty to reconsider the use of these weapons. It is notable that the discussion of using mines as ASW devices disappears for some time after this report, and it seems likely that this conclusion had a detrimental impact on this branch of mining.

From the middle of 1901 *Vernon* devoted considerable resources and effort into the production of an independent mine. Its design was broadly based upon that which had been abandoned in 1895, using a modified version of Jackson's firing mechanism. Here the direct impact of the organisation's strategic preconceptions on the development of technology can clearly be seen. Whilst the decision had been taken by the Admiralty to adopt independent or blockade mines, it is apparent that little real thought had gone into what exactly the navy required.

Part of the problem stemmed from the compartmentalisation of issues such as mining, which saw technical departments like *Vernon* being relied upon to answer broader strategic issues. As Herbert Richmond remarked 'the opinion of *Vernon* is not one which is of particular value strategically. They think in detail and not in mass. They work on subjects such as the design of a Reducer value or a telephone, but do not study war with a big W.'[51] The difficulties came when the failure to understand the broader picture directly impacted the development of technology. In the case of the design of the new independent mine, *Vernon* did not think carefully about what criteria the new design needed to meet. In particular, the design of the mine was adapted in such a way as to try to ensure that it could be made safe in order to raise it after use.[52] This had been a requirement of the navy for all mine designs, but was abandoned as unrealistic for independent mines in 1892. The reasons why it was readopted are unclear; however it suggests that little attention was paid to the circumstances in which mines would be used. Similarly, great effort was put into limiting the effect of countermining on the new weapon; indeed one potential firing pistol was discounted solely because of its susceptibility to countermining.[53] This clearly indicates that the navy, or at least those at *Vernon* carrying out the trials, had not properly considered the issues. Countermining was a feasible mine-clearance technique when mines were confined to narrow channels and shallow waters and when those attempting to clear the mines had a good idea of where the field was. It was simply too resource-intensive to carry out on a large scale. If independent mines were to be used extensively in fast night-time operations, as suggested in Jackson and Bacon's report, then the scope for them being cleared through countermining was very limited indeed.

The impact of this uncertainty on the design of the mine was apparent. C. J. Briggs, who had taken over from H. B. Jackson on the *Vulcan*, carried out trials with the mines. He concluded that:

> the result of the [blockade] mining is generally very unsatisfactory. Many attempts have been made to construct a blockade mine which will answer certain conditions, but the present gear satisfies none of them with any degree of reliance ... . The withdrawal of these mines for the present is therefore suggested.[54]

Vernon immediately replaced this design with a newer version, however the basic fault of trying to achieve too much in one design remained.

The initial spurt of interest in independent mining in *Vernon* quickly dissipated. Despite the resources and trials, no effective design for a service independent mine was produced until 1905, when events elsewhere brought the issue back into clear focus.

The decision to readopt independent mining should have forced the navy to carry out some definite strategic thinking with regard to how and where these weapons would be deployed. The evidence of the ongoing problems of mine design implies that this had not taken place. This is not entirely true; Bacon and Jackson in their report on the Elia mine had laid out the potential for using mines offensively, particularly mentioning the need for speed and stealth in operations near an enemy's coast.[55] John Fisher also showed a continued interest in independent mining after he left the Mediterranean Fleet. Whilst Second Naval Lord, Fisher wrote a paper entitled 'Automatic Dropping Mines for Ocean Use, both for Offensive and Defensive Purposes'. In it he argued that 'the question of the use of these mines as an adjunct to a battle fleet in a fleet action has not been put forward so strongly as desirable as compared with their use in preventing egress or ingress to a port.' Fisher stated that 'there is no question they could be employed with immense effect to protect the rear of a retreating fleet'.[56] These weapons were not, in Fisher's mind at least, purely defensive. He discussed at some length ways in which an admiral could lure his opponent over a minefield, causing widespread destruction. The paper appears to have been inspired by a set of Italian fleet exercises in which a similar set of events took place. Fisher concluded in typical style.

> Briefly, they are offensive mines, and are being largely adopted in foreign navies. Special vessels are necessary for laying them efficiently. If we do not adopt them, we shall lack one weapon possessed by our enemies, which will be used against us and we shall not be able to retaliate in the same manner. No means should be neglected for injuring our enemies.[57]

Fisher was railing against the decision made by Lord Walter Kerr, the First Naval Lord, to adopt independent mines but not to put in place the infrastructure or resources to use them properly. Most notable was the mention given to minelayers, a new class of ship that had just been adopted by the Russian and Italian navies. It is unclear who read Fisher's memorandum, or what their reaction was; the copy which Fisher later gave to the Prime Minister, Arthur Balfour was simply annotated

'Written on 6th Dec 1902 by Sir John Fisher, as Second Sea Lord,—but the proposal was shelved.'

It is clear that whilst the Royal Navy had adopted independent mines in 1901 they remained a peripheral technology. Put simply, the majority within the Admiralty did not accept the contention made by Bacon, Jackson and Fisher that they were an offensive weapon. Instead they were regarded as a defensive one, whose innate role, sea denial, was the antithesis of the founding purpose of the Royal Navy. There was no notion of how independent mines could be used by a power seeking to exercise command of the sea. It is worth noting that the Royal Navy saw this in absolute terms; therefore, even in their role of sealing up enemy's harbours, mines were limited by the difficulty of ensuring that no ships would, under any circumstances, be able to pass through the minefield. The Royal Navy was also largely blind to the threat posed by mines. There appears to have been little acceptance of Fisher's realisation of the suitability of independent mines for ocean use. Mines had always been a littoral weapon; the service was well aware of their potential in this environment but was, in this period, unlikely to deploy the fleet in coastal waters. The Royal Navy did not appreciate how the greatly expanded scope of these weapons could impinge on its strategic intentions, and as such devoted no real effort to addressing these issues.

Any opportunity for a full reconsideration of independent mining evaporated when, in January 1903, the Secretary of State for War, St John Brodrick, raised the question of the continuation of RE submarine mining at British ports.[58] This issue was complex and highly politically charged. On a basic level the Royal Navy did not see any advantage to the army in continuing to spend money on submarine mining defences which it viewed as obsolete. Furthermore, many naval officers were far from comfortable at the idea of such dangerous weapons being in the hands of the army, which it was felt was unable to distinguish an enemy's ship from a British one. The problem lay in the navy's concern that the army had a deeper political motive for the reconsideration of submarine mining. Up until this point it had been accepted that the army would provide for the defence of British ports, something that freed the navy to act offensively. In an era of defence cuts the army was keen to focus its resources elsewhere, whilst the navy was desperate not to get drawn into providing what it described as fixed defences. In this climate the navy had no desire to add to the confusion by reappraising its mining policy. Further uncertainty was added from the end of 1903 as senior military and political leaders began to focus their attention on the deterioration of relations between Japan and Russia in the Far East. Having recently signed a defensive treaty with the Japanese, British leaders were very concerned about the possibility of being dragged into an unnecessary conflict.[59]

The extent to which mining had slipped from naval priorities by 1903 is revealed by a series of documents discussing mining vessels. In October the Controller, William May, raised the question as to whether a replacement for the mining depot ship *Hecla* should be included in the Estimates for the next year.[60] It was decided that such a vessel was not really required and that if necessary a ship could be taken up from the mercantile marine for the purpose. Tellingly, the Senior Naval Lord, Walter Kerr, minuted that 'it must of course be borne in mind that the cost of such a vessel must come off other services, unless, as is unlikely, we can enlarge our estimates.'[61] In an era of stretched budgets the Admiralty were looking to make savings wherever they could and mining offered an obvious target. The DNI, Prince Louis of Battenberg, went on to comment that other, more important, roles were assigned to ships to be taken up from the merchant marine, a telling indictment of how far mining had fallen in priority from the 1880s, when a mining ship had been viewed as an essential part of any fleet.[62] As a result of this decision the Board asked the Transport Department to investigate the availability of vessels to be taken up for mining purposes in the event of war. The focus was on telegraph cable ships, which had the necessary tanks and other fittings for storing and dispensing submarine electric cable. The assumption appears to have been that the Royal Navy would continue to focus on controlled mining, which required such stores, although the issue of where they would be used seems to have been ignored. The matter was then left for some time, and, before any definite action could be taken, war had broken out in the Far East and events there would eventually lead to a dramatic shift in policy. In the meantime it was apparent that mining was no longer being seriously considered by the Royal Navy in the event of war.

For many years mine warfare, in the form of controlled mining, had been at the heart of the Royal Navy's strategic and technical thinking. The service had embraced the technology because it offered a solution to specific challenges and in doing so could be adapted to fit in with the aims and strategic culture of the service. This was never the case with independent mining. Despite the best efforts of certain officers independent mines were simply never perceived to be a weapon which could fit with the way the Royal Navy intended to fight, be that strategically or culturally. It would need events elsewhere to reinvigorate the debate around mining in the Royal Navy.

NOTES

1. The National Archives [TNA], ADM 116/247, 'Automatic Depth Arrangement (Lieut Ottley's)' enclosed in Markham to Admiralty, 26 August 1884, G2586/84.
2. John Beeler, *British Naval Policy in the Gladstone–Disraeli Era 1866–1880* (Stanford: Stanford University Press, 1997), pp. 211–215; John Beeler, *Birth of the Battleship: British Capital Ship Design 1870–1881* (London: Chatham Publishing, 2001), pp. 9–29; and Andrew Lambert, 'The Royal Navy, 1856–1914: Deterrence and the Strategy of World Power', in Keith Neilson and Elizabeth Jane Errington, eds., *Navies and Global Defense: Theories and Strategy* (Westport, CT: Praeger, 1995), p. 78.
3. For a detailed discussion of the Royal Navy and controlled mining see Richard Dunley, 'Technology and Tradition: Mine Warfare and the Royal Navy's Strategy of Coastal Assault 1870–1890', *Journal of Military History*, vol. 80, no. 2 (2016), pp. 389–409.
4. *Torpedo Manual for Her Majesty's Fleet*, vol. II (HMSO, 1882), pp. 2, 3, 74.
5. The weights refer to the charge of wet guncotton contained within the mine. TNA, ADM 186/870, 'Notes on Naval Guns and Torpedoes', 1893, pp. 217–218.
6. *Torpedo Manual for Her Majesty's Fleet*, vol. II (HMSO, 1882), pp. 80–90; Murray F. Sueter, *The Evolution of the Submarine Boat, Mine and Torpedo from the Sixteenth Century to the Present Time* (Portsmouth: Griffin & Co., 1907), pp. 266–280; and G. E. Armstrong, *Torpedoes and Torpedo Vessels* (London: George Bell & Sons, 1901), pp. 101–125.
7. *Torpedo Manual for Her Majesty's Fleet*, vol. II (HMSO, 1882), pp. 142–150.
8. *Torpedo Manual for Her Majesty's Fleet*, vol. II (HMSO, 1888), p. 201.
9. Dunley, 'Technology and Tradition'.
10. TNA, ADM 189/1, Vernon Annual Report 1881, Herbert minute, 26 August 1881.
11. Richard Dunley, '"The Most Resistless and Revolutionary Weapon of Naval Warfare That Has Ever Been Introduced": The Royal Navy and the Whitehead Torpedo 1870–1890', in Michael LoCicero, Ross Mahoney, and Stuart Mitchell, eds., *A Military Transformed?: Adaptation and Innovation in the British Military, 1792–1945* (London: Helion, 2014).

12. E. N. Poland, *The Torpedomen: HMS Vernon's Story 1872–1986* (Private Publication, 1993), Appendix A.
13. TNA, WO 33/19, Final Report, Floating Obstructions Committee, July 1868, p. XXVIII.
14. TNA, ADM 1/6088, 'Commander Fisher's Report of His Visit to Prussian Establishments', 21 August 1869.
15. Churchill Archives Centre (CAC), FISR 10/8, 'A Short Treatise on Electricity and the Management of Electric Torpedoes', p. 88.
16. TNA, ADM 189/4, 'Lieutenant Ottley's Automatic Depth Taking Apparatus for Submarine Mines', 1884, p. 171.
17. *Torpedo Manual for Her Majesty's Fleet*, Volume II (HMSO, 1882), p. 56.
18. TNA, ADM 116/331, Tryon to Admiralty, 13 April 1885, G2445/85.
19. TNA, ADM 116/331, Hood minute, 22 January 1886, G197/86.
20. TNA, ADM 116/331, 'Experiments with Captain Joseph's Mechanical Mine', Fisher minute, 4 January 1887, G6552/86.
21. TNA, ADM 256/31, 'Mines for Blockade Purposes', p. 45.
22. TNA, ADM 12/1232, Cut 59.8, Beresford Report, G8517/91.
23. TNA, ADM 189/11, Vernon Annual Report 1891, 'Experiments with Ottley Mines from HMS Undaunted', pp. 84–92.
24. TNA, ADM 256/31, DNO Papers 1895, 'Mines for Blockade Purposes', pp. 45–46.
25. National Maritime Museum (NMM), CBT/13/1(7), Richmond to Corbett, 20 November 1904.
26. TNA, ADM 189/12, Vernon Annual Report 1892, Ottley to Bourke, 12 April 1892, pp. 98–100; TNA, ADM 256/31, DNO Papers 1895, 'Mines for Blockade Purposes', p. 46.
27. TNA, ADM 189/12, Vernon Annual Report 1892, 'The Question of the Efficiency or Otherwise of Naval Mines', 15 July 1892, p. 101.
28. TNA, ADM 189/12, Vernon Annual Report 1892, 'Introductory Remarks', pp. ix–xi.
29. TNA, ADM 189/12, Vernon Annual Report 1892, 'The Question of the Efficiency or Otherwise of Naval Mines', 15 July 1892.
30. TNA, ADM 189/12, Vernon Annual Report 1892, Admiralty to Hall, 13 May 1892.
31. TNA, ADM 189/13 and ADM 189/14, Vernon Annual Reports 1893 and 1894, 'Blockade Mines'.
32. TNA, ADM 256/31, 'Mines for Blockade Purposes', May memo, n.d., pp. 47–48.
33. TNA, ADM 256/31, 'Mines for Blockade Purposes', Kane and Fisher minutes, 24 and 28 November 1894, p. 48.
34. TNA, ADM 256/31, 'Mines for Blockade Purposes', Bridge and Noel minutes, 28 November and 20 December 1894, p. 48.

35. TNA, ADM 256/31, 'Mines for Blockade Purposes', Richards minute, 28 January 1895, p. 48.
36. For best discussion of the conference and its origins see Alan M. Anderson, 'The Laws of War and Naval Strategy in Great Britain and the United States: 1899–1909' (Unpublished PhD thesis, King's College, London, 2016), pp. 47–140. Also see Scott Andrew Keefer, *The Law of Nations and Britain's Quest for Naval Security: International Law and Arms Control, 1898–1914* (Basingstoke: Palgrave Macmillan, 2016), pp. 95–135.
37. Alan M. Anderson, 'Jacky Fisher and the 1899 Hague Conference: A Reassessment', *New Zealand Journal of Research on Europe*, vol. 11, no. 1 (2017), pp. 53–92.
38. Count Mouravieff to Scott, 30 December 1898, 'Correspondence Respecting the Peace Conference at The Hague, 1899', Parliamentary Papers, C.9534, p. 4.
39. TNA, ADM 116/98, Goschen to Custance, 14 May 1899.
40. TNA, ADM 116/98, Custance Memorandum, n.d. (May 1899).
41. TNA, ADM 116/98, Admiralty to Foreign Office, 16 May 1899 (draft).
42. TNA, FO 412/65, Fisher Memorandum, n.d., enclosed in Paunceforte to Salisbury, 31 May 1899, No. 138, p. 120; TNA, ADM 116/98, 'Peace Conference: Questions Relating to Naval Warfare', Richards Minute, 2 June 1899.
43. TNA, ADM 189/20, Vernon Annual Report 1900, Jackson Report, 5 February 1900, pp. 23–25.
44. TNA, ADM 256/36, DNO Papers 1900, 'Blockade Mines—Use of, for Defence Against Submarine Boats', Fisher Submission, 20 February 1900, p. 105.
45. TNA, ADM 256/36, DNO Papers 1900, 'Blockade Mines—Use of, for Defence Against Submarine Boats', Jeffreys Minute, 14 April 1900, p. 106.
46. TNA, ADM 256/36, DNO Papers 1900, 'Blockade Mines—Use of, for Defence Against Submarine Boats', Custance Minute 23 April 1900, pp. 106–107.
47. TNA, ADM 256/36, DNO Papers 1900, 'Blockade Mines—Use of, for Defence Against Submarine Boats', Kerr Minute, 30 April 1900, p. 107.
48. TNA, ADM 256/37, DNO Papers 1901, Bacon and Jackson Report, 10 January 1901, G430/01, pp. 116–119.
49. TNA, ADM 256/37, DNO Papers 1901, 'Blockade Mine—Particulars of the "Elia"—"Vernon" to Work Out Designs', DNO Minute, 12 February 1901, p. 119.
50. TNA, ADM 256/37, DNO Papers 1901, Bacon and Jackson Report, 10 January 1901, pp. 116–119.

44   R. DUNLEY

51. NMM, CBT/13/1(7), Richmond to Corbett, 20 November 1904.
52. TNA, ADM 189/21–3, Vernon Annual Reports 1901–03, 'Blockade Mines'.
53. TNA, ADM 189/22, Vernon Annual Report 1902, 'Dumas Firing Pistol', pp. 49–50.
54. TNA, ADM 189/22, Vernon Annual Report 1902, 'Briggs Report on Torpedo Course at Platea'.
55. TNA, ADM 256/37, DNO Papers 1901, Bacon and Jackson Report, 10 January 1901, pp. 116–119.
56. British Library (BL), Add Ms 49710, Balfour Papers, 'Automatic Dropping Mines for Ocean Use, Both for Offensive and Defensive Purposes', n.d., ff. 1–2.
57. BL, Add Ms 49710, Balfour Papers, 'Automatic Dropping Mines for Ocean Use, Both for Offensive and Defensive Purposes', n.d., ff. 1–2.
58. For a detailed treatment of this subject see Richard Dunley, 'The Offensive Mining Service: Mine Warfare and Strategic Development 1900–1914' (Unpublished PhD thesis, King's College, London, 2013), pp. 30–61.
59. TNA, CAB 38/4/1, 29th Meeting CID, 4 January 1904.
60. TNA, MT 23/169, May minute, 15 October 1903, T228/04.
61. TNA, MT 23/169, Kerr minute, 17 October 1903, T228/04.
62. TNA, MT 23/169, Battenberg minute, 17 October 1903, T228/04.

CHAPTER 4

Mine Warfare in the Russo-Japanese War: The Royal Navy Perspective

The Russo-Japanese War, which broke out in February 1904, fundamentally changed the debate regarding mines in Britain. It indisputably demonstrated the power of these weapons to alter the course of war at sea and exercise an influence far beyond their size or cost. The war also highlighted the opportunities presented by the technology to act offensively and confirmed the mine's place as a crucial tool in the arsenal of any naval power. The reality of the events in the Far East, as embodied in the reports of the British naval attachés, reinvigorated the discussion of mines within the Royal Navy, but it also served to reinforce the deep cultural suspicion of the weapon, something that further polarised the debate in the service.

The Russo-Japanese War had its origins in the expansion of the two belligerents into the power vacuum left by the gradual collapse of Chinese influence in Korea and Manchuria. Japanese influence on the East Asian mainland grew rapidly following Japan's victory in the Sino-Japanese War of 1894–1895. The major check on its ambitions came from Russia. The Russians, together with France and Germany, had intervened in the Treaty of Shimonoseki at the end of the war to deprive Japan of the Liaodong Peninsula. To add insult to injury the Russians promptly occupied the peninsula themselves and began establishing a major naval base at Port Arthur. These developments meant that it was only a matter of time before Russia and Japan came to blows. From a British perspective this was an economically important part of the world; however, it was the signing of the Anglo-Japanese Alliance in 1902

© The Author(s) 2018
R. Dunley, *Britain and the Mine, 1900–1915,*
https://doi.org/10.1007/978-3-319-72820-9_4

45

which cemented British interest. This alliance dictated that if one party were at war with two or more hostile powers then the other would be obliged to come to their assistance. This was of particular importance due to Russia's alliance with France. Tensions between Russia and Japan rose throughout 1903, with no agreement seeming possible as to their respective spheres of influence in Korea and Manchuria.

War broke out on 8 February 1904, with a surprise Japanese torpedo attack on the Russian Pacific Fleet. This set the stage for what was to be in many ways a very modern war. The Royal Navy, together with the army, began to look at how to get accurate and up-to-date information. The conflict was the first between major powers since 1871 and the first with a strong naval focus since the American Civil War. Information on how the technological revolution which had occurred in that time had affected the battlefield was widely accepted to be of great importance.[1] The primary source for this type of intelligence-gathering were the military and naval attachés attached to the embassies and legations in the major naval powers.[2] As early as November 1903 the First Lord of the Admiralty, the Earl of Selborne, had suggested that, in light of the circumstances, the naval attaché in St Petersburg should 'be sent overland to visit Port Arthur and Vladivostok'.[3] This was rejected by the First Naval Lord, Admiral Lord Walter Kerr, who stated that work in the Far East was the responsibility of the attaché in Tokyo.[4] In April information reached the Admiralty that American and French naval attachés had left St Petersburg for the front. Prince Louis of Battenberg, the DNI, immediately suggested that a British officer should be sent out to follow the course of the war from the Russian side.[5] It was decided that Captain Cresswell Eyres, a young Russophile officer who had recently served in the Naval Intelligence Department (NID), should be dispatched.[6] The course of events combined with the difficult nature of Anglo-Russian relations meant that Eyres had a very unsatisfactory time in the Far East, eventually being captured by the Japanese without achieving anything of note.[7]

Close relations between the Royal Navy and the Imperial Japanese Navy meant that getting access from the Japanese side was somewhat easier. Two British officers, Captains Ernest Troubridge and Arthur Ricardo, were already in Japan, and Troubridge saw a great deal of the early action with the Japanese fleet. Inexplicably both officers then left their posts without Admiralty sanction and returned to England. There appears to have been a series of communication breakdowns between the Admiralty in London, Vice-Admiral Gerard Noel (Commander-in-Chief on the

China Station) and the attachés in Tokyo.[8] The First Lord, who was even more insistent than his professional advisors on having observers in the Far East, was 'raging'.[9] He wrote to Noel that '(t)his matter of Naval Attachés *is* my personal and particular responsibility', and took steps to resolve the issue.[10] Selborne ordered Noel to replace Ricardo with an officer from his fleet and told him that a further officer, Captain John Hutchison, was being sent out from England. Captain William Pakenham, who had replaced Troubridge, was to stay with the Japanese fleet. Selborne concluded by saying that these officers 'are not to be allowed to come away without the most positive orders from the Admiralty.'[11]

The result of this debacle was that a new group of officers served as attachés for the majority of the war. Captains Pakenham and Hutchison were to serve aboard the Japanese fleet, whilst Commander Thomas Jackson,[12] who had been selected by Noel to replace Ricardo, was based in Tokyo. Broadly speaking, the attachés appointed ably fulfilled their roles. Troubridge, whilst revealing a worrying sensitivity in his behaviour regarding leaving his post, appears to have had a strong relationship with the Japanese and his reports were well received.[13] Likewise, Pakenham and Jackson were intelligent and observant officers who won high praise from the Japanese government for their behaviour during the war.[14] Hutchison was very much the silent partner, and did not enjoy his service with the Japanese fleet. He transferred ashore in September 1904 at his own request, being replaced by Jackson, and spent the rest of the war reporting from Tokyo.[15] The British Minister, Sir Claude MacDonald, reported on this move in words which did not reflect well on Hutchison.[16] He did, however, go on to produce a number of useful reports on Japanese land-based preparations.[17]

The close relationship between Britain and Japan at the time meant that the attachés were well received and had unprecedented access to all aspects of the Imperial Japanese Navy. Thomas Jackson remarked to Noel on how open and frank the Japanese were with him and his colleagues, something that compared favourably with the experiences of the military attachés:

> The Naval officers are quite different to the military ones. Our Military Attachés are having great difficulty in getting any information beyond that given to the Military Attachés of all the Powers, but the Naval officers as a rule either say a matter is confidential or else explain it, without all the beating about the bush that the military officers indulge in.[18]

This favoured position enabled the attachés to compile detailed reports on the first major naval war of the twentieth century. The experiences of the Russo-Japanese War as recorded by the attachés would be a crucial element in the formation, justification and criticism of naval policy in Britain through to the outbreak of the First World War.[19]

I

The naval war, broadly speaking, fell into two distinct parts. Following an initial assault, the Japanese fleet blockaded the Russian Pacific Fleet in Port Arthur. The Russians launched occasional sallies resulting in minor actions; however they did not generally contest Japanese command of the sea. A Russian cruiser squadron operating out of Vladivostok to the north caused the Japanese a number of problems, conducting commerce-raiding operations and interdicting supplies between Japan and the mainland. In early December 1904 advances by the Japanese army allowed land-based artillery to destroy the Russian fleet in Port Arthur. This facilitated the second phase of the naval war, in which the Japanese were able to abandon the blockade and prepare to face the Russian Baltic Fleet, which was sailing round the globe to try to reestablish Russian command of the sea. This attempt failed with the crushing Japanese victory at Tsushima, which effectively ended the naval conflict.[20]

The war in its outline and strategy would have been familiar to any student of naval history, but the technology was radically new. One of the most important developments being the prevalence of underwater weapons. This was the first major conflict in which modern underwater weapons were to play a significant role, and the Admiralty in London was keen to see how effective they were in realistic wartime conditions.

The war began on 8 February 1904, when the Japanese launched a surprise torpedo attack on the Russian fleet in Port Arthur.[21] Eleven Japanese destroyers attacked the unprepared Russian fleet lying in the outer harbour.[22] The results were impressive; two Russian battleships and an armoured cruiser damaged, with the former two being forced to ground themselves in shallow water. The attack itself was, however, seen as something of a disappointment. Total surprise was achieved, with the first torpedoes being fired at unprepared ships from a relatively close range. Despite this the torpedoes failed to have the decisive effect which was hoped for, partly because of their still limited range and accuracy.[23] Following the initial assault there were few opportunities to use torpedoes to any advantage. Where they were used in the fleet engagements it was noticeable how difficult it was to achieve any hits. Torpedoes were used by both sides to sink stationary vessels; however striking a moving target was much more challenging. The limitations of speed and range meant that the weapon had far less impact on the course of the naval war than many observers had anticipated. Pakenham would later claim that the torpedo had a crucial indirect impact. He argued:

> I have had to draw the attention of the Admiralty to the extraordinary influence that has been conceded to the ship-borne torpedo in this war. This has been nothing less than that its range—with a bit added to give a margin of safety—has defined the minimum fighting distance for unbeaten fleets.[24]

In spite of these claims, it was apparent to most commentators that the torpedo had not lived up to the suggestions made in certain quarters that it had replaced the gun as the primary arbiter of naval warfare.[25]

The newest of underwater weapons, the submarine, had a rather surprising impact on the war. The Russians had for many years been interested in submarines, and this was reinvigorated by the maturing of the technology from the late 1890s. They had developed a number of small experimental craft by 1904 and some of these were shipped to the Far East. The extent to which these craft were ever operational is unclear; however their presence did exert a considerable moral effect. The Japanese had no submarines at the beginning of the conflict, but expended considerable effort in ordering submarines from America and purchasing designs for construction in home yards.[26] Neither project produced a submarine which was able to have any influence on the war. Despite the lack of operational submarines and the very limited nature of these vessels, both parties in the conflict were at times convinced that the other had submarines active, something that demonstrates the fear created by underwater weapons.

Contrary to the expectations of many, the weapon that came to dominate the first phase of the conflict was the mine. In total, during the war, the Japanese lost two battleships, four cruisers, two destroyers, one torpedo boat and two gunboats to mines, whilst the Russians lost one battleship, one cruiser, two destroyers, one torpedo boat and one gunboat.[27] The extent of these losses, especially when compared to the limited impact of gunfire and torpedoes in the period up until Tsushima, came as a great surprise to all observers. From the outset of the war the Russians and the Japanese laid independent mines in large numbers. Both sides had a design of electro-mechanical mine which they used, the Russian one being based upon the Hertz cell and horn, whilst the Japanese one used a sprung inertia circuit-closer with a dry-cell battery.[28] These weapons were laid with an automatic depth-taking apparatus similar in design to the Ottley or Pietruski gear used by other navies. It appears that they were regularly supplemented with mines extemporised from the opposing fleets, something which helps to explain some of the problems encountered in mining, particularly with regard to safety.[29] Japanese mining operations were generally rather ad hoc affairs, relying on destroyers, small commandeered steamers and, frequently, ship's launches and even temporary rafts.[30] The Russians, by contrast, had constructed some of the first minelayers, the *Amur* class, the lead ship of which served with great distinction in the conflict. It appears likely that they also used some smaller craft to lay mines in the coastal waters, although there is no evidence that they persuaded Chinese junks to perform this role, as was claimed by the Japanese.[31]

The pattern of the early phase of the war, with the Japanese blockading the Russians in port, gave great scope for mining operations to take place in the relatively confined waters around Port Arthur. Initially these were attritional in nature, affecting the light craft from both sides which operated inshore. By April 1904 the Russians had managed to repair the ships damaged in the 8 February torpedo attack and so were at least equal to the Japanese in materiel. Command of the Russian fleet had been taken over by Vice-Admiral Stepan Osipovich Makarov, who was far more willing than his predecessor to take the fight to the Japanese. In light of this the Japanese drew up a plan. On the night of 12 April mines were laid across the entrance to Port Arthur. The following morning a cruiser squadron was placed in full view, in an attempt 'to lure the Russians across the minefield'.[32] The initial phase of the plan failed; Makarov did as expected and sailed out to challenge the Japanese cruisers, passing through the minefield without incident. The Japanese commander, Admiral Tōgō Heihachirō, arrived with the main body of the Japanese fleet and the Russians, not yet desiring a major engagement, turned back. It was on the return to Port Arthur that Admiral Makarov's flagship, the *Petropavlovsk* struck a mine and promptly blew up. The battleship *Pobyeda* also struck a mine and barely made it back to Port Arthur. The incident had a profound impact on the course of the war; the loss of a first-class battleship tilted the balance of forces back in favour of the Japanese. More decisively the Russians lost, in Makarov, the one commander willing and able to challenge the Japanese at sea.[33] From this point on the Russian Pacific Fleet never sought to regain the initiative; its only sorties were intended to try to escape to Vladivostok to the north and, where possible, avoid confrontation with the Japanese. Captain Pakenham summed the event up by declaring that 'it was the day of the infernal machines'.[34]

Barely a month after the loss of the *Petropavlovsk*, mines inflicted on Japan what Pakenham described as the 'ultimate strategic injury'.[35] On the 14 May the Russian minelayer *Amur* laid a small field approximately ten miles offshore in an area commonly known to be traversed by the Japanese blockading squadron. The next day Admiral Nashiba, with his flagship *Hatsuse* and two further battleships, the *Shikishima* and *Yashima*, passed through the minefield. The *Hatsuse* and *Yashima* both struck mines; the flagship, in attempting to limp clear, struck a second mine which detonated the main magazine. Brave efforts were made to save the *Yashima*; however nightfall forced the crew temporarily to abandon her, and she had disappeared by the time the salvage effort was renewed next morning.[36] The potential impact of this event was vast. Pakenham outlined how 'at a single blow, and without corresponding loss to the enemy, Japan finds herself deprived of one third of her prime fighting force'.[37] The Russians did not properly exploit the Japanese loss. Makarov's replacement, Admiral Wilgelm Vitgeft, was unwilling to use his fleet aggressively and the Japanese were able to regroup. The losses were, however, sorely felt by the Japanese throughout the war and they meant that Tōgō had to face the Russian Baltic Fleet at a serious numerical disadvantage.

The Japanese were very concerned about the potential impact of the sinking of these two ships, not only on Russian strategy, but also on the morale at home. The *Hatsuse* had blown up in full view of Russian observers on the hills around Port Arthur and so its loss could not be denied. The *Yashima* had been seen to strike a mine, but she had proceeded south over the horizon before sinking in darkness. The Japanese therefore acknowledged the loss of one battleship, and a small cruiser, *Yoshino*, which had been sunk in a ramming accident earlier in the same day. The crew of the *Yashima* were employed elsewhere and the Captain and officers took up quarters in a torpedo depot ship, from where the books of the *Yashima* remained open, and official correspondence produced, until well after the end of the war. The plan worked very well; the Russians were totally deceived, and continued to report the presence of five Japanese battleships in the region.[38]

The destruction of three first-class battleships fundamentally changed the course of the war at sea. The loss of the *Petropavlovsk* deprived the Russians of the chance to reestablish their superiority in materiel and resulted in the death of the one commander who was willing to contest Japanese command of the sea. The Japanese losses were arguably even more significant. The *Hatsuse* and *Yashima* represented a large proportion of Japanese naval strength and were irreplaceable. Had either the Russian Pacific, or Baltic Fleets been better trained or led, these losses might well have cost Japan the war. Although there were no further losses of battleships after May, mine warfare continued to be an essential and everyday part of the war at sea right up until the time when Port Arthur finally fell. Indeed, as a result of the loss of the two Japanese battleships Tōgō withdrew his main fleet to a secure anchorage and attempted to block Port Arthur through a larger-scale use of mines. This in turn placed additional emphasis on the Russian ability to maintain a clear channel through the Japanese minefields. Following the destruction of the Russian Pacific Fleet the focus on mining slipped, as attention turned to the arrival of the Baltic Fleet. The large number of mines laid, and their tendency to break free from their moorings did, however, mean that they would remain an issue until well after the war was concluded.

II

Unsurprisingly, given the crucial role mines played in the first phase of the war, they were one of the subjects that came to dominate the reports of the British naval attachés. These reports were read by all the key decision-makers in London and formed the basis of the surge in interest, both positive and negative, in mining from 1904 onwards. One of the major problems facing the attachés was their lack of detailed knowledge of mine warfare. None had trained as a torpedo officer, and although they would all have taken part in the Royal Navy's mining exercises it is unlikely that they would have had much experience with independent as opposed to controlled mines. It is possible that the choice of officers reflected an expectation that the key issues in the conflict would revolve around fleet battle and gunnery, but there is no specific evidence on this point, and the confusion surrounding the appointments perhaps makes it unlikely. The impact of this decision was, however, clear. A lack of detailed knowledge meant that whilst the attachés undoubtedly tried their best to provide accurate information to their superiors in London, much of the discussion surrounding mining was confused, something that had a knock-on effect on the debate in Britain.

One of the key questions which regularly recurred in the attaché reports surrounded the ability of mines to successfully sink a first-class battleship. This might seem a strange point considering the weapon's spectacular successes on this front, but there was a deep-seated scepticism among many within the service. This was rooted in the Royal Navy's strong technological and cultural association with the battle fleet and the unwavering belief in its primacy as the arbiter of naval conflict. Traces of such views can clearly be picked up in the reports of the naval attachés, and the course of events served to amplify any doubts regarding the effectiveness of the mine to the audience in London. In the wake of the sinking of the *Petropavlovsk* the Admiralty received reports from Pakenham, who was with the Japanese fleet, and Jackson, in Tokyo. Both reports noted separate explosions from the mine and then the magazine; Jackson went on to note that witnesses 'did not attribute the sinking of the flagship to the direct effect of the mine'.[39] The reports with regard to the loss of the *Hatsuse* also emphasised the importance of the magazine explosion. Indeed a report by Hutchison stated that this fatal explosion took place a minute and a half after the second mine struck, and as such it could have been 'entirely independent of the result of the mine'. Hutchison went on to argue that the secondary explosion on the *Petropavlovsk* was caused by over-sensitive fuses in shells in the magazine.[40] This focus on secondary explosions clearly tapped into the faith placed in the battleship as a technology and the losses were framed as being, at least in part, a result of faulty ship design, or bad explosives handling, rather than a deeper challenge to the position of the battleship.

This tendency was naturally tempered by the context provided by the loss of the *Yashima*, and the serious damage to the *Pobyeda* without any secondary explosions. Pakenham was far from immune to the tendency to focus on the importance of the battle fleet, but the events of April and May 1904 clearly shocked him. He wrote in the first draft of his report on the loss of the two Japanese battleships that 'it tends to drive home and place beyond dispute a lesson which those who put their trust in battle-ships, will be unwilling to learn'.[41] The Japanese attempts to cover up the loss of the *Yashima* had a direct impact on the way the effectiveness of the mine was perceived. In order to assist with their deception the Japanese Admiralty asked that Pakenham's full report on the loss of both ships be withheld until the end of the war. The Japanese were initially very reticent to reveal the loss of the *Yashima*, even to their allies, but by the beginning of June Sir Claude MacDonald secretly informed London of the disaster and one must assume that the other British naval attachés in the region were also aware of it.[42] Their reports, however, were not allowed to mention the sinking and this served to accentuate the tendency, which was already prevalent, to see the loss of these ships as a failure of ship design as opposed to the result of the success of an offensive weapon. Whilst it is clear that the Admiralty in London was aware of the loss of the *Yashima* it is less obvious how, in the absence of Pakenham's detailed report on the subject, it interpreted the information available to it. Without the knowledge as to how the *Yashima* was lost it would have been very easy to overplay the importance of secondary explosions, especially when the attaché reports contained so much conflicting information on what was a relatively new subject. This helps to explain the continuing Admiralty focus on the importance of secondary explosions when considering protection from underwater attack. The Committee on Designs, which met in early 1905 and produced the basic designs for both the *Dreadnought* and the *Invincible*, directly mentioned the loss of both the *Petropavlovsk* and the *Hatsuse* to secondary explosions. The committee placed great emphasis on 'having a magazine under each pair of guns so situated as to be as far as possible from a mine explosion'.[43] This was arguably seen as more important than the watertight subdivision of ships which is commonly associated with underwater protection, and which would have prevented losses such as that of the *Yashima*.

The issue of the effectiveness of mines was further confused by the prevalence of floating, or drifting mines. Mines laid by both sides broke free from their moorings, particularly in rough weather, and they were not designed to either sink or detonate on breaking free, as later mines tended to be. These weapons then drifted on the current and presented a particular hazard as the conflict wore on. The reporting of floating mines was somewhat confused, with many, including the British attachés, believing that belligerents were purposefully using unanchored mines and failing to understand their limited effectiveness. On the 26 October 1904 the Japanese battleship *Asahi*, with Captain Pakenham on board, struck a floating mine. Pakenham commented in his report that the damage, amounting to a few burst valves, 'could hardly have been less'.[44]

This report, together with other examples of minimal damage caused by floating mines, created something of a quandary. How could mine explosions sink the *Petropavlovsk, Hatsuse* and *Yashima* and yet leave other vessels barely marked? Pakenham put this down in large part to the mine striking on the armoured belt, noting that 'the power of thick armour to withstand a heavy explosion will cause no surprise'.[45] In truth thick plate provided a remarkably poor defence against a submerged explosion, as the Royal Navy had discovered in the 1870s, but Pakenham would have been unlikely to have known this, not being a torpedo officer. Another explanation alluded to in the reports was that the mines were of greatly varying sizes. This was most likely to be true, particularly in the case of the extempore mines used by both sides. Pakenham's report on the *Asahi* explosion points, however, to another explanation. The mine struck the main armoured belt of the battleship and Pakenham noted 'nearly the whole force of the explosion appears to have gone upwards, smashing all excrescences or projections on the ship's side'.[46] This is, perhaps, unsurprising for the detonation of a floating mine. Submarine explosions are so powerful because of the density of the medium in which the detonation takes place. A floating mine is only half submerged and thus the force of the detonation would be channelled upwards by the water and the side of the ship. Floating mines, although dangerous to light craft, would have been unlikely to have seriously damaged a heavy warship. Unfortunately the British attachés in the Far East did not have the appropriate background to understand and acknowledge this distinction.

The combination of the recurring discussion of the importance of secondary explosions and uncertainty over floating mines meant that the attaché reports often presented a confused picture of the effectiveness of mines against warships. This provided the scope necessary for the reaction to the reports to be shaped by the culture and experience of the audience in London. Whilst many were entirely convinced as to the continuing impact mines would have on naval conflict, others, drawing on these uncertainties, felt that the influence of mines had been exaggerated. This fed into the preexisting debates within the Royal Navy regarding mines and provided the context for the future development of the technology.

The lack of detailed knowledge of mining and mining processes also impacted on the ability of the attachés to report on the design of mines and minelaying equipment. This was not helped by this being one of the few areas in which the Japanese were not overly willing to give their British guests unrestricted access.[47] This lack of knowledge did not disguise the very obvious danger which was associated with all types of mining operation in the war. The process of laying mines remained a difficult one; early in the war the Russians suffered particularly from the dangers presented by their own mines. Interestingly, Pakenham put this down to the 'size and deep draft of the vessels employed' by the Russians in minelaying, with the Japanese immunity 'attributed to their having followed the opposite course'.[48] The truth of this appears to have been limited; in the later stages of the war the Japanese suffered a notable number of casualties both in the preparation and laying of mines.[49] Indeed, Pakenham reported that the Japanese had, by November, concluded that their mines were 'not sufficiently safe in laying out and not sufficiently sensitive when laid'.[50] Mine clearance posed an even greater challenge for the two navies. Both adopted some form of sweeping technique for the purpose, with the Russians gaining particular experience through their attempts to keep a clear channel out of Port Arthur. This came at a considerable cost and all mine-clearance operations were fraught with danger, a problem which neither side successfully solved.[51]

One of the aspects of mining that was raised in a report from Pakenham was the importance of precision and knowledge. He noted that 'unless securely moored in a situation accurately known, the mine is not only as likely to injure the side that lays it down as it is the enemy, but is a danger to general navigation.' The risks associated with this issue were made very clear when the Russian minelayer *Yenesei* was lost. She sank taking the only plans of the minefield she had just laid with her.[52] Concern about the loss of the *Yenesei* was such that the First Naval Lord, Admiral Lord Walter Kerr, felt the need to request that the Foreign Office obtain further information from the Russians. Ironically, Kerr was more concerned about the release of floating mines when the ship sank than the precise location of the minefield, but this appears indicative of the lack of real knowledge of independent mining in the Admiralty.[53] More generally the reports of the attachés reveal how both laying and sweeping independent mines required accurate navigation and the rapid communication and dissemination of information, in order to minimise the threat these weapons posed.

Despite these issues, discussion of mines and mining occupied a large proportion of the reports produced by the attachés, and the impact they had on the conflict was obvious to both professional and civilian audiences. This focus on mining, together with the comparatively unimpressive results of torpedoes and gunnery, at least until Tsushima, presented a fundamental challenge to the Royal Navy's strategic and cultural association with the battle fleet. Indeed, so stark was this challenge that Pakenham felt the need to address it directly in a report. Unfortunately the only copy of this report known to exist is in Pakenham's personal papers, so we cannot be certain that it was ever sent. In his report Pakenham acknowledged that the events of the war had not conformed to expectations. He accepted that on initial inspection battleships had achieved little in the conflict, '(t)hough costing millions, it seems hard to say what benefit either Russia or Japan has derived from the possession of these dear-bought monsters'.[54] By contrast the mine appeared to be the weapon which was dominating the naval war. These admissions were in themselves indicative of the remarkable change in attitude brought about by the conflict, but Pakenham was keen to emphasise that he did not feel that such lessons were immediately applicable to naval warfare more generally. He suggested that the particular circumstances of the conflict had given the mine 'a prominence to which it is no means entitled'. More generally he suggested that a balanced view needed to be taken, arguing that:

> Command of the sea neither rests, nor promises to rest in any near future, with either battle-ship or small-craft separately: each class has its own special duty, and completeness can only be attained when they are used to compliment each other.[55]

The fact that Pakenham felt the need to write this report, subtly playing down the impact of the mine and reasserting the importance of the battleship, albeit within a balanced naval force, is indicative of how great an influence mine warfare had on the first half of the conflict. It also highlights the perceived polarity in the relationship between the mine and the battleship, something that would continue to be an important factor in shaping the response of the Royal Navy to mining throughout the period.

III

The direct, material, impact of mine warfare in the Russo-Japanese War was easy to see and quantify, whether it be in ships sunk, or men killed. What was more difficult to gauge was the unquestionable impact of the

58   R. DUNLEY

fear created by these weapons on the morale of the forces and the decisions made by their commanders. This issue did, however, come through clearly in the reports of the naval attachés. Captain Pakenham was by, all accounts, a fearless individual who was noted at the time for his sang-froid, and yet even he was perturbed by the constant threat invoked by mines.[56] He commented that:

> A point to which those not taking part in this war seem blind is that naval battles are going on the whole time. In these days it is unnecessary for fleets to meet face to face. When they do, the fighting is obvious and the sound of the artillery appeals to the common herd, but the continuous and deadly struggle that never ceases by day or night passes unrecognised. And yet, glancing back over the events of this war, it may be seen that the danger to life and the losses incurred by mines alone are equivalent in their total result to more than one first class naval action. For braving these neither Admirals or Fleets receive any credit.[57]

Both fleets struggled to come to terms with their losses to mines. The anxiety caused by the suddenness of the strikes, their unknown origin and the lack of an enemy to strike back at, promoted panic. Following the loss of the *Hatsuse* and *Yashima* Pakenham observed this tendency in the Japanese fleet.

> When the *Petropavlovsk* was blown up observers in the Japanese fleet were diverted by the flurry of Russians trying to re-enter their port, and it was surmised their wild firing might be caused by the erroneous idea that a submarine boat was in action against them. The Japanese were now able to see the reverse side of such an incident, and experience in their turn all the doubt and discomfort that had been the portion of the Russians.[58]

The fear created by the mining successes was not restricted to the men. The sinking of the *Hatsuse* had taken place in full view of observers at Port Arthur and the Russians knew that one of the other battleships was at least seriously damaged. This was the perfect moment for them to strike. Instead, Admiral Vitgeft refused to allow his battleships to raise steam. Julian Corbett, in his official history, declared that 'the horror of the mines had possessed him'.[59]

Admiral Tōgō's response was not altogether different. As Pakenham reported '(t)he Russian mines drove the [Japanese] battle squadron into harbour, its only proper place at this stage, where it has since remained, prepared at the shortest notice for a Russian sortie.'[60] Mines forced Tōgō to abandon the concept of close blockade; instead he left light craft off Port Arthur and moved his battle fleet to a safe anchorage at Elliot Island. This approach was combined with a concerted effort to close Port Arthur using mines. Bizarrely, the fear of mines even spread to the other side of the globe, with the Russians sweeping the seas around Kronstadt daily and getting merchant vessels to lead the warships of the Baltic Fleet through narrow channels.[61]

The Royal Navy dispatched attachés to the Far East in order to discover more about the naval conflict, and learn from the experiences of the combatants. With respect to the impact mine warfare had on the materiel and morale of combatants this was relatively straightforward, and there was strong evidence that mines were going to be an important part of naval conflict in the future. The service's relationship with the technology, however, had never been that simple, and it was apparent that the success of mining would raise questions over its morality. This was naturally compounded by the fact that mines were laid in far greater numbers and over a far wider geographical area than had previously been envisaged. The attaché reports, particularly those of William Pakenham, reflected the ambivalent attitude of many in the Royal Navy to the weapon on moral and cultural grounds, despite of its unquestioned success on the battlefield.

The initial discussion of the question of morality with regards to mining came on the subject of floating mines, and fitted into a broader pattern of questioning the values of the Russians. This, certainly with regard to Pakenham, originated from his clear bias in favour of the Japanese, whom he viewed as an island race, not dissimilar from, and in certain respects superior to, the British. Within weeks of the beginning of the conflict, mines that had broken free from their moorings began to be seen in the vicinity of Port Arthur. Pakenham, in particular, took a very partisan view on the subject, arguing that all floating mines were Russian and claiming that had the Russians found Japanese mines drifting 'a good deal would probably have been said about "yellow perils" and "methods of barbarism"'.[62] His reports also contained the implication that the Russians might have been purposefully releasing drifting mines, as they were not contesting command of the sea. This appears to have supported a general assumption that all mines struck in places where the Japanese did not expect minefields must have been floating mines. Instead, it appears certain that the Russians were frequently simply more adept at evading the Japanese blockade than they were given credit for.

Concerns regarding floating mines were quickly augmented by more general worries about the indiscriminate use of mines on the high seas. Following the loss of the *Petropavlovsk* Pakenham mentioned how the Russians believed that the mine which sank her had drifted into her path from a different minefield. He noted that if the sinking was 'caused by the explosion on the site of its original anchorage, of a Japanese mine, [it] was the result of a perfectly legitimate act of war'. By contrast, he argued, if it was the result of a floating mine then 'an entirely new order of things is introduced'.[63] In Pakenham's view the threat of a mine drifting outside of the territorial waters of the belligerents and so threatening civilians or neutrals presented an unacceptable development within warfare. He concluded that:

> It is thus open to question whether the perils entailed by their use upon navigation do not constitute such a menace to neutrals in the exercise of their right to navigate the high seas in safety as to call for an international agreement prohibiting the use of mechanical mines in future wars.[64]

Two weeks later, in the light of the loss of the *Hatsuse* and *Yashima* Pakenham's position had hardened considerably. He stated how, previously, in filling the seas with drifting mines, Russian 'competence as miners has been impeached'. The latest act was, however, different. 'Laying mines in a public fairway, on a vague chance of catching an enemy rather than a neutral, the action shows such a cynical indifference to the general weal as to merit the severest condemnation'. He continued that as 'their misconduct has been crowned with success, it offers a precedent that every navy, under similar temptation, will almost certainly follow, so long as the use of this pernicious form of mine continues [to be] admissible in civilised warfare.'[65] Mine warfare was, by its very nature, indiscriminate and this directly challenged a number of the key principles which were at the heart of Royal Navy organisational culture. This technology undermined the notion of British sovereignty of the seas and even questioned the ability of the Royal Navy to protect British neutral ships in international waters. Thus the success of mining proved difficult for the service to rationalise and led to continuing questions over the legitimacy of the mine as a weapon.

The issue of morality, like that of mining more generally, was at the forefront of attention throughout the first phase of the war. After the fall of Port Arthur, mining incidents became far less common and the subject was discussed less frequently in the attaché reports. The Battle of Tsushima instantly refocused attention both in the region and at home on decisive battle, and battleships. It would be wrong to say that the battle led to previous experiences being forgotten, but it did restore faith in the perception of naval warfare which informed British policy, and shifted the focus away from the unusual events of the previous months.

IV

The Russo-Japanese War offered the Royal Navy a superb opportunity to view a modern naval conflict at close hand, without the risks involved with being an active participant. Despite this, learning lessons from the experiences of others proved far from straightforward. The way in which events in the Far East were reported, and the manner in which these reports were then interpreted was heavily influenced by the cultural preconceptions of the attachés and their audience. The scale of the success of mining did, however, force a renewed discussion on the entire subject. As Vice-Admiral Lord Charles Beresford pointed out to the Prime Minister, Arthur Balfour, the events had 'practically proved the certain danger of under water warfare, a danger we have been in the habit of underrating both in the Navy and in the country.'[66] Perhaps more importantly they had demonstrated the new direction of underwater warfare as facilitated by independent mines. Up until May 1904 mine warfare had been a littoral combat. The weapons were deployed in rivers, or the immediate vicinity of ports, but always within territorial waters. The Russian actions of sinking the *Hatsuse* and *Yashima* demonstrated to the world the potential of independent mines on a much broader canvas. This meant that mining was likely to pose a serious threat to a far wider range of British maritime interests than had been previously supposed. Of equal interest was the manner in which the Japanese used mines offensively. This was a naval power which had successfully achieved and exploited command of the sea. The similarity between British and Japanese strategy was not lost on observers of the conflict, with many, like Pakenham, going further and making geo-cultural connections as well.[67] The extensive and effective use of mines by the Japanese demonstrated in the clearest possible manner that independent mining could be offensive, and was not contrary to the Royal Navy's objective of achieving command of the sea. As ever this reality was shaped through a prism of preconceptions and events at home. Whilst some in the service and beyond fully understood the challenges and opportunities presented by mining as demonstrated in the Russo-Japanese War, others still struggled to see past the basic idea that the mine was fundamentally antithetical to Royal Navy strategy and culture. It was greatly to the detriment of the Royal Navy that it took so long to produce an official history of the conflict; indeed Corbett's excellent work, which brings out these points so clearly, has been all but ignored precisely because it was released a matter of months before the outbreak of the First World War.[68]

In Britain, the Russo-Japanese War attracted a great deal of interest with the course of the war being viewed very positively due to Britain's alliance with Japan and its rivalry with Russia. There remained an element of concern over the risk of Britain being drawn into the conflict through its Japanese alliance; this was reinforced by the anti-Japanese stance of both France and Germany. These fears were not helped by the transit of the Russian Baltic Fleet past many key strategic points in the British Empire and through waters where British supremacy was rarely challenged. The Dogger Bank incident served to heighten the tension and provoked an even stronger Russophobic reaction within British public opinion at all levels.

It was in this atmosphere that the attaché reports were viewed, and unsurprisingly they received considerable attention. A number of the reports were forwarded on to the Prime Minister and the King, who took a keen interest in the events in the Far East and their impact on British policy.[69] The Admiralty immediately viewed them as an important source of information and the NID drew up a number of printed volumes containing edited reports and lists of events, although these lacked any clear analysis.[70] The similarities between the British and Japanese navies in terms of training, materiel and mindset meant that Japanese successes were frequently perceived to be a vindication of the British approach. One area where this was, however, clearly not the case was mine warfare. In June 1904 the Senior Naval Lord, Admiral Lord Walter Kerr, minuted that he had been 'somewhat shaken' by the events in the Far East and he wrote to Noel, stating bluntly; '(t)hey are a terror these mines'.[71] Kerr was a technologically conservative officer who had shown little interest in mining. The extent of the losses inflicted by mines clearly came as a major surprise to him and prompted an interest in how these results had been achieved. On reading a report by Jackson on the loss of the *Petropavlovsk*, Kerr minuted 'I hope that we shall hear in due course how the Japanese laid the mines which sank the *Petropavlovsk*. At the present time there is no clear information on this point, we shall no doubt hear in due course.'[72] The rather more forceful First Lord, the Earl of Selborne responded 'Let us specifically ask the question of Capt Pakenham'.[73] Pakenham dutifully obliged in his report of 31 August.[74]

Outside the Admiralty, the response of the navy to the new form of mine warfare was overwhelmingly negative. In a paper read at the Royal United Services Institute in May 1904 the Reverend T. J. Lawrence, the lecturer in international law at the Naval War College, openly condemned the new practice. He declared that:

> if the Russians deliberately created a mine-field outside their own territorial waters, they violated all just principles, and went far beyond their rights as belligerents. There are no precedents for such an act. If it has been committed it is unique, and it is also outrageous.

Vice-Admiral Sir Robert Harris, who was in the chair, immediately identified this as 'the most important part' of Lawrence's paper. He expressed serious concern at the stray mines which had broken adrift, but was particularly agitated about the prospect of mines being laid in open waters. The Russian action in laying the mines which sank the *Hatsuse* and *Yashima*, was still unconfirmed at the time, but its nature was such that Harris could 'hardly believe it'. He went on to paint a very negative picture of the situation in the event of a war between Britain and France in which the English Channel would be rendered impassable due to mines. Harris concluded: 'I think it is a question for International Law to put an outside limit on the laying of these infernal machines which are as dangerous to the innocent as to the belligerent.'[75]

The events in the Far East as reported by the attachés did prompt renewed discussion of mining, but the results indicate how deeply entrenched suspicion of independent mines was in the culture of the Royal Navy. At the end of 1903 the Admiralty had begun to look at mining policy in the context of the need to find a replacement for the ageing torpedo depot ship, *Hecla*. The conclusion reached was that mining was no longer sufficiently important as to justify the provision of a specific ship, and if necessary one could be taken up from the merchant marine on the outbreak of war. As such the Admiralty asked the Director of Transports to produce a list of suitable telegraph cable ships, something indicative of the continuing focus on controlled as opposed to independent mining. By the time a list had been produced, the events in the Far East had cast a long shadow over the discussions. The widespread use of mines and their impact came as a major surprise, and in May the DNI, Prince Louis of Battenberg, felt compelled to comment. He remarked that the Japanese had used one ship as a combined mining vessel and mother ship for the torpedo flotilla. He went on to say that 'the actual work of dropping mines off Port Arthur was carried out, as far as our present information goes by small vessels somewhat similar probably to our R.E. [Royal Engineers] mining launches.' Battenberg did not, however, see this as particularly relevant. Instead he wrote that:

> it seems doubtful whether it would be our policy to carry out offensive mining operations to the same (or a proportionate) extent as the Japanese. Unless under very exceptional circumstances it should be our endeavour to induce the enemies' ships to come out of harbour and give battle, and not to place obstacles in the way of their egress.[76]

He went on to conclude that if the decision was made to use mines in a similar manner to the Japanese, small vessels 'could be taken up at the time and fitted with extempore appliances which need not be of an elaborate nature.'[77]

Despite these remarks from the DNI the developments in the Far East were considered important enough to warrant a conference on mining to be held in the Senior Naval Lord's room on the 27 May. The naval members of the Board were joined by the DNI, the DNO, the ADT and Ernest Troubridge, who had just returned from his position as naval attaché. The conclusions are in many ways quite remarkable. In spite of the dramatic results achieved by independent mines in the first months of the Russo-Japanese War the conference decided as follows:

> In regard to Blockade Mines. Although no distinct purpose could be assigned for the use of these weapons, it was considered that occasions might well arise in war in which they would be effective, and that it was therefore desirable that a small number should be provided and retained at the principle ports in readiness for shipment in vessels taken up as auxiliaries for the purpose in times of strained relations.[78]

It went on to say that 'it was considered that no elaborate fittings should be necessary in the auxiliaries and that expense should be cut down as low as possible.'[79] The drive for economy was unsurprising given the political climate, but the difficulty in assigning a role to independent mines is more interesting. These remarks together with the earlier comments by Battenberg give a very clear indication of the cultural difficulties facing independent mining. The DNI noted in surprise that the Japanese were using mines widely even though they were on the offensive. In the minds of the majority of British naval officers these were defensive weapons deployed by the weaker power to deny use of the sea to an enemy. This was of course the direct antithesis of everything the Royal Navy stood for. Indeed, although the position the Japanese occupied in the Yellow Sea was very similar to one that the Royal Navy envisaged in European waters, senior officers found it almost impossible to see beyond the simple mantra of sea control. It is also evident that the Admiralty continued to see mines as a littoral weapon, indicated by the intention to use small launches to lay mines, together with an enduring faith in countermining. It does have to be said, however, that mines were not immediately used in open water in the Far East and it would have taken time for this development to be appreciated in London.

Over the course of 1904 the profile of mining rose dramatically as the events in the Far East became public knowledge. Despite this increased awareness very little action was taken by the Admiralty. This was in part due to the ongoing debate over the submarine mine defences run by the Royal Engineers, which was taking place in the Committee of Imperial Defence (CID) at this time. The matter was a very difficult political question and only likely to be further complicated by any reconsideration of the navy's offensive mining policy. In addition, from the early summer it was known that Admiral Sir John Fisher would replace Kerr as Senior Naval Lord, and Fisher made it clear that he intended a radical shake-up of Admiralty policy in a number of areas. The result was that issues were left to drift pending the oncoming storm. There are, however, indications that senior officers were beginning to take mining issues seriously. In September when discussing mine clearance Battenberg remarked that 'the term "Blockade Mine" is to be deprecated since these mechanical mines would be used quite as much to prevent entry as exit' to a port.[80] This marks a considerable turnaround in opinion since May, when similar remarks made by Alexander Bethell, the ADT, were completely ignored.[81] It was not only at the Admiralty that the developments in offensive mining were being noted. Vice-Admiral Charles Beresford, commanding the Channel Squadron, had a long connection with independent mining, and had strongly advocated its use through the 1890s. In December 1904, he wrote to the Admiralty recommending that specialist minelayers be constructed for the service. Unfortunately the detailed record of his comments and the reaction to them appears to have been lost; however it is clear that the Admiralty did not at this stage see the necessity for such a large and costly shift in policy.[82] Despite this, things were beginning to change; in December the Admiralty agreed to an increase in the number of staff on *Vernon* in response to the additional experimental work on mining that was being carried out.[83] These small developments indicated a subtle shift in policy, but for any real progress to be made in developing independent mining as a weapon system, much larger steps were needed.

The Russo-Japanese War provided an excellent opportunity for the Royal Navy to examine the conduct of warfare under modern conditions. The strong similarities between the British and Japanese forces in terms of training, equipment and strategic situation clearly aided this process. With regard to mining it would have been difficult for the navy not to recognise the important role played by these weapons, but all the attachés took time to explore the matter in detail. Despite this the Admiralty in London struggled to come to terms with the impact of independent mining, something that resulted largely from its cultural and strategic preconceptions. This would begin to change with the arrival of Fisher at the Admiralty, but mining would remain a controversial subject within the Royal Navy, strategically, culturally and morally, for some time to come.

NOTES

1. A broader discussion can be found in Richard Dunley, 'The Warrior Has Always Shewed Himself Greater Than His Weapons': The Royal Navy's Interpretation of the Russo-Japanese War 1904–5', *War and Society*, vol. 34, no. 4 (2015); Philip Towle, *The Influence of the Russo-Japanese War on British Military and Naval Thought, 1904–1914* (Unpublished PhD thesis, University of London, 1973).
2. For a detailed analysis of the role of attachés, albeit in slightly different circumstances, see Matthew S. Seligmann, *Spies in Uniform: British Military and Naval Intelligence on the Eve of the First World War* (Oxford: Oxford University Press, 2006).

3. Bodleian Library, Oxford (BLO), Selborne Papers, Selborne Mss 35, Selborne to Kerr, 18 November 1903, f. 232.
4. BLO, Selborne Papers, Selborne Mss 35, Kerr to Selborne, 25 November 1903, f. 233.
5. The National Archives (TNA), ADM 1/7774, Battenberg to Kerr, 7 April 1904.
6. TNA, ADM 1/7774, Thomas minute, 22 April 1904, 'Russian Govt. Has No Objection ...' Docket.
7. TNA, ADM 1/7816, Eyres Reports 10 and 28 February 1905; Towle, *Influence of the Russo-Japanese War*, p. 219.
8. BLO, Selborne Papers, Selborne Mss 41, Kerr to Selborne, 5 April 1904, ff. 86–87.
9. National Maritime Museum (NMM), Noel Papers, NOE/4/A/1, Kerr to Noel, 12 April 1904.
10. NMM, Noel Papers, NOE/4/A/1, Selborne to Noel, 13 April 1904.
11. NMM, Noel Papers, NOE/4/A/1, Selborne to Noel, 13 April 1904.
12. Not, as Peter Halvorsen confusingly claims, H. B. Jackson. See Peter Halvorsen, 'The Royal Navy and Mine Warfare 1868–1914', *Journal of Strategic Studies*, vol. 27, no. 4 (2004), pp. 685–707.
13. TNA, FO 46/577, Balfour minute, n.d., Troubridge Report enclosed in MacDonald to Lansdowne, 17 March 1904.
14. TNA, FO 46/596, MacDonald to Lansdowne, 1 June 1905; TNA, FO 371/84, MacDonald to Grey, 29 June 1906.
15. TNA, FO 46/579, Hutchison to MacDonald, 20 October 1904; National Museum of the Royal Navy (NMRN), Hutchison Diary 1904, Acc. No. 2005/14/3, 31 August, 3, 12 and 17 September 1904, pp. 69, 70, 72 and 74.
16. TNA, FO 46/579, MacDonald to Lansdowne, 21 October 1904.
17. For a detailed discussion of the various attachés see Dunley, 'The Royal Navy's Interpretation of the Russo-Japanese War'.
18. NMM, Noel Papers, NOE/15/A/1, Jackson to Noel, 23 January 1905.
19. Towle, *Influence of the Russo-Japanese War*.
20. David C. Evans and Mark R. Peattie, *Kaigun: Strategy, Tactics and Technology in the Imperial Japanese Navy, 1887–1941* (Annapolis: Naval Institute Press, 1997), pp. 94–128; Julian S. Corbett, *Maritime Operations in the Russo-Japanese War 1904–1905* (Annapolis: Naval Institute Press, 1994).
21. TNA, ADM 231/41, 'Russo-Japanese War: Diary of Naval Events', NID Report 749, 8 February 1904.
22. TNA, FO 46/577, Troubridge Report, 14 February 1904.
23. Corbett, *Maritime Operations in the Russo-Japanese War*, pp. 95–101.
24. BLO, Selborne Papers, Selborne Mss 92, Pakenham to Selborne, 28 November 1905, ff. 61–66; East Riding Archive Centre [ERAC],

Strickland-Constable Papers, DDST/1/5/3/22, Japan/NA Report 14/05, 'A Minimum Range for Fleet Battle', 21 December 1905.

25. British Library (BL), Balfour Papers, Add Ms 49708, Selborne to Balfour, 23 August 1905, ff. 88–91.
26. TNA, ADM 1/7775, Hutchison Report, n.d. 1904, Japan SSO Report No. 9/04, enclosed in Hutchison to MacDonald, 19 November 1904.
27. Corbett, *Maritime Operations in the Russo-Japanese War*, pp. 443–446.
28. TNA, ADM 189/25, Vernon Annual Report 1905, Figures 2 and 3.
29. TNA, ADM 231/43, 'Remarks on the Bombardment of Port Arthur, April 15th, By Kasuga and Nisshin', Pakenham Report, 1 May 1904, NID Report 755.
30. TNA, ADM 231/43, 'Remarks on the Bombardment of Port Arthur, April 15th, By Kasuga and Nisshin', Pakenham Report, 1 May 1904; 'Naval Proceedings from the Capture of Kinchow', Pakenham Report, 19 June 1904, NID Report 755.
31. TNA, ADM 1/7775, 'Naval Proceedings from August 30th to September 16th, 1904', Pakenham Report, 17 September 1904, Japan/NA Report 23/04.
32. TNA, ADM 1/7775, 'Operation of the Japanese Fleet off Port Arthur 12th and 13th April', Pakenham Report, n.d., Japan/NA Report 2/04.
33. Corbett, *Maritime Operations in the Russo-Japanese War*, p. 184.
34. TNA, ADM 231/43, Pakenham Report, 17 April 1904, NID Report 755.
35. TNA, ADM 231/44, 'The Sinking of the Battleships *Hatsuse* and *Yashima*', Pakenham Report, 19 May 1904, NID Report 783.
36. TNA, ADM 231/44, 'The Sinking of the Battleships *Hatsuse* and *Yashima*', Pakenham Report, 19 May 1904, NID Report 783; Corbett, *Maritime Operations in the Russo-Japanese War*, pp. 234–237.
37. TNA, ADM 231/44, 'The Sinking of the Battleships *Hatsuse* and *Yashima*', Pakenham Report, 19 May 1904, NID Report 783.
38. TNA, ADM 231/44, 'The Sinking of the Battleships *Hatsuse* and *Yashima*', Pakenham Report, 19 May 1904, NID Report 783.
39. TNA, ADM 231/43, 'The Sinking of the *Petropavlovsk*', Jackson Report, 7 May 1904, NID Report 755; TNA, ADM 1/7775, 'Operation of the Japanese Fleet off Port Arthur 12th and 13th April', Pakenham Report, n.d., Japan/NA Report 2/04.
40. TNA, ADM 231/43, 'Raid of the Russian Vladivostok Cruisers Resulting in the Sinking of the Japanese Transports on June 15th', Hutchison Report, 28 June 1904, NID Report 755; NMRN, Hutchison Diary 1904, Acc. No. 2005/14/3, 28 July 1904, pp. 23–24.
41. ERAC, Strickland-Constable Papers, DDST/1/5/3/7, Japan/NA Report 8/04, 'The Russo-Japanese War: Japanese Naval Losses', 15 May 1904.

4 MINE WARFARE IN THE RUSSO-JAPANESE WAR ... 69

42. TNA, Satow Papers, PRO 30/33/7/3, Campbell to Satow, 20 May 1904; TNA, FO 46/596, MacDonald to Lansdowne, 1 June 1905.
43. Committee on Designs: Proceedings, P. K. Kemp, ed., *The Papers of Admiral Sir John Fisher*, vol. I (London: Navy Records Society, 1960), p. 220.
44. TNA, ADM 231/44, 'Naval Proceedings from October 20th to November 10th, 1904', Pakenham Report, 11 November 1904, NID Report 772. For a personal description of the event see ERAC, DDST/1/8/1/9, Pakenham to Margaret Strickland-Constable, 7 November 1904.
45. TNA, ADM 231/44, 'Naval Proceedings from October 20th to November 10th, 1904', Pakenham Report, 11 November 1904, NID Report 772.
46. TNA, ADM 231/44, 'Naval Proceedings from October 20th to November 10th, 1904', Pakenham Report, 11 November 1904, NID Report 772.
47. TNA, ADM 231/43, 'Remarks on the Bombardment of Port Arthur, April 15th, By Kasuga and Nisshin', Pakenham Report, 1 May 1904, NID Report 755.
48. TNA, ADM 231/43, 'Naval Proceedings from the Capture of Kinchow', Pakenham Report, 19 June 1904, NID Report 755.
49. TNA, ADM 231/43, 'Naval Proceedings from the Capture of Kinchow', Pakenham Report, 19 June 1904, NID Report 755; TNA, ADM 231/44, '19th August to September 15th, 1904', Hutchison Report, NID Report 772.
50. TNA, ADM 231/44, 'Diary of Proceedings 10th October to 25th December 1904', Jackson Report, NID Report 772.
51. TNA, ADM 231/44, 'Diary of Proceedings 10th October to 25th December 1904', Jackson Report, NID Report 772.
52. TNA, ADM 231/43, 'Remarks on the Bombardment of Port Arthur, April 15th, By Kasuga and Nisshin', Pakenham Report, 1 May 1904, NID Report 755.
53. TNA, FO 17/1654, Kerr to Sanderson, 22 February 1904, ff. 144–145.
54. NMM, Pakenham Papers, PKM/2/1/9, 'Battleship, Small Craft and Under-Water Attack'.
55. NMM, Pakenham Papers, PKM/2/1/9, 'Battleship, Small Craft and Under-Water Attack'.
56. BLO, Selborne Papers, Selborne Mss 46, MacDonald to Selborne 18 January 1905, ff. 97–99.
57. TNA, ADM 231/44, 'Naval Proceedings from October 20th to November 10th, 1904', Pakenham Report, 11 November 1904, NID Report 772.

58. TNA, ADM 231/44, 'The Sinking of the Battleships *Hatsuse* and *Yashima*', Pakenham Report, 19 May 1904, NID Report 783.
59. Corbett, *Maritime Operations in the Russo-Japanese War*, p. 235.
60. NMM, Noel Papers, NOE/8/B, 'Narrative of Naval Proceedings from the Landing of the Second Army to the Capture of Kinchow'.
61. 'The Baltic Fleet', *The Times*, 10 June 1904, p. 5, col. B; *The Times*, 25 October 1904, p. 3, col. A.
62. TNA, ADM 1/7775, 'Bombardment of Port Arthur by *Kasuga* and *Nisshin*', Pakenham Report, 15 April 1904, Japan/NA Report 3/04.
63. TNA, ADM 231/43, 'Remarks on the Bombardment of Port Arthur, April 15th, By Kasuga and Nisshin', Pakenham Report, 1 May 1904, NID Report 755.
64. TNA, ADM 231/43, 'Remarks on the Bombardment of Port Arthur, April 15th, By Kasuga and Nisshin', Pakenham Report, 1 May 1904, NID Report 755.
65. TNA, ADM 231/44, 'The Sinking of the Battleships *Hatsuse* and *Yashima*', Pakenham Report, 19 May 1904, NID Report 783.
66. BL, Balfour Papers, Add Ms 49713, Beresford to Balfour, 25 May 1904, ff. 139–145.
67. See for example Liddell Hart Centre for Military Archives (LHCMA), Corbett Papers, Box 2, 'Lecture Notes: Russo-Japanese War', Lecture 1.
68. John B. Hattendorf and Donald M. Schurman, 'Introduction', in Julian S. Corbett, *Maritime Operations in the Russo-Japanese War 1904–1905* (Annapolis: Naval Institute Press, 1994).
69. TNA, ADM 1/7775, Unsigned Minute, 9 June 1904, on docket 'Reports (Nos. 2 & 3) by Capt Pakenham'.
70. See Diary of Events and Attaché Reports, TNA, ADM 231/41-4, NID Reports 749, 755, 772 and 783.
71. TNA, ADM 1/7717, Kerr Minute, 6 June 1904, 'Function of Submarine Mines in War'; NMM, Noel Papers, NOE/4/A/1, Kerr to Noel, 10 June 1904.
72. TNA, ADM 1/7775, Kerr Minute, 22 June 1904 on 'Sinking of the Petropavlovsk', Jackson Report, 7 May 1904.
73. TNA, ADM 1/7775, Selborne Minute, 26 June 1904.
74. TNA, ADM 231/44, 'How the Japanese Laid the Mines Which Sank the Petropavlovsk', Pakenham Report, 31 August 1904, NID Report 772.
75. Rev. T. J. Lawrence, 'Problems of Neutrality Connected with the Russo-Japanese War', *Royal United Services Institute Journal*, vol. 48, no. 318 (1904), pp. 915–937; T. J. Lawrence, *War and Neutrality in the Far East* (London: Macmillan, 1904), pp. 93–111.
76. TNA, MT 23/169, Battenberg Minute, 4 May 1904, T335/04.
77. TNA, MT 23/169, Battenberg Minute, 4 May 1904, T335/04.

78. TNA, MT 23/169, Kerr Memo, 2 June 1904, T335/04.
79. TNA, MT 23/169, Kerr Memo, 2 June 1904, T335/04.
80. TNA, ADM 1/7833, Battenberg Minute, 29 September 1904.
81. TNA, MT 23/169, Bethell Minute, 11 May 1904, T335/04.
82. TNA, ADM 12/1405, Cut 59.8, 'Mining Vessels: Construction of for British Navy', 12 December 1904.
83. TNA, ADM 12/1417, Cut 59.8 'Experimental Work in Mining', 2 December 1904.

CHAPTER 5

The Russo-Japanese War: Outrage and Reaction

Mine warfare, unlike the submarine, was not a technology which commanded much public attention in Britain at the turn of the twentieth century, although many observers who followed British defence policy would have been aware of its existence. When placed next to the futuristic submarine, mines appeared distinctly old-fashioned and unlikely to have a dramatic effect on any future naval conflict. As elsewhere, this perception was only compounded by a general ignorance of the different types of mines and the possible ways in which they could be deployed. The events of the Russo-Japanese War thus came as a major surprise to the British public, which watched the conflict in the Far East closely and was usually well informed of naval matters. The influence of the mine was entirely unexpected and evoked very strong reactions, initially of shock, which turned quickly into outrage and anger. This response was heavily influenced by perceptions of both British identity and morality in the maritime sphere. Naturally this led in turn to pressure on the British government to act, firstly in its role as 'sovereign of the seas', and latterly as a bastion of civilisation and morality within the realm of international law. The reactions of the British public, which in large part mirrored those of the naval and political elites, helped shape British policy on the subject of mining in the lead-up to the Second Peace Conference at The Hague in 1907.

The first decade of the twentieth century saw popular interest in Britain in naval matters, and in defence subjects more generally, reach a peak. It is thus unsurprising that the outbreak of a major conflict

© The Author(s) 2018
R. Dunley, *Britain and the Mine, 1900–1915*,
https://doi.org/10.1007/978-3-319-72820-9_5

between Britain's ally, Japan, and its long-time rival, Russia, sparked a frenzy of media activity. This was assisted by the development of wireless, and the improvement of telegraph communications which allowed news to reach London within hours. Detailed reports on the conduct of the war could be found dominating large parts of the British press, with many of the major papers having correspondents on the ground in the Far East. This is not to suggest that all of the reports were entirely accurate. If the British naval attachés frequently struggled to see through the fog of war, the newspaper reporters often found it impenetrable. This was not helped by the highly partisan nature of many of the newspapers and their correspondents. Most, although not all, sided with the Japanese against Britain's age-old adversary the Russians, and this clearly came through in their reports.[1]

Despite the spotlight of media attention being shone on the naval conflict the subject of mining barely received a mention in the first two months of the war. It was the sinking of the *Petropavlovsk* that was to radically change this. The first reports of the loss in British newspapers came in the evening press on 13 April 1904 from statements issued in St Petersburg. The situation was far from clear but it was reported that 'the vessel is supposed to have struck a torpedo, probably during manoeuvres'.[2] By the next morning the message was a little clearer and *The Times* stated, remarkably accurately, that '(t)he battleship Petropavlovsk struck a mine, which exploded, and the vessel capsized'.[3] The assumption was that Marakov had 'fallen a victim not to the enemy, but to one of his own mines. These weapons of war have proved very deadly in this struggle—but deadly only to their own side'.[4]

Despite the accuracy of the initial reports there was a marked unwillingness in the newspaper commentaries to take the Russian accounts at face value. Rear-Admiral John Ingles, writing in the *Daily Telegraph* suggested that 'I think it will be found that, when later telegrams come to hand, the Russian flagship had been badly mauled in battle before she got torpedoed and sunk'.[5] The editorial in *The Times* also noted that it seemed 'hardly conceivable that a single mine could send a battleship to the bottom with such fearful rapidity'.[6] By the time the evening newspapers came out in London, the tone of the reports had shifted perceptibly. Both the *Pall Mall Gazette* and the *St James's Gazette* reported the story that the Russian warship had not struck a mine, but instead was 'surrounded by torpedo boats' and 'struck by no fewer than five torpedoes'. An unnamed naval officer also cast doubt on whether any single weapon could cause 'such immediate and terrible destruction'.[7] The confusion continued, with widespread reports that there had been a major naval engagement between the Russians and the Japanese, and that the sinking of the *Petropavlovsk* may have resulted from the action of Japanese submarines. *The Daily Chronicle* even went so far as to suggest that '(a) ll information tends to prove that it was not a mine nor torpedo that was responsible for the ship's destruction', seemingly suggesting an unrelated internal explosion had caused the loss.[8] In the light of these various claims many felt that 'one may be forgiven a certain scepticism about the mines, which are said to have accounted not only for the loss of the flagship and the Admiral, but also for the severe damage to the "Pobieda"'.[9]

The situation in the waters off Port Arthur in the first months of the war was very confused, something not helped by the limited access the belligerents gave to journalists. In the light of this it is apparent that some confusion over the events surrounding the loss of the *Petropavlovsk* was to be expected. This does not, however, entirely explain the fundamental unwillingness of the British press to accept the most likely story, that, as was suggested by the Russian government, the *Petropavlovsk* had struck a single mine and blown up. The doubts were rooted in part in an ignorance of the technology. Few really understood how mines worked and where they could be deployed, and this fed through into questions over their effectiveness. Perhaps more importantly the scepticism regarding mines drew directly from a knowledge of, and association with, the battleship. The British media and public at large had almost as strong an association with the battleship as the symbol of naval power as had the Royal Navy. This continued in the wake of the sinking, with virtually every paper running a short description of the vessel and some having line drawings or plans. Within these reports the *Petropavlovsk* was compared to British battleships, something that not only aided understanding, but also reinforced the association with the Royal Navy.[10] As the newspaper reaction clearly shows, the wider British audience found it virtually impossible to accept that a mine could sink a battleship, something bound up in its connection with these vessels.

The precise causes of the sinking of the *Petropavlovsk* were the subject of much confusion and debate in the British media, but the initial reaction to it was almost universally written in a tone of regret. From the beginning the press described the event as a 'tragedy', referred to Makarov as a 'gallant Admiral' and generally treated the sinking as an accident rather than a successful military operation.[11] The sudden and unexplained loss of a fine battleship was not viewed as part of the regular course of the war, and certainly not associated with a legitimate military attack. *The Daily Chronicle* wrote early on that '(t)his latest disaster is the result of an accident, and the fate of so gallant a commander in so terrible a catastrophe will excite just commiseration'.[12] Indeed, even the Japanese were presented as expressing regret for Makarov's death.[13] Over the course of the week following the sinking the true picture of events became clear, particularly with the publishing of Admiral Tōgō's official despatches. This served to lessen, although did not entirely remove, the scepticism in the British press regarding the effectiveness of mines in this particular case. The Japanese reports also had a very different impact on the tone of the descriptions of the events, something drawn from the fact that they legitimised the sinking as an act of war. The knowledge that the Japanese had specifically planted the mines and then lured the Russian fleet over them enabled the British press to entirely rethink the way they presented the event. No longer was this an accident, to which the course of the war was almost incidental. Instead it was a 'legitimate result of clever Japanese schemes' and at the same time a great act of der-ring-do.[14] The *St James's Gazette* reported on the 'thrilling story of the laying of the mines', whilst *The Daily Telegraph* proclaimed it as an act of 'courage of the highest order, allied with that wonderful combination of Eastern cunning and Western science'.[15] This shift fed into the natural tendency of the British press to favour the Japanese over the Russians, and at times treat them as a proxy for the British.

The perception of mines as a legitimate, if novel, part of the war in the Far East lasted for less than a month. On 20 May news reached London of the sinking of the Japanese battleship *Hatsuse*. Despite early rumours, the Japanese authorities successfully concealed the loss of the *Yashima*. All of the British papers agreed that the destruction of a first-class battleship was a blow of the 'most grievous character', but most concluded that '(i)t has weakened Togo's sword arm, but has come too late to jeopardise his position'.[16] The loss of the *Hatsuse* finally laid to rest any remaining doubts in the press around the effectiveness of mines. Within the reports much attention was focused on the fact that the *Hatsuse* was 'among the finest [vessels] in the Imperial Japanese Navy' and that she had been built in Britain to some of the latest British designs.[17] The fact that she could be fatally damaged by mines, and sink so quickly, caused considerable disquiet. As *The Daily Telegraph* reported:

She embodied all the latest ideas in hull construction which the ingenuity of the naval architect has yet evolved, and her fate is yet another illustration of the frailty of even the strongest vessel when she is attacked in one of her many vulnerable parts by either mine or torpedo.[18]

This sparked into life a debate on the role of the battleship in modern warfare, which had just spread across the Atlantic from the United States. Following the sinking of the *Petropavlovsk* the *New York Sun* had asked '(m)ay it not come to pass, then, that, before this generation has passed, perhaps before long, the great battleships ... will be rendered obsolete and practically only material for the scrap heap?'[19] This quickly flared into a broader debate, with Captain Alfred Mahan weighing in with articles in the *New York Sun* and *Collier's Weekly* suggesting that whilst the battleship may not be doomed, future navies would be comprised of smaller, more numerous ships.[20] The debate was picked up in Britain on 19 May 1904 when Mahan published a version of his article from the *Collier's Weekly* in *The Times*. This, when followed the next day by news of the sinking of the *Hatsuse*, meant that considerable attention was paid to the question of whether mines rendered the battleship somehow redundant or obsolete.

Considering that British naval supremacy was built upon its superior battle fleet, and the broader British technological and cultural association with the battleship, it is unsurprising that all of the major papers found this an unsettling subject to address. *The Times* confronted the issue head-on, suggesting that no 'responsible naval authority' had 'drawn from the events in the Far East the astonishing inference that the days of the "capital ship" are numbered. The proposition seems to us to be little short of unthinkable'.[21] *The Pall Mall Gazette* took a similar position, arguing that, far from undermining the importance of the battleship, the events in the Far East simply confirmed the need for an overwhelmingly powerful British navy. 'The plain moral of all of these disasters is that it is never safe to rely on a slight margin of numerical superiority' especially not when such events 'may turn the scale of naval strength in the balance of which hangs the fate of an Empire'.[22] The paper proceeded to reinforce the political nature of its point with a cartoon showing the Liberal politicians Sir Henry Campbell-Bannerman and John Morley in a rowing boat approaching a mine, with the ironic caption 'Lets have a cheap Navy, John; we'll loose less when they go to the bottom!'[23] Others, particularly in the more Liberal press, felt that the loss of the two battleships did highlight a fundamental weakness in the battleship as a weapon system. This was particularly apparent in editorials in *The Manchester Guardian*, which claimed that 'the largest and most expensive contrivances have produced the smallest results and the most insignificant, the most startling'.[24] They continued, the following day, that '(t)he greatest danger to our naval supremacy, we should say, is the belief that the types of war vessels are now roughly fixed'.[25]

All of the newspapers associated the battleship with the British position and viewed the mine as antithetical to this. Irrespective of the stance adopted on the issue of the future of the battleship, it was universally accepted that the challenge that the mine represented to the battleship was, in effect, the challenge of the foreign to the British. None of the papers discussed the possibility of the Royal Navy using mines in a similar way to the Japanese, nor was it mentioned that both sides in the conflict had deployed mines as part of broader strategies that included the use of battleships. Within the public discussion in Britain, mines and the battle fleet were incompatible, and one of these technologies, mines, was fundamentally un-British. Perhaps ironically, this was best summed up in an article in the Irish Nationalist-supporting *Dublin Evening Telegraph*:

> The great heart of John Bull has been sorely wounded, as usual through the breeches pocket. He rules the waves at tremendous cost, and he is afraid that the expenditure is all in vain. For the Russians have blown up a Japanese battleship with a floating mine, and the bulwarks of Britannia consist of battleships ... . The easy destruction of a battleship is therefore a solemn warning to the boastful Britisher.[26]

I

Reports on the loss of the *Hatsuse* initially focused on the military implications and drew in the ongoing arguments regarding the role of the battleship in naval warfare. Within days this had all been overtaken by a major debate over the legitimacy and morality of the use of mines, something that had begun following the sinking of the *Petropavlovsk*, but was given serious momentum by the Russian deployment of mines in international waters. This was to be the single most important debate shaping British policy towards mines for the following three years.

The first accounts of the sinking of the *Hatsuse* saw a subtle shift in the nature of reports on mines. Whilst the Japanese success in sinking the *Petropavlovsk* had been widely applauded in the British media, at least after they finally understood what had transpired, the loss of the Japanese battleship was presented differently. *The Manchester Guardian* noted in its editorial that '(i)t does seem little better than an accident when a handful of men in a torpedo boat drop a mine at a venture and ten or twelve thousand tons of wrought iron navigated with a prodigious expenditure of brain power and steam run up against it the next day'.[27] Other papers also commented on the sense of chance and accident which surrounded the Russian success, and there was a perception that this was a different and perhaps lesser way to conduct a war.

Most of the newspapers focused initially on the impact of mines on the belligerents, and as such whilst the reports were less jingoistic than those on the sinking of the *Petropavlovsk*, they were broadly neutral in tone. The *St James's Gazette* appears to have been alone in raising concerns about the 'terrible and hidden dangers' to neutral navigation.[28] This remained the case until 23 May when a letter by Admiral Algernon de Horsey was published in *The Times*. De Horsey raised the question as to whether the 'laying of explosive mines in the open sea is admissible by the law of nations'. His own views on the matter were clear, arguing that should it 'prove true that the destruction of the Hatsuse was effected by a mine willfully placed in the open sea, ten miles from land, the act appears to me to have been one of wholesale murder, and its perpetrator *hostis humani generis*.'[29] In the same edition a special report from *The Times*' correspondent in the region stated that the Russians had been attempting to 'sow the whole of the Gulf of Pe-chi-li with floating blockade mines'.[30]

These claims were immediately picked up by the rest of the media in Britain and in the United States, and virtually all further discussion of the mining question revolved around the rights of neutrals. The evening papers on 23 May echoed the commentary in *The Times*, widely condemning the Russians for their 'scattering of infernal machines'.[31] This continued over the course of the following days with reports in many of the major papers attacking what was widely accepted to be the solely Russian practice of laying mines in international waters.[32] Russian explanation of their actions, as reported in the *Daily Express*, did little to ameliorate the situation. The correspondent claimed that 'Russia justifies her action in sowing the Chinese seas with mines by the axiom that "All's fair in war" except anything that is expressly forbidden by the Geneva Convention or international law'.[33] The American media also reported widely on the threat posed by mines to neutral shipping, with reciprocal reports being reprinted in papers on both sides of the Atlantic, something that appears to have only reaffirmed the sense of outrage.[34]

Whilst most papers were content to merely express disbelief at the uncivilised behaviour of the Russians, within the letters pages of *The Times* there developed a more in-depth debate on the subject of the legal status of mining. Drawing directly from de Horsey's remarks, the renowned international jurist Erskine Holland sought to frame the debate as part of a 'perpetually-recurring conflict between belligerent and neutral interests'. Despite this he still found little to justify the use of mines, asserting that 'no international usage sanctions the employment by one belligerent against the other of mines, or other secret contrivances, which would, without notice, render dangerous the navigation of the high seas'. Holland did add the caveat that the definition of territorial waters had not been clearly set out, but it was apparent that he felt the Russians had breached commonly accepted norms in international law.[35] Admiral Sir Cyprian Bridge responded to Holland's remarks with a rather more pragmatic analysis. He suggested that whilst the widespread use of mines might make the position for neutrals 'intolerable', this was not entirely new. Bridge asked rhetorically '(i)s the position of neutrals during our wars with France forgotten?' This is not to suggest that he was a supporter of the use of mines. Instead Bridge posed the question '(i)s the value of mines, used either by the attack or by the defence, great enough to compensate for the direct risk to friendly ships or for the probable consequences of neutral resentment?' The strong implication being that, despite the successes of mines in the Far East, Bridge, who was still an influential naval officer, felt that their use was not worthwhile.[36] This was a fundamentally different position from that being generally proffered, that mines were extremely effective, but immoral and illegal.

Within a short space of time the attention of the British media shifted from outrage at Russian minelaying to demands for action from the British government. *The Manchester Guardian* led the way, with calls for an international convention inspired by the principle to 'rob war of as much of its injustice and cruelty as possible'.[37] The following day the journalist H. W. Wilson wrote a letter in *The Times* pushing a similar agenda, but inspired by slightly different motives. He emphasised the need for the British government to be proactive from a point of view of its own security and was horrified by what he saw as the supine position adopted in Whitehall. Commenting on the reported action being taken by the US government in collecting information on minelaying he wrote, '(h)ow is it that England, a Power so much more effected by such reported infractions of maritime law remains inactive? Is the risk to our Fleet realized of such possibilities as the mining of the Straits of Gibraltar or the Channel'.[38] Wilson's call was picked up in the *Pall Mall Gazette* that evening, which echoed his concerns. The paper felt that:

> it is pretty plain that, what between John Bull's generally easy going nature and his particular anxiety to create no unnecessary friction in this present case, it is not very likely that our government will make any effective protest against proceedings which may create precedents of the utmost danger to ourselves on some future occasion.[39]

The press were not the only ones who began to exert pressure on the British government to take action. Sir William Walrond, the Chancellor of the Duchy of Lancaster, in a speech in his constituency, called for his own government to take 'prompt action' to 'put a stop to the indiscriminate laying of mines'.[40] In the House of Commons both the Irish Nationalist, John Campbell, and the Liberal, John Lawson Walton asked the Prime Minister what action the government was taking on the issue. Balfour responded that the issue was being 'most anxiously reviewed by His Majesty's Government, but do not think that at this moment any public object would be gained by the publication of any communications we have made or indeed by any premature statement on the subject'.[41]

As the course of the war progressed the focus of the British press shifted away from mining onto other aspects of the conflict. This is not to suggest that the issue had been forgotten. Shortly after the Treaty of Portsmouth brought hostilities to a close *The Times* remarked on how the conflict had highlighted the need for a new examination of a number of aspects of international law. Leading among these was the necessity for 'some agreement concerning the use of floating mines in open seas'. The paper reflected the views of most in Britain when it declared that 'it is repugnant to civilization itself and utterly destructive of the legitimate rights of neutrals that any belligerent should have the right to render, say the Channel, impassable to neutral commerce by scattering floating mines broadcast in its waters'.[42] This position, and the expectation that the British government would use all of its influence to achieve an international agreement, dominated popular discourse on mining from the end of the conflict right through until the Hague Conference in the summer of 1907. Mines were widely viewed as a dangerous, uncivilised and fundamentally un-British form of warfare, and one which, it was confidently expected, very severe limitations would be placed upon in all future conflicts.

The British debate on the legality of the use of mines fed directly into the discussions which took place at the Institut de Droit International. This was a private body, which considered issues of international law at a biennial conference. Its elected membership was made up of some of the best-regarded international jurists from across the globe, including many who served as advisors to their respective governments.[43] As such the body's conclusions were seen as an important marker giving an indication of legal opinion on a particular topic, and the reports it produced often served as an informal starting point for official discussions.

The Institut picked up on the potential impact of mining very quickly, and at their session in Edinburgh in September 1904 the Greek lawyer Michel Kebedgy proposed the question of the regulation of mines in international waters as a topic for discussion. It was decided that at the time there was not enough accurate information to usefully discuss the subject, but Kebedgy was charged with producing a report for the next conference.[44] Working with a fellow Greek lawyer as well as colleagues from Italy, Belgium, Germany and France, Kebedgy produced a report for the 1906 conference, which was held in Ghent. The report and the resultant discussion were clearly framed with the forthcoming Hague Conference in mind, and there was considerable debate, particularly over terminology. Despite this there was no question over the main issue at stake. All the members agreed to the principle behind Kebedgy's key resolution, that the laying of floating or anchored mines in international waters should be banned. Although the session ran out of time before it could work through the precise details, the delegates, with a view to the upcoming Hague Conference, voted on and provisionally approved proposals that would have placed very tight restrictions on where mines could be laid, and ensured responsibility lay squarely with the belligerents, not neutrals or non-combatants.[45]

The mining question was also raised at the rival International Law Association. At their meeting in Christiania in 1905 a paper by the Belgian lawyer M. Gaston de Leval was read out, but the issue was not discussed in detail. Gaston de Leval largely concurred with the arguments presented by British international lawyers, that the belligerents could not be allowed to deprive neutrals of their rights to use the high seas.[46] The following year the Association met in Berlin and the German international lawyer Professor Ferdinand von Martitz gave a paper on the use of mines, drawing directly from the events in the Russo-Japanese War. Von Martitz took a very different view on the question from that of any other lawyer up to this point. He noted that:

> No infringement of the principle of freedom of the seas is involved in their [mines] use, for the high seas are not less open to the belligerents for the conduct of hostilities against their opponents than to neutrals for innocent maritime transit.[47]

Instead he suggested that belligerents should simply be responsible for warning neutrals of the dangers, removing the mines after the hostilities, and compensating them for damage suffered from mines that had broken free from their moorings. Although couched in very civilised language, von Martitz's ideas were strongly challenged by the British delegate, Sir Thomas Barclay, who stated that 'I think the greatest atrocity it is possible to conceive is the blowing up of ships by floating mines. Even the blowing up of belligerent ships by floating mines is a horror in itself'. Barclay hoped that the matter would be dealt with 'seriously and definitely' at the Hague Conference. Barclay was supported by the American lawyer George Whitelock, who suggested banning mines altogether.[48]

The discussion of mining at these international meetings was, of course, picked up by the media in Britain.[49] Although there is relatively little analysis within these reports, it is clear that there was a sense of approval of the tight restrictions that they suggested placing on mining.[50] These conclusions, by eminent groups of international lawyers, served to reinforce the belief that this was an issue where the case for action in the form of international regulation was so overwhelming that there could be no realistic opposition to such a move.

II

The popular debate in the United Kingdom on mining stemming from the events of the Russo-Japanese War ran in parallel with a more specific debate between the British government and the country's very considerable commercial interests. This was to place further pressure on the government to act, initially with regard to protests to the belligerents and clearance of mines in the Far East. This would later shift to a focus on the necessity for an international agreement to prevent mines from becoming a major hazard to British commerce in any future conflict.

At the beginning of the conflict the expectation on the part of commercial interests, such as any existed, was that mines would only be laid in territorial waters and would not impact neutral shipping. The first signs that this might not be the case came in May 1904 when reports surfaced in the press that fears regarding mines were effecting navigation. This began in the Far East, with the *Daily Express* reporting that '(t)he terror of the mines has so possessed the Chinese sailors that large numbers refuse to go to sea'.[51] The impact at home was brought into focus the following day by an article in the *Daily Chronicle* which recounted a conversation with 'a gentleman well known in connection with [the] marine insurance business'. The problem posed by mines was felt to be:

> A most serious one for the mercantile world generally as a vessel touching one of these mines would in all probability leave no trace of her fate. There could only be surmise to go on as to her actual fate and in due course she would be posted as 'missing', and underwriters would have to pay a total loss on ship and cargo without a possibility of recovering anything from either of the belligerents.

The difficulties presented by mines were considered to be such that 'underwriters cannot help feeling that this is a matter in which the assistance of the Government through diplomatic channels is most desirable.'[52]

Following this it can hardly have come as a surprise when, the next day, a letter from Henry Hozier, the secretary of the insurers, Lloyds of London, was received at the Foreign Office. Hozier outlined the concerns regarding reports that mines had been 'freely laid' by the Russians and were 'loose and not in any way under control'. Lloyds' specific concern was that the mines 'may cause material damage to shipping for which even Underwriters who do not write war risks may be unable to prove that they are not liable and serious loss may occur'. Hozier requested that the Foreign Secretary take whatever action he felt appropriate on the matter.[53] It is worth noting here that the term floating mine had a different meaning from that used in much of the debate in the newspapers outlined above. Whereas the debate in the media largely revolved around mines specifically laid in the open seas, the primary focus for commercial interests, at least to begin with, was mines that had broken adrift from their anchors.

The Foreign Office initially expressed scepticism over the issue and requested that Lloyds furnish 'information of a reliable nature' before they could take the matter forward.[54] In early June the Admiralty joined the discussion, reporting that they had received concerns from a number of shipowners and they requested that the Foreign Office ask the Japanese government for clarification on the issue.[55] As such the Foreign Office requested information from the Minister in Tokyo, Sir Claude Macdonald. The response from the Japanese was that the threat to neutral shipping had been 'greatly exaggerated' and that efforts were being made to clear those mines that might be a hazard.[56] This satisfied Lloyds, who asked that they be permitted to publish the statement; this was agreed by the Foreign Office on the condition that it remained unattributed.[57]

Despite the confidence expressed by those in London in the statements made by the Japanese government, reports of floating mines endangering neutral shipping continued to filter through. In July 1904 Henry Little, the Acting Consul in Newchwang, wrote to Sir Ernest Satow, the Minister in Peking, requesting that the British fleet take action to clear the mines proliferating in northern Chinese waters.[58] Satow passed the request on to Vice-Admiral Sir Gerard Noel, Commander-in-Chief, China Station, who refused on the grounds that 'it is impossible for the Navy to take any action in this matter whilst war operations continue in these waters'.[59] Back in Britain concern regarding mines had spread to the bodies representing merchant seaman. The Scottish Shipmasters' Association wrote to the Foreign Office in August regarding the 'very real source of danger to merchant vessels peacefully employed and strictly carrying out their neutrality obligations'. They felt it wholly inappropriate that their members were being 'exposed to perils which should belong to vessels only engaged in actual warfare and not to peaceful merchants'. As such the Association requested action on the part of the government to protect their members and British trade in the Far East more generally.[60] The Foreign Office clearly had little time for such a request and dismissed it, merely forwarding them a copy of the notice published by Lloyds in the *Shipping Gazette*, based upon the information received from the Japanese government.[61]

The Foreign Office's scepticism over the nature of the threat posed by mines to neutral shipping was finally shattered in October, when reports came in from the Lloyds agent at Chefoo that the British steamer SS *Kashing* had struck a mine and had barely limped into Wei-Hai-Wei.[62] A report by the ship's captain outlined how a 'drifting contact mine exploded under the port bow', causing major damage. One Chinese seaman was killed, another was missing and four men were injured.[63] Although the damage was comparatively limited this incident forced the Foreign Office to accept that mines were not only a potential problem in a future European conflict, but were a real issue in Far Eastern waters. That is not to say that they saw any short-term solution. As Walter Langley, Senior Clerk in the Far Eastern Department, noted, '(t)he remedy for the floating mine evil can I supposed only be introduced as the result of an International Agreement'. Francis Campbell, the supervising Assistant Under Secretary, minuted his concurrence.[64]

The risk of destruction was not the only impact that the mines had on commerce. From the outset, insurance underwriters were among those most concerned about the threat posed by the weapons, and quickly began to factor this into the war risks premium that they charged shipping in Far Eastern waters. During the course of the conflict the risks regarding mines were bound up in the broader costs relating to the war and so it is difficult to judge how much extra was being paid to insure against this specific threat.[65] Unlike the other war-related risks, those associated with mines continued after the end of the conflict. Indeed as late as November 1907 the Board of Trade informed the Foreign Office that underwriters were still insuring against the risks posed by floating mines for vessels sailing in waters near the Korean Peninsula and Vladivostok. The additional cost of this postwar insurance against mining was charged at the considerable rate of five shillings per cent.[66] The new developments in mine warfare, therefore, not only posed a direct danger to neutral shipping in terms of the risk of striking a mine; they also imposed a heavy financial cost on all of those seeking to trade in Far Eastern waters.

The problems posed by mines to neutral trade in Chinese waters grew as the conflict wore on. Mines were laid on an ever-increasing scale by both sides up until the fall of Port Arthur in December 1904, and a combination of time in the water and winter storms meant that growing numbers of these broke their moorings. On 7 March 1905 agents from three of the largest British trading companies in the Far East,

Jardine Matheson & Co., Butterfield & Swire and Chinese Engineering and Mining Co., wrote to the British Consul General at Tientsin complaining about the issue. They emphasised that the threat from mines had increased and it was only a matter of time before a merchant ship was sunk. As such they requested that the British government take steps to have 'the present danger zone searched and swept by ship's of His Majesty's navy with the aim of destroying as many of these floating mines as possible'. They felt confident that the British government should, and would, take this step 'not only in the interests of trade but in those of common humanity'.[67] It is clear that they viewed it as not merely the right, but the responsibility of the British government to police Chinese waters and protect shipping of all nationalities. L. C. Hopkins, the British Consul General in Tientsin, appears to have broadly agreed with them, forwarding the request to Vice-Admiral Noel, a step endorsed by the Minister, Sir Ernest Satow.[68] Further south in Shanghai, Butterfield & Swire wrote to Sir Pelham Warren, the Consul General, complaining about the same issues. They enclosed a report by the Master of one of their vessels highlighting the 'perfect epidemic' of mines in northern Chinese waters, one of which 'came very near being the cause of our destruction'.[69]

On 15 March Hopkins, the Consul General in Tientsin, reported that the Chinese authorities had taken action as a result of the petitions of local shipping firms. Viceroy Yüan informed Hopkins that he had 'already despatched a war vessel to proceed to the Shantung sea and devise a scheme for exploding floating mines'.[70] British trading companies in the Far East had little faith in the ability of the Chinese to carry out this type of work and their representative body, the China Association, soon became involved. In early April, the Shanghai branch put pressure on Warren for renewed efforts in clearing the mines. As he telegrammed to Satow, they considered the 'Chinese action unreliable', but expressed their 'fullest confidence if [the] work be carried out by [a] British man-of-war'.[71] Later the same day Satow sent a telegram to Noel reiterating the request and emphasising that the 'efficiency of [the] Chinese navy cannot be relied upon'.[72] The admiral, however, saw little reason to reverse his decision of the previous July, and stated that it was 'not practicable [for] His Majesty's Ships [to] undertake [a] thorough and systematic search'.[73]

Warren informed the Shanghai branch of the China Association of the decision on 12 April and unsurprisingly it was not received well.[74]

The following day the branch telegrammed the central office of the Association in London asking that they take the matter up with the government in Britain, in the hope that it would force Noel to take action. Joseph Welch, the secretary, immediately forwarded the telegram on to the Foreign Office. Despite this, and further exhortations later in the month, the Foreign Office refused to deviate from the position adopted by Noel.[75] The Admiralty itself clearly outlined its views in a letter to the Foreign Office, which highlights the different perceptions of the role of the Royal Navy. The Admiralty reported that it was aware of the problem and had produced a number of warning notices to mariners. It, however, could not 'undertake to detail His Majesty's ships for the dangerous duty of seeking and destroying mines on the high seas and in foreign territorial waters'.[76] This contrasts sharply with the position adopted by the British commercial interests as represented by the Shanghai branch of the China Association. At roughly the same time as the Admiralty was stating its position, the branch wrote to London with a very different perception of the responsibilities of the British government. It suggested that 'no value whatever' could be placed on the efforts of the two Chinese warships to clear the mines. It went on that:

> It is believed that our own naval authorities have reserved their search for the immediate zone at Wei-Hai-Wei and are disinclined to go further afield; noting the big priority in British shipping interests, combined with the ambition to always see our navy prominent in matters pertaining to these seas, it is hoped that even yet the matter maybe undertaken by our authorities; the dangers are very real and will continue so for a long time to come.[77]

British companies were not the only ones who felt that it was the responsibility of the Royal Navy to take stronger action. On 10 July Lord Muskerry made a speech in the House of Lords on the 'grave risks to life and property' caused by the mine problem and 'the laxity of the Admiralty in this matter'. He declared of the Royal Navy that '(t)heir time would then be spent in a service to humanity, and as their business is to police the seas, it seems to me that they are sadly neglecting that duty'. Muskerry went on to reflect a sentiment shared by many, suggesting that 'it is a poor thing for British ships to be trusting to foreign navies to protect them from these dangers when we have our own Navy on the spot'.[78]

Part of the problem was revealed in a report produced by Captain Edward Shortland of the cruiser *Hogue*, which was stationed at Wei-Hai-Wei. Shortland wrote his report towards the end of March, but it was not given to Satow until the end of April and did not reach London until June.[79] Both the full report and an abridged version were circulated widely by the Foreign Office and Board of Trade.[80] The report heavily played down the risks posed by mines in the waters around China. Shortland stated that he had received numerous reports of mines from coastal steamers and plotted these on a chart. '(T)he positions of many of them by latitude and longitude are shown to be many miles inland. Several of them are probably the same mine drifting backwards and forwards, and seen by different steamers; many are, I believe floating casks, logs of wood etc'. Shortland concluded that '(u)nder these circumstances I can quite understand how it is easy for the masters of steamers who are not experienced in these matters to report every object they see in the water as being dangerous to navigation. I beg to make this report in order to restore confidence in the various steamers which are navigating these waters.'[81] Unsurprisingly, Shortland's report did nothing of the sort. When the report was read at a meeting of the London council of the China Association there was a sense of outrage. James Henry Scott, senior partner at Butterfield & Swire, 'remarked that Captain Shortland was indulging in a cheap smear at the merchant skipper. As a matter of fact the masters of coasting steamers in Chinese waters were thoroughly competent and trustworthy men, most unlikely to be guilty of the blunders insinuated by Captain Shortland.'[82]

The following day the China Association wrote to the Foreign Office expressing its surprise at the mistakes referred to in Shortland's report and suggesting that these were most likely 'clerical errors'. It went on to emphasise that it did not accept the basic contention that the reports of mines had been exaggerated. In this it was assisted by the fact that on 11 and 12 May two steamers, the British-registered SS *Sobralense* and the Japanese *Maiko Maru*, had been destroyed by mines.[83] Both of these vessels struck mines in the vicinity of Port Arthur, and it is likely that they struck moored rather than floating mines, but the examples still added weight to the Association's demands. Despite this evidence the British government still refused to take the concrete steps demanded by British commercial interests in the Far East. It did, however, appear to increasingly accept the reality of the problems posed by the mines. In September the Foreign Office wrote to the China Association to inform it that further representations had been made to the Japanese government, and that the Japanese were 'doing all in their power to remove the danger to shipping'.[84] Such action had limited effect, and only weeks later the China Merchants' Steam Navigation Co. steamer *Hsieh-Ho* was sunk by a mine off Wei-Hai-Wei.[85]

The nature of the threat posed by mines was such that the termination of the conflict did little to ameliorate the risk. There were continuing demands for action to be taken by British naval forces in the region, but the Admiralty was 'not prepared to depart from [the] principle' that it had established during the war.[86] As late as November 1906 the North of England Protection and Indemnity Association wrote to the Foreign Office requesting information on the clearance of mines and continuing risks. It stated almost apologetically that '(o)ur excuse for thus troubling you, is the fact that British steamers to the value of £23,000,000 are entered in the War Risk Class of this Association and that an ordinary Lloyds policy ... does not cover the risk of mines'.[87] It was informed that efforts had been made to clear mines, but that the Russian Chief of Naval Headquarters' Staff 'could not undertake to say that all had been cleared away'.[88]

In total the United States Navy Department identified fifteen ships 'known to have been destroyed by derelict mines off the China coast, during the years 1904, 1905 and 1906'.[89] British figures, given by David Lloyd George as President of the Board of Trade in response to a Parliamentary Question in August 1907, stated that two British vessels were known to have been destroyed by mines, and a further two badly damaged. He went on to say that '(n)ine neutral vessels, of which three were British, have been reported missing on voyages in the East, but the causes of their loss are of course purely matters of conjecture'.[90] Whilst these figures are not particularly high, they served to highlight the very real risks posed by mines to neutral shipping interests. Considering the limited scope of the Russo-Japanese War, and its comparative geographic isolation from the foci of global trade, the impact of the mines was quite considerable. The potential for a problem on an entirely different scale in the event of a major European conflict was clearly apparent. The action of British commercial interests in continually raising the mining problem with the British government and demanding action overlapped with, and reinforced, the more popular expressions of outrage made in the press regarding the legality of mines. The issues facing shipowners, crews and insurers aligned closely with the arguments made in Britain presenting mines as a threat both strategically and culturally. Within the public discourse the technology threatened British maritime trade as a neutral, and Britain's ability to exert naval power as a belligerent. Furthermore it appeared to pose an uncomfortable challenge to the country's self-appointed position as guardian of the seas. The indiscriminate nature of the weapon, combined with the inability of the Royal Navy to protect its own commerce, led to many viewing mines as a fundamentally un-British weapon.

The regular demands by British companies for action to be taken regarding mines also opened up the debate over the precise role of the Royal Navy. It had long been accepted that the service not only protected British interests abroad, but served as the guarantor of the broader idea of freedom of the seas. It had done so by offering a security umbrella under which trade could take place, but this had generally required comparatively little direct interaction between the navy and commercial interests. The problems caused by mines in Chinese waters and the unwillingness of the Royal Navy to engage with the issue challenged these perceptions of the service. Many in the commercial community, and in Britain more widely, felt that it was the duty of the navy to take action in order to protect British shipping. This fed into a broader debate which was taking place at the time over how the service was supposed to ensure the safety of British commerce.[91] Events in the Far East speak to a cleavage between the internal view within the Royal Navy as to its role and the external perceptions within Britain. Over time the navy would develop a far closer working relationship with commercial interests, but this only developed slowly with regard to mines.

Both the popular outrage regarding the legality and morality of mines, and the more practical demands made by commercial interests, placed pressure on the British government to act. The official response taken in London, which will be outlined in the following chapter, clearly draws considerably from this broader public discourse on the subject; something aided by the fact that most in government shared the concerns that were expressed more widely about the morality of mines and their potential impact on British commercial and strategic positions. This confluence of opinion meant that Britain developed a clear and definite outward position on mining, which in turn fed into the broader discussions around the necessity for a conference to discuss matters of international law following the conflict.

Notes

1. The most obvious exception being Bennett Burleigh, the *Daily Telegraph* reporter, who the Japanese felt was so pro-Russian that he was breaching rules on neutrality. See The National Archives (TNA), PRO 30/33/7/3, Satow Papers, Campbell to Satow, 2 December 1904.
2. 'The War', *The Evening Standard*, 13 April 1904, p. 5, col. A.
3. 'The War', *The Times*, 14 April 1904, p. 3, col. A.
4. 'The Russian Disaster', *The Daily Chronicle*, p. 4, col. B; 'War in the Far East', *The Times*, 14 April 1904, p. 4, col. B.
5. 'Naval Position Today', *The Daily Telegraph*, 14 April 1904, p. 9, col. G.
6. 'The Sinking of the Petropavlovsk', *The Times*, 14 April 1904, p. 7, col. C.
7. 'The Russian Disaster: Petropavlovsk Torpedoed or Mined?', *Pall Mall Gazette*, 14 April 1904, p. 7, col. B; 'The Man and the Hour', *St James's Gazette*, p. 3, col. A.
8. 'Sunk Battleship', *The Daily Chronicle*, 16 April 1904, p. 5, col. D.
9. 'Damnosa Hereditas', *St James's Gazette*, 15 April 1904, p. 3, col. A.
10. 'The Lost Russian Battleship', *The Daily Telegraph*, 14 April 1904, p. 10, col. C.
11. 'The Man and the Hour', *St James's Gazette*, 14 April 1904, p. 3, col. A; 'The Russian Disaster', *The Daily Chronicle*, 14 April 1904, p. 4, col. B.
12. 'The Russian Disaster', *The Daily Chronicle*, 14 April 1904, p. 4, col. B.
13. 'Japanese Regret for Makharoff', *Pall Mall Gazette*, 14 April 1904, p. 7, col. C.
14. 'Japanese Tactics', *The Daily Chronicle*, 19 April 1904, p. 5, col. F.
15. 'Togo's Daring Tactics', *St James's Gazette*, 18 April 1904, p. 10, col. B; 'Naval Position Today', *The Daily Telegraph*, 18 April 1904, p. 10, col. C.
16. 'The Naval Losses', *The Daily Telegraph*, 20 May 1904, p. 9, col. D; 'The Fortune of War', *St James's Gazette*, 20 May 1904, p. 3 col. A.
17. 'Japanese Naval Disaster', *The Daily Chronicle*, 20 May 1904, p. 5, col. B; 'The Lost Japanese Ships', *The Times*, 20 May 1904, p. 3, col. F.
18. 'The Naval Losses', *The Daily Telegraph*, 20 May 1904, p. 9, col. D.
19. 'Are We Approaching a New Naval Era?', *The New York Sun*, 18 April 1904, p. 4, Col. C.
20. 'The Probability of the Survival of the Battleship', *The New York Sun*, 11 May 1904, p. 6, col. E; 'Torpedo Craft vs Battleships', *Collier's Weekly*, 21 May 1904, p. 16.
21. 'It Is a Singular Illustration', *The Times*, 21 May 1904, p. 11, col. C.
22. 'The Unknown Quantity', *The Pall Mall Gazette*, 20 May 1904, p. 1, col. B.
23. 'The Penny Wise Policy', *The Pall Mall Gazette*, 20 May 1904.
24. 'We Are All in Sympathy with Japan Today', *The Manchester Guardian*, 20 May 1904, p. 4, col. A.

5 THE RUSSO-JAPANESE WAR: OUTRAGE AND REACTION 93

25. 'It Is Too Early to Dogmatise', *The Manchester Guardian*, 21 May 1904, p. 6, col. B.
26. 'Mines and Battleships', *Dublin Evening Telegraph*, 25 May 1904, p. 2, col. B.
27. 'We Are All in Sympathy', *The Manchester Guardian*, 20 May 1904, p. 4, col. A.
28. 'The Fortunes of War', *St James's Gazette*, 20 May 1904, p. 3, col. A.
29. 'Mines in the Open Sea', *The Times*, 23 May 1904, p. 8, col. B.
30. 'The War', *The Times*, 23 May 1904, p. 3, col. A.
31. 'The Scattering of Infernal Machines', *Pall Mall Gazette*, 23 May 1904, p. 3, col. B.
32. 'Floating War Mines', *The Daily Telegraph*, 25 May 1904, p. 10, col. A.
33. 'Strewn with Explosives', *The Daily Express*, 24 May 1904, col. B.
34. 'May Mines Be Sent Adrift on the High Seas?', *New York Sun*, 26 May 1904, p. 8, col. B; 'The Loss of the Hatsuse', *The Manchester Guardian*, 25 May 1904, p. 4, col. B.
35. 'Mines in the Open Sea', *The Times*, 25 May 1904, p. 10, col. C.
36. 'Mines in the Open Sea', *The Times*, 30 May 1904, p. 12, col. E.
37. 'The Loss of the Hatsuse', *The Manchester Guardian*, 25 May 1904, p. 4, col. B.
38. 'The Laws of Naval Warfare', *The Times*, 26 May 1904, p. 5, col.
39. 'Counsels of Despair', *Pall Mall Gazette*, 26 May 1904, p. 1, col. B.
40. 'Sir W. Walrond and Floating Mines', *The Times*, 24 May 1904, p. 4, col. D.
41. 'International Law of Warfare', House of Commons Debate, 6 June 1904, *Hansard*, vol. 135, col. 804.
42. 'There Are Few Questions Which More Deeply Effect …', *The Times*, Wednesday 13 September 1905, p. 7, col. E.
43. Benjamin Allen Coates, *Legalist Empire: International Law and American Foreign Relations in the Early Twentieth Century*, (Oxford University Press: Oxford, 2016) pp. 18–21; Stephen C. Neff, *Justice Among Nations: A History of International Law* (Harvard University Press: Cambridge, MA, 2014), pp. 300–302.
44. *Annuaire de L'Institut de Droit International*, vol. 20 (1904), pp. 233–234.
45. *Annuaire de L'Institut de Droit International*, vol. 21 (1906), pp. 88–99, 330–345.
46. *International Law Association: Report of the Twenty-Second Conference Held at Christiania*, 'Questions of International Law Arising Out of the Russo-Japanese War', pp. 83–85.
47. *International Law Association: Report of the Twenty-Third Conference Held at Berlin*, 'The Use of Submarine Mines in Maritime Warfare', pp. 74–77.
48. *International Law Association: Report of the Twenty-Third Conference Held at Berlin*, Discussion of 'The Use of Submarine Mines in Maritime Warfare', pp. 77–80.

94 R. DUNLEY

49. 'Wireless in Wartime', *The Daily Telegraph*, 27 September 1906, p. 10, col. B; 'International Law Association, *The Times*, 2 October 1906, p. 3, col. D.
50. 'The Institute of International Law', *The Times*, 1 October 1906, p. 4, col. C; 'International Law Association, *The Times*, 3 October 1906, p. 3, col. C.
51. 'Strewn with Explosives', *The Daily Express*, 24 May 1904, col. B.
52. 'Mines and Insurance', *The Daily Chronicle*, 25 May 1904, p. 7, col. B.
53. TNA, FO 17/1655, Hozier to FO, 26 May 1904, ff. 430–431.
54. TNA, FO 17/1655, Langley Minute on Hozier to FO, 26 May 1904, ff. 430–431 and FO to Lloyds (draft), 31 May 1904, ff. 460A-1.
55. TNA, FO 17/1655, Admiralty to FO, 7 June 1904, ff. 494.
56. TNA, FO 17/1655, FO to Lloyds (draft) and FO to Admiralty (draft), 13 and 14 June 1904, ff. 549–551 and 554–555.
57. TNA, FO 17/1655, Lloyds to FO and FO to Lloyds (draft), 14 and 16 June 1904, ff. 558–8A and 577; Guildhall Library, MS 31571, vol. 64, Minutes of the Committee of Lloyds of London, 1904.
58. TNA, FO 228/1540, Satow to Noel, 16 July 1904 (draft).
59. TNA, FO 228/1540, Noel to Satow, 26 July 1904.
60. TNA, FO 46/627, McIntosh to Lansdowne, 5 August 1904, ff. 376–379.
61. TNA, FO 46/627, Unsigned Minute [Walter Langley], 12 August 1904, f. 379; FO 46/628, Lansdowne to McIntosh, 12 August 1904, ff. 157–158.
62. TNA, FO 17/1657, Lloyds to FO, 26 October 1904, ff. 173–174.
63. TNA, FO 17/1657, Pickard to Stewart Lockhart, 26 October 1904, enclosed in CO to FO, 9 December 1904, ff. 426-7A.
64. TNA, TNA, FO 17/1657, Langley and Campbell Minutes, n.d., on Lloyds to FO, 26 October 1904, ff. 173–174.
65. 'Lloyds and Marine Insurance Companies', *The Times*, 26 May 1904, p. 13, col. B; 'The Marine Insurance Market', *The Times*, 27 March 1905, p. 12, col. C; 'The Marine Insurance Market', *The Times*, 18 May 1905, p. 14, col. D.
66. TNA, FO 371/212, Board of Trade to Foreign Office, 19 November 1907, 38282/838/10, ff. 526–529.
67. TNA, FO 17/1671, Boyce-Kup, Edkins and Nathan to Hopkins, 7 March 1905, Enclosed in Satow to Lansdowne, 9 March 1905, ff. 81–84.
68. TNA, FO 17/1671, Hopkins to Satow and Satow to Lansdowne, 7 and 9 March 1905, ff. 81–84.
69. TNA, FO 228/1597, Warren to Satow, Enclosing Butterfield & Swire to Warren (copy), 9 March 1905; TNA, FO 671/288, Warren to Butterfield & Swire (draft), 10 March 1905.
70. TNA, FO 17/1671, Hopkins to Satow (copy), 15 March 1905, enclosed in Satow to Lansdowne, 16 March 1905, ff. 123–124.
71. TNA, FO 228/1597, Warren to Satow, 10 April 1905.

72. TNA, FO 228/1585, Satow to Noel (copy), 10 April 1905.
73. TNA, FO 228/1585, Noel to Satow, 11 April 1905.
74. TNA, FO 671/288, Warren to Lavers (draft) 12 April 1905. For further complaints about the issue also see TNA, PRO 30/33/16/8, Satow diary, 17 April 1905.
75. School of Oriental and African Studies (SOAS), CHAS/04/04, China Association 1905-6, Welch to Campbell, Campbell to Welch and Welch to Campbell, 13, 17 and 18 April 1905, pp. 62-65.
76. TNA, FO 228/1573, Adm to FO, 15 May 1905.
77. SOAS, CHAS/04/04, China Association Annual Report 1905-6, Lavers to Welch, 10 May 1905, pp. 67-68.
78. 'Floating Mines', House of Lords Debate, 10 July 1905, Hansard, vol. 149, cc. 49-54.
79. TNA, FO 671/287, Satow to Warren, 24 April 1905, enclosing a copy of the Shortland Report; TNA, FO 17/1671, Satow to Lansdowne, 27 April 1905, enclosing a copy of the Shortland Report, ff. 337-339.
80. TNA, MT 9/776, Floating Mines in Gulf of Pechili, 26 June 1905, M11865; TNA FO 17/1671, Langley minute on Satow to Lansdowne, 27 April 1905, ff. 337-339.
81. TNA, FO 17/1671, Shortland Report, enclosed in Satow to Lansdowne, 27 April 1905, ff. 337-339.
82. SOAS, CHAS/02/03, China Association Minutes of the General Committee and Executive Committee, 28 June 1905.
83. TNA, FO 228/1573, Welch to FO (copy), 29 June 1905.
84. SOAS, CHAS/04/04, China Association Annual Report 1905-6, Campbell to Welch, 12 September 1905, p. 70.
85. 'The Marine Insurance Market', *The Times*, 2 October 1905, p. 15.
86. TNA, FO 371/20, Adm to FO, 9 February 1906, 4993/543/23, f. 183.
87. TNA, FO 371/20, Metcalfe to FO, 23 November 1906, 39444/543/23, f. 195.
88. TNA, FO 371/20, Nicolson to Grey, 20 December 1906, 42939/543/23, f. 195.
89. 'Memorandum on Derelict Mines' enclosed in Newberry to Root, *Foreign Relations of the United States (FRUS) 1906*, vol. 1, pp. 305-307. The accuracy of this list is unclear as it contains some vessels which were damaged but not destroyed.
90. TNA, FO 371/212, Bellairs Parliamentary Question, 7 August 1907, 27316/838/10, ff. 514-515.
91. Stephen Cobb, *Preparing for Blockade, 1885-1914: Naval Contingency for Economic Warfare* (Ashgate: London, 2013).

CHAPTER 6

Mining and International Law: Britain and the Hague Conference

Until 1904, interest in the subject of mining had been restricted to a relatively small circle of professional naval officers. The events in the Far East, both in terms of the naval success of mines and the popular attention the subject attracted, ensured that the issue would go on to receive considerable political scrutiny. Much of this was channelled towards the growing calls for an international agreement banning, or severely limiting, the use of mines in future conflicts. This chapter will explore the official response of the British government and its attempts to achieve an agreement on mining at the Second International Peace Conference held at The Hague in 1907. This outward response was not the only course of action taken by the British government, and following chapters will address the quiet preparations made by the Royal Navy to develop a mining capacity and deploy mines as necessary.

Official concern about the impact of mines on neutrals began in late May 1904, when the Earl of Selborne, the First Lord, asked his First Naval Lord, Admiral Lord Walter Kerr, whether the Admiralty should contact the Foreign Office about making a formal complaint to the Russians. Kerr took a cautious approach. He remarked that '(w)e have no certainty as to their [the Russians] having deliberately placed them, they maybe escapees from Dalny or P. Arthur. I fancy the H. of Commons will have some enquiries on the subject when they meet.'[1] Selborne was keen to push the matter forward and three days later produced a memorandum on questions of international law 'which seem to have an important bearing for us'. He reported that:

© The Author(s) 2018
R. Dunley, *Britain and the Mine, 1900–1915,*
https://doi.org/10.1007/978-3-319-72820-9_6

97

It is alleged that the Russians have been sowing mines broadcast in the open sea far outside territorial waters. We have no proof of this as yet. If it is proved however it would be a very serious matter and one which we are bound to take up. How should we proceed? Should we endeavour to get the US to take action with us?[2]

The issue was discussed later the same day at a meeting of the Committee of Imperial Defence (CID).[3] Intriguingly the Chancellor, Austen Chamberlain, appears to have taken a leading role, and it was decided to appoint a sub-committee to look at a range of issues of international law brought up by the war.[4] The sub-committee was made up of the Earl of Halsbury, the Lord Chancellor; Lord Lansdowne, the Foreign Secretary; Sir Robert Finlay, the Attorney General and Edward Davidson, Legal Advisor to the Foreign Office. Later in June the sub-committee produced its report. With regard to mines it concluded that:

the Committee considered that the belligerent who laid the mines should be held responsible if they were laid outside territorial waters, or if owing to the negligent manner in which they were laid, they found their way into the high seas to the danger of neutral commerce.[5]

This expression of official opinion was strongly worded, but in reality meant little. As has been seen above the British government was unwilling to be drawn into even the most basic level of involvement on this issue, that of mine clearance. Without the prospect of any definite action such remarks were never likely to have any impact on the two belligerents. The British government recognised this and when the CID met on 17 June to discuss the conclusions of the sub-committee it was decided that this, together with certain other matters, 'must be left for consideration until the conclusion of the present war'.[6] Thus, when in October 1904 the American government raised the idea of a second peace conference the British supported such a move, but insisted that any conference would have to wait until the end of the current hostilities.[7]

October 1904 also saw the succession of Admiral Sir John Fisher to the post of First Sea Lord, replacing Kerr. Fisher was a hugely experienced "Whitehall warrior" and was well aware of the potential difficulties which could arise from the politicisation of the subject of mining. It is generally remarked that Fisher himself had never believed in the civilisation of war, and had little time for the international agreements resulting from conferences.[8] He did, however, appreciate the importance of "playing the game", both to garner the support of politicians and the public at home, and to retain the moral high ground in the event of British interests being impinged on by mining in a future conflict in which Britain remained neutral. As such the Admiralty, with the support of at least some senior politicians, adopted not one policy, but two. The first was aimed at addressing public concerns and securing Britain's interests as a neutral, and the other very quietly sought to prepare the navy to face the real challenges highlighted by the events in the Far East.

The multiplicity of issues arising from the widespread use of mines in the Russo-Japanese War was highlighted by a disjointed exchange which took place between Fisher and the Prime Minister, Arthur Balfour, in January 1905. Balfour wrote to Fisher asking whether in the light of what was happening in the war 'a special enquiry' should be made into 'the new problems raised by the wholesale scattering of floating mines'.[9] By way of reply Fisher got Prince Louis of Battenberg, the Director of Naval Intelligence (DNI), to draw up a memorandum which he opened by stating 'I presume the Prime Minister's remarks refer to the effect of floating mines upon the Ocean Waterways open to Neutral Ships, both fighting and trading.' Battenberg went on to raise the question of whether 'floating mines are a legitimate weapon' but cautioned that 'seeing its tremendous latent powers it is not seen how belligerents are to be prevented from using them, wherever strategy demands'. The memorandum did offer the solace that 'by day a good lookout would probably enable a ship to avoid floating mines which are generally on the surface'.[10] Battenberg's response clearly draws on the popular outrage in Britain at the use of mines in international waters and the implications of this for neutral trade. This was an obvious political issue and the DNI expected the Prime Minister to be addressing this concern. The reasoning behind Battenberg's focus on floating mines, meaning those that had broken adrift from their anchors, is unclear. It is possible that he was, like the naval attachés in their early reports, uncertain of the important distinction between floating and moored mines, or it could be simply that these mines were the primary concern of British commercial interests at the time.

Balfour was not happy with Battenberg's response and replied to Fisher, stating that 'I was not so much thinking of neutral shipping as of naval strategy.' Ironically it was the Prime Minister who was keen to address the purely military aspects of the issue, whilst the Admiralty was focusing on the broader political questions. Balfour went on to present the exact argument that had been used for so long in naval circles to justify British inaction on mines. In relation to naval strategy he argued that 'if we were blockading the enemy's port, we should probably not scatter mines at the mouth of his harbour; for, so long as he did not put to sea these would be a greater danger to us than to him.' He concluded that 'it seems to me that these mines are in favour of the weaker belligerent, and therefore, on balance, detrimental to us.'[11] Balfour held not understood the lessons that the Japanese use of mines had for the Royal Navy and how they could, in fact, be used to great effect by a power seeking command of the sea. The ongoing confusion with regard to terminology and the exact nature of the weapons concerned cannot have helped this general groping for understanding.

Battenberg produced a second memorandum in response to Balfour's concerns which presented a rather more coherent, if generally negative, view of independent mining. Battenberg accepted Balfour's assertion that 'mines are in favour of the weaker antagonist and therefore on balance detrimental to us'; however he sought to explain how they might be used. He restated the core principle which imbued the Royal Navy executive branch prior to the First World War; that the service's main aim was 'a second Trafalgar, a great fleet action in which our superior strength in ships will assure us victory'. He went on to argue that blockade mines, as he termed them, did not frustrate this aim, as they would not permanently seal up a harbour. Instead they gave a blockading force ample warning of an enemy's intention to leave port, because of the mine clearance that would have to precede such an exit. Battenberg felt that 'if we use blockade mines at all we shall only do so in places near an enemy's port, which, by reasons of gun-fire &ct that protects them will never be approached by our heavy ships.' Balfour had also raised the possibility of an enemy using independent mines in the locality of British ports to try and inflict damage on the fleet. Battenberg conceded that this was a risk and that in future 'we might even have to countermine ourselves out of our own ports ... as we are the best counterminers in the world we are that much to the good'. He accepted that it would be extremely difficult to persuade any international conference to ban such weapons as, in his opinion, 'against ourselves, all other nations gain by their employment.' He concluded that 'it is most desirable that this problem should be faced without delay'; however, he offered no obvious course of action to address the issue.[12]

This exchange highlights how the development of mining had raised a number of different questions which the British government needed to address in the immediate future. Neither the challenges faced by British commerce in conflicts where Britain was neutral, nor the problems of naval strategy appeared to have obvious solutions, and the question of an international agreement loomed large. Within this the lack of detailed knowledge of mining was clearly a problem. Prince Louis of Battenberg was a highly intelligent officer who, in general, had a strong understanding of both the technical detail and the broader strategic picture. With regard to mines, however, it was obvious that he lacked the knowledge to understand fully the materiel developments and their impact. It is surprising that an officer with as strong an intellectual background as Battenberg failed to extract the true significance of the reports received from the naval attachés with the Japanese fleet. Fortunately for the Royal Navy Battenberg was replaced as DNI in February 1905 by Captain Charles Ottley. Ottley was arguably the navy's foremost expert on independent mines. No one was in a better position to cast light on what was a highly confused issue, especially for the civilian members of the CID.

Within days of taking up his post Ottley had drawn up a detailed memorandum on so-called submarine automatic mines. This paper was to be a crucial document in the development of independent mining in the Royal Navy, but was considered far too revealing to be released to the CID. As such Ottley produced a sanitised version which outlined the position the navy would proffer to their political masters.[13] In this shortened paper Ottley emphasised the '(s)tartling success achieved by automatic mines during the Far Eastern War'. He went on to state that the Admiralty had included provision for 300 mines in the 1905–1906 Estimates, but this was 'a very small beginning'. Fundamentally, the navy wished to know what position the government intended to take on the political questions surrounding independent mining. In this paper Ottley's views were straightforward:

> The fact that Great Britain possesses a mercantile marine far greater than that of any other country would naturally make it very desirable, from the British standpoint, that automatic mines should never be used in any future war, or that in any case their use should be restricted, under

stringent international penalties, solely to the immediate approaches of great naval arsenals.[14]

Ottley did, however, admit that the 'same motives which from a British standpoint, render automatic mines an objectionable mode of warfare, must, from the standpoint of our possible enemies, prove a strong argument for employing them on the widest possible scale.' Thus the DNI concluded that Britain must either persuade the other powers to adopt their view on the subject, 'or (on pain of certain disaster in any future war) we must do as Europe does'.[15]

In mid-April 1905 Fisher pressed for a discussion of the question of independent mining at the CID. The issue was an emotive one, as this letter from the secretary of the CID, Sir George Clarke to Balfour reveals:

> Sir John Fisher is very keen to have the question of the employment of blockade mines discussed at the next meeting. The main point seems to be whether after the war is over, a Hague Conference could be induced to limit the employment of these diabolical things. If their general use comes to be sanctioned in open waters forming highways of commerce, civilization will have taken a step backwards.[16]

The issue came before the committee on the 19 April 1905, and the navy's position, as outlined in Ottley's memorandum, was repeated, focusing on the desire to get an international agreement. The new First Lord, Lord Cawdor, told the meeting that:

> The Admiralty suggest that the following conditions should be imposed by international agreement on the use of automatic mines:- (a) That automatic mines should be furnished with a sinking arrangement which would render them harmless after the lapse of a few months. (b) That, if a mine breaks adrift, it should automatically become harmless. (c) That automatic mines should be laid only in the territorial waters of approach to an enemy's arsenals, and that a notification that this operation had been carried out should be sent to all neutrals.[17]

It was revealed that the navy intended to experiment with mines on a small scale in the 1905 manoeuvres and desired the committee's approval of this, and the broader course of action outlined by Cawdor. The CID 'provisionally approved' the Admiralty policy, although the concept of Britain even practising with these mines was not viewed positively.[18] There appears to have been particular concern that Britain should not be seen to be embracing a weapon on which it would seek to place serious limits in any forthcoming international convention, for fear of accusations of hypocrisy.

I

Despite attentions being focused on a crisis in Europe throughout the summer of 1905, Balfour did not let the issue of mining slip. He instructed Fisher to contact the American government through its naval attaché in London to get the issue raised informally. In October Fisher reported to Balfour that he had done so, and enclosed a letter from Ottley.[19] Both of these documents also contain references to the secret developments which the Royal Navy were undertaking at the time; these will be discussed in context in the following chapters. With relation to the idea of limiting the usage of mines Ottley declared:

> The Conference should certainly be called upon to pronounce an unhesitating opinion on the following points. 1. Is the use of offensive mines a legitimate form of war and if so – 2. Is the use of such mines to be permitted outside the three-mile limit? 3. If the answer to 2. be in the negative; is the use of offensive mines to be permitted off the mercantile ports of an enemy? Or 4. Is it to be confined to the territorial waters of approach to naval arsenals. I submit that 4. is the very utmost limit to which Great Britain should accede. We might go to the Conference with clean hands and might say that we desire to limit the use of offensive mines to the utmost possible extent. We might safely count upon the support of the United States in this view and I believe the same policy would be acceptable to every civilized power.[20]

Fisher suggested that if Balfour still wished to press the mining issue at the Hague Conference then this should form the starting point of negotiations.[21] The Prime Minister agreed, arguing that Britain should use all its influence to place limits on the use of mines.[22] He issued a memorandum stating his desire to have the subject discussed at the conference, and the necessary steps were taken through the British minister at The Hague.[23] Balfour's correspondence does giving interesting insights into the particular concerns which inspired this decision and the ongoing difficulties, especially on the part of politicians, in understanding the technology. In particular he wrote to Sir George Clarke regarding his discussions with Fisher 'about the use of offensive mines, i.e. the floating mines which even now are a peril to neutral commerce in the Far East'.[24] The reference to neutral commerce rather than naval strategy is instructive, as concerns regarding Britain's position as a neutral would dominate the debate going forward. Balfour's use of the term 'floating mines', does, however, suggest that there was still considerable uncertainty in the distinction between buoyant anchored mines, and those which had broken adrift from their moorings.

By October the Treaty of Portsmouth ending the Russo-Japanese War had been successfully concluded and any outstanding issues resolved. As such, attention, both popular and official, began to turn to the planned conference on questions of international law arising out of the conflict. The day after Balfour's memorandum was released Clarke drew up a working paper in an 'attempt to forecast the more important questions which may arise, and to arrive at clear ideas as to British interests regarding them.'[25] Clarke's involvement was by no means universally welcomed. As Willoughby Maycock of the Treaty Department of the Foreign Office wrote, 'Sir George is rather addicted I believe to writing on matters which do not come within his immediate purview which at times is calculated to cause embarrassment and confusion to those who have to deal with the questions'. Furthermore his views on many matters were 'thought to be rather heterodox'.[26] This gives an indication of some of the interdepartmental tensions created by the discussion of the laws of war at an international conference. With regard to mining, Clarke's comments do not appear to have been controversial. He concluded, in a similar spirit to that expressed by the Admiralty earlier in the year and Ottley more recently, that; 'British interests would be best served by the abolition of all uncontrolled mines. Failing this, rules limiting the waters in which they can be used, and requiring that they should be moored in all cases, would be to our advantage'.[27] The Admiralty, on reviewing the paper, expressed its full concurrence.[28] The outward position of the Royal Navy was that, although independent mines could prove useful, it was already confident in achieving its strategic aims. Britain, therefore, had less to lose by the prohibition or limitation of use of these mines, due to her already being the preeminent naval power. Furthermore, the potential danger posed by these weapons to neutral shipping was a sufficient problem to press for their use to be outlawed.

In April 1906 the Foreign Office proposed that a small interdepartmental committee be put together under the Attorney General, Sir John Walton, to discuss matters which might arise at the conference.[29] The committee was made up of Lord Desart, Treasury Solicitor; Edward Davidson, Legal Advisor to the Foreign Office; Cecil Hurst, Assistant Legal Advisor to the Foreign Office; Eyre Crowe, Senior Clerk at the Foreign Office; J. S. Risley, Legal Assistant to the Colonial Office; W. J. Howell, Assistant Secretary of the Marine Department of the Board of Trade; Colonel Francis Davis, Assistant Director of Military Operations at the War Office; Sir George Clarke; and Charles Ottley. The Walton Committee mainly focused on the most controversial issues to be discussed at The Hague, notably the right of capture of private property at sea, and contraband. Mining was, however, also considered, particularly with reference to broader issues around the rights of neutrals. Although no detailed record of the committee's deliberations survive, it is clear that it was keen to engage in the considerable debate which was ongoing at the time between international lawyers regarding positions to be taken at The Hague. The committee considered memoranda prepared by Sir John Macdonnell and Sir Thomas Barclay, both of which tended to focus on neutral rights.[30] They also looked at a report on the rights of neutrals, prepared by a high-power committee of lawyers and politicians, which examined each of the various topics to be discussed at the conference in turn.[31] This report concluded that mines should be banned outright as they 'must from their very nature be a serious peril to neutrals pursuing innocent voyages'.[32] Perhaps most notable were the regular references within all of these discussions to a paper entitled 'The Rights of Neutrals as Illustrated by Present Events'. This had been produced by Sir Edward Fry, an eminent judge and the man who would lead the British delegation at The Hague. As the title implies, the paper examined the issues which were to come before the conference from the perspective of neutral powers. With specific reference to mines, Fry noted that in war the convenience of neutrals should always prevail over that of the belligerents. Thus he concluded that whilst belligerents had the right to use new weapons, such as independent mines, if they 'cannot be used without the infliction of additional burdens on neutrals, they cannot lawfully be used at all.'[33] From the evidence that we have it appears that the interdepartmental committee considered the subject of mining almost entirely from the perspective of Britain as a neutral, rather than as a belligerent.

This is largely confirmed from what we know of the Admiralty's external position on the subject. In June 1906 Captain Edmond Slade, head of the War Course College, produced a memorandum for Captain William Nicholson, the naval assistant secretary of the CID, on the Hague Conference. In it he made clear that although there were possible uses of mines by the Royal Navy, the disadvantages considerably outweighed any advantages. Notably, Slade picked up on the impact mines would have on insurance premiums and the possible broader dislocation of trade that could ensue. He was clearly looking at how best Britain could position itself regarding these arguments and concluded that '(t)he strongest ground we can take is the danger that such mines present to neutrals, and the risk of destroying innocent lives.'[34] Slade was not, at this stage, working inside the Admiralty, but he was very closely connected with key figures within the decision-making process and other evidence points to the fact that the Admiralty was keen to view the majority of the issues to be discussed from the perspective of Britain being a neutral. Eyre Crowe, secretary of the British delegation, and a member of the Walton Committee, later stated in a letter to his wife that the Admiralty had, at the time of the Committee, accepted a focus on neutral rights.[35] Crowe was specifically referring to the right of capture of private property, but this appears to have been a more general approach. The Second Sea Lord, Vice-Admiral Sir William May, wrote to the First Lord, Lord Tweedmouth, outlining what seems to have been the main concern motivating the attitude the Royal Navy adopted towards mines with regard to the conference. May wrote:

> Imagine war between Germany and France, and the former laying down numbers of unanchored mines in certain positions in the Channel or off Brest with the idea of injuring French trade, of course, the result would do more injury to our trade and we ought to and will have to assert ourselves, such a procedure would drive us into war with Germany.[36]

This focus on strengthening the protection for neutrals underpinned the position taken by the Admiralty both in the Walton Committee and then later at the Hague Conference itself. In the end the Walton Committee produced proposals almost identical to those put forward by Clarke in his working paper. It stated that ideally the use of mines would be prohibited altogether, but more realistically it would be limited to territorial waters surrounding naval bases. It also repeated the proposals originally made by Ottley that it should be determined that mines would have to become harmless upon breaking free of their moorings or after a certain period of time.[37]

II

The original intention had been to hold the conference at The Hague in the autumn of 1906; however organisational difficulties meant that it had to be postponed until the following summer.[38] The British delegation for the conference was something of a mixed bag. It was led by Sir Edward Fry, a distinguished lawyer, judge and international arbitrator. Fry, however, had recently turned eighty and had no experience as a diplomat. Fry was supported by Sir Ernest Satow, Lord Reay and Sir Henry Howard.[39] Satow was a career diplomat, who had spent nearly forty years in Japan and China before retiring in 1906. Reay was a Dutch-born politician and colonial administrator who had strong connections with the Liberal government. Howard was the British minister at The Hague, had been a delegate at the First Hague Conference and was heavily involved in the preparations. Ottley was appointed as Expert Naval Delegate to the conference, having recently left his position as DNI. Commander John Segrave was appointed as a naval assistant.[40] Ottley's appointment was not universally welcomed; Sir George Clarke ranted to Lord Esher that 'Ottley is quite unfit physically, [and] mentally, to represent H. M.'s Navy at a great international gathering. He is intellectually much of a flibertigibet [sic] and personally looks too much like a Portuguese Eurasian. It won't do.'[41] This view does not appear to have been widely shared; when Ottley was appointed to the Walton Committee Edward Davidson minuted approvingly that 'it seems to be an instance of the doctrine of "natural selection"'.[42]

It is difficult to gauge the importance placed on the conference by the various British stakeholders, especially the Foreign Office and the Admiralty. Within the professional ranks of the Foreign Office there appears to have been a widespread scepticism about the likelihood or even desirability of coming to arrangements on some of the more difficult topics such as disarmament and the immunity of private property at sea. The Liberal government, perhaps inspired by political necessity, took a more sanguine view, something that infuriated its civil servants.[43] As Eyre Crowe wrote bluntly to a colleague, the Foreign Secretary, Sir Edward Grey resolutely adhered to his proposals, 'though it is difficult to believe that any responsible person can be serious about them.'[44] Clarke was equally dismissive of key aspects of the programme, declaring to Esher that 'I think it is all sap about the capture of private property at sea'.[45]

The position of the Admiralty regarding the conference is rather more difficult to assess, and has been the subject of considerable historiographical debate. In his controversial recent book *Planning Armageddon* Nicholas Lambert has reasserted the traditional position that Fisher had little time for international agreements and planned to 'cynically disregard' any international law that inhibited Britain's freedom of action as a belligerent.[46] Alan Anderson, in the most comprehensive recent analysis of the naval aspects of the Hague Conferences, takes a very different view. He suggests that the Admiralty was heavily involved in all aspects of the conference preparations and took a keen interest in the developments at The Hague.[47] It is clear that the selection of Ottley to represent the Admiralty indicates a genuine interest in the subject. He was a key figure in Fisher's inner circle and this was widely acknowledged by all those involved in the conference.[48] Fisher did, however, later remark to Lord Esher that 'the orders given to the Admiralty delegates are so stringent that they would leave by the next train if our fighting interests are tampered with'.[49] It is, therefore, possible that Ottley was chosen precisely because he knew better than any other officer what those interests were, rather than this signaling a real desire on the part of the Admiralty for progress to be made at the conference. These orders have, however, never been uncovered and as with all of Fisher's statements it is necessary to view this with a certain degree of scepticism. Ottley himself appears to have taken matters seriously. At the height of the conference he wrote to Willoughby Maycock, bemoaning the burden of work and the fact that he was missing grouse shooting in Scotland. He went on, however: '(s) till I would not have missed this conference for a wilderness of grouse. I don't think I ever felt before quite the same interest and intellectual stimulus'.[50]

The actions of the Board, by contrast, show remarkable indifference to the entire subject. Fisher appears to have been on holiday for the majority of the conference and the First Lord, Lord Tweedmouth, similarly was frequently absent from discussions. The officer left to deal with matters at the Admiralty was William May, who whilst a very capable man was not well suited to that type of work. It seems likely that, because Fisher did not expect very much to come of the conference, he paid it little regard. Whether this stemmed, as is claimed by Lambert, from a general disregard for international law, or simply from an expectation that the conference would quickly descend into a stalemate and be unable to achieve any meaningful results, is difficult to tell. It is, perhaps, noteworthy that Edward VII, whose relationship with Fisher was very close, remarked to Satow prior to the conference that 'there w[ou]ld prob[ably] be a good deal of talk without much result'.[51] It is certainly true that senior naval officers were disdainful of the more radical elements of the programme. In December 1906 Battenberg wrote to the former Civil Lord of the Admiralty, Arthur Lee and put the case very clearly:

> All the references to the Hague and Disarmament on the part of the Cabinet are to my mind rubbish, and although I admire those who form it and agree with much that they say and do, I find it difficult to believe that they are sincere in all this Utopian talk. Of course J[ohn]. F[isher]. knows it to be rubbish.[52]

Ottley is on record as expressing similar views. He declared bluntly to May that 'I am quite willing to tear up any number of paper conventions, and run counter to all the jurists in the world ... if British interests demand that necessity.'[53] It is possible that this reflects the duplicitous position adopted by the Admiralty on key issues, seeking to protect Britain's interests as much as possible if she were neutral, whilst being willing to ignore any restrictions if she were involved in a major conflict. However much of the internal documentation clearly shows a genuine interest and concern over the issues, which would seem to have been unnecessary if the above duplicitous position were the accepted policy. In the face of so much conflicting evidence it is unlikely that there can ever be a satisfactory answer to this question.

What is clear is that with specific regard to mines there was a general expectation that something would be achieved. As early as July 1906 *The Times*, in an editorial, felt that an agreement on mines 'should offer no serious difficulty'.[54] On the eve of the conference the journalist and disarmament campaigner W. T. Stead reported that all major powers bar one supported placing severe restrictions on mines, and questioned whether one power should be able to prevent such an agreement.[55] This belief that the impact on neutrals during the Russo-Japanese War, combined with the perceived barbarity of the weapons, would be sufficient to ensure a general agreement extended to the British officials. Within the Foreign Office this was an area where a positive outcome from the conference was expected.[56] The case of the Admiralty is less certain. As has been seen above, leading naval officers had indicated that, because mines could be used effectively against Britain, other nations would be loath to give up this right. Even so it appears that leading figures, including Fisher, expected some form of agreement to be reached.[57]

III

In June 1907 the British delegation left for The Hague. Sir Edward Fry was given, in a formal letter from Sir Edward Grey, the positions which the government desired to be adopted. With regard to mines it stated that 'His Majesty's Government would view with satisfaction the abandonment of the employment of automatic mines in naval warfare altogether.' Failing this it sought the 'strictest limitations' on their use, including their restriction to territorial waters, preferably those surrounding naval arsenals. The mines themselves were to be of such a design as to be rendered safe on their breaking free from their moorings, or after a period of approximately six months.[58]

Before going on to discuss the events that took place at The Hague it is necessary to briefly consider the internal relationships within the British delegation. According to the official correspondence the British plenipotentiaries and their technical advisors worked seamlessly together to further the British case. Private correspondence, particularly that of Eyre Crowe, presents a rather different picture. Crowe served as secretary to the British delegation and appears to have played an increasingly important role in the behind-the-scenes negotiations as the conference progressed. Crowe was half-German and had been educated in Germany; he also spoke fluent French, and often criticised the linguistic skills of the British delegates, particularly Fry.[59] Crowe had married a German, Clema Gerhart, whose sister was married to the German naval delegate at the conference, Admiral Rudolf Siegel. Crowe and Siegel appear to have had a very good relationship, regularly dining together or going out to concerts.[60] Indeed Crowe's strong relations with the German delegates appear to have been part of the reason for his growing influence over the course of the conference. Crowe's correspondence, both to his wife and colleagues at the Foreign Office, gives some of the best descriptions of the events of the conference and in particular the difficulties within the

British delegation. From the outset Crowe reported negatively on the senior plenipotentiaries. He described Fry as 'too much accustomed to the position of dictator', whilst Reay apparently spent his time 'thinking of little else than the discovery of means how to conciliate and lick the boots of all and sundry no matter what your own interests are'.[61]

Crowe had a reputation as a difficult man to work with, and it is possible to dismiss his attacks as the views of a relatively junior official with an inflated sense of his own importance.[62] It is, however, clear that Crowe was accurate when he claimed that Fry, Reay and Satow were in the habit of ignoring the advice of the expert naval, military and legal delegates, and of settling matters in private.[63] Reay in particular was frequently the subject of Crowe's ire. Twice in July he tried to get despatches sent to London purporting to have been approved by Ottley, when in reality Ottley had either not been consulted or had already rejected the idea.[64] By the middle of July the matter had got to the stage where Ottley was forced to write to Tweedmouth on the subject.[65] The First Lord in turn wrote to Sir Edward Grey and matters appear to have improved, although the issue never went away.[66] Private correspondence between Reay and Satow following the conference suggests that this was not simply a matter of poor communication or management within the delegation. Instead both men insisted that too much heed had been given to the views of the Admiralty on matters '*not* technical but judicial', and that 'Ottley was a man who did not know his own mind'.[67] It thus appears that Reay was somewhat disingenuous when, following the conference, he wrote to the Prime Minister, Sir Henry Campbell-Bannerman, that '(t)he relations with my Colleagues were most harmonious'.[68]

Very little has been written about the issue of mining within the historiography of the Second Peace Conference at The Hague.[69] This is somewhat surprising considering the importance placed on the issue by contemporaries. As Rear-Admiral Charles Stockton, former President of the US Naval War College, wrote in 1908, '(n)o subject assigned to the Hague conference seems to have required a settlement and reconciliation more than this one' and the historian Calvin Davis, despite focusing his attention elsewhere, remarked that 'no topic at the conference received more scrutiny'.[70] This was, in part, due to its obvious and immediate relevance. The strong public reaction in Britain had been mirrored in other parts of the world, particularly the United States, and the ongoing issues caused by mines in Far Eastern waters were well known. Towards the beginning of the discussions the Chinese delegation shone further light on the specific problems they faced as a result of mines, issuing a statement to delegates that:

> In spite of every precaution being taken, a very considerable number of coasting trade boats, fishing boats, junks and sampans have sunk as a consequence of collisions with these submarine automatic contact mines, and these vessels have been utterly lost with their cargoes without the details of the disasters reaching the western world. It is calculated that from five to six hundred of our countrymen in the pursuit of their peaceful occupations have met a cruel death through these dangerous engines.[71]

This background meant that mining was one of the topics which received most attention during the course of the conference, and was also perceived to be an area where agreement would be reached.

The first two weeks of the conference were occupied with drawing up draft proposals to be submitted to the committees appointed to discuss the subjects in detail. With regard to mines this work was largely left up to Ottley, together with the American naval delegate, Rear-Admiral Charles Sperry. The American attitude towards mines had first been set out in the US Naval War College volume *International Law Topics and Discussions 1905*. This took a more liberal position than that adopted by the British, suggesting that belligerents had the right to use these weapons, with certain restrictions. The first of these was that unanchored mines had to become harmless after a certain period of time. The second was that any anchored mine that broke free from its moorings had to become safe, and thirdly, mines could only be laid in territorial waters or 'within the area of immediate belligerent activities'.[72] When the General Board of the Navy came to consider the question of what position the American government should adopt at the conference, it modified these proposals slightly, to place greater restrictions on the use of mines. It recommended that the American delegates should push for a total prohibition of the use of unanchored mines. It also implied that the crucial definition of 'the area of immediate belligerent activities' should be limited to a circle, whose diameter was the run of a standard torpedo. This would naturally place very severe restrictions on the use of mines.[73]

The American position formed the basis of a joint proposal to be presented to the Third Commission, which was considering mines. In addition to the original statements Ottley added the stricture that 'the use of mines for the establishment or maintenance of a commercial blockade in the absence of blockading vessels is prohibited'. The American position did not mention the General Board's attempt at defining the 'area of immediate belligerent activities', and so the French requested that this caveat be dropped and the draft proposals should simply state that mines could only be laid 'within belligerent jurisdiction'.[74] This would mean that mines could only be laid in the territorial waters of the belligerent powers, and not in international waters. Sperry would later suggest that he believed that French support for Britain on the issue of mines was 'the outcome of the entente'.[75] Whilst there is no other evidence to support this it is certainly notable that the key British demand regarding mines was introduced by the French. All three parties acceded to these changes and the Japanese delegate Admiral Shimamura expressed his concurrence with the new draft. This draft was then proposed by Ottley to the First Sub-Committee of the Third Commission of the Conference, which was convened to discuss the mining question.[76]

At the same time as working with his fellow naval delegates to produce a draft proposal on mines, Ottley was independently putting together a proposal with regard to torpedoes. On 21 June he wrote to Fry enclosing a draft proposal which he hoped to lay before the conference 'dealing with the restrictions which, in the interests of neutrals, it appears desirable to impose on the use of locomotive torpedoes.' He went on that in his draft the matter 'has been argued entirely from the point of view of neutral powers, and the indubitable fact that any such restrictions would be specially to the advantage of this country has been kept out of sight.'[77] The key principles outlined in Ottley's draft were that the use of torpedoes between sunset and sunrise should be prohibited except within fifty miles of the belligerent coastline, and that only regular warships should be allowed to deploy torpedoes.[78] The motives behind this proposal are far from clear. This subject was not mentioned in the build-up to the conference and was not on the agenda. It also represented a major restriction on an established and accepted weapons system, not something that was generally contemplated. Ottley himself accepted that 'it is probably too much to expect the assent of other powers to any such drastic measures'. Furthermore he admitted that it would make little difference from a naval perspective, as no commander could trust that the enemy would abide by such restrictions.[79] It appears most likely that Ottley put this forward fully aware that it would be rejected, but with the hope of gaining some advantage in the mining discussions.

In any event the Admiralty declared that such restrictions would be unfeasible, and nothing further appears to have taken place.[80]

Following the acceptance of the British proposal as the basis of discussion, the whole question of mining was passed over to a sub-committee for detailed examination. The recommendations of this sub-committee would then be reviewed and voted on by the Third Commission of the Conference. Initially matters appeared to be proceeding well. On 7 July Fry reported to Grey that 'Captain Ottley has gained the impression that, with the possible exception of Germany, all the powers are likely to accept our proposal with a few slight and unimportant modifications.'[81] Three days later Fry went further still, suggesting that there was little danger of the other powers accepting an amendment proposed by Siegel, the German delegate, to allow mines to be used freely in the theatre of war, broadly defined. He went on:

> We have on the contrary learnt that the First German Delegate foresees and reckons with the necessity of having to give his adherence to the British proposals on this subject, as it appears even to him practically and morally impossible for Germany to run the risk of allowing herself to be completely isolated in a matter of this kind.[82]

At the meeting of the sub-committee the next day it was decided to appoint a Comité de Rédaction made up of representatives of the major naval powers to work through the proposals.[83] Unfortunately no minutes of this small examining committee were kept, however the events can be pieced together from Sperry's papers and the report produced by Ottley. Within the committee there were clearly two divergent groups. According to Ottley, Britain, France, Italy and Japan all supported the severe restrictions on mines outlined in the original British draft. By contrast 'Germany and Russia have stood out for the utmost possible liberty to belligerents to deploy these mines, under conditions in which the user is to be the sole and self-constituted arbiter.'[84] It is clear that the discussions were frank, and at times distinctly undiplomatic. Relations between Siegel and Ottley appear to have been particularly bad, with Ottley viewing the German as obstructive and even hinting at his being somehow uncivilised. Siegel, by contrast, objected to the tone adopted by the British representative and there are suggestions that he placed little faith in Ottley's declarations regarding civilised behaviour. Sperry records one such clash in his notes on the meeting of 13 August. When

6 MINING AND INTERNATIONAL LAW: BRITAIN AND THE HAGUE ...   115

discussing the use of mines in a blockade Siegel 'made some caustic remarks addressed at Captain Ottley as to there being no occasion for high-sounding announcements of humane principles'.[85]

German opposition had not been unexpected and could, to a certain extent, be countered. What was far more damaging was the fact that the United States 'wavered in an unaccountable manner' on the key point at issue, the localities in which mines could be laid.[86] Sperry, who had led the initial US Naval War College investigation into the subject of mines, clearly did not approve of the more stringent restrictions implied in the General Board of the Navy's guidance. He had told Ottley at the time of the initial proposal being drafted that he was 'uncertain as to the French proposition'.[87] The British appear not to have taken this seriously and his positioning the Comité de Rédaction came as a real surprise. Sperry firmly opposed any definite restrictions limiting the use of mines to territorial waters. He argued that the large unprotected coastlines of both the US mainland and the Philippines meant that the Americans could not give up this form of defence. He suggested that the increased range of modern naval artillery meant that even a ten-mile limit was not sufficient to protect American interests.

Ottley met privately with Sperry to discuss the matter on 23 August. Ottley was seeking to introduce an amendment whereby mines could be laid outside of territorial waters, but they had to be designed so as to become harmless after just two hours. Sperry declared this to be an 'impossible condition'. It appears that Ottley pressed the issue, forcing the American to state that he had 'well known and legitimate objections.' Sperry 'told him further that because a power made a perfectly legitimate and obvious reservation of the rights of self-defence it could not therefore be accused of seeking an opportunity for a brutal and uncivilized attack upon the other party.'[88] Such was the importance of the American opposition that the British continued to apply pressure on this crucial point. A further meeting was held on 12 September between the leading figures from both delegations. The British 'did all we could to convince them that mines ought not to be laid on the high seas outside of the 3 mile limit'. Once again Sperry resisted firmly, insisting on the right of the Americans to deploy mines within the 'immediate sphere of operations', a term so vague as to be almost meaningless.[89]

Despite these setbacks in the examining committee Ottley seemed to remain positive that a good outcome could be achieved. He concluded his report to Fry saying:

the great majority of the Powers are entirely of our way of thinking on the main principle involved, which is the inalienable right of all neutrals and innocent non-combatants to freely navigate the seas without such jeopardy to life as is inevitably implied in a wholesale and indiscriminate use of automatic mines.[90]

It is worth noting the continuing focus in Ottley's remarks on this issue being one of neutral rights, as opposed to any notion of Britain's interests as a belligerent. Satow, who was the British Plenipotentiary for the Third Commission, took a rather less sanguine view. He recorded on 22 August that after eleven meetings on the subject the parties appeared to be no closer to any form of consensus.[91]

The report of the examining committee came before the Third Commission on 17 September. From the outset it was clear that the Germans would not accept any meaningful limitations on the localities in which mines could be laid. Siegel, who was one of the German delegates, declared that the Germans would reserve the right to lay mines where they saw fit. The example he used is worth quoting at some length as it offers a remarkably clear exposition of German policy, and the reasons why they were willing to stand firm on the issue of mining. The terms he used, 'fleet X' and 'country Y', appear to have been very thinly disguised references to the Royal Navy and Germany respectively.

> A single example may be cited. If a fleet X blockades the coast of country Y, it does so to cut the latter off from all communication by sea. It desires to destroy the country through a slow starvation by depriving it of its means of existence. The country Y would do its best to avoid such a fate and would seek to keep the vessels of the fleet X at as great a distance as possible from its shores. In the case the naval forces are insufficient to attain this object, the State Y finds a valuable auxiliary in mines. But in order to make them more effective it is necessary to carry them to the vicinity of the enemy. However, the fleet X will not always come near the coast: it will perhaps station itself at a distance of twenty miles or more. As Article 3. forbids the employment of mines at a distance greater than three miles and in certain cases ten miles from the coast, the defender finds itself deprived of the only means which would force the enemy fleet to keep aloof from its coasts. This state of affairs would be absolutely inadmissible.[92]

Siegel was wonderfully described by the historian Barbara Tuchmann as having 'the mind of a chess-player trained by a Jesuit', but it appears that the mining issue did not bring out his Machiavellian side.[93] This was a simple and straightforward rejection of British policy. In the votes that took place at the meetings on 17 and 19 September it became apparent that, bolstered by the support of Austria-Hungary, Russia and the United States, the Germans would successfully oppose limits on the location of mines.[94] On the 24 September Fry reported to Grey that the draft convention as amended by the Commission 'discards our restrictions regarding localities in which automatic mines maybe laid.' He went on that although an article prohibiting the use of mines to solely target commercial traffic had been agreed, it was apparent that 'this stipulation is quite ineffective' and had been declared to be as much by Siegel.[95] At the very last moment Santiago Perez Triana, the Columbian delegate, put forward a new proposal placing much greater restrictions on the use of mines. This was discussed on 26 September, and whilst it was unsurprisingly rejected, it did cause considerable ructions within the British delegation.[96] When it became clear that the proposal was not going to get sufficient support Ottley, according to Satow in his diary, 'wanted to get up and talk, and when I refused to let him open his mouth, wished me to reply to Marschall [von Bieberstein, the German First Plenipotentiary], w[hi]ch I refused to do.'[97] The following day *The Times* reported on the events in excoriating language, noting with suitable sarcasm that 'diplomatic etiquette does not apparently allow the naval representative of the greatest naval Power in the world to speak in so august an assembly as a plenary meeting of committee'.[98] Satow immediately came to the conclusion that the story had 'gone from Ottley through Saunders', the correspondent of *The Times* covering the conference. He declared that such 'use of the press is indefensible. I told Sir Ed[ward] Fry what I thought of it'.[99] Judging by Ottley's close relations with the press it appears that Satow may have had legitimate grounds for his complaint.

The debate on mines at the First Sub-Committee of the Third Commission was described by Sperry in a letter to his son as 'the bitterest fight of the Conference'.[100] It is clear that the issue led to major disagreements between the naval delegates of Britain, Germany and the United States, and soured relations more generally.[101] This was not helped by the hostile tone adopted by the British press, particularly towards the Americans. W. T. Stead proclaimed with regard to mines that 'it is impossible to believe that the American government would endorse the action of Admiral Sperry whose attitude at the Hague has been a source of amazement, not to say dismay'.[102] Sperry's resentment that 'the United States has come to be paraded before the world by the English press, along with Germany, as the great patron of the infernal engine' was particularly targeted against Ottley.[103] There was a belief in the examining committee that Ottley was passing information onto the press in order to further his points. According to Sperry the German delegate, Siegel, even went so far as to make an official complaint. By the end, Sperry reported to his son that 'naturally we all had a contempt for Captain Ottley'.[104] It is impossible to tell if there was any truth in the allegations, and it is clear that even if this was the case Ottley was far from being alone in using the press as a weapon at the conference. What this does, however, indicate is the extent of the falling-out between the British and American naval delegates and the bitterness of the disagreement over mining.

Ottley returned to Britain almost immediately after this final discussion at the Third Commission, and it was left up to John Segrave to produce a memorandum outlining the commission's work. He concluded that 'the Convention as it stands cannot be regarded as a satisfactory safeguard to neutral interests in naval warfare.' The reasons for this were clear: within the terms of the new proposals there was 'no limitation as to where mines may be laid, and, therefore, little security for neutral merchantmen on the high seas.'[105] Once again it was the issue of the rights of neutrals that was of particular concern to the British delegation. This report was not well received at the Foreign Office: Assistant Under Secretary Sir Francis Campbell minuted that '(f)or this very unsatisfactory result we are I image mainly indebted to Germany'.[106] Rather ironically, the Permanent Under Secretary, Sir Charles Hardinge referenced the very editorial in *The Times* which Satow had complained about, stating that 'the scathing article ... is amply justified by this result'.[107]

When the convention on mining came before a plenary meeting of the conference on 9 October Satow expressed British regret that it did not place tighter restrictions on the use of mines. He went on to say that the British government considered the convention a 'partial and inadequate solution.'[108] As a result he warned that

> It will not be possible to presume the legality of an action for the mere reason that this Convention has not prohibited it. This is a principle which

6 MINING AND INTERNATIONAL LAW: BRITAIN AND THE HAGUE ... 119

we desire to affirm and which it will be impossible for any state to ignore, whatever its power.[109]

The German First Plenipotentiary, Marschall von Bieberstein, forcefully objected to what he saw as a direct attack on Germany's reputation. He launched into an aggressive speech, ending with the remark; '(a)s to sentiments of humanity and civilization, I cannot admit that there is any Government or country which is superior to the one I have the honor to represent.'[110] Bieberstein's riposte went down badly at the conference. Fry reported to Grey that it 'was delivered in a tone of some irritability' and 'had been held by many of those present to have betrayed unnecessary feeling.'[111] Crowe, in letters to his wife, was less diplomatic. He described Bieberstein's speech as 'personally rude' and said that he gave himself away 'by fitting the cap to his own head'.[112] Furthermore he claimed that 'Germany's attitude about the use of these mines is generally condemned'.[113]

The convention which was finally passed by the conference was a very limited one. It opened with the admission that 'the existing position of affairs makes it impossible to forbid the employment of automatic submarine contact mines'. Britain succeeded in ensuring that unanchored mines and torpedoes became safe shortly after release, and anchored mines could not explode if they broke adrift. Belligerents were also to 'do their utmost to render these mines harmless after a limited time has elapsed'. Quite what was meant by 'do their utmost' was of course left open to interpretation. Contracting powers also undertook to remove any mines which they had laid at the close of any conflict. Perhaps the greatest achievement for British diplomacy came in the form of Article 2, which stated that the laying of mines 'with the sole object of intercepting commercial shipping is forbidden'. Once again, however, these were words with little real meaning, as such an accusation would be impossible to prove. Further limitations on the effect of the convention came in the form of Article 7. This stated that 'the provisions of the present convention do not apply except between contracting powers and then only if all the belligerents are parties to the convention'. This clause meant that the convention would only be in force in conflicts where all the belligerents had ratified it.[114] This was not the case in the First World War, where notably the Ottoman Empire had not ratified any of the Hague conventions, and as such even these limited restrictions were not binding on any power.[115]

IV

The failure of the British delegation to achieve its aims with regard to mines was generally attributed to the Germans. Lord Reay summed up British frustration in a memorandum for the Prime Minister, Sir Henry Campbell-Bannerman:

> the Germans constantly proclaimed their adhesion to lofty humanitarian principles, but whenever it was a case of applying them—as in mines or balloons—they maintained that exigencies of war would prove too strong to give effect to any Convention limiting the use of engines of destruction.[116]

These views were widely held, but Crowe, perhaps partly in response to the difficult relationships within the delegation, also suggested other problems. He accused both Reay and Satow of 'utter incompetence' and 'moral cowardice' in the negotiations, contrasting this with the 'considerable skill' of Siegel and the other German delegates.[117] Without other evidence it is very difficult to either corroborate or dismiss Crowe's claims, but it is impossible to deny the success of German diplomacy on this and other issues.[118]

Having been agreed at the conference, it was necessary for the various conventions to be signed and ratified by the contracting governments. Sir Edward Grey decided to re-form the Inter-Departmental Committee which had sat prior to the conference, in order to evaluate Britain's position and recommend which conventions should be signed.[119] Following the sudden death of John Walton, Lord Desart stepped up to chair the committee and Captain Edmond Slade represented the Admiralty. In March 1908 the committee produced an interim report covering the majority of points, including the convention on mines. It expressed its extreme dissatisfaction at the limited nature of the agreement. This would, it felt, 'have very little effect in preventing belligerents from making use of such engines of barbarity as automatic contact mines or in preserving peaceful shipping and persons from appalling catastrophes'. Once again the focus was very much on neutral rights and referenced Britain's special connection with the sea and maritime commerce. In spite of this the committee deemed it desirable to sign the convention, but was concerned that in doing so it could be misconstrued that Britain recognised all usages of mines, not expressly prohibited, as being legitimate. To prevent this it was suggested that Britain attach a declaration to this effect when signing the convention.[120] As such when, in June 1908, Britain finally signed the conventions of the Hague Conference it expressed reservations with regard to no. 8 and attached a declaration stating that:

> In affixing their signatures to the above Convention the British Plenipotentiaries declare that the mere fact that this convention does not prohibit a particular act or proceeding must not be held to debar His Britannic Majesty's Government from contesting its legitimacy.[121]

By doing this, Britain emphasised that it would contest any use of mines which impeded neutral British shipping, and so retained a comfortable sense of moral superiority. Britain was not alone in expressing reservations. France and Germany both signed the convention; however, they officially expressed reservations with regard to Article 2, concerning the use of mines against commercial shipping. Russia and Sweden were notable as countries who refused to sign altogether, although their precise grievances are undocumented.[122]

The reaction to the failure of the British delegation to achieve its aims regarding mines at The Hague was negative. Sir Edward Fry in his summation letter to Sir Edward Grey wrote that:

> the discussion on the subject of automatic mines have been, as you are aware, protracted, and have resulted in only a very partial adoption of the British proposals. We hope that one result of the debates maybe to awaken public attention to the gravity of the danger which is threatened by the use of mines.[123]

Quite why Fry felt that public opinion needed to be further awakened, or what he thought could be achieved by this is unclear. Mining was one of the topics which was most closely followed by the press in Britain. The reasons for this, in the opinion of *The Times* at least, was clear:

> Of all the questions which have been discussed at the Conference, there is none which concerns this country and its people so profoundly and so nearly as this. We are not only the first of maritime Powers, but the first of maritime nations. Our daily bread is literally at all times upon the waters.[124]

The response in the British press to the issue was clearly a continuation of the reaction against the widespread use of mines in the Far East three years before. The British efforts to place very tight restrictions on these weapons were viewed within the context of the country's perceived place in the maritime world. As such it was commonly felt that '(i)t was clearly our right and our duty to take the initiative in this matter... . But we asked for nothing that would not have equally benefited the whole of the sea-going world.'[125] The opposition to the British efforts, particularly that of the German and American delegations, was roundly condemned. *The Times* blasted that the actions of these nations 'seem to reduced civilised war to the level of organised piracy' and ran a prolonged editorial campaign under headlines such as 'Hypocrisy at The Hague' and 'The Submarine Mines Fiasco'.[126] Even the more esteemed commentators, such Reverend T. J. Lawrence, who taught international law at the Naval War College, attacked those opposing limitation in vehement terms.[127]

Similar sentiments can be found across the British press, with W. T. Stead, arguably the most influential of the correspondents at The Hague, pouring scorn on Sperry in particular, whom he saw as deserting the proper cause.[128] *The Manchester Guardian* was one of the few papers to take a rather different view of proceedings. Whilst wholeheartedly condemning the use of mines, which it said was 'cruel and unjust, and should also be illegal', it felt that 'resistance to these reforms is the penalty that we are paying for our enormous lead in the great engines of war'.[129] Following the closing of the conference, the paper was unable to restrain itself from having a dig at its London-based rival, declaring 'we must recognise that mines, like privateering, are the weapon of the weaker naval Powers, and no good can come of language of such unmeasured violence as the "Times" has used against them'.[130] This attitude, which stemmed from *The Manchester Guardian*'s strong support for disarmament, was highly unusual. Public opinion in Britain clearly still viewed mines as barbaric and uncivilised weapons which posed a major threat to neutral trade and commerce. In doing so, mines struck at the very heart of what many perceived to be the nation's core interests and identity, and so were fundamentally un-British.

Reaction in naval circles was more muted, but of a similar tone. T. J. Lawrence gave a paper at the Royal United Services Institute looking at the results of the Hague Conference. He was disappointed at the lack of action on the mining issue, but felt that it was 'the most conspicuous of the cases where the feeling that the laws of naval warfare ought to be used to equalize advantages all round influenced the decisions of the Conference to the detriment of Great Britain'. Lawrence emphasised that the convention would have little practical effect, noting that it would be a 'curiously simple-minded naval commander' who could not evade its strictures. The discussion following the paper acknowledged the disappointment caused by the failure of the British to achieve what they wanted with regard to mines at The Hague, but also reflected a pragmatism within the service community about the limits of any international convention. Despite this more sober analysis of the issue there remained an undertone of moral judgement around the discussion of mining, something that drew directly on the cultural perceptions of the technology. This was best illustrated by Lawrence's remark about the British delegation's protest at the end of the conference at the failure to place greater restrictions on mines. He declared that '(t)he voice was the voice of Sir Ernest Satow, but the words were the words of England.'[131]

Sir John Fisher was informed about the final settlement at The Haguewhilst he was holidaying at Lake Garda. He wrote to Tweedmouth in almost jubilant terms, commenting on what a failure it had been. He remarked '*How well the Germans have done it!* Choate [the American First Plenipotentiary] tied with black and yellow ribbons to Marschall's chariot wheel would be a lovely picture!'[132] Despite this even Fisher appears to have been surprised by the lack of progress on mines. He remarked in a letter to the King how 'Choate swore to me he was heart and soul against floating mines', and yet had, in Fisher's eyes, been 'completely annexed' by the Germans. It is, however, noteworthy that he went on to say that the Russian Foreign Minister, Alexander Izvolsky told him, with regard to mines, that 'these war restrictions come to nothing when the time arrives.'[133] Whether or not Izvolsky ever divulged such an opinion to the First Sea Lord it is apparent that this was the attitude taken by Fisher, and he was keen to propagate it widely.

The attempt by the British government, with tacit support from the Royal Navy, to get independent mines banned had achieved little. This came as a great surprise to many commentators, and provoked an outpouring of vitriol about the barbarism of those who opposed restrictions. Within the Royal Navy it appears that there was considerable support for the idea of an agreement, but far greater scepticism over the likelihood of anything being achieved. It was felt that arguments of military necessity would ultimately outweigh humanitarian concerns, and so it proved. The extent to which the navy would have placed any faith in limitations, even if agreement had been reached, is difficult to assess. The realities at The Hague appeared to confirm the perception that Germany in particular would go to virtually any lengths to strike at the British navy. This gave further impetus to the British developments in mining, which had up until this point been taking place underneath a cloak of secrecy.

NOTES

1. Bodleian Library, Oxford (BLO), Selborne Papers, Selborne Mss 41, Selborne to Kerr, 29 May 1904, ff. 162–163.
2. The National Archives (TNA), FO 46/624, Selborne Memorandum, 1 June 1904, ff. 215–217.
3. TNA, CAB 38/5/53, 44th Meeting CID, 1 June 1904.
4. Cadbury Research Library (CRL), A. Chamberlain Papers, AC7/5B/1, Davidson to Chamberlain, 1 June 1904.
5. TNA, CAB 38/5/68, 'Note of Conclusions Arrived at by the Sub-Committee Appointed to Consider Certain Questions of International Law Arising out of the Russo-Japanese War', June 1904.
6. TNA, CAB 38/5/61, 46th Meeting CID, 17 June 1904.
7. TNA, FO 412/79, Hay to Signatory Governments of 1899 Hague Agreement and Lansdowne to Choate, 21 October and 7 November 1904, 'Correspondence Relating to Second Peace Conference', Nos. 1 and 3, pp. 1–3.
8. Ruddock F. Mackay, *Fisher of Kilverstone* (Oxford: Clarendon Press, 1973), pp. 218–223.
9. British Library (BL), Balfour Papers, Add Mss 49710, Balfour to Fisher, 23 January 1905, f. 166.
10. BL, Balfour Papers, Add Mss 49710, Battenberg Memo, 24 January 1905, ff. 167–169.
11. BL, Balfour Papers, Add Mss 49710, Balfour to Fisher, 25 January 1905, f. 174.
12. TNA, ADM 116/3093, 'Prime Minister's Inquiries, re Blockade Mines' n.d., 'Naval Necessities II'.
13. TNA, ADM 1/8879, Ottley to Fisher, 21 February 1905.
14. TNA, CAB 38/8/22, 'Submarine Automatic Mines: Memorandum by the Admiralty', 13 March 1905.
15. TNA, CAB 38/8/22, 'Submarine Automatic Mines: Memorandum by the Admiralty', 13 March 1905.
16. BL, Balfour Papers, Add Mss 49701, Clarke to Balfour, 13 April 1905, ff. 132–135.
17. TNA, CAB 38/9/34, 71st Meeting CID, 19 April 1905.

18. TNA, CAB 38/9/34, 71st Meeting CID, 19 April 1905.
19. BL, Balfour Papers, Add Mss 49711, Fisher to Balfour, 20 October 1905, f. 126.
20. BL, Balfour Papers, Add Mss 49711, Ottley to Fisher 14 October 1905, ff. 127–131
21. BL, Balfour Papers, Add Mss 49711, Fisher to Balfour, 20 October 1905, f. 126.
22. TNA, FO 83/2146, Balfour to Fisher (copy) 26 (?) October 1905, enclosed in Balfour to Clarke, 25 October 1905.
23. TNA, FO 412/79, Balfour Memorandum, 25 October 1905, 'Correspondence Relating to Second Peace Conference', no. 49, p. 56; BL, Balfour Papers, Add Ms 49729 Lansdowne to Balfour, 27 October 1905, ff. 202–205.
24. TNA, FO 83/2146, Balfour to Clarke, 25 October 1905.
25. TNA, CAB 38/10/76, 'The Hague Conference: Notes on Subjects Which Might Be Raised by Great Britain or by Other Powers', 26 October 1905.
26. TNA, FO 372/23, Maycock Minute, 23 April 1906, 14063/11592/329, ff. 92–94.
27. TNA, CAB 38/10/76, 'The Hague Conference: Notes on Subjects Which Might Be Raised by Great Britain or by Other Powers', 26 October 1905.
28. TNA, CAB 38/11/20, 'The Hague Conference: Notes on Subjects Which Might Be Raised by Great Britain or by Other Powers with Remarks by the Admiralty', 15 May 1906.
29. TNA, FO 372/23, Maycock, Davidson and Campbell Minutes, 6, 7 and 9 April 1906, 11592/11592/329, ff. 1–4.
30. TNA, CAB 17/85, 'Statement of Laws and Usages of Neutrality', February 1907; TNA, FO 372/23, Fitzmaurice Memorandum, 12 May 1906, 16592/11592/329, ff. 110–114.
31. TNA, FO 372/23, Unknown Minute, 12 November 1906, 37850/11592/329, f. 493.
32. TNA, FO 372/23, 'Draft Reports as to Rights of Neutrals', 37850/11592/329, ff. 501–515.
33. Sir Edward Fry, *The Rights of Neutrals as Illustrated by Recent Events* (London: The Royal Academy, 1906), pp. 5, 8.
34. TNA, CAB 17/85, 'Hague Conference', Enclosed in Slade to Nicholson, 20 June 1906, ff. 259–263.
35. BLO, Crowe Papers, MS. Eng. d. 2901, Crowe to Wife, 21 August 1907, ff. 145–148.
36. National Museum of the Royal Navy (NMRN), Tweedmouth Papers, Mss 254/474, May to Tweedmouth, 11 September 1907.

37. NMRN, Fisher Papers, Mss 252/7/6 'Report of the Inter-Departmental Committee', 21 March 1907.

38. Parliamentary Papers (henceforth PP), 'Correspondence Respecting the Second Peace Conference Held at The Hague in 1907' (henceforth Hague Correspondence), Isvolsky to Benckendorff, 25 May 1906, p. 7.

39. PP, 'Hague Correspondence', Grey to Fry, 12 June 1907, p. 11.

40. TNA, FO 412/86, Adm to FO, 8 and 15 April 1907, 'Correspondence Relating to Second Peace Conference', Nos. 208 and 221, pp. 148, 155.

41. Churchill Archives Centre (CAC), Esher Papers, ESHR 10/40, 9 April 1907.

42. TNA, FO 372/23, Davidson Minute, 29 May 1906, 17912/11592/329, f. 237.

43. For Liberal attitudes to disarmament see Andre T. Sidorowicz. 'The British Government, The Hague Peace Conference of 1907, and the Armaments Question', in B. J. C. McKercher, ed., *Arms Limitation and Disarmament: Restraints on War 1899–1939* (Westport: Praeger, 1992).

44. TNA, FO 800/23, Crowe to Villiers, 21 February 1907, ff. 284–287.

45. CAC, Esher Papers, ESHR 10/40, 9 June 1907.

46. Nicholas Lambert, *Planning Armageddon* (Cambridge, MA: Harvard University Press, 2012), p. 99.

47. Alan M. Anderson, 'The Laws of War and Naval Strategy in Great Britain and the United States: 1899–1909' (Unpublished PhD thesis, King's College, London, 2016), pp. 197–200, 202–207, 214–215.

48. TNA, FO 372/75, Grey to Fry, 18 July 1907, 42742/268/329.

49. CAC, Esher Papers, ESHR 10/42, Fisher to Esher, 17 October 1907.

50. TNA, FO 372/70, Ottley to Maycock, 12 August 1907, 26717/268/329.

51. TNA, PRO 30/33/16/10, Satow Diary, 7 May 1907.

52. Courtauld Book Library (CBL), Lee Papers, CI/LEE/6/1, Battenberg to Lee, 1 December 1906.

53. NMRN, Tweedmouth Papers, Mss 254/477/6, Ottley to May, 15 September 1907.

54. 'The Next Peace Conference', *The Times*, 23 July 1906, p. 4.

55. 'First Impressions of the Second Hague Conference', *Review of Reviews*, vol. 36, no. 211, July 1907, p. 35.

56. This is clearly shown by the surprise and frustration at the eventual lack of progress. See TNA, FO 372/74, Hardinge and Campbell Minutes, 2 October 1907 and n.d., 32663/268/329.

57. For an indication of this see his surprise at the lack of results in Arthur J. Marder, *Fear God and Dread Nought: The Correspondence of Admiral of the Fleet Lord Fisher of Kilverstone*, vol. II (*FGDN II*) (London:

Jonathan Cape, 1956), Fisher to the King, 8 September 1907, no. 82, pp. 129–131.

58. PP, 'Hague Correspondence', Grey to Fry, 12 June 1907, p. 14.
59. BLO, Crowe Papers, MS. Eng. d. 2901, Crowe to Wife, 7 July 1907, ff. 44–48.
60. Sibyl Crowe and Edward Corp, *Our Ablest Public Servant: Sir Eyre Crowe*, 1864–1925 (Merlin: Braunton, 1993), p. 209.
61. TNA, FO 800/69, Crowe to Tyrrell, 23 June 1907, ff. 128–133.
62. Nigel J. Brailey, 'Sir Ernest Satow and the 1907 Hague Peace Conference', *Diplomacy and Statecraft*, vol. 13, no. 2 (2002), p. 201. For a rather different view see Crowe and Corp, *Our Ablest Public Servant*, pp. 203–214.
63. BLO, Crowe Papers, MS. Eng. d. 2901., Crowe to Wife, 17 and 18 June 1907, ff. 8–9, 10–12; TNA, FO 800/69, Crowe to Tyrrell, 23 June 1907, ff. 128–133.
64. BLO, Crowe Papers, MS. Eng. d. 2901., Crowe to Wife, 2 and 8 July 1907, ff. 36–37, 49–51; TNA, FO 800/69, Crowe to Tyrrell 2 July 1907 ff. 136–145.
65. NMRN, Tweedmouth Papers, Mss 254/501, Ottley to Tweedmouth, 16 July 1907.
66. TNA, FO 800/87, Tweedmouth to Grey, 18 July 1907.
67. TNA, PRO 30/33/11/12, Satow Papers, Reay to Satow, 5 December 1907; TNA, PRO 30/33/11/15, Satow Papers, Satow to Reay, 29 November 1907.
68. BL, Campbell-Bannerman Papers, Add Ms 41242, Reay to Campbell-Bannerman, 22 October 1907, ff. 259–260.
69. There is some discussion with specific legal history of mine warfare. See Howard S. Levie, *Mine Warfare at Sea* (Dordrecht: Martinus Nijhoff, 1992), pp. 23–53. Also see Scott Andrew Keefer, *The Law of Nations and Britain's Quest for Naval Security: International Law and Arms Control, 1898–1914* (Basingstoke: Palgrave, 2016), pp. 215–220.
70. C. H. Stockton, 'The Use of Submarine Mines and Torpedoes in Times of War', *The American Journal of International Law*, vol. 2, no. 2 (1908), p. 277; Calvin DeArmond Davis, *The United States and the Second Hague Peace Conference: American Diplomacy and International Organisation 1899–1914* (Durham, NC: Duke University Press, 1975), p. 244
71. James Brown Scott, *The Proceedings of The Hague Peace Conferences: The Conference of 1907*, vol. 3 (New York: Oxford University Press, 1920), p. 400.
72. *US Naval War College: International Law Topics and Discussions 1905* (Washington: Government Printing Office, 1906).

73. National Archives and Records Administration (NARA) (I), Record Group 80, Folder 438–7, Dewey to Bonaparte, 27 September 1906.
74. Library of Congress (LOC), Sperry Papers (MSS 40923), Box 10, Folder 2, 'Notes of Conversation with Captain Ottley R.N.: Mines'.
75. Naval War College (NWC), Record Group 8/2, Box 94, Folder 9, 'Submarine Mines: Report of the US Naval Delegate Plenipotentiary to the Secretary of State', 20 October 1907.
76. TNA, FO 412/87, 'Correspondence Relating to Second Peace Conference', Fry to Grey, 28 June 1907, no. 5, p. 6.
77. TNA, FO 412/86, 'Correspondence Relating to Second Peace Conference' Ottley to Fry, 21 June 1907, no. 326, Inclosure 1, pp. 271–272.
78. TNA, FO 412/86, 'Restrictions on the Use of Locomotive Torpedoes at Night', no. 326, Inclosure 2, pp. 272–274.
79. TNA, FO 412/86, Ottley to Fry, 21 June 1907, no. 326, Inclosure 1, pp. 271–272.
80. TNA, FO 412/86, Admiralty to Foreign Office, 28 June 1907, no. 346, p. 324.
81. TNA, FO 412/87, 'Correspondence Relating to Second Peace Conference', Fry to Grey, 7 July 1907, no. 30, p. 93. On German opposition see TNA, PRO 30/33/16/10, Satow Diary, 4 July 1907.
82. TNA, FO 412/87, Fry to Grey, 10 July 1907, no. 44, p. 158.
83. TNA, FO 412/87, Fry to Grey, 14 July 1907, no. 68, p. 227.
84. TNA, FO 412/89, 'Correspondence Relating to Second Peace Conference', Ottley to Fry, 1 September 1907, no. 7, Inclosure 1, pp. 33–38.
85. LOC, Sperry Papers (MSS 40923), Box 10, Folder 2, 'Third Commission, First Sub-Commission, Comité d'Examen'.
86. TNA, FO 412/89, 'Correspondence Relating to Second Peace Conference', Ottley to Fry, 1 September 1907, no. 7, Inclosure 1, pp. 33–38.
87. LOC, Sperry Papers (MSS 40923), Box 10, Folder 2, 'Memorandum for Members of the Third Committee'.
88. LOC, Sperry Papers (MSS 40923), Box 10, Folder 2, 'Mines Memorandum of Conversation with Capt. Ottley, Friday, 23rd August 1907'.
89. TNA, PRO 30/33/16/10, Satow Diary, 12 September 1907.
90. TNA, FO 412/89, 'Correspondence Relating to Second Peace Conference', Ottley to Fry, 1 September 1907, no. 7, Inclosure 1, pp. 33–38.
91. TNA, PRO 30/33/10/16, Satow Papers, Satow Memorandum, 22 August 1907.

92. Brown Scott, *Hague Peace Conferences*, vol. 3, p. 381.
93. Barbara W. Tuchmann, *The Proud Tower: A Portrait of the World Before the War 1890–1914* (New York: Macmillan, 1966), p. 260.
94. Brown Scott, *Hague Peace Conferences*, vol. 3, pp. 378–445.
95. TNA, FO 412/89, 'Correspondence Relating to Second Peace Conference', Fry to Grey, 24 September 1907, no. 83, p. 520.
96. TNA, FO 372/74, 'Colombian Proposal Respecting Automatic Mines', 24 September 1907, 31986/268/329.
97. TNA, PRO 30/33/16/10, Satow Diary, 26 September 1907.
98. 'Hypocrisy at The Hague', *The Times*, 27 September 1907, p. 9.
99. TNA, PRO 30/33/16/10, Satow Diary, 29 September 1907.
100. LOC, Sperry Papers (MSS 40923), Box 5, Folder 2, Sperry to his son, 6 October 1907.
101. Davis, *United States and the Second Peace Conference*, p. 244.
102. 'The Second Conference at The Hague', *Review of Reviews*, vol. 36, no. 213, September 1907, p. 249.
103. LOC, Sperry Papers (MSS 40923), Box 5, Folder 2, Sperry to his son, 6 October 1907.
104. LOC, Sperry Papers (MSS 40923), Box 5, Folder 2, Sperry to his son, 6 October 1907.
105. TNA, FO 412/90, 'Correspondence Relating to Second Peace Conference', 'Memorandum by Commander Segrave', 28 September 1907, no. 1, Inclosure 1, pp. 1–3. Scott Keefer's recent suggestion that Britain got most of what it wanted from the convention is wide of the mark, Keefer, *Law of Nations*, pp. 219–220.
106. TNA, FO 372/74, Campbell Minute, 2 October 1907, 32663/268/329.
107. TNA, FO 372/74, Hardinge Minute, n.d., 32663/268/329.
108. Brown Scott, *Hague Peace Conferences*, vol. 1, p. 275.
109. Brown Scott, *Hague Peace Conferences*, vol. 1, p. 275.
110. Brown Scott, *Hague Peace Conferences*, vol. 1, p. 276.
111. TNA, FO 412/90, 'Correspondence Relating to Second Peace Conference', Fry to Grey, 14 October 1907, no. 23, p. 342.
112. BLO, Crowe Papers, MS. Eng. d. 2902, Crowe to Wife 8 (9?) and 12 October 1907, ff. 83–86, 89–92.
113. BLO, Crowe Papers, MS. Eng. d. 2902, Crowe to Wife 8 (9?) October 1907, ff. 83–86.
114. PP, 'Convention Relative to the Laying of Automatic Submarine Contact Mines', 'Final Act of the Second Peace Conference at The Hague', pp. 77–81.
115. James Wilford Garner, *International Law and the World War*, vol. I (London: Longmans & Co, 1920), pp. 18–25.

130 R. DUNLEY

116. BL, Campbell-Bannerman Papers, Add Mss 41242, Reay Memo, ff. 261–266.
117. BLO, Crowe to Wife, Crowe Papers, MS. Eng. d. 2902, 28 September 1907, ff. 50–57.
118. For an external, if not impartial critique of British diplomacy at the conference see 'The Second Peace Conference at The Hague: Observations of a Disillusioned Crusader', *Review of Reviews*, vol. 36, no. 212, August 1907.
119. TNA, FO 372/117, 'Peace Conference: Inter-Departmental Committee', 17 January 1908, 1787/1787/329.
120. TNA, CAB 37/92/43, 'Peace Conference: Inter-Departmental Committee: Interim Report', 27 March 1908.
121. PP, 'Final Act of the Second Peace Conference at The Hague', 'Reservations', p. 148; PP, 'Further Correspondence Respecting the Second Peace Conference Held at The Hague', Grey to Fry, 18 June 1908, p. 2.
122. PP, 'Final Act of the Second Peace Conference at The Hague', 'Table of Signatures', pp. 140–143.
123. PP, 'Correspondence Respecting the Second Peace Conference Held at The Hague in 1907', Fry to Grey, 16 October 1907, p. 19.
124. 'Marine Mines at The Hague', *The Times*, 2 September 1907, p. 7, col. D.
125. 'Hypocrisy at The Hague', *The Times*, 28 September 1907, p. 9, col. B.
126. 'Submarine Mines', *The Times*, 22 August 1907, p. 8, col. A; 'Hypocrisy at The Hague', *The Times*, 28 September, 1907, p. 9, col. B; and 'Peace Conference: The Submarine Mines Fiasco', *The Times*, 1 October 1907, p. 3, col. A.
127. 'Submarine Mines and the Preparation of Business for Future Hague Conferences', *The Times*, 10 September 1907, p. 5, col. D.
128. 'The Harvest of The Hague', *Review of Reviews*, vol. 36, no. 214, October 1907, pp. 352–353.
129. 'There Has Been an Interesting Discussion at The Hague...', *The Manchester Guardian*, 17 August 1907, p. 8, col. B.
130. 'It Would Be Affection to Deny...', *The Manchester Guardian*, 21 October 1907, p. 6, col. B.
131. T. J. Lawrence, 'The Hague Conference and Naval War'. *Royal United Services Institute Journal*, vol. 52, no. 362, April 1908, pp. 479–509.
132. NMRN, Tweedmouth Papers, Mss 254/450, Fisher to Tweedmouth, 14 October 1907.
133. Fisher to King, 8 September 1907, FGDN II, no. 82, pp. 129–131.

CHAPTER 7

The Strategic Shift: The Origins of British Mine Warfare

Following the unexpected impact of mine warfare in the Russo-Japanese War, the British government devoted considerable effort in attempting to place very strict limitations on the use of the weapon in international law. This policy had widespread support, not only among the British public, but also within naval circles. It fed directly from the perception that mines were fundamentally antithetical to the Royal Navy's mission as embodied in its organisational culture, and Britain's role more broadly as a maritime power.

The argument put forward by the British at The Hague was grounded in a perception of the priority of the rights of neutrals over those of belligerents, and a broader appeal to humanitarian principles. At times the rhetoric deployed by the British delegates, and more especially by the British media, presented the mining question as one of civilisation. Those who defended the right to use mines more widely were condemned as endorsing barbaric forms of warfare, not befitting a modern civilised state. Some of those who opposed the attempts to limit the use of mines sought to cast doubt on the sincerity of the British claims to humanitarian principles. They pointed out that the British were more than happy to claim the moral high ground on issues such as mining, where the liberal, humanitarian position aligned with their own interests.[1] On other issues, particularly around blockade, Britain was willing to block proposals which appealed to the same principles on the grounds that they potentially damaged her vital interests.[2] Whilst the German and American delegates were right to question the extent to which Britain

© The Author(s) 2018
R. Dunley, *Britain and the Mine, 1900–1915*,
https://doi.org/10.1007/978-3-319-72820-9_7

131

was willing to exploit the moral high ground to her advantage in discussions on mining, it is also apparent that much of the feeling displayed, both in the navy and in Britain more broadly, was genuine. Widespread use of mines was sincerely believed to be inhumane and to represent a step back in the broader mission of the time for the limitation and civilisation of warfare.

In the light of this situation it is thus remarkable that the Royal Navy had, long before the failure at The Hague, developed plans and infrastructure to deploy mines on a scale never previously envisaged, and in a way that stood in complete contradiction to the position it adopted in public. Unsurprisingly the Admiralty did not take the decision to follow such a culturally divisive and politically dangerous policy lightly. It was driven by a specific set of strategic circumstances in a possible naval conflict between Britain and Germany. It was this strategic challenge that forced the Royal Navy to set aside the difficulties relating to independent mining and facilitated the institutionalisation of the technology into the service. Success in the Russo-Japanese War had highlighted the potential threat posed by mines, but it was the strategic challenge that was necessary for this to be reinterpreted as a potential opportunity. The institutionalisation of the technology overcame some of the cultural challenges facing mining within the Royal Navy, and would in time facilitate a more open evaluation of the merits of the mine as a weapon.

The Admiralty's decision to adopt a policy which would have been in contravention of the limited agreement reached at The Hague, let alone the far more wide-ranging restrictions which the British had attempted to place on mining, offers an interesting point of reflection on contemporary views on international law. In her very influential works, Isabel Hull has argued that German views on international law were fundamentally different to those of the Western allies in the First World War. At the heart of this is the idea that the Germans placed a far higher value on the concept of military necessity. Indeed, Hull argues that '(t)he uniquely strong concept of military necessity held by military and civilian leaders and shared by German academics suspended the laws of war upon the subjective judgment of military officers'.[3] The actions of the British Admiralty with regard to mines in the decade before the outbreak of war offers a very different perspective on the question of military necessity, and strongly suggests that, in this area at least, the idea of German exceptionalism can be taken too far.

I

The fundamental reassessment of the use of independent mines by the Royal Navy was driven by two distinct, if related challenges, both of which came to prominence in the period 1904–1905. The first of these was the question of how to fight a conflict with the growing naval power of Germany. The second was how best to support France in a broader European conflict against the Germans. These issues are generally conflated in the historiography, but represented two separate strands within Royal Navy strategic planning, and each posed its own problems.

Growing German naval armaments combined with a confrontational foreign policy meant that the Royal Navy had been thinking seriously about the prospect of war with Germany since 1902.[4] At first sight, it appeared to be a straightforward challenge. Britain enjoyed an overwhelming naval superiority which would enable it to dictate the course of the war, and fight in a manner and on terms favourable to her. The situation was best described by the German Chancellor, Bernhard von Bülow, in a letter to Friedrich von Holstein. '(W)e are practically powerless against England. By capturing our colonies and shipping, destroying our navy and trade and paralyzing our industry, England could within a foreseeable time force us into a disadvantageous peace.'[5] Closer examination of the issue revealed difficulties for the British, which stemmed in large part from the existence of the Kiel Canal. This strategic artery provided the Germans with an internal line of communication between the North Sea and the Baltic. It meant that if the British wished to operate off both German coasts it would be necessary to either have two separate forces, both of which were superior to the entire German fleet, or find a method of closing the canal.

The second strategic challenge developed far more rapidly in the summer of 1905. The signing of the Entente Cordiale in 1904 had placed Anglo-French relations on an improved footing, but it was the dual impact of Russian defeat in the Far East and belligerent German foreign policy regarding Morocco that revolutionised the strategic situation. The turmoil in Russia meant that the balance of power on the continent shifted markedly in Germany's favour. France, lacking the support of her powerful eastern ally, was not capable of acting as a suitable counterweight to the strength of Germany and Austria-Hungary. Fearful of German domination on the continent Britain began to align itself, informally at least, alongside France to maintain the equilibrium. This was largely a diplomatic alignment, but events in the summer of 1905 forced British military planners to think seriously about how they could best support France against German military might. Crucial within this was a realisation of the priority of the land conflict. In a straight Anglo-German war, Germany's inability to strike at Britain's crucial interests meant that a more limited campaign based around the destruction of overseas trade and the capture of colonies could be sufficient to force an advantageous peace. This would clearly not be the case in a conflict involving France. As such the Royal Navy was forced to consider how best to divert German efforts away from the French border, and ultimately defeat Germany before the German army overwhelmed France.

To achieve its policy aims the Royal Navy had two main strategic tools, economic warfare and littoral operations. The navy's primary weapon had always been the economic blockade. Historically, closing off a country from international trade had a serious impact on the economic well-being of that country. This vulnerability was widely considered to have grown with the globalisation of both supply chains and markets, and European industrialisation. Furthermore, the increasing dependence of the highly urbanised European states on food imports from the New World seemed to suggest that such a strategy could be decisive.[6] This policy would have undoubtedly formed the central plank of any strategy for an Anglo-German war, but there was considerable doubt over whether it could be relied upon to defeat Germany sufficiently quickly in the event of a conflict in support of the French.

The crucial distinctions between planning for a straight Anglo-German war and planning for a conflict in support of France, have frequently been overlooked in the historiography. Contemporary naval officers had a much clearer grasp of the situation and quickly looked to littoral operations as a possible solution. Admiral Sir Arthur Wilson, commander of the Channel Fleet, wrote a memorandum on potential strategy at the height of the Moroccan Crisis in June 1905. In it he stated that 'no action by the Navy alone can do France any good.'[7] Wilson was desperately concerned that Britain could be forced into a highly disadvantageous peace following a collapse of French military power similar to that of 1870. The issue had political as well as military aspects. If Britain were allied with France in a major war against Germany the political pressure, from both home and abroad, on the government to take steps beyond a blockade would be irresistible. This point was made by the historian and strategist Julian Corbett in his correspondence with the DNI, Charles Ottley, in early July 1905. Ottley was forced to concede that, 'you are absolutely right we should *have to* throw an expeditionary force ashore on the German coast *somewhere* in addition to any naval action we might take. No other attitude would be worthy of our traditions or would be acceptable to France.'[8]

Both strategic options open to the navy, the economic blockade, or direct littoral warfare, relied on the implementation of a close blockade. In relation to the strategy of direct action this was essential in restricting the movements of enemy warships and providing the security for the operations to take place. The requirement with regard to the economic blockade was a legal rather than a practical one. For a port or coastline to be placed under blockade it was required, under the rules set out in the Treaty of Paris in 1856, to be what was described as effective. By this it was meant that the blockading force should be placed so as to be able to interdict all seaborne trade between that coastline and the outside world. If this was not the case then no legal blockade could be mounted and all neutral vessels would have to be allowed to continue trading with, in this case, Germany, so long as they were not carrying contraband. Such a step would seriously limit the effectiveness of any blockade.

The problems thrown up by these new strategic situations would force the Royal Navy to look for novel ways to achieve its strategic goals, and mine warfare would become central to this. For the first time independent mining would find a strategic role within the service, something that would lead to its rapid adoption and institutionalisation in spite of the continuing cultural opposition to the technology. The willingness of the Admiralty to embrace mine warfare, at the same time that the British public was reacting so badly to the use of mines in the conflict in the Far East, and that the British government was planning its campaign to get the weapons banned, indicates how important mines were perceived to be. It also highlights the gap between international law and military necessity, something usually associated with Germany rather than Britain.

II

The rapid expansion of German naval forces led the Admiralty, in 1902, to reexamine the strategic position with regard to a possible war between Britain and Germany. Commander George Ballard, working within the NID, was asked to produce a memorandum on 'the strategic situation in the North Sea with reference to the development of the German

Fleet and the completion of the Baltic Canal.'[9] The reference to the Kiel (Baltic) Canal is important as it was to represent a major difficulty in naval planning throughout this period. If the British wanted to mount a close blockade of the German coasts in order to implement an effective economic blockade then they either required two fleets, both superior to the German fleet, or they needed to block the entrance to the Canal. This issue was taken up by the planners at the NID and the solution they came up with was to use blockships (sunken hulks) to close off the channel of the River Elbe, into which the Kiel Canal flowed. The closing of the exits of the canal would enable the British to rely on torpedo craft to maintain a close blockade of the German North Sea ports, safe in the knowledge that German heavy vessels would not be able to challenge them. This provided considerable flexibility to the British main fleet to support incursions into the Baltic without risk of the German fleet entering the North Sea and coming between the British and their bases. Through such an arrangement it was felt that the Royal Navy could operate successfully on both sides of the Jutland Peninsula.[10]

In July 1904 this entire structure of operations was undermined by the Hydrographer. In a memorandum, which appears to no longer exist, he wrote of the considerable difficulties in blocking the exits to the Kiel Canal due to the width of the channel, the absence of any fixed reference points and the constantly shifting sandbanks. In conclusion he bluntly declared that 'any attempt to block the Elbe by sinking ships in it is almost certainly doomed to failure'.[11] This conclusion, which was supported by the First Naval Lord, Admiral Walter Kerr, left the navy without a strategy for conducting a war with Germany. If the entrance of the Elbe could not be blocked then the British could not mount a close blockade of either German coast without having two fleets superior to the German one. If the British had attempted to blockade the North Sea coast only, then the main fleet would have been required to support the flotilla in case the German fleet came out. Such a plan would leave the way open for the German fleet to exit the Baltic via the Skaw and come between the British fleet and their home ports; this was of course unacceptable. The only way a close blockade could have been mounted was by withdrawing the British fleet from the Mediterranean, thus providing a sufficient level of superiority over the Germans. The state of Anglo-French relations at this time rendered such a move impossible.

The ongoing crisis in the Far East and the possibility of Britain being drawn into a conflict with the Dual Alliance, particularly after the

Dogger Bank incident, appears to have stopped any further consideration of the German question in 1904. This is not to suggest that the perceived threat from Germany had in any way diminished. Indeed Admiral Sir John Fisher, who replaced Admiral Lord Walter Kerr as First Sea Lord in October 1904 considered the Kaiser to be 'scheming all he knows to produce war between us and Russia.'[12] In early 1905, as the risk of war with the Dual Alliance appeared to be abating, the possibility of a naval war with Germany began to receive further thought. In February Captain Charles Ottley, the new DNI, wrote to the Hydrographer requesting the issue of new charts of the Germany North Sea and Baltic coasts to all the major forces in home waters. He remarked that '(t)he approaches to the Elbe, Weser and Jade are particularly interesting, and, on the Baltic side, a general chart of the approaches to Kiel would probably be very welcome'.[13]

Ottley also immediately began thinking about how best to resolve the issue thrown up by the Hydrographer's remarks on the use of blockships in the Elbe. The entire British naval strategy regarding Germany relied on the ability to close the entrance to the Kiel Canal, and Ottley quickly came up with a solution in the form of mining. In February 1905 he drew up a detailed memorandum on independent mining. A number of different versions of this paper exist, aimed at different audiences. The most revealing was prepared for the Board of Admiralty, and a copy was sent in early March to Sir George Clarke, the Secretary of the CID.[14] It began by outlining the use of mines in the Russo-Japanese War and the failures of British mining. It quickly went on to reveal that Ottley and Fisher were considering using independent mines on a scale and in a manner never previously envisaged. The report was annotated in Ottley's hand, saying that it contained 'most secret enclosures', including a map of the German North Sea coast. With the aid of the map, it outlined a plan in the event of a naval war between Britain and Germany for a mining campaign against the German North Sea ports in which 2000 mines would be laid in 4 lines in the Heligoland Bight.[15] For Ottley the advantages of the new scheme were clear. Unlike the earlier proposal to sink blockships in the channels leading from German ports, mines would not permanently close these exits, but they would mean that any excursion of the German fleet would have to be preceded by a slow and visible minesweeping operation. Using the experience of the Japanese in the Far East, Ottley demonstrated how this would enable the British to have far greater flexibility as to where they deployed their main fleet.

This strategy was clearly designed in response to the perceived failures in the concept of close blockade in this context. The flexibility provided by such a policy would enable the British main fleet to be located in the middle of the North Sea, offering a far greater range of strategic options, particularly regarding the Baltic.

The military rationale behind the proposed mine barrage was obvious, but Ottley was, from the outset, keen to promote another far more controversial benefit. He remarked positively that the policy would rapidly mean that 'Germany would loose the whole of her seaborne trade while ours is free to go on'. Within an economic warfare strategy the ability to close off trade by neutral vessels as well as that by belligerents had always been a key consideration. This was one of the main reasons for the Admiralty's attachment to the policy of close blockade, in spite of the major difficulties this posed. The mine barrage would sidestep all these issues, allowing the Royal Navy to mount an efficacious economic blockade without having to implement a close blockade. The indiscriminate nature of mines meant that they would be just as effective at destroying neutral shipping as they would be in sinking either German flagged vessels or warships. The legal niceties would be swept aside by the realities of war.[16] The economic blockade had always been the primary offensive weapon of the Royal Navy in a European war. The difficulties surrounding close blockade posed a serious threat to the navy's ability to exert power and the mine barrage offered an elegant and simple solution.

Ottley was fully cognisant of the potential impact of this policy and would later acknowledge that the mine barrage plan could result in 'the wholesale sinking of neutral and non-combatant ships.'[17] The Admiralty was well aware of how controversial this policy would be, not only in Britain, but among the broader international community. As such Ottley looked to events in the Far East as justification for such action. He noted in the memorandum that 'the only efforts to safeguard neutral and mercantile shipping in the Far Eastern war, have taken the shape of notices to mariners which have been issued from time to time prescribing certain waters as *dangerous*.'[18] It would be simple enough for the British to follow such a precedent and it would clearly have no impact on the effectiveness of the policy. Ottley, however, failed to openly acknowledge the fine but crucial distinction between what he was proposing and the events in the Far East. Russian and Japanese mines may have been laid in international waters and damaged and sunk neutral vessels, but they had always been laid with the purpose of destroying opposing warships. He was, for the first time, suggesting that mines should be used to establish a commercial blockade in a situation where it was not really possible to establish an effective legal blockade.

At this time British public opinion had come out very strongly in opposition to mining, and the British government had begun to consider how it could get the weapon banned in international law. This memorandum reveals the gulf in attitudes between the Admiralty, considering the issue from the perspective of military necessity, and the more moral positions adopted publicly. Ottley's justification of this policy was brutally realistic. He declared that such actions may be 'repugnant to men of our own race. But we cannot afford ourselves the satisfaction of taking it for granted that a similar abhorrence of this mode of warfare prevails abroad'. This claim to a policy of preemptive retaliation was in truth merely a cover for the recognition of the primacy of military necessity in planning. Ironically Ottley's greatest success at the Hague Conference two years later would be the outlawing of exactly the type of commercial blockade which he was proposing in this memorandum.

The concept of using mines as an integral part of an economic blockade strategy, designed specifically to get around the difficulties associated with maintaining a legal blockade, was extraordinarily radical. It involved using a technology that many within the Royal Navy and the country at large saw as barbaric, in order to prevent neutral and non-belligerent commerce. For this reason the proposal was never explicitly outlined and the readership for Ottley's full memorandum was very small. Instead the DNI produced a different version of his paper for the CID, from which all mention of the mine barrage had been expunged.[19] Indeed, the only surprise is that the full paper, originally drawn up for the Board alone, was sent to Sir George Clarke in the first place, something that is indicative of the position of trust that was still held by the Secretary of the CID at this stage.[20] Similarly the copy of the Ottley memorandum printed in the 1905 'Naval Necessities' was a much fuller document than that given to the CID, but still lacked the vital sections concerning using mines against Germany, and the impact on German trade. As is so often the case, what is left out of a document tells us far more about what was important to the Admiralty than what was included. It is obvious that Fisher and Ottley considered the entire topic of mining too controversial to be officially endorsed; this did not, however, prevent serious action being taken within the navy.

III

The first indication that Ottley's plans for independent mining were being taken seriously comes from the second volume of 'Naval Necessities' which Fisher put together in March 1905. As well as including an amended copy of Ottley's memorandum Fisher chose to highlight mining in his introduction. In the first section, entitled 'Immediate Necessities', he wrote:

> Then there remains the most pressing of all services still to be dealt with— the organisation of the mine-laying service. This must be separate, silent and secretive. Too much time has been lost already. Here we see 5,000 of these offensive floating mines laid down off Port Arthur, covering a wider space than the English Channel, and we, so far, have none, nor any vessels yet fitted! What a scandal! For a purpose unnecessary to be detailed here, it is absolutely obligatory for us to have these mines instantly for war against Germany. They are an imperative immediate strategic necessity, and must be got at once.[21]

The connection between this statement and the new mine barrage strategy against Germany is clear. What is interesting about this remark is the emphasis on mining being 'separate, silent and secretive'. As we will see this was a constant theme in Fisher's attitude towards mining and the effect of this policy has been to disguise the importance of the subject to Fisher's Admiralty. Indeed Ruddock Mackay has used this comment to highlight how little, as he saw it, Fisher did to promote mining.[22] Nothing could be further from the truth, but the extensive preparations made have, until now, been entirely missed by historians.

The Ottley memorandum was very important as it provided, for the first time, a strategic scenario in which the Royal Navy would use independent mines on a large scale. For this to be turned into a reality the navy needed to acquire the materiel necessary to carry out such an operation. Although independent mining had officially been reintroduced in 1900, progress on developing and acquiring suitable equipment had been slow. For four years *Vernon* tried to develop a new mine, but struggled with the design of the firing pistol. Finally in 1904 a design of pistol, produced by Lieutenant A. H. Quicke and Mr. F. Scarff, was trialled, adopted and twinned with a spherical mine case, which was fitted with 120-lbs of guncotton to form what became known as the Naval Spherical Mine.[23] Thus, by early 1905, the Royal Navy finally had a specifically designed independent mine with which it could begin to equip its fleets.[24]

With the design of mine finally set, the immediate challenge was financial. Mines, particularly of the type adopted, were pieces of precision engineering, and as such were expensive. In an era of stretched budgets mining had, for many years, been a low priority. Even when independent mining was officially readopted in 1900 few financial resources were devoted to it. Following the events in the Russo-Japanese War interest grew and in the 1904–1905 Estimates, £28,000 had been set aside for mining stores, a considerable sum in comparison to the previous dearth of funds. Even this, was, however only a fraction of the amount that would be required to provide sufficient mines for the navy's potential requirements.[25] The abolition of controlled mining by the Royal Engineers at British ports provided the navy with a windfall in terms of supplies and equipment, but none of these were immediately suitable for independent mining. The question of how best to exploit these resources had begun to be investigated in early 1905 but at this stage there appears to have been a distinct lack of urgency surrounding the subject.[26] The question of providing the mines was not the only challenge facing the navy; the issue of how best to lay them also required addressing. Some initial trials using a torpedo gunboat took place in early 1905, but again this was only on a small scale.[27]

The spring of 1905 saw a sudden expansion in the practical work needed to implement an independent mining strategy. This clearly stemmed directly from the conclusions of Ottley's memorandum, and Fisher's statement in 'Naval Necessities' that mines were 'an imperative immediate strategic necessity.'[28] This must, however, be placed in the context of what the navy were telling their political masters. The sanitised version of the Ottley memorandum, produced for the consumption of the CID, clearly presented mining in a very negative light, declaring it to be 'to the incalculable detriment of that seaborne commerce which is the very breath of our national life'.[29] Ottley requested that the CID come to a decision on whether the navy should be allowed to conduct 'some practice in the laying of automatic mines' or whether this was felt to undermine Britain's moral position, as the subject moved towards an international conference. The committee concluded that the navy could practice on a small scale.[30] This was clearly a long way from the internal discussions in the Admiralty in which Fisher and Ottley saw mining as a key aspect of a war strategy against Germany. Despite this limited disclosure to the CID, and the obvious political risks involved, the Admiralty remained keen to take the practical steps necessary for it to implement its mine warfare strategy. The major restraining factor was money, and there is evidence that the First Sea Lord sought to address this. On the 14 March Fisher wrote to the Chancellor, Austen Chamberlain, enclosing a paper entitled 'Automatic Dropping Mines for Ocean Use, both for Offensive and Defensive Purposes'.[31] The letter makes it clear that the two men had discussed the subject previously and Fisher was seeking to convince Chamberlain of the merits of mines. The enclosed document had been written by Fisher in December 1902 and outlined the potential benefits of using mines in fleet actions. Naturally it made no mention of any form of mine barrage. An identical document can be found in the Balfour Papers, but without any accompanying letter.[32] It seems reasonable to assume that the papers were sent at the same time. It is clear that Fisher was trying to convince the Chancellor and Prime Minister of the importance of mines and it seems certain that his motivation for doing so was financial. It is noteworthy that he relied on a paper produced three years previously, setting out how mines might be used in fleet actions, rather than any reference to the mine barrage strategy. This clearly remained too controversial to be placed in front of politicians at this time. Unfortunately we have no information as to whether Fisher was successful in his attempt to squeeze more money out of the already hard-pressed Treasury and so it is difficult to tell if it had any immediate impact on mining development. It is impossible to separate out spending by the Royal Navy on mining from other expenditure within Vote 9 of the Navy Estimates, something that also includes torpedoes and all related subjects. In Table 7.1, an attempt has been made to produce indicative figures to show spending on mining. The data is derived from the accounts of the Royal Laboratory, which was where all new mines and mining equipment purchased by the navy were produced prior to the outbreak of war. This information gives only a very narrow view on mining expenditure—for example it does not include any of the money spent on converting the gunboats for minelaying—but does give a useful indication of trends. These figures provide a clear picture of the dearth of funds available for mining, especially independent mining, prior to 1905. Unfortunately, the decision to focus investment on converting the supply of Royal Engineers mines into independent mines means that the figures are highly distorted for the period 1905–1907. That work was

Table 7.1   Royal Navy expenditure on mining and torpedo supplies produced by the Royal Laboratory

	1902–1903	1903–1904	1904–1905	1905–1906	1906–1907	1907–1908	1908–1909	1909–1910	1910–1911	1911–1912	1912–1913	1913–1914
Independent mining	£1967	£832	£1524	£17,495	£52,833	£46,339	£72,391	£76,918	£49,692	£30,418	£53,042	£31,430
Controlled mining	£16,216	£23,470	£11,576	£2651	£0	£98	£0	£0	£0	£0	£165	£0
Boat mining	£94	£0	£52	£0	£0	£0	£0	£0	£0	£0	£0	£0
Miscellaneous mining	£6905	£1218	£2090	£4766	£2651	£4729	£6201	£6307	£9998	£14,285	£13,184	£8934
Total mining	£25,184	£25,521	£15,244	£24,913	£55,484	£51,168	£78,592	£83,225	£59,690	£44,704	£66,392	£40,365
Torpedoes	£1550	£318	£3271	£1393	£1344	£3117	£6123	£3427	£4322	£11,314	£14,002	£15,008
Total	£26,735	£25,840	£18,516	£26,307	£56,829	£54,286	£84,715	£86,652	£64,013	£56,019	£80,395	£55,373

Data extracted from the Account Books of the Royal Ordnance Factories. The National Archives (TNA), SUPP 2/3-14 largely carried out by *Vernon* and the dockyards, and so is not captured in the data from the Royal Laboratory.

In spring 1905 the sense of urgency regarding the mining issue quickly spread through the Admiralty. Towards the end of March the DNO wrote to Captain Charles Briggs, of *Vernon*, stating that a decision on the use of Royal Engineers' equipment was 'urgently required'.[33] It was soon decided that one type of mine was suitable for naval use and these should be converted into independent mines.[34] The conversion of these mines had clearly become a high priority and the £28,000 available in the Estimates was allocated to this purpose.[35] This move would take some time, and events in Europe continued to cause concern. For a while there appeared to be a number of separate but concurrent crises in Europe and the prospect of one of them spilling over into war seemed real. Fisher and Ottley would have been well aware of the risk of a war breaking out before the materiel was ready to implement a mining strategy. This led to a sudden burst of activity aimed at ensuring that the navy had sufficient equipment. Due to limited manufacturing facilities there was no way the navy could expedite the production of the new mines and firing pistols. Instead, Fisher dictated that 300 Service electro-mechanical mines should be readied for instant use.[36] This mine was an adaptation of the 76-lb electro-contact controlled mine, which had until very recently been the standard service issue and was designed to protect an advanced anchorage. The electro-mechanical adaptation of this mine, instead of being connected by a cable to a battery on shore, was fitted with the battery inside, so that it could be used as an independent mine. It was considered a highly unsatisfactory weapon and had been condemned as dangerous as early as 1892.[37] These mines had supposedly been replaced by the new design, but the urgency of the situation meant that the First Sea Lord considered it necessary for them to be not only retained, but fitted out ready for use.

Such was the pressure to have mines available immediately that Briggs reported to the Admiralty that the Royal Engineer mines could be converted into electro-mechanical mines, which, although producing a less satisfactory weapon than the conversion into mechanical independent mines originally proposed, could be carried out far more rapidly.[38] The urgency of the matter meant that Briggs felt it necessary to break with the usual procedure of forwarding his correspondence through the Commander-in-Chief at Portsmouth, and wrote direct to the DNO.[39] In response Captain Alexander Bethell, the Assistant Director of Torpedoes

(ADT), minuted that due to the advantages of the blockade (mechanical) mine pistol he did not think it necessary to approve the suggestion at the present. He went on to say that 'this idea should be borne in mind in case an urgent demand was made for blockade mines in large quantities before sufficient of the R.E. mines have been converted.'[40]

In addition to ensuring an adequate supply of mines, the barrage strategy relied on the availability of a number of large minelayers. In a report on the 3 May Briggs recommended that the Royal Navy's torpedo gunboats could be fitted out as minelayers if necessary, pending the results of recent trials.[41] Whilst this idea was by no means depreciated it was apparent to those at the Admiralty that they would require a greater number of vessels and that they would have to be of a larger capacity. For this reason Bethell contacted the Director of Transports asking for information on ships that could be taken up from the merchant marine. He stated that 'the vessels would require to be from 500 to 1000 tons with a flush upper deck aft and of a high speed.' Bethell emphasised the urgency with which these craft would be needed, noting that 'this request refers to an emergency such as a period of strained relations with some powers'.[42] The request fitted perfectly with the plan developed by Fisher and Ottley to deploy a large-scale mine barrage against Germany immediately on the outbreak of war. The vessels chosen were largely cross-Channel steamers, being fast, of shallow draft and with a flush deck enabling mine rails to be run along their entire length. The Controller, Captain H. B. Jackson, reinforced the importance not merely of having the information, but of selecting eight vessels which could be taken up immediately. He minuted later in May that 'the matter is rather urgent'.[43]

If anyone at the Admiralty remained under any misapprehension as to the importance of these developments they were soon corrected by a memorandum Fisher sent to the naval members of the Board, the DNO and DNI. The First Sea Lord stated that, reliant on the satisfactory conclusion of the trials, a number of torpedo gunboats should be set aside for minelaying. In addition, a list of suitable merchant vessels should be prepared and steps taken to ensure 'that a sufficient number are always likely to be in our Home Ports at all times of the year.'[44] He went on that:

it may be argued against the use of the Gunboats that they form an integral part of our war scheme against France. This is true, but the use of these mines will, in all probability, not be of such immediate importance in this particular eventuality and that in the case of war with Germany when the mines would be most urgently required the Gunboats would not be of such great importance.[45]

This memorandum makes it obvious that in May 1905 Fisher intended to use independent mines on a large scale in the event of a war with Germany. The importance of the matter was reinforced by his remark at the end of the paper stating that he wished 'to know weekly the progress made in the whole question of mines and the preparations for laying them out.'[46] At a time when Fisher, and the Admiralty as a whole, were under enormous pressure from the combination of a radical programme of reforms and a series of international crises, it is noteworthy that mining issues remained a primary concern.

The sudden adoption of an offensive mining strategy meant that a large number of mines were needed immediately. Using the £28,000 in the Estimates Bethell ordered 300 of the RE mines to be converted into independent mines with a mechanical firing pistol. The day after Fisher wrote his memorandum on mining vessels Bethell submitted a proposal for a further 700 mines to be converted in 1905, bringing the total cost up to £90,000, the maximum he thought could be wrung out of the budget for that year.[47] Precisely where this additional money had come from is unclear and there is the possibility that it was included following Fisher's communications with the Chancellor on the subject of mining.

Fisher accepted Bethell's proposal, but clearly felt that more needed to be done. The following week an influential committee met at his request to discuss the entire issue of mine provision in more detail. The committee was chaired by Ottley and contained Bethell; Reginald Bacon, Fisher's naval assistant and technical guru; Charles Madden, Assistant to the Controller; and Wilfred Henderson. The committee decided that Britain's most likely enemies were Germany, Russia and France, or possibly combinations of two out of the three. They focused heavily on the former and stated that '(t)he committee therefore consider that with Germany as an enemy our policy should be to run lines of mines across the mouths of these rivers [Elbe, Weser and Jade] in such a way as to leave no passage for any vessels larger than torpedo craft'.[48] This effectively confirmed the policy put forward in Ottley's February memorandum. The committee did decide that the mines should be laid slightly further from the German coast, resulting in more mines being needed.

Thus the committee reported that 3000 mines 'would be immediately required, in the event of war with Germany'.[49] Additional circumstances, including conflicts against Russo-German and Franco-Russian alliances were considered, although in considerably less detail than operations in the Heligoland Bight. Intriguingly the report mentioned the possibility of using mines off Dutch, Danish or Scandinavian ports. This could have meant doing so after a German invasion, which was seen as a realistic possibility especially in the Dutch and Danish cases, and would have presented a major threat to British security. There remains, however, the possibility that this was a veiled reference to the use of mines to interdict trade flowing through neutral ports into Germany. Neutral ports were known to be a major weakness in any economic blockade strategy and the use of mines to this end was, as we shall see, far from inconceivable.[50] In all the committee decided that the navy should possess at least 10,000 mines ready for immediate use, the majority of which were to be kept 'under Admiralty direction for offensive operations against definite localities.'[51] Unfortunately the original report of the committee has been lost and the only surviving copy is that printed in the 1905 'Naval Necessities'. We cannot tell how closely this matches the original; however it is worth noting that the copy of Ottley's February memorandum reproduced in the same volume was carefully sanitised to remove its more controversial elements. This might explain why no mention was made in the committee's report of the commercial aspects of the proposed mining operations.

According to the report, the Board of Admiralty had previously agreed that 1000 mines would be acquired under the 1904–1905 Estimates, with another 1000 under those of the following year. The committee suggested that provision for a further 2000 mines should be included in the 1905–1906 Estimates to bring the total available up to 4000 as this 'would provide for the most urgent case, viz., the mining of the mouths of the German North Sea rivers, and leaving 1000 over for fleet purposes.'[52] Although the original docket containing the reaction to the committee's report has not survived, we know from the Admiralty Record Office digest that the proposals were approved.[53]

Fisher's decision to print the report of the Ottley committee in the 1905 'Naval Necessities', together with his other remarks in the volume, further indicate that he fully endorsed the strategy being put forward by his DNI. That is to say that by May 1905 the Royal Navy had adopted a new strategy which it intended to implement in the case of

148   R. DUNLEY

a war between Britain and Germany. At the heart of this strategy was a large mine barrage, which was to be laid immediately on the outbreak of war. This strategy had been designed to circumvent the problems of implementing a close blockade of the German North Sea coast. In doing so it would not only limit the movement of the German fleet, but would also act as a complete bar on seaborne trade in and out of German ports even though Britain would not be able to mount a legal blockade. The decision to adopt this strategy stood in complete opposition to Britain's outward position on independent mines. The barrage was to be laid in international waters with little or no regard for the rights of neutrals or non-belligerents. Furthermore, even Ottley, the author of the strategy, frequently expressed his horror at the indiscriminate nature of the weapons and their likely impact on civilians and neutrals. That the leadership of the Royal Navy felt that this was an appropriate step to take clearly indicates the extent to which, in the eyes of these figures, military necessity overrode humanitarian principles.

Barely had the ink dried on the new strategy when the situation in Europe demanded a rethink. The summer of 1905 saw relations between France and Germany at breaking point over events in Morocco. Following the resignation of the French Minister of Foreign Affairs, Théophile Delcassé, the Admiralty was forced to consider, for the first time, the possibility of fighting a war against Germany in alliance with France. On 24 June Fisher asked Ottley to draw up a statement on a potential British naval policy in such a circumstance. Unfortunately the file containing the correspondence regarding this issue has not survived and the only information we have is that quoted by Arthur Marder, who looked at the archives before they were weeded. Nonetheless the material we have is very interesting. Ottley immediately noted on 'the exceptionally favourable circumstances of this moment'; by which he meant that Britain would not have to worry about any other naval powers, and indeed would have the assistance of the French fleet.[54] Marder states that the rest of Ottley's memorandum developed the idea of implementing an economic blockade of Germany. Beyond this the Admiralty were to have little involvement, with Admiral Arthur Wilson, the Commander-in-Chief, Channel Fleet, dictating strategy in home waters. Ottley went on to say that Wilson should be asked whether he intended to close the entrance of the Elbe with blockships and what his requirements were with regard to mines. It is extremely frustrating that due to the absence of the original document we do not know the precise context in which these remarks were made and so cannot really draw any inferences from them. Despite this the memorandum sheds considerable light on Ottley's previous mine barrage proposal. Firstly, Ottley's surprise at the novelty of the situation confirms that the earlier proposal was drawn up envisaging an Anglo-German war, or one in which Germany was allied with France or Russia. It also gives considerable support to the idea that the mining proposal was produced with the main intention of interdicting commerce. On 1 July 1905 Ottley wrote to the historian and strategist Julian Corbett stressing what he considered to be the power of such an economic blockade. He wrote that 'the blockade of the German ports today would sever an artery, essential—it seems to me—to the financial existence of Germany'.[55] It appears very clear that Ottley intended, at this stage, to remain content with an economic blockade of Germany in the event of war and there is no reason to think that this was not the case when he wrote his February memorandum.

Ironically, Ottley seemingly perceived that the potential French support meant that mines were no longer essential. He noted that 'remembering the immense strategic advantage of the French harbours so close to the mouth of the Elbe, I believe there would be no practical difficulty in proclaiming and maintaining an effective blockade of the entire German seaboard.'[56] Evidently Ottley envisaged a close blockade of the German coast at this time, as this was the only way in which the British could proclaim and maintain 'an effective blockade' under the terms of international law. The proximity of neutral ports, particularly Esbjerg in Denmark, meant that for a blockade to be legal the blockading forces had to remain close to the German coast. Furthermore the obvious implication of Ottley's statement was that, without the French harbours, such an undertaking would be difficult, and this was where the mine barrage planned for an Anglo-German war would have fitted in. The precise benefits provided by the French harbours is, however, less clear. Dunkirk was the furthest east of the naval bases, and this was no closer to the mouth of the Elbe than Harwich.

Ottley's memorandum was immediately sent down to Arthur Wilson at Portsmouth. His response of the next day highlighted how little thought Ottley had put into the subject. The old admiral starkly set out how the new strategic position left Britain beholden on the result of the land campaign on the French border. If this was lost then the destruction of German trade, or the capture of colonies, mattered little. As such he maintained that the Royal Navy needed to take steps which would influence the course of the land campaign through offensive action on the German coast. He went on that '(a)s the main object would be to draw off troops from the French frontier, simultaneous attacks would have to be made at as many different points as possible.'[57] Central to this policy would be the establishment of a close blockade on both sides of the Jutland Peninsula. This would have been facilitated, as Ottley had noted, by the 'overwhelming' nature of the allied 'naval preponderance'.[58] The French alliance would have freed up the majority of the British Mediterranean fleet and support could also potentially have come from French naval units themselves. Unfortunately we do not have the precise details of Wilson's response with regard to mines, but it is obvious that he saw scope for them within this policy of littoral warfare. It is noteworthy that no record can be found for any steps taken with regard to the acquisition of the blockships mentioned in Ottley's memorandum, whilst it can be shown that very specific mining arrangements were set in place. In fact Wilson's response made it clear that he did not see permanently closing the exit to the Elbe as being of particular importance. Instead he remarked that 'the course that seems to me most worthy of consideration would be an attempt to capture the Works at the mouths of the Elbe and Weser by a combined military and naval expedition'.[59] This is not to suggest that Wilson was not interested in using blockade mines; all the evidence points to the contrary. They would have proved very effective in temporarily closing off certain channels, and providing advanced warning of any planned German sortie in the shape of minesweepers. This policy had been adopted with great success by the Japanese fleet and it had not passed unnoticed in London.[60] Such a use of mines would grant the British fleet far greater freedom, and it was hoped, allow amphibious operations to be mounted with relative security.

The shift in the nature of planning and urgency of the threat naturally had an immediate impact on mining preparations. In particular the Admiralty became very concerned that war would come before the new mines had either been built or converted from the Royal Engineers' stores. The type of close blockade envisaged by Wilson would see mines deployed in a different setting than the mine barrage proposed by Ottley in the event of an Anglo-German war. Wilson's desire to operate close into the shore and undertake littoral operations meant that mines would be used to close specific channels, most likely within German territorial waters. This was how the Japanese had used mines off Port Arthur

7 THE STRATEGIC SHIFT: THE ORIGINS OF BRITISH MINE WARFARE   151

and the Admiralty was aware of their potential in this role. The key point with this type of operation is that the number of mines required would be much smaller than that needed for Ottley's large mine barrage. Despite this the international situation was such that the navy were worried that war would come before the mines were ready. As such the Admiralty put in place a contingency which would allow it to deploy mines on a smaller scale in the event of war. This planning relied on deploying the old-fashioned service mine with an electro-mechanical pistol. This proposal was clearly taken very seriously, with all details being worked out, even down to the level of the exact make-up of the crews for the minelayers, with those laying electro-mechanical mines needing a greater number of skilled personnel due to the delicate nature of the appliances.[61] This is remarkable considering that the electro-mechanical mine was a totally obsolete weapon, and one which had been declared unsafe for use 13 years previously. The decision to reintroduce it is indicative of the level of desperation felt in the Admiralty at this time and the obvious importance of mining within its strategy.

IV

War was averted in the summer of 1905, but the Admiralty continued pressing forward with the preparations for its offensive mining strategy. By October these had reached a stage where the navy needed some definite answers to questions of national policy regarding mine warfare. To this end Fisher decided to inform the Prime Minister, Arthur Balfour of the new strategy. Balfour was a close confidant of Fisher's, but it appears that even he had been kept in the dark over the developments up to this point. To provide an overview of the situation regarding mining Fisher sent the Prime Minister a letter he had received from Ottley a few days previously. On initial inspection the DNI's letter appears somewhat incongruous, repeating large amounts of information already known to the First Sea Lord, and carefully setting out arguments both for and against the use of mines. In reality it appears almost certain that the letter was written for the specific purpose of being forwarded on to the Prime Minister and this detailed exposition was for his benefit. This was a tactic Fisher used regularly to convince his readers that the material he was sending them was a genuine expression of policy and not solely intended for their benefit.[62] His exhortation to 'please burn' in his covering letter to Balfour fits into this pattern.[63]

Ottley's letter began by setting out how one of the most pressing requirements for the navy was 'perfecting of our organisation for the instant employment of the large numbers of offensive mines which we shall shortly possess, on the outbreak of war'. He noted that following the widespread use of mines in the Russo-Japanese War 'we shall under present arrangements do likewise off the estuaries of large rivers in certain contingencies'. Ottley went on to say that further detailed arrangements needed to be made, remarking:

> that 16 merchant steamers at least will be needed to lay the 3,000 mines required for one single very probable operation. No such colossal mining operation has ever hitherto been attempted within the dark hours of a single night, and nothing less should be aimed at.

There can be no doubt over what Ottley was referring to. The figure of 3000 mines corresponds exactly with the number decided upon by the Ottley committee earlier in the year for a mine barrage in the Heligoland Bight, whilst the suggestion that it needed to be completed immediately upon the outbreak of war drew directly from Fisher's statements on British strategy against Germany. Confusingly, and for no obvious reason, Ottley referred to blocking the estuary of the Danube, rather than the Elbe, but in his covering letter Fisher told Balfour '(w)hen Ottley says the Danube you know what river he really means!'[64]

The DNI then went on to address the key point from the perspective of the navy. Writing mainly for his political audience, he remarked that:

> such action on our part, resulting as it might easily in the wholesale sinking of neutral and non-combatant ships, would probably bring down upon us a storm of indignation from the rest of Europe, and would probably be very unfavourably viewed by a considerable section of our own people[.]

This went to the heart of the mining dilemma. Fisher and Ottley had adopted mining because they saw it as a particularly effective solution to a difficult strategic problem. They did so with full knowledge that it was in breach of the accepted patterns of warfare at the time. It came down to a question of whether the demands of military necessity would override the moral and legal principles of the nation. The Admiralty, perhaps unlike its German counterpart, unquestionably felt compelled to involve the civilian government in this debate, but nonetheless it had still invested considerable time, effort and resources in facilitating this strategy and expected a rapid answer.

Ottley's letter concluded by discussing whether the British government should press the mining issue at the upcoming Hague Conference and what position it should adopt. This further reveals the duality in the navy's response towards mining. The Admiralty had developed a detailed plan to use mines in a way that Ottley fully admitted would dramatically impact on civilians and neutrals. Yet he still felt compelled to caveat his statements by saying that as the 'originator of the offensive mine idea', the much more limited use of the weapon in the Far East 'far oversteps the limits I had ever contemplated for it, and I do not believe that any such wholesale employment is likely to be sanctioned by the public opinion of Europe'. It is difficult to tell the extent to which these comments were specifically directed at Balfour, but given similar statements elsewhere, and Ottley's actions at The Hague, it would seem that both expressions were sincere. This gives an indication of how contested this issue was, even within the mind of one of the navy's leading strategists.

Fisher, perhaps unsurprisingly considering what is known of his character, appears to have been less concerned by the possible legal and moral restrictions on mining. He obviously felt that he needed to get the Prime Minister's approval of the policy he was adopting, but had no desire to raise the issue more widely, where the scruples of politicians might inhibit his freedom of action. As such he told Balfour that '(i)t is *not* desirable to bring it before the Defence Committee. Only a few people know that we shall soon have *10,000* of these mines ready!'[65] The Admiralty had deliberately sanitised its previous statements to the CID regarding mines and Fisher felt no obligation to provide any further information at this point. The First Sea Lord was, however, keen to find out whether Balfour had decided 'to press this business of the Hague Conference'. He was aware that it would be political suicide to argue for the abolition of independent mines whilst the Royal Navy was openly building its capability on that front. At the same time, Fisher wanted to include an additional £250,000 for mines in the next Estimates and practise with them in the manoeuvres. He concluded that if the government felt compelled to pursue the mining issue at the Hague 'I think we could go easy, arrest with what we shall have ready and only practice on so small a scale as not to attract notice.'[66] Unlike Ottley, Fisher did not appear to have any problems with deploying mines in a fashion that would potentially kill neutrals and non-combatants. Instead he was solely concerned with managing the political situation through restricting knowledge of the Admiralty's intentions and hiding its preparations from the rest of the world.

Balfour's reply confirmed that the government would be pursuing the matter at The Hague and that Britain would seek strict limitations on the use of mines. It made no mention of the strategic aspects of the issue, which appear to have been held over.[67] This decision meant that mining developments within the Royal Navy had to be kept relatively quiet, as any significant moves would lead to calls of hypocrisy at the conference table. This policy was further reinforced when Balfour's Unionist Government was replaced in December 1905 by a Liberal ministry that contained members of a distinctly pacifist hue.

V

The decision to press for serious restrictions to be placed on mines at the Hague Conference meant that the Admiralty needed to proceed quietly in its mining developments, but it certainly did not prevent further progress. Ottley's letter to Fisher stated that 'the name of the officer in command of the mine-laying flotilla is ready to submit to you'.[68] The officer selected for the job was Commander Herbert Orpen and he took up his post as Commander of the Offensive Mining Service a couple of weeks later on 6 November.[69] It is difficult to discern who drove Orpen's selection for this role, or whose patronage network he fell under. Orpen had served as a Sub-Lieutenant under Fisher aboard the gunnery training school *Excellent* as far back as 1883–1884, but did not appear to have had any connection with the First Sea Lord since.[70] More recently he had come to the attention of H. B. Jackson, when the latter was commanding the Plymouth torpedo school, *Defiance*, and it seems probable that the then Controller recommended Orpen for the post.[71] Latterly Orpen had been commanding the *Pandora* in the Channel Fleet, and as such would have been known to Wilson, who showed a keen interest in mining developments at this time. Whilst it is difficult to tell who drove Orpen's appointment it is very clear that he rapidly joined the ranks of officers swimming in the proverbial 'Fishpond'.

The following day a crucial meeting was held at the Admiralty to discuss the entire subject of mining. The significance of the meeting can be gauged by the personnel involved. In addition to Fisher those present were Vice-Admiral Sir Charles Drury, the Second Sea Lord; Captain H. B.

Jackson, the Controller; Captain Frederick Inglefield, the Fourth Sea Lord; Admiral Sir Arthur Wilson, commander of the Channel Fleet; Captain Charles Briggs of *Vernon*; Captain Alexander Bethell, ADT; Captain Charles Ottley; Captain Reginald Bacon, Naval Assistant to the First Sea Lord; Captain Henry Oliver of HMS *Mercury*, the navigation school; Captain George Ballard, the Assistant Director of Naval Intelligence (ADNI); Commander Herbert Orpen; Commander Godfrey Tuke, Intelligence Officer, Channel Fleet; and Commander Thomas Crease.

The meeting began with a statement on mining by Briggs, presumably to bring those who had not been party to the recent developments up to date. Briggs outlined how, over the summer, 300 electro-mechanical mines had been prepared 'for immediate use as blockade mines'. He also informed the meeting that preparations had been made to convert four gunboats to carry the mines. Briggs noted that these mines were only a 'makeshift', in case insufficient mines of the new design were ready, a policy clearly adopted out of fear that the navy would have gone to war in the summer without an independent mine. The relatively small number of mines fits into the strategy for a close blockade set out by Wilson in the event of a war with Germany in support of France. Briggs went on to say that these preparations were stopped in September, when it became clear that war was not likely, and it was decided to wait and focus on the new style of mines.[72]

The discussion paper drawn up for the meeting addressed the question of how best to lay mines. It noted that '(l)ately some across Channel steamers have been under consideration, and eight have been selected as being quite suitable and have a sea-going speed of not less than 18 knots'. It went on:

> The great drawback to the employment of these or any other hired vessels for this work is the serious delay necessarily involved in taking them up and fitting them at a critical time. It is estimated that about a fortnight would be required to prepare these vessels and as they could not well be fitted as mine-layers until war is inevitable, it is, therefore, unlikely that they would be ready at the most important moment, *i.e.*, the actual outbreak of hostilities.[73]

For these reasons the paper proposed the conversion of ships of the *Latona* (or *Apollo*) Class of protected cruisers.[74] The two main advantages given were that 'these vessels can be prepared for service without attracting outside attention' and 'they would be ready when required, the only delay being that due to preparing the ship for steaming.' This gives a very clear indication of the position of mining at this time. The subject was obviously considered sensitive enough that secrecy was required, whilst it was essential that the minelayers be ready at the outbreak of war. If there was any doubt on this matter then the paper forcefully concluded that 'the hired steamer plan would undoubtedly cheaper if we have no war', however they 'may not be available at the supreme moment when mines are most required, that is on the sudden outbreak of hostilities'. As such their use was 'out of the question'. This rejection of a potential economy at a time when the Estimates were under intense pressure is indicative of the importance given to mining. It is almost certainly not a coincidence that this language is characteristically Fisherite in tone. There can be little doubt of the First Sea Lord's personal interest in and attachment to this subject, and it is highly likely that the paper was penned by Fisher himself.

Considering the nature of this discussion paper it is unremarkable that the committee agreed with its conclusions. The discussion in the meeting clearly focused around the issue of where to deploy mines and how they fitted into the broader strategic situation. The minutes are exceptionally cryptic, but the meaning behind them remains obvious. Point C read:

> Suppose two double lines of mines should require to be laid in different places, the Commander in Chief concerned should consider the exact places in which the mines should be laid being assisted by Captain A.[sic] F. Oliver as to the pilotage aspects of the question.[75]

Point D went on to clarify that the lines of mines under consideration would be about two miles long and the mines would be laid 150 feet apart. For this it was estimated that eight minelayers would be required. The issue of whether blockships were also necessary was discussed but no conclusion was reached, the mines being considered 'the most important point'. As if any doubt existed as to the operation proposed, it was decided that 100 of the new mines should be sent to Berehaven in March 1906 for Wilson to experiment with mining the entrances to a harbour. Although it is never directly spelt out, the laying of double lines of mines and the expectation that they would only be two miles long definitely indicates that the intention was to try and semi-permanently

7 THE STRATEGIC SHIFT: THE ORIGINS OF BRITISH MINE WARFARE   157

block the exits of a port or ports. The nature of the strategic situation at the time strongly suggests that this operation was being considered with reference to the exits of the German North Sea ports and the Kiel Canal. The size of the minefields and the discussion of blockships indicates that these mines were to be laid close into the shore and in a definite channel; as such the Germans would most likely be aware of their existence and have few difficulties in sweeping them. The only scenario in which such a deployment would make sense would be as part of a larger operation which would see the mines protected by flotilla craft, backed if necessary by the fleet. This interest in mining within the context of a close blockade scenario naturally connects with the urgent action taken in the summer to ensure a supply of mines when the navy was considering Wilson's strategy for littoral operations in a war in support of France. It also connects with the recent scholarship which has re-emphasised the continued importance of a close or observational blockade within Royal Navy strategy throughout the Fisher era.[76]

The discussion of this strategic situation was immediately followed by a decision to press ahead with the conversion of all 2000 Royal Engineers mines, and that this should be augmented by a further 2000 new mines, with 'the work being hastened to the utmost extent'.[77] Fisher further reinforced the urgency of this issue in a meeting of the Estimates Committee later the same week. He stated that it was 'of the utmost importance that a full supply of these mines should be obtained as soon as possible'. Remarkably considering the situation, Fisher said that this should be done almost regardless of cost, saying that any expense additional to the sums allocated could be found out of other Votes.[78] The decision to acquire a large number of mines and do so with expediency is all the more surprising in the light of Balfour's letter, less than two week previously, making it clear that he intended to pursue the mining question at the Hague Conference. Fisher clearly felt it appropriate to press on with the mining preparations in the expectation that, one way or another, the navy would be able to implement its strategies.

The decision of the committee immediately raises the question of why the First Sea Lord wanted such a large number of mines as a matter of real urgency. The scenario discussed in the meeting on 7 November of laying double lines of mines off enemy harbours would not require anything close to the 4000 mines being ordered. Instead, it seems too much of a coincidence that this is the exact number recommended by the Ottley Committee as being necessary for a war with Germany. The vast majority of these were set aside by the committee to mount the large-scale mine barrage off the German North Sea coast.[79] It appears that the navy were, at this time, envisaging two distinct strategies for war against Germany depending on the circumstances. The first, clearly, was for a situation like that which had arisen in the summer, in which Britain would be allied with France against Germany. In this scenario a close blockade was being considered for exactly the reasons set out by Wilson in his letter of the 27 June. For this the navy was considering using mines to close the exits of enemy harbours and restrict the movement of their fleet. It is, however, apparent that this was not the only set of circumstances being considered by the Admiralty. With hindsight it is very easy to suggest that the alignment of Britain with France was obvious, and as such assume that this was the dominant assumption of planners. In truth this does not appear to have been the case. In a memorandum drawn up only days after the immediate crisis had passed, in July 1905, Ottley wrote of 'the special circumstances arising out of the recent Morocco embroglio', and described the European political situation as 'unusual'.[80] Thus, in addition to looking at strategies to conduct a war in a French alliance, the Royal Navy was also still considering the previous questions surrounding an Anglo-German war. In such a scenario it is clear that Fisher wanted to be able to lay the large mine barrage proposed by Ottley as part of an economic blockade of Germany.

The failure on the part of many historians to separate these two strands within Admiralty strategic thought at this time has led to much controversy. Nicholas Lambert has argued that the navy had no real interest in littoral operations, which he christened the 'reckless offensive', and that it instead focused from 1905 on the economic blockade.[81] He uses Ottley's mine barrage as part of the evidence for this assertion.[82] He does not, however, appreciate that this was only being proposed in the event of an Anglo-German war, not one involving the French. As we have seen, the preparations made throughout the summer and autumn of 1905 show that the Admiralty was continuing to plan to mount littoral operations on the German coast in support of the French in the event of war. Shawn Grimes has taken the opposite view to Lambert, and maintained that the navy were focused on amphibious operations in the Baltic. Whilst there is undoubtedly some truth in this argument, he fails to pick up on the detailed preparations outlined above. In particular the centrality of mining, and the ongoing separation between the two strategic options, are entirely missed.[83]

7 THE STRATEGIC SHIFT: THE ORIGINS OF BRITISH MINE WARFARE   159

Over the course of 1905 mining had gone from being a peripheral technology largely ignored within the Royal Navy, to being an important component of the service's strategies for fighting its most likely opponent. This shift led to new developments in materiel and a focus on providing this in sufficient quantities to facilitate the strategic outlook. Behind this lay even more remarkable developments. The Royal Navy had viewed independent mining with a mixture of suspicion and disgust for almost half a century, and yet in the space of under a year the strategic situation forced the service to overcome its cultural distrust of the technology. Furthermore the navy embraced mining in the full knowledge that the policy it was adopting represented a complete rejection of the accepted norms of civilised warfare and stood in direct opposition to the views of the British public and the stated aims of the British government. That the Admiralty continued to pursue this course of action is indicative of the attitudes of its leading figures, who ultimately felt that military necessity would trump any moral or legal obligations that might place restrictions on the use of mines by the Royal Navy.

NOTES

1. Library of Congress (LOC), Sperry Papers (MSS 40923), box 10, folder 2, 'Third Commission, First Sub-Commission, Comité d'Examen' and 'Mines Memorandum of Conversation with Capt. Ottley, Friday, 23 August 1907'.
2. For British awareness of the importance of this perception see British Library (BL), Add Ms 52514, Campbell-Bannerman Papers, Grey Minute on Ponsonby to Grey, 25 July 1907.
3. Isabel V. Hull, *A Scrap of Paper: Making and Breaking International Law During the Great War* (Ithaca: Cornell University Press, 2014), pp. 317–318; Isabel V. Hull, '"Military Necessity" and the Laws of War in Imperial Germany', in Stathis Kalyvas, Ian Shapiro, and Tarek Masoud, eds., *Order, Conflict and Violence* (Cambridge: Cambridge University Press, 2008).
4. Matthew S. Seligmann, 'Switching Horses: The Admiralty's Recognition of the Threat from Germany, 1900–1905', *International History Review*, vol. 30, no. 2 (2008), pp. 239–258.
5. Norman Rich and M. H. Fisher, eds., *The Holstein Papers: The Memoirs, Diaries and Correspondence of Friedrich von Holstein 1837–1909*, vol. 4 (Cambridge: Cambridge University Press, 1963), Bülow to Holstein, 15 December 1904, no. 869, pp. 317–319.
6. Avner Offer, *The First World War: An Agrarian Interpretation* (Oxford: Oxford University Press, 1989); Nicholas Lambert, *Planning*

160   R. DUNLEY

Armageddon: British Economic Warfare and the First World War (Cambridge, MA: Harvard University Press, 2012).

7. A. K. Wilson to Fisher, 27 June 1905, quoted in Arthur J. Marder, *The Anatomy of British Sea Power: A History of British Naval Policy in the Pre-Dreadnought Era, 1880–1905* (London: Frank Cass, 1964), p. 504.

8. National Maritime Museum (NMM), Richmond Papers, RIC/9, Ottley to Corbett, 3 July 1905.

9. The National Archives (TNA), ADM 1/8997, 'Remarks on the Framing of Certain Plans for War with Germany Now at the Admiralty', Ballard Memorandum, Attached to Ballard to Fisher, 3 May 1909.

10. TNA, ADM 116/3093, 'Naval Necessities II', 'The Organisation for War of Torpedo Craft in Home Waters', Battenberg Memorandum, n.d., Summer 1904.

11. Hydrographer's Memorandum, 6 July 1904, quoted in Marder, *Anatomy*, p. 481.

12. Arthur J. Marder, *Fear God and Dread Nought: The Correspondence of Admiral of the Fleet Lord Fisher of Kilverstone*, vol. II (*FGDN II*) (London: Jonathan Cape, 1956), Fisher to Lady Fisher, 30 October 1904, p. 47, n. 2; and Ruddock F. Mackay, *Fisher of Kilverstone* (Oxford: Clarendon Press, 1973), p. 316.

13. UK Hydrographic Office (UKHO), Hydrographic Department Minute Book, No. 66, Ottley Memorandum, 27 February 1905, Ottley Minute, 26 April 1905 and Fisher Minute, 27 April 1905, f. 242.

14. TNA, CAB 17/24, 'Submarine Automatic Mines', 12 February 1905.

15. TNA, CAB 17/24, 'Submarine Automatic Mines', 12 February 1905.

16. TNA, CAB 17/24, 'Submarine Automatic Mines', 12 February 1905.

17. BL, Add Ms 49711, Ottley to Fisher, 14 October 1905, ff. 127–131.

18. TNA, CAB 17/24, 'Submarine Automatic Mines', 12 February 1905.

19. TNA, ADM 1/8879, 'Submarine Automatic Mines', 13 March 1905; the official copy can be found in CAB 38/8/22.

20. TNA, ADM 1/8879, Ottley to Fisher, 21 February 1905.

21. Peter Kemp, ed., *The Fisher Papers*, vol. 2 (London: The Navy Records Society, 1964), 'Naval Necessities II', p. 8; an early draft of this introduction was sent to Arthur Balfour in early April 1905, see BL Balfour Papers, Add Ms 49710, 'Naval Necessities' n.d. (April 1905), f. 246.

22. Mackay, *Fisher*, pp. 376–378.

23. TNA ADM 189/24, Vernon Annual Report 1904, p. 80; ADM 189/25, Vernon Annual Report 1905, p. 62.

24. For a more comprehensive analysis of the development of the independent mining materiel see Richard Dunley, 'The Offensive Mining Service: Mine Warfare and Strategic Development in the Royal Navy 1900–1914' (Unpublished PhD thesis, University of London, 2013), pp. 128–131.

25. TNA, ADM 1/7897, Eardley Wilmot Minute, n.d. (April 1905).
26. TNA, ADM 1/7897, Bethell to Briggs, 30 December 1904; Briggs Memo, 13 January 1905 and Bethell Memo, 19 January 1905.
27. TNA, MT 23/169, Briggs to Douglas, 21 February 1905; ADM 12/1417 Cut 59.8 'Minelaying Trials', 20 April 1905; ADM 189/25, Vernon Annual Report 1905.
28. Kemp, *Fisher Papers II*, 'Naval Necessities II', p. 8.
29. TNA, CAB 38/8/22, 'Submarine Automatic Mines', 13 March 1905.
30. TNA, CAB 38/9/34, CID Meeting 71, 19 April 1905; CAB 38/8/22, 'Submarine Automatic Mines', 13 March 1905.
31. Cadbury Research Library (CRL), A. Chamberlain Papers, AC44/4/41–42, Fisher to Chamberlain, 14 March 1905.
32. BL, Balfour Papers, Add Ms 49710, 'Automatic Dropping Mines of Ocean Use, Both for Offensive and Defensive Purposes', n.d., ff. 1–2.
33. TNA, ADM 1/7897, Shirley Litchfield to Briggs, 28 March 1905.
34. TNA, ADM 1/7897, Briggs to Jellicoe, 6 April 1905 and Bethell Memorandum, 14 April 1905.
35. TNA, ADM 1/7897, Eardley Wilmot Minute, n.d. (April 1905).
36. TNA, ADM 1/7897, Adm to CinC Portsmouth (Draft), 29 April 1905.
37. TNA, ADM 189/12, Vernon Annual Report 1892, 'The Question of the Efficiency or Otherwise of Naval Mines', 15 July 1892.
38. TNA, ADM 1/7897, Briggs to Jellicoe, 6 May 1905.
39. TNA, ADM 1/7897, Briggs Note, Briggs to Jellicoe, 6 May 1905.
40. TNA, ADM 1/7897, Bethell Minute, 8 May 1905.
41. TNA, ADM 1/7897, Briggs to Douglas, 3 May 1905.
42. TNA, MT 23/169, Bethell to Boyes, 3 May 1905.
43. TNA, MT 23/169, Jackson Minute, 23 May 1905.
44. TNA, MT 23/169, Fisher Memorandum, 7 May 1905.
45. TNA, MT 23/169, Fisher Memorandum, 7 May 1905.
46. TNA, MT 23/169, Fisher Memorandum, 7 May 1905.
47. TNA, ADM 1/7897, Bethell Minute, 8 May 1905.
48. TNA, ADM 116/3093, 'Naval Necessities II', 'Supply of Automatic Submarine Mines to the Fleet', 1905.
49. TNA, ADM 116/3093, 'Naval Necessities II', 'Supply of Automatic Submarine Mines to the Fleet', 1905.
50. Bodleian Library, Oxford (BLO), Selborne Papers, Selborne Mss 21, Wilson to Selborne, 6 March 1904, ff. 9–10.
51. TNA, ADM 116/3093, 'Supply of Automatic Submarine Mines to the Fleet', 'Naval Necessities II', 1905.
52. TNA, ADM 116/3093, 'Supply of Automatic Submarine Mines to the Fleet', 'Naval Necessities II', 1905.
53. TNA, ADM 12/1417, Cut 59.8, 'Use of Mines in RN: Admiralty Policy'.

54. Ottley Memorandum, 26 June 1905, quoted in Marder, *Anatomy*, pp. 502–503.
55. NMM, Richmond Papers, RIC/9, Ottley to Corbett, 1 July 1905.
56. NMM, Richmond Papers, RIC/9, Ottley to Corbett, 1 July 1905.
57. Wilson to Fisher, 27 June 1905, quoted in Marder, *Anatomy*, pp. 504–505.
58. Ottley Memorandum, 26 June 1905, quoted in Marder, *Anatomy*, pp. 502–503.
59. Wilson to Fisher, 27 June 1905, quoted in Marder, *Anatomy*, p. 505.
60. TNA, CAB 17/24, 'Submarine Automatic Mines', 12 February 1905, f. 26.
61. TNA, ADM 1/7897, Bethell Minute, 19 August 1905.
62. Richard Dunley, 'Invasion, Raids and Army Reform: The Political Context of "Flotilla Defence" 1903–1905', *Historical Research*, vol. 90, no. 249 (2017), pp. 613–635.
63. BL, Balfour Papers, Add Ms 49711, Fisher to Balfour, 20 October 1905, f. 126.
64. BL, Balfour Papers, Add Ms 49711, Ottley to Fisher and Fisher to Balfour, 14 and 20 October 1905, ff. 126–131.
65. BL, Balfour Papers, Add Ms 49711, Fisher to Balfour, 20 October 1905, ff. 126–131.
66. BL, Balfour Papers, Add Ms 49711, Fisher to Balfour, 20 October 1905, ff. 126–131.
67. TNA, FO 83/2146, Balfour to Fisher (Draft), 26 (?) October 1905, enclosed in Balfour to Clarke, 25 October 1905.
68. BL Balfour Papers, Add Ms 49711, Ottley to Fisher, 14 October 1905, ff. 127–131.
69. TNA, ADM 12/1417, Cut 59.8, 'Offensive Mine Service', 6 November 1905.
70. TNA, ADM 196/42/144, Orpen (Chatterton) service record.
71. TNA, ADM 196/88/98, Orpen (Chatterton) service record, Jackson remark, January 1897.
72. National Museum of the Royal Navy (NMRN), Fisher Papers, Mss 252/2, 'Blockade Mines' 7 November 1905, Memoranda Attached to 'Report of Navy Estimates Committee', 16 November 1905.
73. NMRN, Fisher Papers, Mss 252/2, 'Blockade Mines', 7 November 1905, Memoranda Attached to 'Report of Navy Estimates Committee', 16 November 1905.
74. The *Apollo* Class were small protected cruisers built under the 1889 Naval Defence Act for trade protection, armed with two 6' and six 4.7' guns and displacing 3600 tons. Norman Friedman, *British Cruisers of the Victorian Era* (Barnsley: Seaforth Publishing, 2012), pp. 156–157.

75. NMRN, Fisher Papers, Mss 252/2, 'Blockade Mines', 7 November 1905, Memorandum Attached to 'Report of Navy Estimates Committee', 16 November 1905.

76. Shawn T. Grimes, *Strategy and War Planning in the British Navy, 1887–1918* (Woodbridge, Suffolk: The Boydell Press, 2012); David Morgan-Owen, '"History Is a Record of Exploded Ideas": Sir John Fisher and Home Defence, 1904–10', *The International History Review*, vol. 36, no. 3 (2014), pp. 550–572.

77. NMRN, Fisher Papers, Mss 252/2, 'Blockade Mines', 7 November 1905, Memorandum Attached to 'Report of Navy Estimates Committee', 16 November 1905.

78. TNA, CAB 1/6, 'Appendix: Minutes of Proceedings' in 'Report of the Navy Estimates Committee', 16 November 1905.

79. TNA, ADM 116/3093, 'Supply of Automatic Submarine Mines to the Fleet', 'Naval Necessities II'.

80. TNA, ADM 116/866B, 'Preparation of Plans for Combined Naval and Military Operations in War', July 1905, ff. 142–143; other copies of this paper can be found in CAB 17/5 and CAB 17/95.

81. Lambert, *Planning Armageddon*, pp. 44, 59–60.

82. Lambert, *Planning Armageddon*, pp. 53–55.

83. Grimes, *Strategy and War Planning*, pp. 61–71.

CHAPTER 8

Development and Institutionalisation: Offensive Mining 1906–1909

Over the course of 1905 the attitude of the Royal Navy towards mining underwent a complete transformation. The Russo-Japanese War had dramatically exposed the potential of the weapon, but it was the connection of the technology to an accepted strategic goal that facilitated the change in the organisation's views. This began with the Ottley mine barrage scheme designed for an Anglo-German war and soon expanded to include plans for the use of mines in the event of a war in support of France, as had appeared likely in summer 1905. The sudden interest in deploying mines on a considerable scale meant that the Royal Navy began to invest time and money in developing the materiel necessary to implement these plans. This chapter will explore the technical developments and how these connected to the evolving strategic situation as the Royal Navy planned for a war with Germany. It will also show how the initial introduction of mining into the service, driven by a set of specific strategic circumstances, led to a more general re-evaluation of the merits of the mine as a weapon, particularly at a tactical level. Growing exposure to mining did begin to reshape cultural perceptions of the weapon within the service, offering the potential for a broader institutionalisation of the technology. This was, however, a slow process.

© The Author(s) 2018
R. Dunley, *Britain and the Mine, 1900–1915*,
https://doi.org/10.1007/978-3-319-72820-9_8

165

I

The sudden rise of interest in mining in 1905 meant that some of the arrangements made to facilitate the new strategy were of a temporary nature. In early November steps were taken to place mining on a sounder footing. The meeting on 7 November settled crucial questions regarding the minelayers, and Commander Herbert Orpen had been appointed the previous day to take charge of the new Offensive Mining Service.[1] Orpen immediately joined a group of relatively junior officers in the Admiralty who enjoyed the trust and support of the First Sea Lord. As part of this role Fisher asked Orpen to chair a secret committee looking at fleet auxiliaries, a category which, perhaps because of Orpen's position, was taken to include the new minelayers. The committee was driven directly by Fisher's desire for 'instant readiness for war' and he felt that the auxiliaries were a crucial part of this. He told the Board that he considered it his 'personal responsibility' and that in undertaking the work on the committee 'Commander Orpen would act on his behalf'.[2]

The Orpen Committee produced its report on 1 February 1906, and it was clearly considered highly confidential. This report would later be referred to as 'the secret pamphlet' and the copy surviving in the Fisher Papers at Churchill College, Cambridge has, 'only to be issued by order of Sir John' scrawled across the top.[3] This, together with Fisher's intimate involvement in the production of the report, suggests that it was an authentic expression of Admiralty opinion at the time. It discusses a whole range of issues relating to fleet auxiliaries, including the new minelayers. Naturally much of the committee's work reflected the conclusions reached at the meeting in November the previous year, but it does appear to signal a slight shift in the planned use of mines. The previous expectation, as outlined by Fisher, of laying large numbers of mines immediately on the outbreak of war had been replaced by a more cautious approach. The committee concluded that '(a)s any mining operations must be deliberately undertaken, there will always be ample time to get the minelayers to the front as required'. They also commented on the slow and unarmed nature of the vessels selected and suggested they would need escorting. Finally, with regard to mine depot ships, a class of vessel that had previously been associated with controlled mining, Orpen suggested that they could be used early in any conflict as 'storage depôts for the minelaying ships ... . They could follow soon after the minelayers when the latter proceed to the front for offensive operations, and replenish them several times from the one cargo at the scene of the action'. All of this points very strongly to the expectation of deploying mines on a large scale as part of littoral operations on the enemy's coastline. This fits easily within the new scholarship highlighting the Admiralty's continued focus on the close blockade within planning in this period.[4]

The report also gave a brief suggestion of the potential uses of the new mines. The two conflict scenarios considered were wars with a Russo-German or Franco-Russian alliance, although it does not appear that any of the mines were intended for use against the Russians in either situation. Notably no mention was made of a war in support of France, the scenario which had arisen in the summer of the previous year. In the case of war with Germany, Orpen suggested that 6000 mines would be needed for rapid deployment. He envisaged 3000 of these being laid off the German North Sea coast, precisely the number which had been identified by the Ottley committee as necessary for a large mine barrage in the Heligoland Bight.[5] More intriguingly, Orpen also stated that 3000 mines would be need to be laid off the coasts of Denmark, Holland and Scandinavia.[6] The Ottley committee had also made reference to this possibility, but there appears to have been a hardening of expectations on this front. These mines may have been intended for use in the event of a breach of neutrality, but the scale of the operation and clear expectation that it would have to be carried out suggest that there may have been an ulterior motive. The Royal Navy had for some time appreciated that mines were the perfect weapon with which to circumvent the difficulties in enforcing a blockade created by trade in neutral bottoms and through neutral ports. Mining Dutch and Scandinavian waters would provide a perfect solution; it would stop trade without having to worry about the legal niceties bound up in issues such as continuous voyage and absolute and conditional contraband. The difficulty would be getting the British government to approve.

A further committee on auxiliaries was formed later in 1906 under the chairmanship of Captain Henry Jones, ADNI, with Orpen as one of its members. The committee said little that was new regarding mining, apart from developing the previous suggestions of using mine depot ships to refill the minelayers. The committee decided that the task was such that ships should be taken up specifically for the purpose, and a new category of auxiliaries referred to as mine-carriers was created. One of these vessels would be attached to each minelayer; the mine-carriers would be capable of carrying 1000 mines with all of their associated equipment and have the facilities to transfer these mines to the mine-layers. The purpose of these vessels was to allow the minelayers to lay a large number of mines without having to return to a British port. These vessels were, however, to be unarmed, and the transfer of mines from the mine-carriers to the minelayers would be a time-consuming process that would have to take place in sheltered waters. This clearly fits into a scenario in which the Royal Navy intended to employ a large-scale mine barrage as part of a wider littoral warfare strategy which included the creation of an advanced base.

In early 1906 the first minelayer was converted. *Iphigenia*, a small protected cruiser of the *Apollo* class, ordered under the 1889 Naval Defence Act, had been intended for trade defence duties on foreign stations.[7] By 1905 she had come to the end of her effective life in that role. In order to convert her into a minelayer she had her armament removed and replaced by two rails running in parallel on her aft deck. The work was carried out at Portsmouth, following which she was commissioned 'for special service with the Channel Fleet' under the command of Admiral Arthur Wilson.[8]

Throughout the summer of 1906 *Iphigenia* undertook a series of trials which were completed satisfactorily, with only slight modifications recommended by her commanding officer, Algernon Heneage.[9] As a result, attention turned to providing further minelayers, although it was decided that four vessels in total, instead of the five recommended by the first report of the Fleet Auxiliary Committee, would be sufficient.[10] Orpen therefore submitted 'that 3 more vessels of the *Iphigenia* Class be ear marked for this service, one being taken in hand now.'[11] The Controller, H. B. Jackson, supported this decision and arrangements were made for the conversion of the *Thetis* at Chatham. The selection of the other two vessels was to wait until the finalisation of the 1907–1908 Estimates.[12] In November the Admiralty informed the Commander-in-Chief, Nore, of the work to be carried out and stated that the *Iphigenia* would immediately proceed to Chatham where she should be berthed alongside the *Thetis* whilst the work was completed. They went on to state that 'the alterations are to be carried out as far as possible by the artificers of the *Iphigenia* assisted by those of the *Thetis*'.[13] This direct stipulation is somewhat unusual, and there appears to be a motivation behind it beyond simple economy. In the original decision to convert the cruisers, the fact that this could be done without attracting attention had been an important factor. This clearly continued to play a role, and if anything became more important with the succession of the Liberal government and the proximity to the Hague Conference. In all disclosures made to Parliament at this time these vessels remained second-class protected cruisers, and whilst they were recorded as having been taken in hand by the dockyards, there was no indication given as to the nature of the work.[14] It was only from 1908 onwards, after the Hague Conference had taken place, that references to the cruisers as minelayers appear in the official parliamentary documentation. Due to the potential political embarrassment both at home and overseas, the Admiralty were keen that British mining retained a low profile.

At the beginning of 1907 discussions were opened as to which two vessels should be selected to complete the agreed complement of four minelayers. Captain John Jellicoe, the DNO, wrote an interesting minute in which he directly linked the conversion of the minelayers to the availability of mines. He stated that the *Iphigenia* and *Thetis* would 'provide for the first two units of 1000 mines'; however as another 1000 were now on order, a third vessel was immediately required.[15] Jellicoe's minute expressly linked each minelayer with a tranche of 1000 mines. This is a direct reference to the intention to accompany each of the vessels with a mine-carrier, capable of taking the entire complement of mines. It also gives indirect support to the notion that this entire structure was being created for the expressed purpose of carrying out large-scale mining operations away from the British coast. If this were not the case then the mine-carriers would be unnecessary, as would the connection of each minelayer with a specific group of mines. In any other scenario it would be sufficient for all of the mines to be kept at the home ports, from where the minelayers could resupply as necessary. After consultations between the DNO, the DNI and the Controller it was decided that the *Latona* should be the third cruiser to be converted into a minelayer and orders to that effect were sent out in spring 1907.[16]

II

The Royal Navy focused considerable attention throughout 1906 and early 1907 in getting the new Offensive Mining Service into a position where it could carry out the tasks expected of it in wartime. The ongoing conversion and construction of mines, the conversion of the new minelayers and the decisions regarding the taking-up of mine-carriers all fit into this process. At the same time questions over where to deploy mines, and for what purpose, continued to arise in the context of the ongoing strategic debates.

Following a lull in autumn 1905, tensions between Germany and France flared again in the run-up to the Algeciras Conference, and in December and January a number of informal meetings were held in Whitehall discussing potential British strategy in the event of war. Within these discussions the Admiralty proposed an amphibious naval strategy, whilst the War Office proffered a couple of early iterations of the so-called 'continental commitment'.[17] Of more direct relevance for the present study, the first meeting of the conference called for a number of major questions to be answered by each department. These questions addressed some of the most important issues around the creation of a combined strategy, including 'the naval strength necessary to impose a controlling superiority on the German battlefleet' and 'possible landing places on the German coastline'. It is thus noteworthy that, among the seven questions asked of the Admiralty was that of 'whether and where blockade mines might be employed'.[18] Unfortunately, distrust and inter-service rivalry meant that the committee broke down, with Fisher withdrawing Ottley, the Admiralty representative, before any answers to the questions were provided.[19] Despite this, the fact that the question was asked demonstrates once again that the issue of mining was being discussed at the very highest level of strategic planning and it was considered to be an important potential weapon in a war against Germany.

A year later, on 14 December 1906, Fisher created a new committee to draw up detailed plans for war against Germany.[20] The committee was chaired by George Ballard, with Maurice Hankey, future Secretary of the CID, as secretary. The identities of the other two members are unknown except for a reference in Hankey's biography describing them as mining and gunnery experts respectively.[21] Unfortunately the identity of the mining expert on the committee has never been discovered; however there is a strong possibility that it was Herbert Orpen. Orpen was almost unique in being an officer of suitable rank who could have been described as a mining expert at this time. We also know that he had previously been appointed to one of Fisher's secret committees and retained the trust of the First Sea Lord. There is no indication in the service records of any of the officers involved, but Orpen was certainly still based at the Admiralty and was spending a considerable amount of time at Portsmouth, where the committee was based. Whether or not Orpen was the individual concerned, the selection of an officer identified as a mining expert for a role on the committee gives a clear indication that the subject was expected to be one of considerable importance within the planning produced.

From the outset, the committee worked 'under Fisher's immediate inspiration' with Ballard meeting with him on a weekly basis. Ottley and Edmond Slade, the President of the War College, were both also intimately involved in the process.[22] The personnel on the committee, Fisher's direct involvement and its failure to appear on any official Admiralty list of committees all points to this being a serious planning body. Despite this evidence it has, until recently, been widely held that the plans were some form of smokescreen.[23] Recent work on the subject has rejected this theory, and a new consensus has emerged that the report produced by the committee was a true expression of Admiralty strategic thinking, although should not be viewed as prescriptive plans.[24]

The continuity in personnel from previous Admiralty planning means that it is unsurprising that the thinking of the new committee followed very similar lines to that displayed in earlier discussions. Indeed, Ballard would later describe the committee's work as more of a synthesis of ideas already formed by the NID than a wholly new creation.[25] What is, however, unusual is that the committee did not put much faith in the principle of offensive mining. Plan A/A1[26] proposed a distant blockade in the English Channel and northern North Sea.[27] This would isolate Germany from the majority of her overseas trade, would cut off her merchant marine and would help protect British commerce. The committee concluded that 'the effect on German interests would undoubtedly be very considerable'. This was despite the fact that the navy, under international law, would be unable to prevent neutral ships from trading with Germany as they were not close enough to the coast to declare a blockade. The limited amount of neutral tonnage was felt to negate this problem, as there were simply not enough ships to replace those of Britain and Germany.[28] No mention was made of using mines as a deterrent tool in this commerce war, despite these notions being implicit in the earlier plans for a mine barrage. Indeed the plans produced by the committee are noteworthy for their strict adherence to both the letter and the spirit of international law throughout. The only role envisaged for the minelayers was in conjunction with the fleet, 'mining the entrances of the enemy's naval ports after the hostile battlefleet had put to sea'.[29] To do this they were to cruise in conjunction with the armoured cruisers and destroyers.

Plans B/B1 and C/C1 within the Ballard committee report both relied on the blocking of the western entrance of the Kiel Canal in order to facilitate the concentration of forces in the Baltic. This idea had been central to Admiralty planning for an offensive campaign in the event of an Anglo-German war since 1902. It had also been a vital part of the plans for a war in support of France set out by Arthur Wilson in 1905. Within both planning streams, mines had been viewed as an important component of any operation to block the German North Sea exits. The Ballard committee, however, came to very different conclusions. It argued:

> There appears to be only one method by which such an obstacle can be provided, and that is by a line of sunken hulks. Mines are not reliable unless they can be constantly watched to prevent removal, and the larger the force with which the enemy can cover his sweeping operations, the larger the watching force must be to prevent them. In this instance the enemy could bring his whole battle squadron up for the purpose, and we could therefore only protect our mines by bringing up a battle squadron on our side, which would stultify the whole object in view, i.e. to keep our battle fleet concentrated elsewhere. It was clearly demonstrated at Port Arthur that mines will not keep a fleet in port which is determined to get out. Moreover, when mines are dropped in a very strong tideway they are apt to drag and to become a danger to friend or foe. And there is one more argument against them in the case of the Elbe, and that is the fact that, although laid primarily to deal with the enemy's ships of war, they would be placed in a great commercial route. Whether this would be recognised as legitimate or not by neutrals is an open question, but in any case we could not protest against Germany laying mines in the Thames if we ourselves laid them in the Elbe.[30]

This rejection of mining in all its forms represents an extraordinary turn-around from the attitude previously shown on the subject and poses a number of difficult questions. Foremost among these is the question of why the committee placed so much faith in blockships. The idea of using sunken hulks to block the exit of the Kiel Canal had been central to Admiralty planning in 1904, but had been dismissed out of hand by the Hydrographer. It is evident that no major change had taken place in the geography of the Elbe in the meantime. Indeed when the idea was raised once again in 1908 by the Strategy Committee, a relatively junior group of officers drawing up plans at the War College, the response was equally damning. The Hydrographer, F. Morton-Field, concluded that even if the Elbe channels could be blocked:

> it is not anticipated therefore that a channel blocked by sunken vessels would necessarily remain blocked for any considerable length of time and that the action of nature would before very long remove obstructions so far as effectively blocking the channel for navigation is concerned.[31]

Ballard had been at the NID when the original plan to use them was rejected, and Ottley's mine-barrage proposal was specifically designed to get around this issue. It is, therefore, inconceivable that the committee was not aware of the flaws in this plan. The only reasonable conclusions are, firstly that Ballard and Ottley did not agree with the Hydrographer's conclusions and felt they could press on with this proposal anyway; or secondly, that this was included as a cover for another similar operation which for various reasons could not be outlined in the plans. It is worth noting that no evidence has been found that the Admiralty ever looked into how it would go about acquiring the large number of vessels (over 100) required. This latter point is particularly interesting as the records of the Admiralty Transport Department have survived relatively intact and frequently contain information which no longer exists in the main Admiralty series, especially regarding the details of vessels to be taken up in wartime.

For these reasons there is the possibility that the subject of mining was still considered too sensitive to go beyond a very limited audience, and the discussion of blockships was inserted as a paper substitute for mining. Given the context of Fisher's relationship with Lord Charles Beresford, and the expectation that Beresford would use the plans to attack the Admiralty, this is not inconceivable.[32] Furthermore we know that the printed copies of the plans that survive are not a complete representation of the original report.[33] There is, however, no direct evidence to support this idea, so it cannot be more than speculation. Either way the question of how the navy would block the North Sea exit of the Kiel Canal to facilitate a Baltic strategy was not fully worked through, and would remain the great unknown in Admiralty planning through until the end of the First World War.

Setting aside the possibility that these plans were not a true reflection of the Admiralty's position on mining, they offer an important insight into the continued ambivalence of many naval officers towards the weapon. The committee's discussion over the potential legality of the use of mines in areas where commercial shipping would be affected is particularly noteworthy, reflecting the strong belief in the importance of protecting the rights of non-belligerents. Its conclusion, that the Royal Navy should avoid laying mines in such locations, stands in complete opposition to previous Admiralty policy. The report quotes another, unnamed, senior naval officer discussing potential German mining in the Thames. The officer suggested that 'the placing of mines in a great commercial route—even if it lay in the territorial waters of the enemy— would raise such a protest at the hands of neutrals that no Power could afford to attempt it'.[34] This was clearly written without the knowledge that the Admiralty themselves had for some time been considering a much more extreme policy. The scenario the officer was discussing would see mines laid in belligerent waters off a key naval base which happened to also be on a major commercial highway. As such they were far less radical than the mine barrage in the Heligoland Bight, which would have placed mines in international waters, yet Ottley and Fisher had never viewed the destruction of neutral shipping as anything other than an advantage.[35] This serves to highlight the continued divergence of views between officers within the Royal Navy on the legality and morality of the use of mines, particularly where they would affect neutrals and non-belligerents.

III

Contested views on whether mines were an appropriate weapon were not restricted to the Royal Navy, and the political environment became even more hostile following the election of a Liberal government in 1905. This brought about a distinct change in the political climate in which the Royal Navy operated. Fisher had been very careful to build a close relationship with Arthur Balfour, the outgoing Unionist Prime Minister, who had taken a strong interest in defence matters. The same could not be said for his replacement. Sir Henry Campbell-Bannerman was a progressive, more interested in domestic reforms than defence or foreign policy. His desire for the reduction of defence expenditure found ample support from the radical side of his party, which had distinct pacifist tendencies. The change of government naturally had a major impact on the navy, particularly by increasing pressure on the Estimates. Campbell-Bannerman and the radical wing of the Liberal Party were also strongly in favour of arms reduction through international treaty and placed greater emphasis on the proposed peace conference at The Hague.[36] These political factors had a direct effect on the development of mining within the Royal Navy. As has already been mentioned the Admiralty felt it necessary to be somewhat economical with the truth when it came to informing Parliament of the steps being taken. The conversion of the *Apollo*-Class cruisers was not disclosed, and mining was simply not mentioned in statements made by the First Lord, or debates in either House. It is of course very difficult to tell how far this subtle deception extended, but it is clear that the navy was not keen on broadcasting what progress it had made in independent mining to a wide audience.

The new political landscape also had an impact on the technical development of mining. The most obvious issue was that the Admiralty seriously limited the scope for training and exercises with mines. In 1912 one of the officers then commanding a minelayer remarked that, 'when the minelayers were first commissioned, owing to the confidential character of the material ... practices with service mines and automatic sinkers was forbidden.'[37] Whilst exercises with a practice sinker attached to a buoy were allowed, this would have been a poor substitute for the real thing. This does not appear to have been the only stricture placed on the offensive mining service by the Admiralty in its early years. The minelayers operated very much apart from the rest of the fleet. Whilst this was to be expected due to the experimental nature of both the subject and the vessels, its extent appears noteworthy. The strongest indication of how far the minelayers were removed from the usual service structures is revealed in a letter written by Beresford to the Admiralty in 1908 in which he requested:

> that I maybe furnished with the results of any trials which have taken place with these vessels up to the present time. I have not had any experience with these vessels and have no information as to their capabilities and without this it is difficult for me to assign these vessels duties which will elucidate points as to their value.[38]

Of course, one has to bear in mind the state of animosity that existed between Fisher and Beresford at this time, and the First Sea Lord's

176   R. DUNLEY

tendency to withhold information from those he considered enemies. It is still, however, remarkable that two and a half years after the formation of the offensive mining service, the most senior British admiral afloat had no information regarding minelaying. This is, of course, compounded by the fact that Beresford had always held a strong interest in mining and his continuing ignorance of developments is indicative of the veil of secrecy which shrouded the subject.

The failure of the Hague Conference to achieve any meaningful progress regarding banning mines, or placing serious restrictions on their use, removed part of the necessity for secrecy, and prompted a reconsideration of the whole subject. At the beginning of 1908, having allowed the press furore over the German intransigence at The Hague to die down, the Admiralty returned to the subject. On 8 January Edmond Slade, the new DNI, met his predecessor Ottley to discuss The Hague, where the latter had been the British naval advisor.[39] It appears highly likely that the focus of attention was on mining, as later in the same day there was a meeting held in the Board Room to discuss the subject. In addition to all of the usual figures, those present included Bernard Currey, the ADT, and Herbert Orpen, who had confusingly changed his surname to Chatterton at the end of 1906.[40] The Admiralty, throughout his time as Captain in Charge of Minelayers, seemingly viewed the names as interchangeable, creating a somewhat schizophrenic identity. The meeting itself was crucial, and important steps were made in expanding and incorporating the mining service into the fleet at large. Slade recorded in his diary

> At a meeting in the Board Room it was decided to bring the stock of mines up to 10,000 and to have 6 minelayers + one spare total 7—Home Fleet to practice at their cruises on 8th Ap and end of May and to have mining operations on a large scale on 8th July.[41]

These steps represented both a large financial expenditure on mining, and a commitment to bring it into the fold of fleet exercises and tactics. This decision, coming so soon after the failure of the Hague Peace Conference, gives further confirmation, if any were needed, of the impact political considerations had on the early development of independent mining. The decision to double the size of the offensive mining service also supports the idea that the navy retained an interest in mining beyond that outlined in the Ballard plans. In an era of extreme budgetary pressure it is highly unlikely that Fisher would have supported a proposal to invest heavily in a weapons system that the navy did not intend to use in its most plausible combat scenario.

Both of these points are further reinforced by remarks made by the First Sea Lord on a draft of the 1908–1909 Estimates. This document was being prepared at roughly the same time as the decision to expand the mining service was taken, and an early version made mention of this. It remarked that '(t)he Mining Service has been considerably strengthened and important mining exercises have been carried out by the principal fleets'. It went on to note that further development was expected in the next year. Fisher took exception to this. He crossed this section out and minuted 'omit as undesirable to make public as we are far ahead of other nations'.[42] Unsurprisingly, the final copy of the text contained no reference to mining.[43] This gives an interesting insight into Fisher's perspective on mining, which he clearly felt to be developing well. It also shows that the veil of secrecy surrounding the subject had not been entirely lifted by the conclusion of the conference at The Hague. It is difficult to avoid the conclusion that this was largely due to the important role which the Admiralty expected mines to play in war policy.

In May 1908 orders were given for the *Apollo* and *Andromache* to be the next two cruisers converted into minelayers; however, pressure on the dockyards meant that work did not begin until near the end of the year.[44] The *Intrepid* and *Naiad* made up the complement of seven minelayers; they were converted under the 1909–1910 Estimates, and completed in the summer of 1910.[45] With respect to mines the Royal Navy had 4900 in 1908, with a further 2200 ordered following the meeting on 8 January for the 1908–1909 Estimates. An additional 2000 were to be ordered under the 1910–1911 Estimates, with the remaining 900 out of the total of 10,000 to come the following year.[46] The dramatic increase in expenditure on mining from 1906–1907 onwards comes through very clearly in Table 7.1, which shows the cost of new mining supplies produced by the Royal Laboratory. These numbers show a step change in expenditure on independent mines from 1906–1907, with a further sharp increase from 1908–1909. This later change can be partially explained by the fact that some earlier expenditure had gone on converting Royal Engineers' mines, which is not included in these figures. However the scale of the increase supports the idea that the navy redoubled its investment in mining following the failure at The Hague.

IV

In the summer of 1908, driven largely by the ongoing dispute between Fisher, the First Sea Lord, and Beresford, Commander-in-Chief, Channel Fleet, the Admiralty issued a new set of war orders. Previous policy had seen the Admiralty draw up potential war plans, but, in theory at least, it left the final decisions in the hands of the admirals afloat.[47] This had seemed a realistic proposition when Arthur Wilson had been in command, but relations between Fisher and Beresford were such that it was felt a more prescriptive approach was required.[48] The resultant war orders were issued on 1 July 1908, and outlined a traditional strategy of mounting an observational blockade of the German North Sea coast with torpedo craft, backed at a safe distance by the fleet.[49] Within this scenario, control of the Heligoland Bight was to be exercised by the flotilla, and the role of mining in these plans was minimal. They reported that:

> the mine-layers will join the squadron in the Heligoland Bight and will be under the orders of the Rear-Admiral Commanding the Cruiser Squadron, ready to mine the entrances to the Elbe and Jahde Rivers should the German Fleet come out, thus hindering its return. As a general rule mines will not be used except for this purpose.[50]

These war orders, in contrast to the Ballard plans, only addressed the first phase of the conflict. They contained no discussion of the strategic rationale behind the operations, nor any indication of whether the Admiralty still envisaged pushing forces into the Baltic. As such we cannot tell whether it remained its intention to block the North Sea exit of the Kiel Canal, and if so whether this was to be with blockships or mines. More broadly, however, it is clear that there was still a strong interest in this subject; the Strategy Committee discussed the issue on a number of occasions and it was the latter's enquiry which led to the latest rebuttal of the blockship approach by the Hydrographer.[51]

The July 1908 war orders did not remain in force for long. In March 1909 Admiral Sir William May replaced Beresford as the senior admiral in home waters when he hoisted his flag as commander of the new Home Fleet. At the same time he was issued with a new set of war orders, referred to as War Plan GU.[52] These documents, which have only recently come to the attention of historians, were based on the somewhat surprising assumption that Britain may have to fight a German-American alliance. Beyond this they largely conform to that which had gone before, relying on an observational blockade of the German North Sea coast, with the torpedo flotilla being pushed forward into the Heligoland Bight. In a slight alteration to the previous war orders it was proposed to establish two advanced bases, off the Dutch and Danish coasts respectively, from which submarines and destroyers could be resupplied.

In connection with mining, these orders offer tantalising hints but very little detail. Out of the five minelayers which had, at this stage, been converted, the *Apollo*, *Andromache* and *Thetis* were to assemble at Sheerness and operate under the orders of the Commander-in-Chief. The only information given was that they would conduct 'minelaying work on the German coast in connection with the operations of the fleets in German waters'.[53] The other two minelayers, *Iphigenia* and *Latona*, were also to assemble at Sheerness, but they would operate under the direct instruction of the Admiralty and no hint is given as to their mission. In addition to the minelayers, three mine-carriers were to be taken up once the order to mobilise was given.[54] Two of these were to be at the 'disposal of the Commander-in-Chief, Home Fleet, to replenish his minelayers either at the front or in some British harbour as he may require'. The third mine-carrier was to operate with the other two minelayers, and similarly had to await Admiralty instruction.[55] Certain aspects of this arrangement appear self-evident. The three minelayers and two mine-carriers would, one assumes, operate out of the two advanced bases, one mine-carrier being based at each. They would most likely be involved in laying either some small fields to limit the range of options available to the Germans, or possibly a larger barrage which would eventually enable the British to withdraw from their forward position. The intentions with regard to the other two minelayers are far more difficult to deduce. It is possible that the Admiralty felt that they would be better placed than the Commander in Chief to spot tactical opportunities to use mines, for example laying mines in the path of a retreating German fleet. Equally the Admiralty may have had specific intentions to use the vessels to deploy mines for other, strategic, purposes.

War Plan GU gives some indication of continued interest in using mining as part of Admiralty planning, and this is supported by certain contemporaneous exercises. In July 1908 the minelayers had practised loading mines from the Naval Ordnance depot at Sheerness in order to test out war arrangements. This exercise was satisfactory and in his report Chatterton recommended that 'practical experience with a mine carrier is desirable.'[56] This proposal was accepted and arrangements were made for the summer of 1909.[57] Such a suggestion was significant as it required the hiring of a merchant vessel, a costly undertaking, and one the Admiralty very rarely condoned. The exercises took place in August, immediately following the summer manoeuvres, using the collier SS *Boscawen*. Just prior to their start the Admiralty sent a telegram to the Commander in Chief, Portsmouth stating that 'the whole evolution regarded as a test of war procedure stop Undue publicity is to be avoided'.[58] The procedure had two stages, the first being the loading of the *Boscawen* with 900 mines held at Portsmouth. Once this was completed the *Thetis* and *Latona* would load their complement of 100 mines each from the mine-carrier. The exercise went off without a hitch and the results appear to have been broadly satisfactory. The *Boscawen* was loaded in fifty-four hours and immediately following the completion of this she was placed alongside the minelayers. The *Thetis* and the *Latona* then received their complement of mines from her, the former loading in three hours and twenty minutes in daylight, and the latter taking three hours and forty minutes, mostly after dark.[59]

The loading of the minelayers appears to have been considered satisfactory and no further comment was passed on the matter. With regard to the loading of the mine-carrier the Superintendent of Ordnance Stores (SOS) requested clarification 'as to whether 60 hours can be allowed for the loading of each mine carrier and if not by what number these hours should be reduced.'[60] Herbert King-Hall, the Director of Naval Mobilisation, responded that 'the mine carriers should be loaded in the shortest possible time and if it is feasible to reduce the time occupied to less than 60 hours it should be reduced by as much as possible.'[61] In the end it was not found to be possible to reduce the time taken much below the 60 hours projected. It is clear, however, that this delay was seen as a problem and the Admiralty Digest records that 'arrangements for replenishing minelayers before the loading of mine carriers in the Thames District is complete. Action to be taken by the N.O.O. [Naval Ordnance Officer] Woolwich on issue of warning telegram.'[62] The provision of the mine-carriers would naturally take a little time. In addition to the loading of the mines it is obvious that there would be some delay resulting from the actual process of taking up the ships from the merchant marine and these then having to proceed to either Portsmouth or Chatham. This would however be small. Indeed, when it was noted that facilities should be constructed for the additional crew envisaged on the mine-carriers, King-Hall effectively vetoed it, pointing out the 'undesirability ... of delaying the ships'.[63] What is truly noteworthy is that the Admiralty saw the necessity of providing for the resupply of the minelayers even before the mine-carriers were ready. The time frame for the organisation and loading of the mine-carriers could be measured in days and not weeks and yet it was still not going to be soon enough for the minelayers. It is difficult to know precisely what conclusions to draw from this information with regard to the Admiralty's mining policy. It appears to confirm that the mine-carriers were an integral part of a potential wartime operation which would be carried out very soon after the outbreak of any conflict. What the aims of such an operation were remains difficult to distinguish, but the scale, over 3000 mines being readied for immediate use, is strongly suggestive of some form of mine barrage. Whatever conclusions are drawn in this respect it is obvious that the Royal Navy wished to retain the option to deploy mines on a large scale away from British waters.

Further evidence pointing towards the retention of some form of mine barrage strategy comes from a very different source. Edward Inglefield had been head of the Trade Division of the NID until 1906, when he retired to take up a highly paid position as Second Secretary at Lloyds of London, the insurance market.[64] He retained exceptionally close links with the Admiralty and was well acquainted with all aspects of naval strategy. Inglefield also proved a great source of information to the Admiralty on a number of fronts. On 19 October 1909 Inglefield wrote to Vincent Baddeley, Assistant Principal Secretary to the Admiralty, discussing his recent visit to Germany and his transit of the Kiel Canal. Inglefield, clearly at Admiralty request, had considered the possibility of setting up a spy in one of the towns bordering the canal to report on the movements of the German fleet, but he said that an Englishman living there would quickly be noticed. He went on to discuss the process of widening the canal and the potential of using blockships to close it. With reference to this he concluded that whilst it would be easy enough to block the canal if tramp steamers could be got past the forts, he did not see how this would be possible. As such he concluded that '(i)t will then remain to block the channels on the Weser with submarine mines.'[65]

The nature of Inglefield's remark shows that this strategy was one which was anticipated by a well-informed observer, albeit one who was now formally outside the Admiralty.

The offensive mining service had been established in response to the development of a mine-barrage strategy in the event of war with Germany. By summer 1905 the technology had become a crucial component in both of the Royal Navy's most likely wartime scenarios, an Anglo-German war and a war against Germany in support of France. The confused state of planning and the limited survival of the archival material means that by 1907 the situation is far less clear. If taken at face value, the Ballard plans suggest that the Admiralty had moved away from the idea of the widespread use of mines, with these being replaced by other means of blocking the German fleet in. Despite this, the continued investment in mining and the surrounding infrastructure demonstrates that the Admiralty was at the very least keen to retain the option of using mines in a strategic fashion; unfortunately the precise details of how and to what end are unclear.

V

Initial Royal Navy interest in mining developed in 1905 as a direct result of the fact that the technology appeared to offer a solution to a specific strategic challenge. This provided enough impetus to overcome the service's traditional opposition to independent mines, rooted in its organisational culture. That did not, however, mean that this opposition disappeared. Many naval officers retained a deep scepticism over the suitability of the weapon for use in any scenario by an organisation looking to exercise command of the sea. This opposition on the part of some officers proved extremely resilient, persisting well into the First World War. Despite this there are clear indicators that the perceptions of mining were changing in the years following 1905 as the technology was slowly institutionalised and its potential was better understood. This process was central to a gradual shift in the focus of mining within the Royal Navy, from being an exceptional technology with a strictly limited strategic role, to an accepted part of a modern fleet, with as many tactical as strategic applications.

The real impetus for this shift came in 1908, when, following the failure of the Hague Conference, the Royal Navy began to lift the very tight restrictions which had previously been placed on mining, and incorporated the mining service into the fleet more generally. At the meeting held at the Admiralty on 8 January it was concluded that 'Home Fleet to practice at their cruises on 8th April and end of May and to have mining operations on a large scale on 8th July'.[66] These exercises would be among the first occasions on which the minelayers operated with the fleet, and signified a growing interest in the possibility of using mines on a tactical as well as a strategic level.

The selection of the Home Fleet for these experiments appears to have been purposeful. As Battenberg told Arthur Lee, 'the old antagonism between him [Fisher] and Beresford now induces Fisher to do everything to aggrandize the Home Fleet whilst belittling the Channel Fleet'.[67] The mining exercises simply provided Fisher with another such opportunity. In April, Beresford, commanding the Channel Fleet, wrote to the Admiralty requesting that 'a mining vessel and a division of submarines be attached to the Channel Fleet in order that mining and submarine exercises maybe carried out with them.' He concluded the letter saying that '(b)eing responsible for the defence of Home Waters in wartime, I wish to bring these two questions [relating to the use of mines and submarines] before their Lordships.'[68] Naturally this served to rile Fisher, and the Admiralty response took the form of a blunt refusal followed by a statement that 'the Board of Admiralty is the sole authority for the conduct of war, whether in Home Waters or elsewhere.'[69] The issue would not go away and on 24 April Slade remarked on the situation in his diary.

> There is a lot of friction going on again between Lord C and Sir J. The former asked for a mining vessel and submarines but has only had a rude reply. What the result will be is only to be conjectured, but he will not sit down under the rebuff. Sir J is frightened at what he has done and is wanting orders to be made out so that there shall be no chance of Lord C saying that he does not intend to use the mining ships that are going to be sent to him for the manoeuvres.[70]

The reference to the manoeuvres is a crucial one, as it is clear that mining was considered a central part of the 1908 scheme. Sir Francis Bridgeman, commander of the Home Fleet, was to take charge of the Red fleet, whilst Beresford commanded the Blue fleet. The aim of Blue was to prevent Red from uniting its two separated battle fleets, and if possible to defeat them in detail.[71] Blue was given two minelayers and Red one; Blue was also given the services of Captain Chatterton (Orpen).[72] As was mentioned by Slade in his diary, a clear emphasis was placed on mining in the instructions given to Beresford. They explicitly stated that:

> such experience is desired not only in the laying and removal of mines near coasts and harbours, but also in regard to proposals which have been made to drop mines in the path of an advancing fleet in the open sea and it is desirable to make use of any opportunities which may present themselves in the course of the exercises for elucidating these points.[73]

It is apparent from these instructions that the Admiralty now saw mining as potentially fulfilling a number of different functions going beyond the initial interesting in blocking operations. The exercises were designed to provide information on these points, but in doing so they also provided mining with much-needed visibility to officers outside the Admiralty. One of the challenges of all attempts to use mines in exercises was how to know which areas had been mined, and whether a ship had been 'sunk'. In order to facilitate the proper use of mines in the 1908 exercises serious attention was focused on this subject. The Captain of *Vernon*, Douglas Gamble, was appointed as a Special Mining Umpire, and set up in an office in Queensferry. He was to map out all areas mined and swept, and try and draw some conclusions as to the impact of mines on the manoeuvres.[74]

Despite all of this effort the manoeuvres proved to be a bit of a disaster. Beresford and Bridgeman, too concerned to avoid the risk of defeat, made no real effort to find each other. Slade remarked in his diary that 'Admiral Bridgeman appears to be doing nothing at all except making useless promenade and burning coal. It is not at all satisfactory'. Meanwhile Beresford tried to make political capital out of the affair, claiming he could have landed 100,000 men on the British coast. The DNI concluded 'I am very much disappointed with the results of manoeuvres generally, neither Admiral has enhanced his reputation and the lessons to be learnt from it are nil.'[75] Neither side appears to have taken any real interest in the minelaying vessels given to it, and very little useful experience was gained in this direction. The official umpire's report noted caustically that:

> (t)he Blue fleet did not make any attempt to lay mines off the Forth when the Red fleet retired there, although instructions were given in the special idea B. to this effect, and special mining vessels were attached to Blue fleet. Anything that would have delayed the exit of the Red fleet even by half an hour at the critical moment might have turned the scale.[76]

It is not clear whether Beresford purposefully ignored the whole subject of mining in these manoeuvres as a form of silent retribution, but considering the state of his relations with Fisher at the time it is by no means inconceivable. The failure of the two admirals to utilise the minelayers should not, however, detract from the fact that the Admiralty was clearly keen to develop the mining service and devoted considerable effort in trying to achieve this.

Immediately following the conclusion of the manoeuvres a mining committee was set up under the presidency of Rear-Admiral George Callaghan, who was then commanding the Fifth Cruiser Squadron attached to the Home Fleet.[77] The initiative for the committee appears to have come from the fleet, and focused on minesweeping rather than minelaying. The concept was rapidly embraced by the Admiralty, which expanded both its personnel and brief. The result was a very strong committee put together to look into all aspects of mining in the Royal Navy. Callaghan was supported by two of his captains from the Fifth Cruiser Squadron, Dudley de Chair and Henry Oliver. De Chair had led some of the early experiments into minesweeping, whilst Oliver had previously been involved in offensive mining due to his appointment as Captain of the Navigation School.[78] Chatterton and Commander Burne of the *Iphigenia* represented the mining service, whilst Bernard Currey, the ADT, Douglas Gamble from the *Vernon*, Osmond de Brock, ADNI, and A. G. H. W. Moore, the Naval Assistant to the First Sea Lord, made up the complement. Considering its origins it is unsurprising that the committee mainly focused on minesweeping, and its recommendations on this front provided the foundations of British policy up until 1914. The discussion of minelaying appears to have been much more limited, but it did put forward an important recommendation. In the final report dated 16 November 1908 the committee stated that 'it is to be considered that the type of vessels at present available is not altogether suitable'.[79] Instead it recommended the construction of a new design of vessel possessing the qualities of shallowness of draft, handiness, seaworthiness, unsinkability and high speed.[80] The report went on to say that:

186   R. DUNLEY

the latter quality is most essential, as it is considered these vessels should *not* need an escort, but should as the opportunity offers, or on being warned by destroyers of a chance, be able to make a dash and be able to trust in their speed to give them a fair chance of escape if chased.[81]

There is no evidence to suggest that any progress was made in pursuing this recommendation before the outbreak of war. A report on the progress in mining the following year by Oliver, who had replaced Moore as Naval Assistant to the First Sea Lord, stated that Fisher decided to 'carry out its recommendations as far as financial considerations permitted.'[82] It is very clear that the stretched naval budget would not cover the cost of a series of new minelayers at this time. This recommendation, and the report's justification of it, does however offer an interesting insight into the role expected to be played by the minelayers.

When, in 1905, mining began to be considered more seriously it was addressed as a strategic issue. The intention had been to use mines as an essential part of a plan to enable the British to obtain and exploit command of the sea to further strategic ends. These potentially included the seizure of an island off the German North Sea coast, the penetration of the fleet into the Baltic or the rigorous enforcing of an economic blockade. From 1908 there appears to have been a growing interest in using mines in a tactical as well as a strategic manner. In the instructions given to Beresford prior to the 1908 manoeuvres it is clearly stated that the Admiralty wished to gain information on the possibility of using mines in fleet actions.[83] Observant readers will recall that Fisher had proposed examining the use of mines in such contexts as early as 1902, but the idea had been shelved.[84] The reason why it was not really discussed in the period 1905–1908 is unclear; however it is possible that the restrictions on the minelayers exercising with the fleet prevented a close examination of the subject.

The report of the mining committee clearly foresaw the potential of using mines in such situations. Perhaps it is unsurprising that a committee which originated in the fleet, and was led by an officer who was a well-regarded fleet commander, looked at the matter from the perspective of the battle fleet. The proposal set out by the committee was for an exceptionally fast mining vessel, which could be used with the fleet. It would rely on speed to both get it into positions to deploy mines, and then to extricate itself, something the converted cruisers were entirely incapable of. In this role mines could be deployed with facility both in the expected path of an enemy's fleet, or in an attempt to cut off its retreat.[85] It is clear that the committee were not alone in seeing the potential of such a tactic and in 1909 the DNO wrote a memorandum on whether manoeuvres should be carried out to examine the potential of using mines offensively in fleet actions.[86] Unfortunately this paper, along with so many others pertaining to all areas of Admiralty policy, appears to have been destroyed in the systematic weeding carried out on the archives. This is particularly frustrating in this instance, as it could have been very instructive to see the reaction of Rear-Admiral Sir John Jellicoe, then Controller, to this proposal by his subordinate. It seems reasonable to suggest that Jellicoe's wartime concerns regarding mine traps had their origins in one of these early discussions. In the end it is not even clear if the manoeuvres proposed by the DNO were carried out; however there was certainly no perceptible deviation in Admiralty policy at this time.

The growing interest, both in the Admiralty and in the fleet, in exploring new ways in which mines could be deployed, particularly in a tactical rather than strategic scenario, is indicative of the shifting attitudes towards the weapon. The Royal Navy initially only accepted the technology because it fulfilled a specific strategic requirement. Whilst interest in fulfilling this requirement remained, the growing exposure of the fleet to the technology allowed some naval officers to come to terms with mining and consider other ways in which they could use the technology in pursuit of the organisation's goals. This process should not be overstated: there were still many within the service who saw mines as a complete anathema, and the primary focus of the mining committee remained on minesweeping rather than minelaying. Despite this, the gradual institutionalisation of the weapon is important and it serves to demonstrate how familiarity can slowly break down even the most entrenched of cultural beliefs regarding technology.

January 1910 saw not only the retirement of Admiral of the Fleet Sir John Fisher as First Sea Lord, but also the end of Chatterton's time as commander of the offensive mining service. On the submission of his final report the Admiralty expressed its satisfaction at the developments which had been made under his guidance.[87] In many respects it is easy to see why. On the succession of Algernon Heneage to the post, which was renamed Captain in Charge of Minelayers, the offensive mining service consisted of five minelayers, with a further two under conversion. The navy had stocks of approximately 7000 mines, with a further 2000 about to be ordered. In addition detailed arrangements had been made for the taking-up of mine-carriers in the event of war, and transferring mines between the vessels had been practised, with further similar exercises planned.[88] This represented a major step forward in capability from the time of Chatterton's appointment in November 1905.

More broadly, the position of the technology had changed markedly over the four years. The initial direct connection with the Royal Navy's main wartime strategy, which facilitated the adoption of mining, had faded. The service clearly continued to see an important strategic role for mining, and invested heavily in the technology, but any evidence of precisely how this fitted into the war plans of the later Fisher Admiralty has been lost. At the same time there was a growing acknowledgement of the potential of mines among naval officers outside of the Admiralty. This shift helped the service to begin to think about mines in a new way, in a tactical, rather than strategic context. It also formed part of a gradual process of institutionalisation, which saw mining and the minelayers become a more accepted part of the fleet. This process should not, however, be exaggerated; many naval officers still viewed mines as fundamentally antithetical to both the Royal Navy's strategic identity, and to British maritime culture more generally.

NOTES

1. The National Archive (TNA), ADM 196/42/144, Herbert Orpen (Chatterton) Service Record.
2. National Museum of the Royal Navy (NMRN), Fisher Papers, Mss 252/2, 'Auxiliaries to the Fleet in Wartime', 16 November 1905, Memorandum Attached to 'Report of Navy Estimates Committee', 16 November 1905.
3. For reference to the secret pamphlet see TNA, ADM 1/7877, Report of the Fleet Auxiliary Committee, February 1907; Churchill Archive Centre (CAC), Fisher Papers, FISR 8/16, 'Report on Fleet Auxiliaries', 1 February 1906.
4. Shawn T. Grimes, *Strategy and War Planning in the British Navy, 1887–1918* (Woodbridge, Suffolk: The Boydell Press, 2012), Chapter 3; Matthew Seligmann, 'The Renaissance of Pre-First World War Naval History', *Journal of Strategic Studies*, vol. 36, no. 3 (2013), pp. 454–479; and David Morgan Owen, 'Cooked up in the Dinner Hour?, Sir Arthur Wilson's War Plan, Reconsidered', *English Historical Review*, vol. 130, no. 545 (2015), pp. 865–906.

5. TNA, ADM 116/3093, 'Supply of Automatic Submarine Mines to the Fleet', 'Naval Necessities II'.
6. CAC, Fisher Papers, FISR 8/16, 'Report on Fleet Auxiliaries', 1 February 1906.
7. Norman Friedman, *British Cruisers of the Victorian Era* (Barnsley: Seaforth Publishing, 2012), pp. 156–157.
8. TNA, ADM 144/27, Admiralty to CinC Portsmouth, 6 January 1906.
9. National Maritime Museum (NMM), Brass Foundry (BF), Ships Cover 218, 'Report on Mine Fittings', 29 October 1906, f. 33/1.
10. NMM, BF, Ships Cover 218, 'Report on Mine Fittings', Tudor Minute, 18 October 1906, f. 34.
11. NMM, BF, Ships Cover 218, 'Report on Mine Fittings', Orpen Minute, 19 October 1906, f. 34.
12. NMM, BF, Ships Cover 218, 'Report on Mine Fittings', Jackson Minute, 24 October 1906; Marshall Minute, 20 October 1906, f. 34.
13. NMM, BF, Ships Cover 218, 'Report on Mine Fittings', Adm to CinC Nore (Copy), 23 November 1906, f. 34.
14. Parliamentary Papers (PP), 'Navy Dockyard Expense Accounts 1906–7', 12 March 1908.
15. NMM BF, Ships Cover 218, Jellicoe Minute, 17 January 1907, f. 37.
16. NMM BF, Ships Cover 218, Jackson Minute, 9 March 1907, f. 36a.
17. The best overall account remains Neil William Summerton, *The Development of British Military Planning for a War Against Germany* (Unpublished PhD thesis, University of London, 1970), Chapter 3.
18. TNA, CAB 18/24, 'Notes of a Conference held at Whitehall Gardens, 6 January 1906'.
19. CAC, Esher Papers, ESHR 4/1, Fisher to Esher, n.d., f. 14.
20. NMM, Ballard Papers, Mss/80/200, Box 1, G. A. Ballard, 'Record of Business, Letters, Etc', 14 December 1906.
21. Maurice Hankey, *The Supreme Command 1914–1918*, vol. I (London: George Allen & Unwin, 1961), p. 39.
22. TNA, ADM 1/8997, Ballard Memorandum, 'Remarks on the Framing of Certain Plans for War with Germany Now at the Admiralty', n.d. (May 1909); Maurice Hankey, *The Supreme Command 1914–1918*, vol. I (London: George Allen & Unwin, 1961), p. 39.
23. Paul Haggie, 'The Royal Navy and War Planning in the Fisher Era', *Journal of Contemporary History*, vol. 8, no. 3 (1973), pp. 113–131; Ruddock F. Mackay, *Fisher of Kilverstone* (Oxford: Clarendon Press, 1973), pp. 366–371; Christopher Martin, 'The 1907 Naval War Plans and the Second Hague Peace Conference: A Case of Propaganda', *Journal of Strategic Studies*, vol. 28, no. 5 (2005), pp. 833–856; and Nicholas Lambert, *Planning Armageddon: British Economic Warfare and*

the First World War (Cambridge, MA: Harvard University Press, 2012), pp. 76–77.

24. Matthew Seligmann, 'Naval History by Conspiracy Theory: The British Admiralty Before the First World War and the Methodology of Revisionism', *Journal of Strategic Studies*, vol. 38, no. 7 (2015), pp. 8–12; Grimes, *Strategy and War Planning*, Chapter 3.

25. TNA, ADM 1/8997, Ballard Memorandum, 'Remarks on the Framing of Certain Plans for War with Germany Now at the Admiralty', n.d. (May 1909).

26. Plan A indicated an Anglo-German War and A1 a War in which there was a French alliance. There was in truth little differentiation between these plans.

27. TNA, ADM 116/1043B, 'War Plans: Plan A', Box 1, ff. 124–138.

28. TNA, ADM 116/1043B, 'War Plans: Plan A', Box 1, ff. 136–138; Lambert, *Planning Armageddon*, pp. 82–84.

29. TNA, ADM 116/1043B, 'War Plans: Plan A', Box 1, f. 134.

30. TNA, ADM 116/1043B, 'War Plans: Plan A', Box 1, 'War Plans: Plan C', f. 152.

31. TNA, ADM 116/866b, 'Blocking a Channel in a Tideway', 22 May 1908, ff. 247–249. Also see UK Hydrographic Office [UKHO], Special Minute Book 2, 'Memorandum to the DNI Relative to the Blocking of Wide Channels', 22 May 1908.

32. Grimes, *Strategy and War Planning*, pp. 85–86; Nicholas Lambert, *Sir John Fisher's Naval Revolution* (Columbia: University of South Carolina Press, 1999), pp. 177–182; and Lambert, *Planning Armageddon*, pp. 74–76.

33. Lambert, *Planning Armageddon*, p. 72.

34. TNA, ADM 116/1043B, Box 1, 'War Plans: Introductory Remarks', f. 112.

35. BL, Add Ms 49711, Ottley to Fisher, 14 October 1905, ff. 127–131.

36. Andre T. Sidorowicz, 'The British Government, the Hague Peace Conference of 1907, and the Armaments Question', in B. J. C. McKercher, ed., *Arms Limitation and Disarmament: Restraints on War 1899–1939* (Westport: Praeger, 1992), pp. 1–4.

37. NMM, Dannreuther Papers, DAN/133, 'The Theory and Practice of Submarine Mining as Practiced by His Majesty's Ships', 25 March 1912.

38. TNA, ADM 116/1090, Beresford to Admiralty, 10 June 1908.

39. NMM, Slade Papers, MRF/39/2, Slade Diary, 8 January 1908.

40. NMM, Currey Papers, CRY/24, Currey Diary, 8 January 1908.

41. NMM, Slade Papers, MRF/39/2, Slade Diary, 8 January 1908.

42. NMRN, Fisher Papers, Mss 252/17/67, 'Statement of the First Lord of the Admiralty Explanatory of the Navy Estimates 1908–1909' (Draft).

43. NMRN, Fisher Papers, Mss 252/17/83, 'Statement of the First Lord of the Admiralty Explanatory of the Navy Estimates 1908–1909'.
44. NMM BF, Ships Cover 218, 'Est'd Cost of Converting Certain Vessels to Minelayers', 21 May 1908, f. 61.
45. NMM BF, Ships Cover 218, 'Est'd Cost of Converting Certain Vessels to Minelayers', Flint Minute, 27 April 1909, f. 62.
46. TNA, ADM 1/7995, 'Information as to Minelayers', n.d.
47. George Ballard, 'Admiral of the Fleet, Sir Arthur Knyvet Wilson', *The Naval Review*, vol. XII (Private Publication, 1924), pp. 44–45.
48. NMM, Slade Papers, MRF/39/2, Slade Diary, 8 January, 2 and 22 June 1908.
49. For a detailed discussion of these war orders including their veracity see Grimes, *Strategy and War Planning*, pp. 115–126; Richard Dunley, *The Offensive Mining Service: Mine Warfare and Strategic Development in the Royal Navy 1900–1914* (Unpublished PhD thesis, University of London, 2013), pp. 189–192.
50. TNA, ADM 116/1043B, box 2, 'War Plan: Germany Enclosure to A. L. 1 July 1908 Sent to CinC Channel Fleet', f. 135.
51. NMM, MRF/39/2, Slade Diary, 22 February, 19 November 1908.
52. For detailed discussion of these documents see David Morgan-Owen, '"History is a Record of Exploded Ideas": Sir John Fisher and Home Defence, 1904–10', *The International History Review*, vol. 36, no. 3 (2014), 565–568; Dunley, *Offensive Mining Service*, pp. 192–203.
53. NMRN, Crease Papers, Mss 253/84/3, 'Copies of War Orders Issued to Captains of Minelayers Apollo, Andromache and Thetis', 'War Plan GU: War Orders for the Commander-in-Chief of the Home Fleet', n.d.
54. NMRN, Crease Papers, Mss 253/84/3, 'Permanent Auxiliaries', 'War Plan GU: War Orders for the Commander-in-Chief of the Home Fleet', n.d.
55. NMRN, Crease Papers, Mss 253/84/3, 'Mine Carrier Ships', 'War Plan GU: War Orders for the Commander-in-Chief of the Home Fleet', n.d.
56. TNA, MT 23/234, Chatterton to Colville, 8 July 1908.
57. TNA, MT 23/234, Unaddressed Chatterton Letter, 3 April 1909.
58. TNA, MT 23/234, Admiralty to CinC Portsmouth, 13 August 1909.
59. TNA, MT 23/234, Chatterton Report, 24 August 1909.
60. TNA, MT 23/234, Chevallier Minute, 6 November 1909.
61. TNA, MT 23/234, King-Hall Minute, 12 November 1909.
62. TNA, ADM 12/1467, Cut 59.8, Supply of Mines to Minelayers, n.d., 1909.
63. TNA, MT 23/234, King-Hall Minute, 11 February 1910.
64. Lambert, *Planning Armageddon*, pp. 28–29.
65. TNA, ADM 116/940B, Inglefield to Baddeley, 19 October 1909.

66. NMM, Slade Papers, MRF/39/2, Slade Diary, 8 January 1908.
67. Courtauld Book Library [CBL], Lee Papers, CI/Lee/6/1, Battenberg to Lee, 20 January 1907 (Quoted) and 11 April 1907.
68. TNA, ADM 116/942, Beresford to Admiralty, 11 April 1908.
69. TNA, ADM 116/942, Admiralty to CinC Channel Fleet, 16 April 1908.
70. NMM, Slade Papers, MRF/39/2, Slade Diary, 24 April 1908.
71. TNA, ADM 116/1090, 'Fleet Exercises', July 1908.
72. TNA, ADM 116/1090, Admiralty to CinC Channel Fleet (Draft), n.d. (15 ?) June 1908.
73. TNA, ADM 116/1090, Admiralty to CinC Channel Fleet (Draft), 6 June 1908.
74. TNA, ADM 116/1090, Slade Minute, 26 June 1908, 'Special Mining Umpire'.
75. NMM, Slade Papers, MRF/39/2, Slade Diary, 18, 23 July 1908.
76. NMM, Noel Papers, NOE/11/B, 'Memorandum on Fleet Exercises in the North Sea July 1908', n.d.
77. TNA, ADM 1/7994, Adm to Bridgeman (Draft), 1 August 1908.
78. NMM, De Chair Papers, DEC/2/5, De Chair Draft Memoir, pp. 62–66.
79. TNA, ADM 1/7995, 'Report on Mining', 16 November 1908.
80. The same characteristics had led to the initial selection of cross-Channel steamers for conversion into minelayers, and would later become embodied in HMS *Abdiel*.
81. TNA, ADM 1/7995, 'Report on Mining', 16 November 1908.
82. TNA, ADM 1/7995, 'Progress in Mine-Sweeping', 3 December 1909.
83. TNA, ADM 116/1090, Admiralty to CinC Channel Fleet (Draft), 6 June 1908.
84. BL, Balfour Papers, Add Ms 49710, 'Automatic Dropping Mines of Ocean Use, both for Offensive and Defensive Purposes', n.d., ff. 1–2.
85. TNA, ADM 1/7995, 'Report on Mining', 16 November 1908.
86. TNA, ADM 12/1467, Cut 59.8, 'Use of Mines Offensively in Fleet Actions', n.d., 1909.
87. TNA, ADM 12/1479, Cut 59.8, 'Offensive Mine Service', 25 January 1910.
88. TNA, MT 23/259, 'Fleet Auxiliaries'.

CHAPTER 9

Strategic Flux and Technical Failure

The 1907 Hague Conference devoted considerable attention to the question of the legality of the use of mines. Following long and, at times, acrimonious, discussions a convention was drawn up and eventually signed, albeit with certain reservations, by the major powers. This did not, however, represent an end to the issue. The delegates, acknowledging that there was no unanimity on the mining question, agreed in Article 12 to reopen the issue at the next conference. This naturally gave scope for a wider public debate, initially around the terms agreed in 1907, and then looking forward to how these could be built upon at a future conference.

In 1908 Rear-Admiral Charles Stockton, former President of the US Naval War College and delegate at the London Naval Conference, penned an article on the mining question for the *American Journal of International Law*. Stockton, in contrast to the initial reaction in Britain, took a rather sanguine view on the mining convention signed at The Hague. He noted that 'the rules ... adopted do not go as far as the United States and many other powers, including Great Britain, desired', but did not necessarily view this as a failure. His inclusion of the United States in this statement would certainly have raised a few eyebrows in London, where the American support for Germany in resisting tighter restrictions on mining was seen as one of the greatest surprises and failures of the 1907 conference. Despite this, Stockton concluded that the convention was 'something where nothing before existed, and at least a

© The Author(s) 2018   193
R. Dunley, *Britain and the Mine, 1900–1915*,
https://doi.org/10.1007/978-3-319-72820-9_9

milestone on the way to a more complete correction to the evils with which it deals'.[1]

Stockton's views were not shared across the international law community. In the late summer of 1908 the Institut de Droit International held, in Florence, its first biennial meeting following the Hague Conference. The Institut had, at its previous meeting in Ghent, adopted a stringent set of proposals to restrict the use of mines. Following the failure of the Hague Conference to agree anything approaching the proposals suggested by the Institut, the issue arose again. Edouard Rolin, who had replaced Michel Kebedgy as the rapporteur on the subject, firstly proposed a new text of the resolution adopted at Ghent, amending it to include the agreements reached, and language used at The Hague.[2] He then went on to suggest that the Institut had a number of options, ranging from dropping the subject altogether through to initiating a complete new examination. The Institut, following some discussion around the question of territorial waters, approved Rolin's new text whilst acknowledging the need for further debate.[3]

Two years later at Paris Rolin reported on the work of a commission set up to study the question further. This went back to first principles, noting the tendency of contemporary international law to limit the rights of belligerents in order to protect those of neutrals and non-combatants. Rolin questioned this tendency, reaffirming the rights of states to engage in conflict, but with regard to mining added that 'the non-belligerents also have their rights, essential rights, among which are the security of commerce and peaceful navigation'.[4] It was this that informed the commission's work and the proposals it presented to the Institut in 1910. By far the most important restriction which the Institut had adopted at Ghent in 1906 had been the banning of the use of mines, moored or otherwise, in international waters. British attempts to get similar agreements at the Hague Conference had failed, but the commission still saw this as essential. It declared that the 'modern principles of international law require that the peaceful use of the sea remains free for all nations. We are therefore convinced that the Institut will maintain the absolute prohibition [of mining] in the open sea'.[5] The commission put forward eight articles for discussion at the Institut, of which the first, restricting the use of mines in international waters, was by far the most important. At the meeting of the Institut in Paris there was a detailed discussion lasting over several days on both the principles and the technical details of the question. In particular there was a long debate over whether controlled mines needed to be restricted in the same way as independent mines, something that eventually led to a reservation being inserted on this point. The disagreement meant that the Institut ran out of time to discuss and vote on the articles in its 1910 meeting and the final votes were held over to the next meeting.[6] Rolin's report to the Madrid gathering in 1911 introduced the final articles to be voted on. In its preamble it set out clearly what had previously taken place at Paris, and why the Institut had adopted the positions it had. The discussion in 1910 had highlighted where the Institut fundamentally disagreed with the principles behind the decisions taken at The Hague. It argued that 'the sacred interests of neutrals and the interest of the whole of humanity' dictated that mining in the high seas be banned. As Rolin stated, the 'momentary interest of the belligerents could not legitimize acts that are threatening for the security of world trade and who knows for the safety of their own trade once the war is over'.[7] This prioritisation of the rights of neutrals over those of belligerents goes to the heart of the debate that had been taking place around mining for the previous seven years. The decision of the Institut to focus on neutral and non-belligerent rights is in many respects unsurprising considering that the organisation could look at questions from a more abstract point of view, free from the political and military questions that dominated the views of state governments. One should not, however, forget that the organisation included many of the most influential international jurists, including leading British figures. The 1910 meeting, which had reached these conclusions, was chaired by Erskine Holland, and Lord Reay, former British Plenipotentiary at the Hague Conference, spoke regularly. The views of such individuals carried considerable weight not only in the British press and public opinion, but also with policymakers. Thus the continued resistance of the Institut to accept the limited agreement on mining reached at The Hague should not be seen merely as an academic stand taken by an organisation out of touch with the realities of the situation.

Mining was not the only issue which came to the attention of the Institut in the wake of the Hague Conference. Following the limited success achieved at The Hague and the resultant London Naval Conference in establishing a clear set of laws of war at sea, the Institut decided to investigate the matter fully before the Third Peace Conference, scheduled for 1915. In 1910 it appointed a small committee to investigate the question. Issues were considered briefly in 1911 and Paul Fauchille was appointed to lead a small group to draft a manual of naval warfare analogous to the

Oxford Manual of Land Warfare. It was hoped that this would then form the starting point for state-level discussions at the next Hague Conference.[8] The issues were briefly discussed in Christiania in 1912 but virtually the entire 1913 session, held once again at Oxford, was devoted to a full discussion of the draft manual. Five articles in the manual dealt with mining, and were effectively taken directly from the articles agreed in Paris and Madrid. There was some debate around the specifics of the minor articles, but the key article, which stated that 'it is forbidden to lay automatic contact mines, anchored or not, in the open sea', was passed without discussion.[9] The agreement of the *Oxford Manual of Naval War* by the Institut in 1913 was seen as a major step forward. The organisation's continued hard line on the mining question ensured that the debate over the legality of using mines on the high seas was not going away, and would naturally arise again at any future conference discussing the laws of naval warfare.

Considering the importance of the subjects under discussion and the calibre of the figures involved it is unsurprising that British policymakers paid close attention to the activities of the Institut. Following the Christiania meeting in 1912 the British Minister, Mansfeldt Findlay, sent back a detailed despatch on the activities of the conference. He adopted a somewhat irreverent tone, remarking on the 'display of a good deal of rather objectless eloquence' and he concluded by saying that the 'constant succession of dinners' and presence of so many 'pleasure bent' ladies 'must go far not only to impair the work of the meeting of the Institut but also the digestions of its distinguished members'. Despite this Findlay still gave a full account of the meeting and his despatch was seen by Sir Eyre Crowe, Assistant Under-Secretary, Cecil Hurst, Assistant Legal Advisor, and the Foreign Secretary, Sir Edward Grey.[10] The development of the *Oxford Manual of Naval War* also received direct attention from decision-makers in Whitehall. In early 1914 the Foreign Office was given a copy of the final text by Professor Oppenheim, and it had it printed. The Manual had clearly been the subject of discussions between Cecil Hurst and Sir Graham Greene, the influential Admiralty Secretary, and a dozen copies of the document were sent to the Admiralty.[11] Unfortunately despite the obvious interest no record of discussions can be found in the surviving Admiralty archives. This makes it very difficult to assess how seriously the navy took the manual, or how it fitted into their debates on naval law.

The discussion of the Institut's work was largely framed in the context of preparations for the Third Hague Peace Conference, which was due to take place in 1915. The attention of the British government was first directed to the issue in 1912, when Sir Eyre Crowe produced a memorandum outlining potential issues that might be raised and discussing the process for investigating these questions. Crowe noted that the question of the laws and usages of naval war was certain to feature prominently and the issues discussed by the Institut were likely to be raised by other powers at the conference.[12] The Foreign Office looked to establish a number of high-power committees to investigate fully each of the broad areas of discussion. These attempts were largely frustrated by what Crowe described as 'the succession of grave political events which has occupied HMG for several years past', but it is clear that the government took the issue very seriously.[13] This was despite a certain scepticism, particularly apparent on the part of Crowe, towards the whole process. He bemoaned that '(i)t may be taken for certain that a great effort will be made on the part of the continental Powers to curtail in every possible way the freedom of belligerents in a naval war'.[14] Elsewhere he declared that '(i)n fact the whole conference is likely to be more gratifying to the more nebulous pacifists than profitable to the participating governments'.[15] In spring 1914 the Foreign Office drew up a memorandum for the Cabinet on the proposed arrangements for the conference, once again highlighting the work of the Institut and suggesting that 'their deliberations form a valuable indication of what other countries may be expected to bring forward'. In particular they noted that 'the whole subject of the Laws of War at Sea has gained prominence from the work of the Institute of International Law at their meeting at Oxford last year'.[16] The events of summer 1914 meant that none of the detailed discussion of British policy for the conference took place. It is, however, clear that the government expected, in part because of the work of the Institut, that questions of the laws of naval warfare would dominate discussions and among these there would be further debates on the question of mining. The continued interest in mining throughout this period highlights the perceived importance of the subject to both policymakers and the informed public more generally. The British government may have been heartened to see that there remained a strong movement in support of the tighter restrictions on mining which they had proposed at the Hague Conference in 1907, but there is little sign that they expected a radical change in the positions adopted by the other powers. Thus it appeared that mining was going to remain a difficult and contested issue in international law for some time to come.

I

The legal uncertainties surrounding mining were in many respects mirrored by developments in strategy. In January 1910 Sir John Fisher was replaced as First Sea Lord by Sir Arthur Wilson. Within traditional historiography this has been viewed as a major turning point, with Wilson reverting to a strategy of close blockade in the event of war with Germany.[17] Recent scholarship has demonstrated that Fisher had not abandoned close blockade in the way previously assumed, and so the shift in strategy was in fact far less marked.[18] Despite this, there were clear developments in policy which took place towards the end of 1910, the most important of which was the abandonment of the idea of establishing advanced bases for destroyers and light craft on the German coast.[19]

In January 1911, as a result of this shift in policy Admiral Sir William May, Commander in Chief, Home Fleet drafted new orders for his Commodore (T), Edward Charlton. These reaffirmed a commitment to a close blockade strategy despite the difficulties produced by a lack of advanced bases. They went on to say that '(t)he three minelayers, *Apollo, Andromache* and *Thetis* ... are also assigned for operations on the German coast and may be employed under the Commodore (T).' Unfortunately it stated that '(n)o detailed instructions can be laid down beforehand for the employment of the minelayers or submarines', which leaves us with little clarity about exactly what they were intended to do.[20] Some indication of the expected role of mining in such a close blockade strategy can be gleaned from the *Cruiser Manual* Part II produced by the Admiralty later in 1911. This devoted considerable attention to the impact of both mining and submarines on blockade strategy. The document presented a very traditional view on the utility of mines declaring that 'as we hope to be the strongest sea power in any probable war, it seems likely that the use of mines by us will be very limited, for it is of paramount importance that the movements of our own ships should be as free as possible'. Despite this, it was felt likely that mines would be of use in closing certain channels, in mining the entrances to enemy harbours when their fleet was at sea, and most intriguingly 'off an enemy's defended ports, to completely stop his water borne commerce'.[21] This document ably sums up the navy's pragmatic acknowledgement of the potential of mining to assist with a number of strategic problems tempered by a continued scepticism over the broader concept of the weapon.

9 STRATEGIC FLUX AND TECHNICAL FAILURE   199

This dichotomy played out in planning with regular references to the use of mining, especially in a blockade context, but a continued unwillingness to specify precise roles for this.

We can glean some further information on the potential uses of mines from a memorandum entitled 'Remarks on Offensive Minelaying' which appears to have been written by Algernon Heneage, Captain in Charge of Minelayers in October 1910. Unfortunately the official copy of this memorandum no long exists and the only version remaining is one contained in the papers of Tristan Dannreuther, commander of one of the minelayers. This means that we have no official reaction to Heneage's remarks, but they do shed some light on the expectations of the mining service about its potential role. The memorandum begins in much the same way as the *Cruiser Manual*, stating that:

> (c)onsidering this subject from the point of view of the power that is strongest at sea, and also the one that must live by sea communication and therefore must keep harbours open continuously and do the utmost to keep the sea open to her sea-borne trade it appears that the use of mines is restricted to a definite number of objectives.[22]

The author then goes on to list five potential strategic and tactical uses for mines within the Royal Navy. The first of these involved laying mines off the enemy's coast 'to hamper the enemy's strategy to the extent of dissuading him from making feints of putting to sea with the object of causing panic in this country.' The second was simply the closing of a channel not being used by the British fleet, or trade. The third potential was the laying of a minefield behind an enemy fleet which was known to be at sea, whilst the fourth was mining the expected path of an opposing fleet in a fleet action. The final scenario involved 'blocking the exit to the enemy's harbour in order to preclude the possibility of interruption of some operations that we maybe undertaking, such as the seizing of a base on the enemy's coast.'[23]

Scenario two is the least interesting; it fits a very traditional pattern of using mines in local waters to deny the enemy the potential of exploiting them, particularly in relation to protecting anchorages. It was a common policy, dating back to the 1870s, to seek to close off all except the major entrances to a protected harbour to limit the options available to an enemy. Scenarios three and four were both tactical in nature and involved the integration of mining into a fleet action context. Options one and five by contrast were undeniably strategic in their scope and aims. Scenario one sought to use mines to protect British interests and was broadly defensive, in its intentions if not its execution. The final case was an offensive strategy from the outset and saw mines as a crucial aspect in British operations on the German coast.

Heneage then went on to examine the feasibility of undertaking each of these courses of action at that time. Clearly the blocking of a channel as set out in case two could be achieved with comparative ease. In relation to the use of mines in fleet actions, the report argued that the minelayers were, realistically, too slow to be involved in the movements of modern fleets. Furthermore it raised questions as to the desirability of laying mines broadcast in open waters, especially when their precise location may be difficult to establish. It goes on, however, to say that the possibility of mining the retreat of an enemy's fleet 'seems one of the most important methods for us to practice.' Case one, trying to restrict the enemy's movements through large-scale use of mines did not appear to the author to present any major problems; however he did emphasise the importance of the inshore squadron in protecting the minelayers and the need to practice with them. Intriguingly the report did not link cases one and five, although their aims, of preventing the enemy from exiting his harbours and thereby interfering in British use of the sea, were the same. Instead it stated that, in the method of execution at least, case five was identical to the steps required to mine the retreat of the enemy's fleet.[24]

This report is the only known prewar example of a mining officer outlining the potential uses of mines in this broad strategic and tactical manner. As such it offers an interesting insight into how the mining service saw itself and gives an indication of the roles it expected to play in wartime. In this regard it enables us to speculate, with some degree of confidence, on the types of work the mining service would have carried out under the war plans produced by Sir Arthur Wilson's Admiralty. The interest in tactical uses of mines should come as no surprise, especially following the increasing integration of the mining service with the fleet. The two strategic scenarios are, however, more interesting, in part because of what they say about the broader strategic picture. The use of mines to protect against German excursions was a concept which, as we will see, came to prominence following the abandonment of the close blockade in 1912 and would remain a key theme in naval thinking throughout the war years. That this was being considered in October

1910 perhaps suggests that faith in the close blockade as the sole solution for sealing in the German fleet came under challenge earlier than is commonly acknowledged. Case five by contrast appears to fit far more easily into the traditional interpretation of Wilson's strategy, with a focus on offensive operations on the German coast to seize an advanced base. It is noteworthy for this study that mining was still perceived to be a potentially important part of such a strategy; the concept suggested by Heneage looks in many respects similar to ideas suggested by Wilson in 1905 and 1906.

In December 1911 the Admiralty further amended the war orders, issuing a document entitled 'Notes on Operations in the North Sea'. No copy of this document appears to have survived, but in January 1912 the new Commander-in-Chief, Home Fleet, Vice-Admiral Sir George Callaghan penned a memorandum outlining his reservations. Much of this dealt with the practicalities of mounting a close blockade. Once again it appears that mining was included in the new orders, but with little in the way of specifics about exactly what the Admiralty's intentions were. Callaghan noted in his conclusion that he did not understand certain aspects of the plans, one of which was 'the use of mines at the mouths of the German rivers.' What the purpose of such operations would have been is as much a mystery to us as it was to Callaghan.[25]

The situation was further confused when, in April 1912, the Admiralty abandoned close blockade, the principle that had been running through planning for decades. There had been a growing movement of opinion among senior officers, not least Callaghan, highlighting the risks of close blockade in modern warfare, but the decision to abandon the strategy was still a risky one and appears to have been made very suddenly.[26] Within wider naval policy the close blockade served two crucial roles; it acted as an observational screen which would provide warning of any excursion by German warships and it ensured an effective legal blockade which would be the basis of the economic warfare strategy. Neither of these roles could be easily abandoned and the Admiralty spent much of the following years attempting to find suitable replacements.

The close blockade was replaced by a set of war orders issued in April 1912 which have become known to historians as the intermediate blockade. The idea was to replace the close blockade with five cruiser squadrons and 4 flotillas 'stationed from Stavanger [Norway] to the Hook of Holland'. These vessels would intercept any ships entering or leaving the German ports, whilst the fleet could cruise safely in Scottish waters.[27] This plan was tested out in the 1912 manoeuvres and proved a disaster. The cordon did not do its job properly and proved highly vulnerable to concentrated enemy attacks. The proposals were promptly scrapped.[28] The situation was one of immense confusion. On 2 May Callaghan had withdrawn the war orders which had been issued to the minelayers, instructing them to mobilise and proceed to Sheerness and await the Commander-in-Chief's orders.[29] These had not been replaced by the end of December 1912, leaving the minelayers with no instructions in the event of war.[30] This was indicative of the broader problems facing naval planners. It was widely accepted that a close blockade was too risky, but none of the alternatives appeared to fit the service's strategic requirements.

One attempt to reconcile these multiple strategic problems came from George Ballard, who had recently returned to the Admiralty as Director of Operations Division (DOD) within the new War Staff. In September 1912 he produced a paper in which he tried to rectify some of the flaws in the intermediate blockade strategy that had been highlighted by the recent manoeuvres. Ballard outlined the basic strategic position, discussing the option of a close blockade. On this issue he supported the new consensus, arguing that the threat from torpedo craft and mines combined with logistical and coaling problems was insurmountable. He concluded that 'no plan of close blockade on a large scale is considered worthy of attention … until suitable submarines have been built in sufficient numbers for the purpose'. Interestingly Ballard did not condemn the principles behind the intermediate blockade in anything like the same terms; indeed he argued that it was the only effective way of defending British interests. According to his report, if the close blockade were abandoned then an observation force was required in the North Sea to provide the intelligence necessary to prevent the Germans from operating at will. Ballard saw the failure of the intermediate blockade in the recent manoeuvres in tactical as opposed to strategic terms, and as such he tried to resolve these problems. On a basic level he noted that the concentrated strength of the watching force varied in inverse proportion to the length of the line being watched. There were, therefore, two options; either to increase the number of vessels in the cordon, which was difficult economically, or shorten the length of the line being watched. Clearly Ballard could not reduce the geographical distance between the Norwegian and Dutch coasts. It therefore appeared that the only option was shifting the observation line closer to the German coast, negating the point of abandoning the close blockade:

unless artificial restrictions of any kind can be devised which will interfere with the enemy's freedom of movement when at sea. Mines offer the only known method of effecting [*sic*] this last object and the question of resorting to mining on a wholesale scale is at least worthy of close attention as a possible solution of an otherwise difficult problem.[31]

Ballard noted that there were no restrictions under international law on placing mines in open waters, and the Germans could not object to the British taking advantage of the position the Germans took at The Hague. He noted that the navy had a 'large and increasing stock of mines in store (more than 9,000)' which represented 'an accumulation of available war material for which no definite function has hitherto been assigned'.[32] Thus mining was potentially a cheap solution for a difficult problem. It is interesting to note that Ballard chose not to mention his earlier involvement in similar discussions around mining, including those in which the present stock of mines were ordered. His precise motives for remaining quiet are unclear.

With reference to the mines the DOD noted that the stock was sufficient to 'run a line of nearly 160 miles in length with the mines 100 feet apart.' Unfortunately due to the loss of the chart attached to this memorandum we do not know the precise line proposed, but it appears that it ran north or north-east from the coast of Holland, leaving only the gap between the end of the line and the Norwegian coast open. Ballard concluded that the laying of the mines 'without the knowledge of the enemy, might prove an effectual barrier to his movements in the direction in which they lay, by causing the loss of the first ship that struck it and establishing a strong moral effect.' This having been achieved it would 'reduce the length of line to be watched by the observing force by nearly 2/3rds'. Ballard also saw additional benefits in slowing any potential invasion force by ensuring they were preceded by minesweepers, and in possibly sinking German submarines looking to patrol off the British coast. Finally he stated that:

> the mines would probably provide a useful auxiliary to our commercial blockade. This blockade can never be more than partially effective as long as neutrals have a method of evading it by showing a Dutch port as their destination on their papers and sailing again thence for a German port. But if a steamer or two on the way from Rotterdam to Hamburg were blown up off the Texel, the traffic to German ports would almost certainly cease at once.[33]

This remark is intriguing in a number of ways. Firstly it suggests that one of the navy's foremost planners believed that the intermediate blockade being discussed would be viewed as an effective legal blockade, something that appears far from certain. As will be explored in more detail later, if the blockade was not deemed effective then neutral vessels could legally sail past the British navy into German ports, so long as they were not carrying contraband, and thus would not have needed to pretend to be destined for Holland. Secondly it once again reinforces the point that, despite its public protests over the possibility of using mines against neutral commerce, behind closed doors the Royal Navy was still considering doing just that.

Ballard did foresee certain problems with his scheme; firstly, the question of the Germans sweeping the mines. He did not see this as a major issue, as he concluded that it would take weeks for the Germans to clear the line completely and if the mines merely forced the German fleet to be led by minesweepers they would be fulfilling their task by considerably slowing their progress. Ballard does not appear to address the question as to how the British would know of German actions in this regard if, as he proposed, the scouting forces were solely focused in the one third of the observation line which was left unmined. More seriously he does not appear to have considered that after discovering the line the Germans could sweep a small section of it, and use this as a secret entrance through which the British would be unwilling to follow them. Admittedly this would have been far more challenging practically than in theory, as in the open sea without any markers it would have been very difficult for the Germans to know precisely where the swept channel was. Ballard did see certain practical difficulties with his proposal, the largest being the limitations of the minelayers. He calculated that the current minelayers would require fifteen separate trips to reload, and the whole process would take a month. Quite where these figures come from is not apparent, but it was obvious that the process would be slow. The solution Ballard proposed was converting more old cruisers, noting that 'in any case the present stock of mines is disproportionately large to the number of vessels fitted to lay them.'[34]

In the conclusion to his report Ballard admitted that his idea was not perfectly worked out, but suggested that it offered such advantages that the subject was 'worthy of the urgent attention of the Board'. Unfortunately we do not have detailed records of what happened to the report, or the views of other members of the Admiralty. What is clear is that the Board rejected the idea. The war orders which were sent to Callaghan at the end of 1912 saw a rejection of the entire concept of intermediate blockade, and an acceptance of the distant blockade strategy.[35]

It is very difficult to tell the extent to which Ballard's proposals were considered and whether they were looked at on their own merits. It is entirely feasible that the experiences from the manoeuvres had so damaged the concept of an intermediate blockade that the entire idea was rejected outright. This having been said, the plan had obvious flaws and, in truth, few real merits. As Ballard had noted in the 1907 War Plans, mines did not pose an impermeable barrier; instead they served to inflict loss on and slow the progress of an enemy, so limiting his ability to use the sea. It is very apparent that Ballard's desire to repackage mines and push them into a role they did not fit was indicative of the strategic problems facing the Admiralty at this time.

In 1924 George Ballard wrote a piece in the *Naval Review* on the prewar Naval War Staff. In it he mentioned that a plan had been 'drawn up for mining the Heligoland Bight and Straits of Dover, not dissimilar in its main features from the scheme actually adopted in the late stage of the war'; in this he was referring to the Northern Barrage. He stated that the scheme received no support from senior officers; however Winston Churchill, the First Lord of the Admiralty was initially interested. His interest supposedly waned upon hearing of the cost of the 50,000 mines required.[36] Arthur Marder in *From the Dreadnought to Scapa Flow* also mentions such a scheme. Marder typically does not provide a reference, but his wording suggests that Ballard's *Naval Review* piece might well have been the source.[37] It seems likely that Ballard was referring to his 1912 mining plan, or some evolution thereof, when writing this article twelve years later. No documentary evidence can be found to support Ballard's 1924 statements regarding mining and his remarks in the same piece on minesweeping are fundamentally incorrect. Thus it appears probable that Ballard was either misremembering events, or was attempting to put a favourable sheen on his time at the War Staff by connecting it to the Northern Barrage, a scheme many believed should have been adopted much earlier in the war. Either way associations made by modern historians between Ballard's 1912 mining proposals and the Northern Barrage should be treated with some scepticism.[38] The 1912 plans were a very specific proposal designed to rescue the intermediate blockade concept. Without considerably more thought and a massive increase in resources they were always going to prove unworkable. Taken at face value Ballard's 1924 claims suggest that such issues were worked through and costed; there is, however, no contemporary evidence to support this.

The decision taken at the end of 1912 not to explore options such as those put forward by Ballard to modify the intermediate blockade, and instead to adopt what has become known as the distant blockade, resolved a number of major tactical issues. The removal of British vessels from being regularly stationed off the German coast limited the risk of torpedo or mine attack, whilst the concentration of forces meant that the likelihood of units being destroyed piecemeal was reduced. These benefits came at a cost in terms of strategy. The removal of British forces from the southern North Sea meant that the navy needed to find a new way to control the movements of both German warships and neutral merchantmen. The problems regarding the economic warfare strategy were particularly difficult. The navy had known for a number of years that they would struggle to intercept goods flowing into neutral ports such as Rotterdam even if their intended final destination was Germany. This problem was in part mitigated by the knowledge that, through the use of blockade, the navy could restrict the importation of all goods into the major German North Sea harbours. The abandoning of the close blockade undermined this second plank of British economic warfare strategy. Under international law, unless an effective blockade was declared, neutral ships could import non-contraband goods into German harbours in wartime. To make matters worse Britain had, at both the Hague and London Naval conferences, pushed for as tight a restriction on the definition of contraband as possible. Put together this severely undermined Britain's ability to exert economic pressure on Germany.[39]

The question of how Britain could maximise the impact of its economic warfare strategy was already under discussion when the decision was taken to shift to a distant blockade. In January 1911 the Prime Minister, Herbert Asquith, had set up a sub-committee of the CID, commonly referred to as the Trading with the Enemy Committee, under Lord Desart to investigate the issues. The committee devoted considerable attention to the question of imports through neutral ports. Whilst it concluded that this was 'a matter of the utmost importance in connection with the questions now under consideration', it was deemed 'not within the functions of the sub-committee to deal with these questions'.[40] The full CID came to discuss the sub-committee's report in December 1912 and the subject of trade through neutral ports was the central issue. Intriguingly, despite the fact that the Admiralty were, at the time of the CID meeting, drafting new war orders based on the distant blockade, this was not divulged to the committee. As such they did not address the even more pressing question of trade in neutral bottoms through German ports.

The Chancellor, David Lloyd George, was the first to speak up on the question of neutral ports and, considering that this account comes from the sanitised official minutes, it is clear that all members spoke their mind on the subject. Lloyd George declared that:

> the geographical position of the Netherlands and Belgium made their attitude in a war between the British Empire in alliance with France and Russia against the Triple Alliance one of immense importance. If they were neutral and accorded full rights of neutrals, we should be unable to bring any effective economic pressure upon Germany. It was essential that we should be able to do so.[41]

Asquith raised the obvious legal questions about whether it would be acceptable to treat these countries as belligerents despite their declared neutrality. The Chancellor responded 'this country could not afford to wait and see what those countries would do. The question must be agreed and settled now ... these measures were essential to our success in war.' These debates mainly focused on Holland, as it was commonly accepted that in any war with France, Germany would be forced to breach Belgian neutrality. Churchill largely agreed with Lloyd George but thought that the problem had been overstated. He suggested that the increased risk faced by neutrals trading in the North Sea in time of war would sufficiently restrict the flow of goods, and raise prices to such an extent that the blockade would still remain effective. It is not clear to what extent he was being partisan and defending what was now the navy's primary war strategy or whether he did believe the risk had been overplayed. Churchill did, however, let on that the Admiralty did not in the event of war expect either Holland or Belgium to remain neutral, which would of course eliminate the problem.[42] Churchill's final comment to the CID meeting on 6 December was suitably blunt. He declared with regard to Holland and Belgium that 'their neutrality was out of the question. They must either be friends or foes.'[43]

From January 1912 George Ballard had, courtesy of his position as DOD, sat on the with the Enemy sub-committee. He had, from his previous stints at the Admiralty, a very good idea of the challenges surrounding naval strategy, and became a regular contributor in the committee's discussions. On 9 February, during the course of discussions on German exports, the issue of neutral ports in Holland and Belgium was raised. Ballard remarked that:

> he anticipated that the naval operations in the North Sea might not unlikely render peaceful navigation east of the Straits of Dover dangerous and cause insurance premiums to and from ports in these countries to rise very high.[44]

From here it is only a very small step to go from expecting that naval operations would make the North Sea dangerous to neutrals, to taking steps to make sure that it would be. At some stage following the CID meeting on 6 December 1912 Ballard had a discussion with Battenberg, newly appointed as First Sea Lord, on the issues of both trade through neutral ports and trade in neutral bottoms to Germany. On 6 February he penned a memorandum outlining his proposal.[45] Ballard began by stating why:

> the actual effect of our naval pressure on Germany in war will ... be greatly minimized by neutral action. We may drive the German mercantile flag off the seas but neutral shipping will go far towards filling the vacancy and the trade which is our real objective will only suffer such diminution as arises from the lesser carrying capacities of neutral mercantile marines and the greater freightage brought about by reduced competition. Our offensive grip will be feeble at best.[46]

The only way Ballard saw 'to overcome this unsatisfactory state of affairs' was by 'resorting to the use of mines.' What he proposed was remarkable; he suggested laying two small minefields, one across the Straits of Dover just east of Calais (M1), and the other off the Dutch coast near Terschelling (M2). Neither minefield exceeded 14 miles in length and they were designed so that the existing 7 minelayers could lay each in one night with no need to reload.[47] Clearly these small minefields would only have a limited effect on shipping; however Ballard proposed to issue a proclamation at the same time as laying the fields. This was to state that 'a certain specified area will contain mines and that vessels entering into it do so at their own risk.' As Ballard commented:

> such a notice will probably provide a very effective check upon traffic through the proclaimed area, whether the mines were actually laid or otherwise, and as the stoppage of trade is the main purpose in view, the proclaimed area might, with advantage to our plans, be much more extensive than the area actually mined.

The area proposed to be declared as dangerous extended all the way from the Straits of Dover to the west coast of Denmark, encompassing all of the Belgian, Dutch and German coastlines and most of the southern North Sea, excluding the British coast.[48] Ballard argued that 'the object of such a proclamation would be to produce a paralysing moral effect on trade in the eastern part of the North Sea, including the approaches to Dutch and Belgian ports.' He went on to suggest that it would be worth considering mining the Kattegat so as to stop all trade passing into or out of the Baltic, although this would only be possible if Russia was allied with Britain.

Ballard's mining proposal was immediately passed to H. B. Jackson, who was Chief of Staff (COS) in the War Staff. He supported the scheme and remarked that he did not think that 'the enemy would credit us with such an operation'.[49] Ironically the image of vehement opposition to all aspects of mining which the British had developed at The Hague would perhaps act as something of a smokescreen for such a campaign. Churchill agreed and suggested that the matter should be discussed at a conference.[50] Unsurprisingly, no record of any conference appears to have survived, but the results must have been positive. By April 1913 Ballard had drawn up detailed orders for the scheme, which were then submitted to the COS and First Sea Lord. The only officer outside of the Admiralty who was to be informed of the new plan was Callaghan. Sealed orders were to be sent to the Captain in Charge of Minelayers, which he was to open on receipt of a specific telegram from the Admiralty. All other ships were also to receive sealed instructions to be opened on the outbreak of war, which would inform them of the precise location of the mines. Ballard had also drafted a Notice to Mariners to inform the mercantile marine of the proclamation with regard to the southern North Sea.[51] Jackson and Battenberg approved these orders immediately. Due to difficulties regarding the wording of the Notice to

Mariners, the final proof was not approved until August.[52] In November the Hydrographer reported that 14,500 of the Notices to Mariners had been printed for issue in the event of war, together with copies of the sealed instructions for the fleet.[53] On 10 December the orders were issued to Callaghan and sealed orders sent to Thomas Bonham, Captain in Charge of Minelayers.[54] This represented the first time that direct operational orders had been given to the Captain in Charge of Minelayers and was thus an important step forward in the development of mining as an independent branch of the navy. Unfortunately such was the secrecy surrounding this whole mission, that no one had consulted an officer familiar with the mines regarding the operation. This was to have implications later on. At this point, however, it is important to note that a proposal to implement a mining policy immediately on the outbreak of war had been accepted and the orders issued. All that was required was a telegram from the Admiralty to the minelayers at Sheerness and the operation would have been undertaken.

A number of recent historians have examined these proposals in varying degrees of detail. Surprisingly none have understood the motives behind the policy and recognised that it was not only agreed, but the orders were issued and minelayers ready.[55] The claims that are made by all the historians who have looked at this subject, regarding the lack of resources and the absence of additional funding, entirely miss the point. As Ballard made clear in his original proposal the total number of mines to be laid in fields M1 and M2 was comparatively small, with the vast majority of the 10,000 in store being retained for other uses. Furthermore the fields were specifically designed around the limitations of the minelayers; they were neither large nor in dangerous locations. This policy was important, fully feasible and ready to be implemented immediately upon the outbreak of war with Germany.

One aspect of Ballard's proposals which has barely received a mention, either by his contemporary colleagues or by more recent historians, is that of their legality. This is particularly noteworthy, both as a reflection on the attitudes of senior naval officers, and in the light of the debates that would take place on the outbreak of war. It is worth emphasising that this scheme showed flagrant disregard for the principles regularly espoused by the British government on the mining question, and was technically in breach of the limited convention signed at The Hague. More to the point Ballard was well aware of both of these facts, and wrote openly about them. He remarked that Britain's attempts 'on behalf of neutral interests' to ban mining on the high seas had failed. He went on to point out that the actual convention 'imposes no restrictions whatever' on the use of mines 'except that they must not be used with the *sole* object of intercepting commercial navigation'. Ballard's emphasis on the word 'sole' is revealing. He suggested that his minefields might have some military value and therefore they did not 'violate in any way the terms of the Convention'. It seems unlikely even Ballard himself was persuaded by this argument, something confirmed by the following paragraph in which he suggested that, because the Germans resisted British attempts to restrict the use of mines at The Hague, 'they will only have themselves to thank'.[56] This was hardly likely to stand the scrutiny of an international lawyer, and entirely ignored the fact that the scheme would impact trade into neutral Dutch and Belgian ports, as well as German ones. Ballard's moral principles come out little better. He accepted that there was a possibility of causing a loss of life to non-combatants, but declared 'from a humanitarian point of view, the objections can be wholly met if a public proclamation is issued'. Responses to the use of mines in the Russo-Japanese War and later protests against German actions suggest that it is unlikely Britain would have acquiesced to any other power behaving in this high-handed way on the open seas. From both the legal and the moral perspective it is clear that the Admiralty was interested in what it could get away with, rather than abiding by either the letter or the spirit of the law. The Royal Navy may not have liked mines, but when it saw that they could be useful it was still willing to let military necessity override legal niceties.

A clear appreciation of the dubious legal position of this British policy sheds new light on the wider questions regarding attitudes towards international law. Isabel Hull briefly discusses this new British mining policy, but appears to have missed its significance. She ignores the fact that it demonstrated that the Royal Navy was willing to breach the only meaningful restriction on mining introduced by the 1907 Hague Conference, and instead focuses on the fact that many in Britain still viewed the weapon as barbaric.[57] By contrast she later condemns the German Foreign Office for concluding, at the end of 1914, that a general warning could meet the humanitarian and legal concerns around the loss of neutral and non-combatant lives in a mine and submarine blockade. In doing so she omits to note that the British reached the same conclusion in peacetime, and had even gone so far as to print the Notices to Mariners in preparation.[58] A clearer understanding of this policy highlights that the British were far more willing to bend or even break the restrictions of international law if they felt they could get away with it. In doing so it suggests that, in this area at least, the clear distinction drawn by Hull and others between the Allies, who were broadly law-abiding, and the Germans, who were driven by concepts of military necessity, are perhaps overplayed.

The adoption of Ballard's mining scheme in 1914 appears to have facilitated a more open-minded consideration of mining, and there are strong hints that the navy was intending to look again at the entire question that summer. In April the Admiralty Secretary sent out letters to the flag officers in home waters saying that a conference would be held at the end of the summer's review, which was taking place at Spithead. The officers were asked to put forward proposals for issues to be discussed.[59] When the programme outlining the questions for the conference was released point A1 was 'the use of moored mines in war—(a) Used Offensively off the enemy's coast (b) Used defensively off our own ports and war anchorages, to afford protection against hostile vessels, destroyers, submarines &c'. Unfortunately unlike many of the other topics listed it was not felt necessary for the Admiralty to provide a precis of the subject. We do, however, know that the topic was put forward for discussion by the Admiralty itself, suggesting that the issue was being seriously reconsidered.[60] Due to the lack of detail we cannot say who within the Admiralty was sponsoring this proposal. On the outbreak of war Churchill, Battenberg and Doveton Sturdee, the COS, all rejected the use of mines, so it is possible that this proposal came from a more junior officer.[61] The conference was scheduled for 24 and 25 July; however it was postponed at the last minute due to the European political crisis, and was, for obvious reasons, never rescheduled.[62] Precisely what would have been discussed is not clear, but it is intriguing that there was a renewed interest in using mines in a defensive manner, for the first time since the abolition of controlled mines in 1905.

III

The four and a half years from the retirement of Sir John Fisher as First Sea Lord in January 1910 to the outbreak of war were ones of flux in terms of the legal and strategic position of mining, but by mid-1914 there appeared to be potential for progress on both fronts. The same could not be said for the tactical and technical aspects of mining within the Royal Navy.

At the beginning of 1910 Algernon Heneage replaced Herbert Chatterton as Captain in Charge of Minelayers, and his command was an active and increasingly integrated part of the fleet. Mining had undergone an extraordinary renaissance since 1905, with a rapid expansion of both materiel and men. This expansion naturally created a need to practise with and evaluate the equipment and policies of the mining service. The first years of Heneage's command saw the continuation and expansion of the mining exercises carried out with units of the Home Fleet. These were important as they raised the profile of the mining service within the navy more broadly and they also offered useful practical experience. These were supplemented by regular practice within the mining service, which tended to be on a smaller scale and more technically focused.[63] This rapid progress did not suggest that the Admiralty's usual focus on economy had disappeared. Mining practice was carefully monitored and all mines, in common with torpedoes, had individual logbooks in which issues and repairs were recorded. Considerable time and effort was spent on recovering the mines after they had been laid. Tristan Dannreuther, Commander of *Intrepid* noted with satisfaction that in 1911 no mines had been lost and under half a dozen sinkers remained unrecovered.[64] Due to concerns about the recovery of mines no exercises took place in the three winter months, and night practice appears to have been limited. A characteristic exercise took place in October 1910 at the Firth of Dornoch with four minelayers and seven battleships from the Home Fleet. Over the course of three days the minelayers laid 115 mines just outside the entrance of the Firth. The battle fleet then passed over the minefield, both with and without accompanying minesweepers, and conclusions were drawn as to the effectiveness of the mines, and the sweepers.[65] One of the principle difficulties associated with any mining exercise was ascertaining whether a mine had fired. Naturally, in exercises the mine would not contain a charge, and the process of recovering the mine would, in itself, invariably fire the pistol, making it impossible to tell whether the mine fired when struck, or merely when recovered. The answer to this problem came in the form of the reintroduction of blowing charges, a small fitting placed on the outside of the mine, but connected to the pistol, and designed to release and then smoke when the mine was fired.[66] Similar devices were first used in the late 1870s with electro-contact mines, for the same purpose. The October exercises were the first in which these devices were used and it was reported that they worked well, and proved a useful tool in ascertaining when the mines had been struck.[67]

The development of blowing charges for independent mines allowed the mining service to monitor when mine pistols fired far more successfully than previously. These were used for the first time on a large scale in the October 1910 exercises and the results were not entirely satisfactory. Whilst it was found that the Quicke-Scarff pistol, more generally referred to as the service pistol, would fire if struck by a ship, it also had a serious defect. It was found that 'the pistol may fire in a heavy seaway if the mine is laid close to the surface'. In addition it was found that mines would frequently break adrift in similar conditions, potentially posing an additional hazard. Captain Heneage saw the problem of premature firing as one which could be resolved through improving the hydrostatic valve on the mine. The pistol was designed so it would only fire if the mine was below a certain depth, something that relied upon a hydrostatic valve. Clearly this system was not working in the difficult conditions of a heavy seaway, and Heneage believed this could be improved. In the meantime, and considering the other issues relating to the mines breaking free, he recommended that mines 'should not be laid at least higher than ten feet L.W.O.S. [Low-Water Ordinary Springs], unless purposely laid against smaller craft when the risk of this [premature explosion] and breaking adrift must be taken.'[68] This stipulation would not have been a major problem had the British been hoping to deploy their mines mainly in the Baltic or Mediterranean, where there was a very limited tidal range. The coastal regions of the southern North Sea and English Channel, however, have very large tidal ranges, and as such mines so laid would have been too deep to strike many craft for the majority of the tidal cycle. Furthermore the strengthening of the German flotilla, in respect of both destroyers and submarines, made it far more likely that the mines would be laid to specifically target shallow draft vessels. Clearly this situation was not sustainable going forward, and further attention would have to be paid to both the design of the mine pistol, and the anchoring arrangement.

As a result of these discomforting conclusions a series of trials were carried out by *Vernon* throughout 1911.[69] In October Heneage reported on one of the trials, which involved replacing the 7/8ths-inch mooring cable with a 1¼-inch cable. This modification had the desired effect in preventing any of the mines breaking adrift in a seaway, but Heneage also recommended a redesign of the method of attachment of the cable to the mine. He went on to note that there was 'a serious fault in the present pistol as previously reported … if bad weather occurs the pistol is liable to fire through the action of the sea alone'. Heneage's suggestion with regard to the mining pistol is very interesting. He recommended 'modifying the mine on the line proposed by Commander Cobbe, so as to necessitate the bumping of projections on the mine to fire it'.[70] In a different section of the same Vernon Annual Report, the issue of the mining pistol was considered directly and it was concluded that 'probably the only certain means of overcoming the difficulty is to adopt a mine which depends for firing on the bending or fracturing of projections on the mine.'[71] There can be no doubt that the design being referred to was that of a Hertz horn, the iconic mine pistol adopted by both the Germans and the Russians, and which would eventually become the standard design for contact mines across all navies. The report went on to say that 'suggestions for effecting this with a minimum number of alterations have been made by Commander Cobbe and Lieutenant Sandford'. Unfortunately the full report enclosing these officers' suggestions has, it appears, been weeded. The conversion of a mechanical mine relying on a pendulum inertia system into an electro-mechanical mine using a chemical battery would not have been easy and the precise nature of their proposal is not known. At the end of this report it was mentioned that 'a very simple device has, however, since been suggested by Captain Heneage, and it is probable that this will be tried first'.[72] In the meantime *Vernon* had also conducted experiments with two foreign designs of mine, namely the Elia and Novero, both of which had a mechanical pistol relying on an inertia ball. The report gives no analysis of the results of this trial, but the designs appear not to have found favour as no further trials took place at this stage.[73]

In 1912 experiments were undertaken with the modifications to the mines as recommended by Captain Heneage. The principle behind these was very simple; the pendulum-based internal firing mechanism which made up the Quicke-Scarff pistol was removed. Instead the hydrostatic value was mechanically held out by a spindle onto which large 'whiskers' were attached, which extended out several feet to either side of the top of the mine. The principle behind the pistol was that when struck the relative motion between the mine and the whiskers served to sheer the pin onto which the whiskers were attached. This freed the hydrostatic valve, which was then pressed in by the water surrounding the mine, and in doing so fired it.[74] The idea behind the design was very simple, and it had the obvious advantage that it required very little material to convert the existing mines to the new design. As such fifty modified mines were given to the minelayers for testing. At the same time as the Heneage pistol was being tested *Vernon* purchased a number of foreign mines to test their suitability and compare them with the British equipment. The types tested were the Carbonit mine, a commercial version of the German Service mine using Hertz horns, a Vickers mine of various different iterations and the French Sautter-Harlé design.[75] The full nature of the tests is not revealed in the reports; however the Carbonit mine and the Service mine fitted with a Heneage pistol were found to be superior to the other designs. The report concluded that:

> The Carbonit Mine was thought to be, on the whole slightly superior, but taking into consideration the greatly increased cost and the fact that the launching arrangements are entirely different, its introduction into the Service was not recommended.[76]

The Carbonit mine was recorded as costing approximately £200 per unit, as compared to £80 for a Vickers mine and £60 for the Service mine fitted with the new Heneage pistol. The breakdown of these costs is not clear; specifically, it is unknown whether the cost for the Service mine was for the conversion of existing stock from the Quicke-Scarf pistol to the Heneage pistol, or whether this was for an entirely new mine. The fact that the Vickers mine was more costly than the Service mine despite containing a charge barely half the size suggests it might have been the former. Whatever the details it is apparent that the decision not to adopt the Carbonit mine was taken for reasons of economy. In early 1913 the Heneage pistol was officially adopted and the requirement to adapt the existing mine stock was acknowledged.[77] The priority for this work, however, appears to have been relatively low. In a report attached to the 1913–1914 Estimates it was noted that:

> Recent improvements in foreign mines and the shortcomings in our own—which are of a comparatively old design—have moreover indicated the necessity for improving existing mines by degrees as the work can be taken in hand and the money allotted.[78]

It does not appear that any attempt was made to prioritise the modifications to mines, even after the decision was made to lay minefields in the opening phases of a war with Germany. To what extent those involved in the decision-making, notably H. B. Jackson, Ballard and Churchill, were aware of the true nature of the deficiencies of the mining stock cannot be demonstrated. It should of course be remembered that in the proposals adopted, mines were primarily used as a moral deterrent, and therefore absolute reliability was not as essential as in other roles. It is, however, very surprising that the replacement of mooring cables was not given high priority, as the prospect of floating mines which had broken adrift from their moorings was one which the navy took very seriously. The most likely explanation is offered by Philip Dumas, who became Assistant Director of Torpedoes (ADT) in July 1914. He recorded in his diary that 'the mooring ropes are too small' but 'The Treasury refused to change them until they were worn out'.[79]

This interlude offered the best prospect of a radical reconsideration of British mining materiel in the prewar period. The deficiencies in the existing mining stock were realised and measures put in place to try and resolve them. The outbreak of war demonstrated that the conclusions reached in this process were not wholly accurate, and the action taken proved to be too little and too late. It is apparent that the German Carbonit mine had performed well in the tests conducted, which is unsurprising considering the pedigree of the design. What is more difficult to explain is how the British Naval Spherical mine fitted with a Heneage pistol was perceived to have performed almost equally well. It should be remembered that, considering how tightly the naval budget was stretched at the time, any decision to adopt an entirely new mine would have most likely resulted in the mining service being without an operational mine for a number of years. The extent to which these types of factors influenced the conclusions reached by the officers running the experiments cannot be known. In the long run these decisions would, however, have very serious consequences, as the navy did not embark on a wholesale reconsideration of the issue when money became available on the outbreak of war.

These technical issues were to have an immediate and direct impact on the mining strategy outlined by George Ballard in early 1913 and adopted by the Admiralty later that year. In late spring 1914 the new Senior Officer, Minelayers, Captain Mervyn Cobbe, was told of contents of the secret orders issued to the minelayers the previous year. It appears certain that this was the first time that any of the officers of the minelaying squadron had been consulted as to the proposed operation. Cobbe immediately realised that the minefield M1, across the Straits of Dover, was entirely unfeasible. With the Naval Spherical mine and Service sinker the mine would drag in tides running at over three knots, and the greater the depth of water the more likelihood of the mine dragging. If a mine was dragged by the tide it was only a matter of time before the mooring cable would snap. Through the narrow part of the Channel where the line M1 was supposed to be laid the tide ran at over four knots. The result of laying a field in this location would be mines dragged down the Channel and gradually breaking free, posing a hazard to all seaborne traffic. To emphasise his point Cobbe concluded with a note saying 'an efficient minefield cannot at present be laid in the position indicated.'[80] At the same time Cobbe also wrote a memorandum on 'the serious defects in our mining apparatus requiring urgently to be remedied'. He repeated the failings of the Service pistol and the necessity to have the Heneage modification fitted to all 10,000 mines in stock. Cobbe also noted that only 2000 mines had been fitted with the modified sinker to carry the 1¼-inch mooring cable. He remarked that the remaining mines 'cannot be counted on to remain "in situ" after one day of bad weather.'[81]

It took the Admiralty some time to respond to Cobbe's memoranda, but on 1 August they issued an amendment to the previous war order, which stated that line M3 should replace line M1. Minefield M3 was to be seven miles long and be located well to the east of M1, between the Fairy Bank and the East Dyck Bank near Ostend.[82] It is probable that the delay in sending the orders came from the necessity of issuing all vessels in home waters with a sealed package containing the details of the new minefield, which would be opened on Admiralty instruction. Cobbe's new orders did not make any mention of altering the depth at which the mines were ordered to be laid. The original orders stated that they should be laid at five feet below LWOS, which was less than the seven feet which Cobbe had stated as the minimum depth at which the mines fitted with the original pistol could be laid.[83] He therefore felt it necessary to send the War Staff a copy of a memorandum he had drawn up outlining where tidal conditions would allow mines to be laid and what the impact of the tide was on the depth of the mine. In the enclosing letter he stated that 'the reason for arranging that mines shall not at any time be less than seven feet from the surface is because the mines with a pendulum [Quick-Scarff] pistol will fire at a less depth than this'. He went on to inform the Admiralty that each minelayer 'is at present supplied with 12 mines having the Heneage Pistol and 88 with the pendulum pistol'.[84] This letter was sent ten days after the British Declaration of War on Germany and effectively represents the final step in the pre-war development of offensive mining in the Royal Navy. It highlights the obvious failure in detailed planning, in which those drawing up the plans did not have the expert knowledge to be able to develop them properly. It also shows the problems associated with excessive secrecy. There was over a year between the plans for minefields M1 and M2 being approved and Cobbe informing the Admiralty of the problems of these orders. If the officer in charge of the minelayers, whether that be Cobbe or his predecessor Thomas Bonham, had been involved in the process at an earlier stage the difficulties would have been resolved sooner. As it was the Royal Navy entered the war with its one major mining policy fatally flawed.

The years leading up to the outbreak of the First World War were difficult ones for the Royal Navy, and the mining branch was no exception. Fisher's departure had left a service divided and faced with a dearth of senior officers capable of continuing the reforming process. The lack of clear leadership meant there was a strategic vacuum which effectively lasted from early 1910 until 1913. The absence of a clear framework of war policy had a profound effect on offensive mining, which was once again left as a peripheral technology with no obvious role. The development of the policy of distant blockade saw mining return to the centre of naval strategy. The adoption of a plan to use mines as the front line in a commercial blockade was driven as much by the dictates of international law as purely military concerns. It did, however, fit within the general British policy of using mines to facilitate the navy to exploit its command of the sea as a strategic weapon. In addition to the strategic flux, the mining service had major technical problems from 1910 onwards. The Quick-Scarff pistol, which was found to be a failure, represented the final evolution of a design dating back to 1890 and which had originally focused on the Mediterranean. It incorporated far too many outdated assumptions on mines and their use and its failure was unsurprising. When examining this issue the mining service had a perfect opportunity to finally abandon the old technology and start with a new design. That they did not, despite acknowledging that the Carbonit mine was the best mine available, can mainly be put down to the financial implications of such a decision. Wartime experience would, however, raise serious questions as to the processes through which *Vernon* and the mining service tested their equipment. The failure of the prewar navy to appreciate and resolve the problems surrounding the naval spherical mine and the Heneage pistol would have implications lasting until the end of 1917. The failure of the Admiralty to address even the concerns that were raised by the mining service, notably regarding the pendulum pistol and the mooring cables, is somewhat strange. This was a result of the failure of communication between the Admiralty and the mining service. The Admiralty would not have been aware that the limitations on the mining materiel were such that they would have a direct impact on the proposed mining policy, until Cobbe raised the issue in 1914. The actual role for mines in the commercial blockade policy was relatively small, and because nobody informed the Captain in Charge of Minelayers of the plan the Admiralty was left believing the mines to be capable of fulfilling this role. It is obvious that this was a period of extreme financial pressure, and issues such as modifying mining stocks were relatively low priority if it was believed that the existing mines would do the job passably well. The end result was that the mining policy in support of the commercial blockade was not feasible in the summer of 1914.

NOTES

1. C. H. Stockton, 'The Use of Submarine Mines and Torpedoes in Times of War', *The American Journal of International Law*, vol. 2, no. 2 (1908), pp. 276–284.
2. *Annuaire de L'Institut de Droit International*, vol. 22 (1908), pp. 156–158.
3. *Annuaire de L'Institut de Droit International*, vol. 22 (1908), pp. 222–227.
4. *Annuaire de L'Institut de Droit International*, vol. 23 (1910), p. 178.
5. *Annuaire de L'Institut de Droit International*, vol. 23 (1910), p. 181.
6. *Annuaire de L'Institut de Droit International*, vol. 23 (1910), pp. 429–457.
7. *Annuaire de L'Institut de Droit International*, vol. 24 (1911), p. 273.
8. *Annuaire de L'Institut de Droit International*, vol. 25 (1912), pp. 41–45.
9. *Annuaire de L'Institut de Droit International*, vol. 26 (1913), p. 227 and *passim*.
10. The National Archives [TNA], FO 372/375, 'Institut de Droit International', 3 September 1912, 37656/37656/330.

9 STRATEGIC FLUX AND TECHNICAL FAILURE

11. TNA, FO 372/548, 'Manual of Institute of International Law', 16 January 1914, 5366/876/329.
12. TNA, FO 372/373, 'Third Peace Conference', 12 February 1912, 6208/6208/329.
13. TNA, FO 372/449, 'Peace Conference', 6 June 1913, 26431/3234/329.
14. TNA, FO 372/449, 'Peace Conference', 6 June 1913, 26431/3234/329.
15. TNA, FO 372/449, Crowe Minute, 13 March 1913, 11619/3234/329.
16. TNA, CAB 37/119/48, Third Peace Conference, 24 March 1914.
17. Nicholas Lambert, *Sir John Fisher's Naval Revolution* (Columbia: University of South Carolina Press, 1999), pp. 203–211; Arthur Marder, *From Dreadnought to Scapa Flow: Volume I The Road to War 1904–14* (Barnsley: Seaforth Publishing, 2013), pp. 370–372.
18. Shawn Grimes, *Strategy and War Planning in the British Navy, 1887–1918* (Woodbridge, Suffolk: The Boydell Press, 2012); and David Morgan Owen, '"History Is a Record of Exploded Ideas": Sir John Fisher and Home Defence, 1904–10', *The International History Review*, vol. 36, no. 3 (2014), pp. 550–572.
19. See correspondence referenced in National Maritime Museum [NMM], May Papers, MAY/10, 'Received From Admiral Sir William May by Admiral Sir F. C. B. Bridgeman' Section III, 25 March 1911; Also see TNA, ADM 12/1478, Cut 50 Home Fleet 'War Orders and War Plans', 'Advanced Destroyer and Submarine Bases in Wartime–Cancelled' and 'War Orders: Blockade of Heligoland Bight'.
20. TNA, ADM 116/3096, 'Heligoland Bight Blockade Squadron: Preliminary Orders for Commodore (T) in Command', 23 January 1911.
21. TNA, ADM 186/5, Cruiser Manual Part II, pp. 8–11.
22. NMM, DAN/190, Dannreuther Papers, 'Remarks on Offensive Minelaying', 'Fleet Mining Exercises', October 1910.
23. NMM, DAN/190, Dannreuther Papers, 'Remarks on Offensive Minelaying', 'Fleet Mining Exercises', October 1910.
24. NMM, DAN/190, Dannreuther Papers, 'Remarks on Offensive Minelaying', 'Fleet Mining Exercises', October 1910.
25. NMM, DAN/190, Dannreuther Papers, 'Remarks on Offensive Minelaying', 'Fleet Mining Exercises', October 1910.
26. See TNA, ADM 116/3096, Bridgeman minute, 9 April 1912 on Admiralty to Callaghan (draft).
27. TNA, ADM 116/3096, 'Orders to Flag Officers with an Explanatory Memorandum', n.d.
28. Grimes, *Strategy and War Planning*, pp. 176–178; Lambert, *Fisher's Naval Revolution*, pp. 263–265; and David Morgan Owen, 'An Intermediate Blockade? British North Sea Strategy 1912–1914', *War in History*, vol. 22, no. 4 (2015), pp. 478–502.
29. NMM, DAN/190, Dannreuther Papers, Callaghan to CO Minelayers, 2 May 1912.

30. NMM, DAN/190, Dannreuther Papers, Dannreuther to CO Minelayers, 28 December 1912.
31. TNA, ADM 116/866B, 'Remarks on War Orders for an Observation Force in the North Sea in Connection with the Lessons of the 1912 Manoeuvres', 16 September 1912, f. 289.
32. TNA, ADM 116/866B, 'Remarks on War Orders for an Observation Force in the North Sea in Connection with the Lessons of the 1912 Manoeuvres', 16 September 1912, f. 289.
33. TNA, ADM 116/866B, 'Remarks on War Orders for an Observation Force in the North Sea in Connection with the Lessons of the 1912 Manoeuvres', 16 September 1912, f. 290.
34. TNA, ADM 116/866B, 'Remarks on War Orders for an Observation Force in the North Sea in Connection with the Lessons of the 1912 Manoeuvres', 16 September 1912, ff. 285–293.
35. TNA, ADM 137/818, 'War Plans', 16 December 1912, ff. 8–24; Grimes, *Strategy and War Planning*, pp. 176–179.
36. George Ballard (1924b), 'The Naval War Staff, 1912–14', *The Naval Review*, vol. XII (1924), p. 455.
37. Marder, *Dreadnought to Scapa Flow* I, p. 328.
38. Nicholas Black, *The British Naval Staff in the First World War* (Woodbridge, Suffolk: The Boydell Press, 2009), p. 62; Peter Halvorsen, 'The Royal Navy and Mine Warfare 1868–1914', *Journal of Strategic Studies*, vol. 27, no. 4 (2004), pp. 701–702.
39. For a detailed discussion of these issues see Matthew Seligmann, 'Failing to Prepare for the Great War? The Absence of Grand Strategy in British War Planning Before 1914', *War in History* (2017), e-publication.
40. TNA, CAB 16/18A, 'Report of the Trading with the Enemy Sub-Committee', 10 September 1912, p. 6.
41. TNA, CAB 38/22/42, 120th Meeting of CID, 6 December 1912.
42. TNA, CAB 38/22/42, 120th Meeting of CID, 6 December 1912.
43. TNA, CAB 38/22/42, 120th Meeting of CID, 6 December 1912.
44. TNA, CAB 16/18A, Fifth Meeting of the Trading with the Enemy Committee, 9 February 1912, p. 79.
45. TNA, ADM 116/3412, Ballard minute, 6 February 1913, 'Proposal for the Use of Mines in an Anglo-German War', f. 493.
46. TNA, ADM 116/3412, 'Proposal for the Use of Mines in an Anglo-German War', 6 February 1913, ff. 495–503; another copy of this document, albeit wrongly dated can be found in ADM 137/818.
47. For a chart of the proposed minefields see TNA, ADM 137/863, Chart 3, 'Proposed Lines of Mines off Dover and Terschelling and Proposed Proclaimed Area', n.d.; the official historians clearly assumed this chart to date from 1914 and not 1913, which explains its location.

48. TNA, ADM 116/3412, 'Proposal for the Use of Mines in an Anglo-German War', 6 February 1913, ff. 495–503,
49. TNA, ADM 116/3412, Jackson Minute, 11 February 1913, 'Proposal for the Use of Mines in an Anglo-German War', f. 494.
50. TNA, ADM 116/3412, Churchill Minute, 23 February 1913, 'Proposal for the Use of Mines in an Anglo-German War', f. 493.
51. TNA, ADM 116/3412, 'Orders Regarding Mines', 30 April 1913.
52. TNA, ADM 116/3412, Churchill Note, 16 May 1913; Minutes to Hydrographer, 14 July and 6 August 1913, ff. 521 and 524.
53. TNA, ADM 116/3412, Hydrographer Memorandum, 21 November. 1913, f. 540.
54. TNA, ADM 116/3412, Admiralty to CinC Home Fleet, 10 December 1913 and 'War Orders: Senior Officer Minelayer Squadron', ff. 551–554.
55. Grimes, *Strategy and War Planning*, pp. 185–187; Lambert, *Fisher's Naval Revolution*, pp. 270–272; Nicholas Lambert, *Planning Armageddon: British Economic Warfare and the First World War* (Cambridge, Massachusetts: Harvard University Press, 2012), p. 181; and Christopher Bell, *Churchill and Sea Power* (Oxford: Oxford University Press, 2013), p. 44.
56. TNA, ADM 116/3412, 'Proposal for the Use of Mines in an Anglo-German War', 6 February 1913, ff. 495–503.
57. Isabel V. Hull, *A Scrap of Paper: Making and Breaking International Law During the Great War* (Ithaca: Cornell University Press, 2014), pp. 155–157.
58. Hull, *Scrap of Paper*, p. 219.
59. TNA, ADM 137/1939, Graham Greene to Flag Officers, 29 April 1914, f. 9.
60. TNA, ADM 1/8380/150, 'Agenda for War Conference'.
61. Imperial War Museum [IWM], PP/MCR/96, Dumas Diary, 1 October 1914; IWM, Battenberg Papers, DS/MISC/20, Reel V, 'Notes on Mining', 18 October 1914, No. 367B.
62. Churchill Archives Centre (CAC), CHAR 13/37/54, Churchill Papers, Battenberg to CinC Home Fleet, 24 July 1914.
63. NMM, DAN/133, Dannreuther Papers, 'The Theory and Practice of Submarine Mining as Practiced by His Majesty's Ships', 25 March 1912, ff. 20–22; TNA, ADM 189/30, Vernon Annual Report 1910, p. 107.
64. NMM, DAN/133, Dannreuther Papers, 'The Theory and Practice of Submarine Mining as Practiced by His Majesty's Ships', 25 March 1912, f. 22.
65. NMM, DAN/190, Dannreuther Papers, 'Fleet Mining Exercises', October 1910.
66. TNA, ADM 189/30, Vernon Annual Report 1910, 'Blowing Charge for Spherical Mines', pp. 110–111.

67. NMM, DAN/190, Dannreuther Papers, 'Fleet Mining Exercises', October 1910.
68. NMM, DAN/190, Dannreuther Papers, 'Fleet Mining Exercises', October 1910.
69. TNA, ADM 12/1491, Cut 59.8, Effects of Tide on Depth of Mines, 10 February 1911; TNA, ADM 189/31, Vernon Annual Report 1911, 'Trial of Mines in a Seaway', pp. 77–78.
70. TNA, ADM 189/31, Vernon Annual Report 1911, 'Trial of Mines in a Seaway', pp. 77–78.
71. TNA, ADM 189/31, Vernon Annual Report 1911, 'Mines with External Firing Arrangements', p. 78.
72. TNA, ADM 189/31, Vernon Annual Report 1911, 'Mines with External Firing Arrangements', p. 78.
73. TNA, ADM 189/31, Vernon Annual Report 1911, 'Trials with the Elia and Novero Mines', p. 78.
74. TNA, ADM 189/32, Vernon Annual Report 1912, 'Captain Heneage's Pistol', p. 52.
75. TNA, CAB 37/121/136, 'Notes on Naval Mines', October 1914; TNA, ADM 189/33, Vernon Annual Report 1913, 'Trials of Carbonit and Vickers Mines', pp. 72–76.
76. TNA, ADM 189/33, Vernon Annual Report 1913, 'Trials of Carbonit and Vickers Mines', pp. 72–76.
77. TNA, ADM 189/33, Vernon Annual Report 1913, 'Captain Heneage's Pistol', p. 66.
78. CAC, CHAR 13/23/13, Churchill Papers, 'Notes by Heads of Departments: Minelaying and Minesweeping', 2 January 1913.
79. IWM, PP/MCR/96, Dumas Diary, 4 October 1914.
80. TNA, ADM 137/843, 'Remarks on Mining', 15 May 1914, ff. 22–23.
81. TNA, ADM 137/843, 'The Serious Defects in Our Mining Apparatus', 15 May 1914, f. 24.
82. TNA, ADM 137/843, 'Instructions to Inspecting Captain of Minelayers' (Copy), 1 August 1914, f. 17.
83. TNA, ADM 116/3412, 'War Orders for Senior Officer Minelayer Squadron', ff. 511–513.
84. TNA, ADM 137/843, Cobbe to Admiral of Patrols, 14 August 1914, ff. 19–21.

CHAPTER 10

The Test of Conflict

At the time of Britain's declaration of war on Germany on 4 August 1914 the Royal Navy was, in certain respects, well positioned for the conflict. The fleet had been assembled, the period of strained relations had facilitated preparations being made, and the basic strategic outlook was largely settled. There were, however a number of areas where the picture was less positive, and mining was undoubtedly one of these. The Royal Navy had, as recently as December 1913, developed a new mining strategy aimed at commerce flowing into neutral and German North Sea ports. On the outbreak of war, however, this carefully-worked-out scheme lay in tatters. The failures of mining materiel discussed at the end of the last chapter meant that the minefields originally proposed could not be laid, due to the strength of the tide and potential for premature firing due to the effect of swell. Attempts at resolving these problems in August revealed the clear breakdown in communication between the Admiralty and the minelaying service. Thus on the outbreak of war the Royal Navy did not have a workable mining policy.

This failure was in fact less significant than one might imagine. Over the course of the first half of 1914 changes of personnel within the Admiralty meant that interest in mining had waned. The replacement of Admiral Sir Henry Jackson as COS and Captain George Ballard as Director of Operations Division (DOD), by Vice-Admiral Sir Doveton Sturdee and Rear-Admiral Arthur Leveson respectively, removed the individuals who had been most interested in pursuing a mining strategy. Both Sturdee and Leveson tended to view mining through the prism

© The Author(s) 2018
R. Dunley, *Britain and the Mine, 1900–1915*,
https://doi.org/10.1007/978-3-319-72820-9_10

225

of traditional Royal Navy organisational culture, and as such saw little prospect of the service employing mines. This position clearly influenced the First Sea Lord, Prince Louis of Battenberg, who, despite approving the mining scheme agreed in December 1913, appears to have remained diffident at best. When, soon after the outbreak of war, the new ADT, Captain Philip Dumas, 'enquired as to the likelihood of mining' he was told by Sturdee and Battenberg that 'it was not our policy to lay mines'.[1] As such it appears unlikely that, even had the difficulties surrounding the prewar mining scheme been worked out, the Admiralty would have decided to implement it. This appears to be confirmed by the fact that no steps were taken to work through the difficulties outlined by Cobbe. The decision not to pursue this policy is instructive. The scheme involved the use of a very small number of mines in carefully selected locations where it was considered it was unlikely the navy would want to operate. It was designed as a potential solution for the problems of trade in neutral ships and through neutral ports; neither of these issues had gone away, and the navy had no other solutions at the time. The policy had the potential, therefore, to achieve a substantial result for a minimal cost. The fact that the Admiralty were unwilling to even consider this highlights the extent of ideological opposition to mining that remained within the service.

This opposition was not shared by everyone either inside or outside the service, and immediately before the outbreak of war the Admiralty received a proposed mining scheme from an unlikely quarter, the armaments firm Vickers. On 27 July 1914 a senior figure within Vickers, most likely Sir Trevor Dawson, wrote to the First Lord, Winston Churchill. This letter provided information on supposed German intentions to mine extensively in the English Channel and Irish Sea on the outbreak of war. It also set out a countermeasure, a 'suggested attack with Vickers Submarine Mines on the first night of the war'.[2] Unfortunately we are lacking some of the details of the scheme, but it appears that Vickers were offering the Admiralty 4500 mines to be laid in the Heligoland Bight.[3] The Admiralty response largely focused on the information regarding possible German action, but the Director Intelligence Division (DID), Rear-Admiral Henry Oliver, did discuss the proposal to mine the German coast. Oliver pointed out that the precise locations selected by Vickers for the mines were not the most suitable, and raised other navigation-based issues. Frustratingly he made no comment on the wider aspects of the scheme, nor did he connect it to the similar mining strategy which he had helped draw up in 1905. There appears to have been no further discussion of the Vickers proposals, and no action was taken. Without more evidence it is impossible to tell whether this was a reasoned decision or simply an outright rejection of mining.

Within the navy there was some interest in exploring the options for offensive minelaying. In September Commander F. D. Arnold-Forster drew up two memoranda for the Admiralty outlining the potential uses of mines. The first addressed the 'possibilities of laying a small number of mines ... off the mouths of the Elbe, Weser or Lister Deep ... on the assumption that it was necessary to keep the enemy's more open waters clear for our own operations'. The second addressed the scenario in which it was considered that the benefits of closing off the Heligoland Bight altogether outweighed the disadvantages of limiting British actions, and so proposed a much larger mine barrage.[4] Arnold-Forster outlined how these operations could be carried out with the limited forces available to the minelaying service at the time, in terms of both mines and vessels. The reaction of the Admiralty was instructive; the DOD, Arthur Leveson, suggested Arnold-Forster be congratulated on 'two well thought out papers which are of considerable value if a mining policy were going to be adopted'.[5] Arnold-Forster may have been 'pleased' on receiving a letter of appreciation from the Admiralty; however, it does not appear that he would have been surprised by their inaction regarding mines.[6]

As was noted at the end of the previous chapter the navy had, in July 1914, intended to hold a conference at Spithead bringing together all the leading figures from the Admiralty and the fleet to discuss matters of strategy, tactics and materiel. The conference was initially postponed, and then cancelled as the July Crisis morphed into war. The outbreak of the conflict, however, made many of the issues to be discussed even more pressing, and so in September 1914 a conference was held at Loch Ewe between senior officers from the Grand Fleet, and the First Lord and members of the War Staff. One of the issues on the agenda for the original Spithead conference had been the potential role of offensive mining, and this was carried over to the Loch Ewe gathering. Specifically the officers were to discuss the potential for 'mining [the] approaches to Heligoland', as part of broader discussions around offensive operations on the German North Sea coast.[7] We do not have a detailed account of the discussions, but Admiral John Jellicoe, the Commander in Chief of the Grand Fleet, drew up a memorandum on the decisions reached. With regard to mining Jellicoe reported that it was '(d)ecided that it was not advisable to mine the Heligoland Approaches under present conditions, and that the mines in the minelayers should be unprimed'.[8] The decision not to pursue a mining strategy, and more tellingly to unprime the mines, demonstrates the extent to which the service had come to reject the technology. The Loch Ewe conference had served to reinforce the fact that the navy did not have answers to all its strategic problems in 1914, and prewar discussions had shown that mining at least had the potential to address some of these. The fact that the navy went beyond simply deciding not to deploy mines immediately, but unprimed the weapons and repurposed the minelayers as supplementary cruisers for the fleet, demonstrates the extent to which the organisation's ideological and cultural attitudes towards mines drove its strategic approach towards the technology.

I

In the early months of the war the Admiralty was not the only body debating the merits of mine warfare; the topic was also the subject of considerable discussion within the Cabinet. The Germans had deployed mines from the first days of the conflict, with almost immediate impact. On 5 August the light cruiser *Amphion* engaged and destroyed the German auxiliary minelayer *Königin Luise*, but early the next morning struck one of the mines laid by the German ship, and sank.[9] The reaction of leading political figures was unsurprising. The Prime Minister, Herbert Asquith, recounted the event to his confidante, Venetia Stanley, concluding that '(m)ines are a hellish device wh[ich] every civilised nation except the Germans wanted to abolish at the Hague years ago.'[10] This condemnation of the use of mines from a moral and pseudo-legal perspective fits into a clear pattern of British prewar political views. When the matter was discussed the following day in the Cabinet this language continued to be used, but a more pragmatic analysis was already developing. The Colonial Secretary, Lewis Harcourt, recorded in his notes that '(c)ontact mines [are] contrary to [the] usage of war. We should warn all Foreign shipping not to enter [the] minefield. This will make an effective blockade of Rotterdam. We want to keep Norwegian neutral flag from going to Rotterdam'.[11] Harcourt was undoubtedly a 'dove' within the Cabinet, having initially opposed the decision for war, and resisted attempts by Churchill to blockade neutral ports.[12] Thus his conclusion that mines, however abhorrent, could be used to block neutral ships trading between two neutral ports is remarkable. At this stage it is, of course, important to remember that the mines concerned were German, and the British were merely informing, or misleading, neutral mariners as to the dangers. The principle, however, of mines or at least the threat of mines being used to interrupt legal neutral commerce was accepted.

The wider issues of how to exert economic pressure on Germany continued to be discussed in Cabinet. The crucial questions were firstly: how, in the absence of a legal blockade, to stop trade in neutral ships with German ports; and secondly how to stop goods flowing into neutral ports such as Rotterdam and then proceeding up the Rhine to Germany. In a meeting on 13 August the Foreign Secretary, Sir Edward Grey, pushed for an aggressive economic warfare strategy; however it was widely accepted that 'we must not make a breech of Internat[ional] Law ... we must not stop U.S. ships going to Rotterdam' and 'we cannot make contraband of food for the civil population'.[13] These restrictions, as had been known prior to the war, would seriously limit any British economic warfare policy. In his notes from the Cabinet the following day Harcourt recorded that the issue was becoming more pressing because the 'neutral scare about mines in the North Sea is passing away'. This meant that more neutral vessels were likely to be heading towards Rotterdam and Hamburg, bringing vital supplies for the German economy. The Cabinet discussed a number of potential solutions to circumvent this impasse. Crucially, these included the option that 'we lay mines ourselves and blow up some neutral ships to deter others'.[14] This is a remarkable statement. Britain had, for the previous ten years, adopted the position that the use of mines outside of territorial waters should be prohibited, due to its potential impact on neutrals and non-combatants. The Admiralty had, on a number of occasions, explored the idea of using mines as part of a commercial blockade, but had always expected opposition from politicians. Thus, the fact that a Liberal Cabinet, with no prompting from professional naval officers, had within ten days of the outbreak of war come to consider the use of mines is extraordinary. It is all the more so, as the use of mines envisaged was not only illegal under the very limited Hague Convention, but was also specifically targeting innocent neutral traders.

Over the following days the debate over how best to respond to the economic warfare challenge continued. Meanwhile a memorandum was received from the US Secretary of State, William Bryan, objecting to the

Admiralty declaration that, due to German minelaying, the Royal Navy retained the right to respond in kind.[15] This was discussed in Cabinet on 17 August, and appears to have tipped the scales against the idea of using mines to stop neutral trade.[16] As Asquith wrote to Stanley, '(t)he Americans protest, in the interests of neutral shipping, against our following the German example & laying down mines in the North Sea. As you know I am all against this provocative and rather barbarous mode of procedure'.[17] Instead Asquith looked to pursue a scheme proposed by Walter Runciman to buy up neutral tonnage, and so prevent it from carrying supplies to Germany.

Following this decision the issue of mining disappeared from Cabinet discussions for the remainder of August, but returned again in September driven by a fundamentally different set of priorities. When the decision was taken to send the British Expeditionary Force to France, it was agreed to leave two of the six divisions in Britain for home defence. This was, at least in part, provoked by a fear of German raids. By mid-September the political and military pressure to send these troops to France was becoming overwhelming, but few believed the threat of an attack on the east coast had passed. Of particular concern was the location of the Grand Fleet in Scottish and later Irish waters, something that ensured its safety against submarine attack, but meant it would struggle to intercept any German force. As a solution the Secretary of State for War, Lord Kitchener, proposed 'laying mines all along our East Coast' to protect against any raids.[18] The reaction of Churchill and the Admiralty is not recorded, but can easily be imagined; weeks later the former would dismiss Jellicoe's call for minefields in British waters for ASW purposes as the 'passive fouling of waters by mines'.[19] The Cabinet discussed the issue, and according to Lewis Harcourt, 'decided against mines on our own coast, but agreed to mining German and Dutch shores and [the] mouths of [the] Scheldt and Rhine.'[20] It is apparent from this that the discussion soon broadened out from the raids issue raised by Kitchener to reconsider the use of mines against neutral trade following through Antwerp and Rotterdam. Asquith's account of the meeting to the King stated that mining was agreed 'in principle' and that the issue was to be considered by the Admiralty.[21] The opposition to mining in the Admiralty appears to have prevented any further action being taken at this point.

The following week a third element was added into the equation: the German submarine menace. On the morning of Tuesday 29 September

Churchill met with Asquith, apparently to discuss the threat posed by submarines to the transport of troops across the Channel. It is apparent that in this context the First Lord was willing to acknowledge the potential use of mines. At the same time it became known in London that the US State Department had drawn up an 'offensive despatch' on Britain's treatment of neutral trade.[22] This led to a 'long conference' of Asquith's inner circle being held that afternoon.[23] Following this the Prime Minister wrote to the First Lord:

> I have been thinking over our conversation this morning, and what you said about *mining* has been reinforced by the conference a few of us had later as to the American attitude in regard to the Declaration of London &c. I am strongly of [the] opinion that the time has come for you to start mining, and to do so without stinting, and if necessary on a Napoleonic scale. I don't know what supply you have of the infernal machinery, but I feel sure you cant do better that make the most ample provision, and use it freely and even lavishly.'[24]

This letter, together with the Admiralty records, suggests that it was primarily the submarine threat which finally pushed Churchill into accepting a mining strategy.[25] Asquith, however, as he revealed to Venetia Stanley, viewed the issue through the prism of the neutral trade problem. He wrote:

> The Americans are making themselves disagreeable about the seizure & detention of cargoes sent in their ships ostensibly to Holland, but for German consumption. Naturally we don't want a row with them, but we cannot allow the Germans to be provided for. I am reluctantly convinced that the only thing to be done is to sow the Eastern part of the North Sea with mines – right down between Rotterdam & Flushing. I have been urging this strongly on Winston, & I think he is disposed to take the same view.[26]

The matter was finally agreed by the Cabinet the following day.[27] This decision, taken a mere eight weeks after the declaration of war, represents a crucial watershed in the discussions of this issue. Prior to the war the British government had maintained a clear legal and moral position in opposition to any mining in international waters. This included the use of mines for clear military purposes. The reasons they gave were based around the impact of mining on legal, neutral commerce and the potential for the deaths of innocent, neutral seafarers. The proposals agreed at the end of September highlight how quickly the rising tide of belligerence overcame prewar British legal and moral concerns. Claims by Isabel Hull that this was 'a purely military response to the submarine threat' are wide of the mark.[28] These proposals were, in the eyes of the Cabinet at least, driven by the desire to stop trade between neutrals. It was known that this trade could not be stopped within the current international legal framework, and the American protests were confirming the diplomatic risks of attempting to do so. Thus attention was turned to mines. Whilst the use of mines specifically to target commerce was technically illegal, German and American opposition at The Hague had rendered the restrictions virtually meaningless. This allowed the British government to act in precisely the way they had feared other nations would, prior to the outbreak of war. They sought to utilise the loopholes in the flawed convention signed at The Hague to prevent neutral trade that they could not legally interrupt. In doing so, they were willing to accept the likelihood that neutral seamen would be killed by British mines. The speed with which the British Cabinet came to reach this decision is remarkable. Asquith's abhorrence of mines as a weapon was clearly revealed in his letter to Venetia Stanley of 6 August, and yet within a week the Cabinet was discussing whether to use mines to 'blow up some neutral ships to deter others'.[29] Ironically the fact that it took so long for this policy to be adopted was largely due to the cultural resistance of the Royal Navy to the idea of laying mines, something wholeheartedly embraced by its political leader, Winston Churchill. Eventually, however, the bellicose attitude of the Liberal Cabinet forced the navy into accepting a mining strategy.

II

Despite the Cabinet decision regarding mines it is clear that Churchill retained reservations. Very early in the morning of 1 October he telegrammed Jellicoe informing him that the politicians were 'pressing us very strongly [to] institute [an] extensive mining policy'. He asked for Jellicoe's opinion 'on Naval grounds excluding political [issues] of a big mining policy'. He was also keen to know if the admiral preferred mines to be laid in the English Channel, or more offensively in the Heligoland Bight.[30] Early the following morning Jellicoe replied, giving his qualified support for mining in the 'narrow seas' around the British Isles, but viewing mining in the Heligoland Bight as 'not worth the materiel expended' due to the perceived facility with which the Germans could sweep the mines.[31] It appears Churchill had made up his mind even before Jellicoe's response, and instructed Battenberg and Sturdee to proceed with a mining operation at the east end of the English Channel, which took place in the first week of October.[32] The decision was clearly taken in great haste and with little consultation with those in charge of mining. Captain Philip Dumas, the Assistant Director of Torpedoes, recorded in his diary for 2 October that he went '(t)o see Winston, who staggered me by saying he was laying mines tonight in the Straits of Dover. As all our mining was dropped and our mines, sinker and mooring ropes are worthless the results must be failure.'[33] Dumas' concerns were soon borne out. The prewar mining policy had been abandoned due to failures of materiel. The decision made by Sturdee and Battenberg that the navy would not undertaking mining meant that fixing these issues had been a low priority, and little had been achieved. To compound matters there had been no consultation over the location of the field, much of which was in an area of exceptionally strong tides, virtually guaranteeing the failure of many of the mines. Over the next few days it became apparent that there had been a considerable number of premature explosions and mines were starting to break away and drift down the Channel.[34]

Despite the laying of mines being forced upon the Admiralty by the Cabinet, there was a resigned acceptance of the necessity of the measure among many naval officers. Notably, they tended to view the step as a response to German submarine activity as opposed to a measure against neutral trade, which had in fact been the primary motive for Asquith in forcing Churchill's hand. This military purpose allowed officers to rationalise the decision as one of necessity. George Ballard had been involved in Admiralty planning regarding mining throughout the prewar period, including proposing measures very similar to these steps. Despite this his reaction to the decision was far from upbeat, and clearly indicates the contested position which mines occupied in the views of naval officers. As he explained to his mother:

> I daresay you noticed in yesterday's paper that the Admiralty, or rather the Government, had announced that they had found it necessary to lay mines in a certain area to the north east of the Straits of Dover … . I don't like mines. They are a vile instrument of war. But there is an honest and a

dishonest way of using them. If you place mines in a certain sea area and tell the whole world that they are there no ship can some to grief except by willful disregard of your warning. That is the honest way. The Germans on the other hand scatter mines wholesale and say nothing about it. The result has been the loss of many peaceful merchant ships belonging to countries which are not engaged in the war. That is the dishonest way.[35]

The fact that British mining was largely targeted at neutral trade was either ignored, or had simply passed Ballard by. Regardless of the continued reservations of naval officers, and the widespread failure of British mines, it is apparent that the operations had piqued Churchill's interest. The day after the first mines were laid he ordered Dumas to obtain 15,000 new mines for delivery by the next summer. As the ADT noted this was not a simple request, as the navy had no efficient design of mine, and the disbanding of *Vernon* left him with little in the way of guidance.[36] On the 4 October Dumas met with leading figures from the armaments firm, Vickers, and the following day placed orders for 7500 mines of the service pattern and 7500 Vickers Elia mines. The latter was a commercial design that Vickers had licensed off an Italian naval officer who had been working on mine designs for well over a decade.[37] It seems clear that Dumas was far from confident over the decisions he had taken and later stated that he had sought to get hold of plans of the German Carbonit mine, but had been unsuccessful.[38] Dumas, at the time, however, bragged in his diary about having 'staggered' everyone and managing to spend £2 million in one day.[39] True to character this was something of an exaggeration; the actual figure, agreed by the Treasury on 6 October, was a mere £1.5 million.[40] Even in the context of wartime expenditure this was still a very large sum of money, and it is noteworthy that this decision took place before the return of Lord Fisher to the Admiralty. On his return he would bemoan that '(a)pparently not one single mine was ordered in the 4 years since I left Admiralty'.[41] This was not true, and the mines that would be laid during his tenure as First Sea Lord came in large part from this order.

Churchill's interest in mining did not stop with the purchase of new mines. Despite spending much of the following week in Antwerp, the First Lord soon returned and looked to embark on an extensive new mining campaign. This time his attention had turned to neutral trade, and presumably perceiving this to be the only way of strengthening the blockade that was likely to meet the approval of the Cabinet, he suggested mining the entrances of the Scheldt and Rhine. As Harcourt noted 'this would block the port of Rotterdam', and in doing so be a virtual declaration of war on the Netherlands.[42] At the same time a report had come in from Sir Francis Oppenheimer, British commercial attaché in The Hague, that the Dutch government were increasingly pro-Allied, and it was decided to wait before taking action.[43] It was seemingly with this in mind that Churchill investigated the availability of French mines and minelayers. He wanted to know this information 'before coming to further decisions about mining in the N[orth] Sea'.[44] In the end the French minelayers were used to lay a field off the Belgian coast east of Ostend.[45] They were chosen in part because they drew less water than their British equivalents, but Churchill also appears to have been concerned that the still substantial British stocks of mines would be insufficient to cover operational requirements until the new mines began to be delivered.

Ironically by the time these operations were carried out at the end of October and early November Churchill's brief interest in mining appears to have faded. On 13 October, following the rejection of his suggestion to mine the Rhine and the Scheldt, others in Cabinet, notably Kitchener, proposed mining the Heligoland Bight instead.[46] Churchill rejected this idea, asserting that the area was too large to mine effectively. Unfortunately someone in Cabinet had the accurate figures and suggested that 5000 mines would provide a double line across the Bight. This was exactly the concept proposed by Charles Ottley almost a decade earlier. Charles Hobhouse, the Postmaster General, clearly confused the Cabinet discussions of 12 and 13 October, writing that 'the P[rime]. M[inister]. and K[itchener]. are very anxious to block the entrance to the Scheldt by mines on an extensive scale', when he meant the Heligoland Bight. His observations on why Churchill was so adamant in his refusal to agree to such an operation were, however, far more astute. He wrote that:

> W.S.C. [Churchill] objected very strongly, nominally because he had only 2500 mines and couldn't, as he said, get any more, but really because he thought a minefield w[oul]^d block in the German fleet, and prevent or postpone the *réclame* of a naval victory.[47]

The issue flared again the following day when, as a result of a sighting of a German U-boat off the Isle of Wight, Churchill wanted to redirect the troop transports to French Atlantic ports. Kitchener objected, and so Churchill developed his point regarding the difficulty of stopping submarines and the inability to block them into the Heligoland Bight. At this point, as Hobhouse recalls, Asquith provocatively asked '"You mean we have lost command of the sea" To this bald and true deduction from his remarks W.S.C. [Churchill] took great umbridge.'[48] It is clear that both Kitchener and the Prime Minister were still pressing for further mining off German coasts. Churchill had absorbed much of the Royal Navy's culture over his years as First Lord, and his distrust of mining reflects this. His professional colleagues at the Admiralty shared the attitude. The same week Sturdee rejected a similar plan put forward by Herbert Richmond, who recorded in his diary that 'he produces the old stale claptrap that what we want is not to keep the enemy in but to get him out and fight'.[49] The Royal Navy organisational culture raised the idea of decisive battle into an almost unchallengeable mantra, and for many mining continued to represent an obstacle to achieving this 'second Trafalgar'. With regard to Churchill specifically, Hobhouse's critique that this position was driven, largely, by the desire for the acclaim such a victory would bring, is undoubtedly accurate.

Churchill clearly appreciated the weakness of his position on this issue and a few days later produced a memorandum for Cabinet. In it he tried to outline the Admiralty view on mining. He split the topic into two sections, the first regarding ambush mining, and the second blockade mining. He largely dismissed the concept of ambush mining as a tool of the weaker power, and a largely ineffective one, owing to the limited scale of mining and the rapid discovery of new minefields. The areas where he saw potential for ambush mining were in the context of a fleet action and through the laying of small fields to interrupt and deter neutral commerce. By contrast Churchill argued that blockade mining was a tool that could be used by superior fleets, citing the example of Admiral Tōgō in the Russo-Japanese War. However, he cautioned that minefields could easily be swept and therefore blockade mining was ineffective unless a 'close and constant watch' was kept on the minefields. This, he claimed, was no longer possible due to the action of submarines, and as such blockade mining was not a policy open to the Royal Navy. Furthermore mining off the German coasts would inhibit British action, most notably that of the submarines. Here the First Lord began to reveal his true colours, declaring that '(t)he weak passive immobile defence of mines cannot for a moment be compared as a military measure with the enterprising offensive of submarines'. This was completely fanciful. In the very difficult conditions of the Heligoland Bight a functioning minefield would invariably be far more effective than a submarine, particularly with the approaching bad weather and limited visibility of winter. Instead this statement draws upon the Royal Navy's cultural rejection of mining as a technology which did not fit with the concepts of how the organisation should fight. Churchill concluded the memorandum with the defensive statement that '(t)he experience of the last three months seems to justify the partial and limited reliance put by the Admiralty upon mining as a method of warfare'.[50] This outright rejection of mining by the navy's political leader did serve to quieten the demands for further mining from other members of the Cabinet. This created its own problems, with Kitchener pressing for units of the Grand Fleet to be moved south in order to respond to any German raids.[51] Churchill steadfastly resisted Kitchener's attempts to force him into either mining or splitting up the Grand Fleet. Instead he laid out the same arguments as had been used throughout the prewar invasion debates.[52] This did little to ease the Secretary of State for War's concerns and he produced a memorandum for the Cabinet in response to Churchill's mining document pressing for some form of naval action.[53] This was discussed at Cabinet on the 21 October but Asquith felt that 'Winston made a very good defence of his policy' and so the matter slipped from view.[54]

The First Lord's sudden swing back in opposition to mining was felt in the Admiralty as well as Cabinet. On 22 October Dumas was called into a 'Conference with the First Lord who was offensive regarding the whole subject [of mining] and he kept asking why didn't you tell me where I have considered that the whole gear was out of date and inefficient [I] ended by saying well I'll draw up another paper for you and this time I wont mince matters'.[55] The resultant document produced by Dumas and his predecessor, Rear-Admiral Edward Charlton, was a bald statement of the materiel failings of British mining. It provided nothing in the way of analysis of the usages of mines, and made no mention of the stocks ordered by Dumas earlier in the month. The decision to print this document for distribution to the Cabinet is surprising and may have been taken by Churchill to remove any further pressure from his colleagues for more widespread mining. This idea is given further credence by the apparent editing of the document prior to printing. Dumas' diary entry for the 23 October records that the paper was 'telling the plain truth and exposing all the causes, amongst others, Winston [Churchill],

[Frederick] Tudor, [John] Jellicoe and [John] Fisher, of our mining failure. They may well beat me about this but I've had my say'.[56] It is difficult to reconcile this with the rather bland statement that was put before the Cabinet. A certain element of caution must be used when relying on Dumas' account, as he was prone to exaggeration, but the First Lord's attitude can perhaps be deduced from the entry on 27 October when Dumas received a 'memo[randum] from W[inston]C[hurchill] to Charlton and myself in the endeavour to find a scapegoat for the mines when it is really he who is to blame.'[57] After a brief moment when mining was at the centre of British strategic discussions, the materiel failings and the First Lord's change of heart appeared to have once again relegated the issue to a backwater. However a radical change in Admiralty personnel occurring at the same time meant that this situation would not last for long.

III

In the eyes of the public, and politicians, the navy was not considered to have performed well in the early months of the war. The escape of the *Goeben*, the failure to destroy the ships of the German East Asia Squadron, and the loss of the three cruisers to the submarine U9 left many feeling the Admiralty had lost control of the war. This was compounded by a press campaign against Battenberg on account of his German birth. At the end of October it became clear that change was needed, and the First Sea Lord was persuaded to resign. The bigger question was over who would replace him. Despite opposition from a number of quarters, including the King, it was eventually agreed that Admiral Lord Fisher should return to the Admiralty. Within days he was joined by Admiral Sir Arthur Wilson was an unofficial advisor, but acted in the role of an additional Chief of Staff. This change in personnel, which was soon followed by the replacement of Sturdee as COS by Henry Oliver, revolutionised the Admiralty. Asquith noted that 'one felt at once the difference made by the substitution of Fisher for poor L.B.— *élan*, dash, initiative, a new spirit'.[58] Similar views were held by many in the Admiralty, whilst at least some of Asquith's Cabinet colleagues saw the return of these two old salt horses as a check on their impulsive political leader.[59]

The advantages of bringing the two most respected prewar naval leaders back into the Admiralty were obvious, but there were always likely to be difficulties. All three men had effectively run their respective administrations and questions of authority, particularly between the positions of First Lord and First Sea Lord, were always likely to arise. Vice-Admiral David Beatty summed up the views of many when he wrote to his wife that 'I cannot see Winston & Jacky Fisher working very long together in harmony. They will quarrel before long.'[60] Of particular relevance here is that all three men also brought with them distinct, if at times overlapping, ideas of how the war should be prosecuted. It was the evolution and interrelation of these three strategic concepts that would drive mining policy over the subsequent six months.

The Royal Navy's adoption of the distant blockade strategy had always posed something of a problem for Churchill. A naturally aggressive figure, he struggled to accept the passive nature of the new strategy, and from the outset sought new ways to take the offensive. The idea which he seized upon was the capture of a German island, usually either Borkum or Sylt, for use as an advanced flotilla base. This concept had been widely considered within Royal Navy planning, but was dropped by 1909 as it was considered the German defences were too strong. Under Churchill's orders a small group of officers led by Rear-Admiral Sir Lewis Bayly reconsidered the idea in 1913, but resistance from the new War Staff was strong.[61] Churchill pressed for the idea to be reexamined once again in the summer of 1914, but events soon overtook this.[62] Despite the absence of a further investigation First Lord remained wedded to the idea.[63] Soon after the outbreak of the conflict Churchill began promoting a different strategy based upon British naval intervention in the Baltic, including potential amphibious operations using Russian troops.[64] These ideas had obvious antecedents in previous British planning and were likely inspired by Churchill's discussions with Fisher. The ideas were dealt a major blow by Russian defeats on the eastern front, and even a much reduced scheme was rejected by naval officers at the Loch Ewe Conference.[65] It should be noted that at this stage the Baltic scheme was entirely separate from Churchill's advanced base idea. Churchill, unlike earlier planners, was not looking at how to close the North Sea exit of the Kiel Canal so as to enable the concentration of British forces in the Baltic. Instead he hoped to soon be able to 'form two strong fleets, one in the North Sea and one in the Baltic.'[66] The latter would come either from the removal of British and French ships from the Mediterranean following Italian intervention on the Allied side, or preferably due to the destruction of the German fleet in battle.[67] The failure of either of these

240   R. DUNLEY

scenarios to come to fruition in autumn 1914 would drive Churchill's strategic vision in new directions.

The arrival at the Admiralty in early November of both Fisher and Wilson brought two very forceful characters into the centre of the planning debate, with clear ideas of how the war should be fought. Fisher had viewed the Baltic as the key theatre in any war with Germany for many years, and his prewar policy had invariably been framed with that in mind. These ideas were immediately brought back into the Admiralty, where they had a considerable amount in common with Churchill's earlier schemes. The same cannot be said for their ideas about controlling the German North Sea coasts. Fisher saw the answer to this challenge in an extensive mine barrage. As he complained in October:

> There are heaps and heaps of d—d stupid things being done and vital things being left undone. E.g., the German Fleet should be mined in as Togo mined in the Russian Fleet at Port Arthur. Not that he didn't want them to come out, but clearing the channel by the Russians gave him the warning signal they were coming out! and his base, like Jellicoe's, was unavoidably and necessarily hundreds of miles away. As fast as the Russians picked up mines Togo put down fresh ones. Thousands upon thousands of mines were thus used! And the mines with wire entanglements are the only bar to submarines.[68]

Although the evidence for this period is fragmentary it appears that Fisher viewed the mine barrage as a prelude to British naval operations in the Baltic. Such a scheme had the obvious and additional benefit that it helped to close down neutral trade flowing into German ports. The parallels between these ideas and those adopted by Fisher in 1905 could not be clearer.

The issue of neutral trade had exercised the new First Sea Lord for many years and one of Fisher's first actions on his return to the Admiralty was to attend a conference of the key political and naval figures, at which, as Asquith recorded, 'our main topic was the closing of the North Sea to all vessels'.[69] Recent claims that immediately prior to this meeting Fisher ordered fresh minefields to be laid as part of an economic warfare strategy are wide of the mark.[70] The field which was supposed to be laid on the night of 3 November was designed to be an extension of French mining which had taken place over the previous month.[71] The aim of this was to prevent German naval units from using the port of Zeebrugge, and there is no indication either of Fisher's involvement or of an economic warfare motivation.[72] There is some confusion as to whether this field was ever actually laid, with the official history of British mining stating that it was, and the later Naval Staff Monograph claiming the operation was cancelled due to the German raid on Yarmouth the day before.[73] As the contemporary documentation does not appear to have survived, it is unlikely we will ever know for certain.

More broadly it is clear that whilst Fisher did unquestionably view mines as part of the solution to the problems around the blockade and neutral trade, this was not the only issue he had in view. In particular he supported growing calls for mines to be used to prevent the worst excesses of German submarines and offensive mining and this brought him into conflict with Churchill. Following the loss of the battleship *Audacious* to a mine laid off the north coast of Ireland, Jellicoe decided that 'the time has arrived to mine the Heligoland Bight', reversing the position he had adopted at the beginning of the month.[74] This suggestion was rejected by the Admiralty, which replied that '(y)our proposals as to mining have been carefully considered but the work done by our submarines in the Bight has been of such importance that it is undesirable to add to their dangers by laying mines whose positions must be very uncertain'.[75] Although both Churchill and Fisher initialled this telegram, the content suggests it was written by the former. Days later Jellicoe wrote again requesting permission to mine areas off the Scottish coast believed to be used by submarines and their tenders.[76] Two days later Fisher wrote to Jellicoe reporting that he would 'expedite to the utmost patrols and mining against submarines'.[77] This was then effectively vetoed by the First Lord, who minuted '(t)his policy cannot be adopted without further discussion. The activity of armed trawlers is in every respect superior to the passive fouling of waters by mines w[hic]h are most ineffective against submarines'.[78]

The debate over the use of mines against submarines fitted in closely with the ideas being proposed by Sir Arthur Wilson.[79] Wilson, unlike either Fisher or Churchill, primarily viewed strategy from the perspective of the fleet. His policies lacked the grand vision of a Baltic project, and instead focused on British command of the sea. In particular he was concerned over the threat posed by German submarines. This issue had preoccupied Wilson for some time, and his prewar solution came in the form of a close blockade in order to catch submarines in shallow waters before they could dive. This policy had been tested in manoeuvres, with limited results, and opposition to Wilson's ideas was widespread. Despite this, in early September 1914 Churchill and Battenberg had held a meeting with Wilson in which the latter outlined his scheme to seize Heligoland. The motives behind their policies could not have been more different, but Churchill clearly saw the overlap with his advanced base scheme, and asked Wilson to set his plans to paper. The memorandum he produced lays out exactly why Wilson saw it as necessary to take the offensive step of seizing the island of Heligoland, and in particular details a new element of his thinking, the use of mines.

> The best means of destroying the enemy's submarines is to lay and maintain mines systematically in the channels at the mouths of the rivers and this cannot be done while Heligoland commands the approaches. If we lay the mines the enemy would quickly sweep channels through.

He went on to say that destroyers, aircraft and submarines based out of the island should be used to prevent the enemy from sweeping the mines. These minefields, backed by the flotilla, would then form the primary defence of the island, preventing the Germans from coming out to mount an attack.[80] A version of this scheme was proposed by Churchill at the Loch Ewe conference later in September and the condemnation of the naval officers present was unanimous, and interest in the concept faded.[81] Wilson, however, continued to be preoccupied with the submarine problem, and viewed mines as the most likely solution.[82] When he returned to the Admiralty in early November he brought the ideas with him and continued to work on his Heligoland scheme.

Over the course of the first month of the Churchill–Fisher–Wilson triumvirate at the Admiralty it appears that, whilst all three were working on distinct strategic ideas, there was some cross-fertilisation.[83] In particular, at a meeting of the War Council held on 1 December 1914, Churchill presented a scheme for seizing an advanced base. The arguments he put forward were remarkably similar to those put forward by Wilson, presenting the concept as one which ensured home defence. Fisher, who seems to have been surprisingly supportive of the idea, even pointed out the advantages with regard to protection against submarines.[84] It is noteworthy that neither Churchill nor Fisher mentioned the use of mines, something that had been central to Wilson's schemes, and the document Churchill drew up the following day indicates he had his eye on the island of Sylt, not Heligoland. Despite this there were obvious overlaps between the ideas.

Over the course of the following month Churchill developed this idea into a far wider strategic endeavour, linking his concept of an advanced base with the Baltic scheme, to create one complete concept for the naval war. As he explained to Asquith and the former Prime Minister Arthur Balfour:

> If it is impossible or unduly costly to pierce the German lines on existing fronts, ought we not, as new forces come to hand, to engage him on new frontiers, and enable the Russians to do so too? The invasion of Schleswig-Holstein from the sea w[oul]d at once threaten the Kiel Canal and enable Denmark to join us. The accession of Denmark w[oul]d throw open the Baltic and enable the Russian armies to be landed within 90 miles of Berlin; and the enemy, while being closely held on all existing lines w[oul]d be forced to face new attacks directed at vital points, and exhaust himself along a still larger perimeter. The essential preliminary is the blocking of the Heligoland Debouch.[85]

Churchill remained as convinced as ever that capturing a German island as an advanced base was essential, but his justification for this had changed. He no longer saw the flotilla as the sole weapon. Instead, seemingly drawing on Wilson's ideas, he argued that the Royal Navy must 'mine on the most extensive scale the channels and rivers of the German coast; and from their advanced base must prevent the mines from being removed'.[86] Churchill's conversion to mining was not, however, driven by the same strategic imperatives as Wilson's, and instead was the necessary result of the merging of the advanced base and Baltic strategies. The initial advanced base concept had simply been designed to allow Britain to secure an overwhelming preponderance of flotilla strength on the enemy's coast, to maintain an observational blockade and engage the enemy flotilla.[87] If challenged by the entire High Seas Fleet, the forces would be supported by the British Grand Fleet. Part of the idea behind the scheme was to draw the German battle fleet out so it could be engaged and destroyed. The addition of the Baltic component to the scheme removed this backstop. Under Churchill's new proposals the entire purpose of 'the closing of the Elbe' was to facilitate 'the domination of the Baltic'.[88] However, if the British fleet needed to be within striking range of the Heligoland Bight in order to support the flotilla, they could not also be in the Baltic. The only solution was, as prewar planners had concluded, to more permanently close the exit from the Kiel Canal, and the only means available to do so were mines or blockships. The Admiralty appear to have finally accepted the objections presented by the Hydrographer's Department to the various blockship schemes proposed over the previous decade, which left only mining as an alternative.

Over the course of December 1914, as Churchill was developing his plan for a naval campaign, his First Sea Lord was working up a different set of proposals. Fisher's support for the seizure of an advanced base at the War Council meeting appears to have been rather out of character.[89] Virtually all the other evidence available suggests that Fisher saw mining, rather than offensive flotilla operations, as the key to closing off the Heligoland Bight. On 14 December Fisher outlined his proposals to his friend, the author and strategist, Julian Corbett, asking the latter to produce a document explaining the rationale behind Fisher's Baltic scheme.[90] This outlined the broad principles behind the proposal, namely that British control of the Baltic would cut off German trade and allow Britain to threaten or actually conduct amphibious operations. It then went on to state that the 'first and most obvious difficulty attending such an operation is that it would require the whole of our battle force, and we could not at the same time occupy the North Sea effectively'. This was exactly the same problem Churchill had faced with his scheme, but the First Sea Lord, by contrast to his political master, did not see the answer in an advanced base. Instead he argued that the only course of action was to 'sow the North Sea with mines on such a scale that naval operations in it would become impossible'. The memorandum suggested that questions regarding the morality of the scheme could be overcome, largely by presenting it as retaliation for German mining. The scheme's impact on British naval operations could be limited by focusing the mining in a certain geographical area.[91] Considering this document represents one of the closest things we have to a detailed outline of Fisher's Baltic Project, the prominence of mining within it is noteworthy.

There are elements of Fisher's scheme which appear to be ill thought-through. Notably Corbett immediately pointed out one 'rather obvious objection.... if it is possible us to make the North Sea untenable with mines, is it not even more possible for the German to play the same game in the Baltic'.[92] No answer to this was forthcoming, and Fisher's biographer has used this and other evidence to suggest that the First Sea Lord may have never intended the scheme to be carried through.[93]

As will be seen, the evidence from the perspective of mining does not support that contention, but it is possible that Fisher was at least as concerned with closing the North Sea to neutral trade and enemy submarines, and feigning threats to Denmark and the Baltic, as he was with the actual pushing of the Grand Fleet through the Straits.

The basic outline of Fisher's mining scheme as part of his broader Baltic Project is well known to historians. What is less well known is that from the first days he entered office he set about putting the materiel in place to execute such a scheme. As has already been noted, Churchill ordered 15,000 new mines just prior to Fisher's return, but no efforts were made to provide suitable minelayers. Fisher knew that he could not rely on the original converted cruisers to carry out his operations. They were too slow, and could carry too few mines to be effective. As he wrote to Churchill, they would 'be butchered if they go out'.[94] He immediately realised that the solution lay in converting a number of fast, shallow-draft passenger liners, something that has distinct echoes of the policy he pursued during the Morocco crisis in the summer of 1905. More generally Fisher needed someone at the Admiralty to co-ordinate mining policy. It is not clear whether he did not trust Philip Dumas, the ADT, or whether the scale of the work was simply such that fresh blood was needed.[95] Either way the First Sea Lord soon identified Commander Forster Delafield Arnold-Forster, who had been commanding one of the original minelayers, and by late November the latter was transferred to the Admiralty.[96] By this time Arnold-Forster had already been scouring the south coast looking for suitable vessels for conversion to minelayers.[97] The small cross-Channel steamer *Paris* was immediate identified and conversion work was started.[98] Beyond this the task proved more difficult, with the list drawn up by the Admiralty Transport Department including eminently unsuitable vessels such as the big Cunard liners *Lusitania* and *Mauritania*.[99] Eventually three vessels under construction in Glasgow were identified. *Princess Irene* and *Princess Margaret* were being built for the Canadian Pacific Railway, were capable of 23 knots and could carry 500 mines.[100] The smaller *Biarritz* was also under construction for the Eastern and Chatham Railway Company, and was good for the same speed, but could only carry 200 mines.[101] The larger, but slower liner *Orvieto* was taken up in early January, soon followed by the *Angora*, a smaller turbine-driven vessel similar to those under construction in Glasgow.[102] The work on completing and converting these vessels was given the highest priority; as the Admiralty wrote to the contractors, the 'work [is] very urgent must by prosecuted by day and night shifts and with all possible despatch'.[103] The aim was to have the three fast ships building at Glasgow completed by 1 March. It is clear that there was strong pressure from the Admiralty in this direction, and Arnold-Forster was desperate to meet this.[104]

The minefields laid in October had revealed serious defects in British mines, and there was a concerted effort to ensure that the new mines under construction by Vickers would be efficient.[105] Arnold-Forster spent considerable time at the Vickers plant and testing facility at Crayford in an effort to rectify any problems. The selection of the new minelayers fits precisely with what would have been required to carry out the type of mining operations discussed by Fisher in this period. The drive to have them completed, and to ensure the mines and crews were ready so the vessels could be operational in late spring 1915 also fits with the admittedly limited evidence that we have regarding when the First Sea Lord wanted to begin such operations. Historians have frequently pointed to Fisher's construction programme as concrete evidence that he was serious about some form of Baltic project.[106] It is clear that the same can be said for the mining aspects of the scheme.

Within the Admiralty, the development of three overlapping, but separate war plans by the triumvirate running the organisation soon began causing problems. The War Staff whose job it would have been to plan any such operation were almost united in their opposition to all three schemes. Fisher's naval secretary, Captain Thomas Crease, would write eighteen months later that it fell to Henry Oliver to mediate between the men. Oliver was 'very methodical, very cautious and very canny, utterly without initiative and imagination ... he was just what was wanted to keep a drag on the impulsive methods of his 1st Lord and 1st Sea Lord'.[107] Oliver himself, albeit writing at a distance of nearly half a century, would recall 'I hated all these projects, but had to be careful what I said. The saving clause was that two of the 3 were always violently opposed to the plan of the third under discussion'.[108] This situation meant that none of the proposals made any real headway in terms of planning. To try to move things forward both Fisher and Churchill devoted considerable effort to trying to convince each other, and Jellicoe, of the merits of their respective schemes. The key point within this was the question of mining. In December Fisher wrote to Jellicoe outlining his views on the North Sea situation and the necessity for mining:

I imagine you are going to be asked by Cabinet orders what is your opinion as to so mining the German fleet into its anchorages that it can't get out into the North Sea without giving the warning signal of the clearing the approaches of mines just precisely similar to Admiral Togo putting mines down off Port Arthur which the Russians had to clear away before coming out and so giving Togo warning whose base was many hundreds of miles away as you know.[109]

Although the precise context of this discussion is unclear, with no specific mention in any surviving records of Cabinet meetings, it appears likely that this was a reaction to the raid on Scarborough, Hartlepool and Whitby. The proposal, however, fitted precisely with Fisher's Baltic scheme. At the same time the First Sea Lord was also attempting the more difficult task of persuading Churchill. The later remained unconvinced. He wrote that whilst he did not object in principle to laying minefields in the Heligoland Bight, 'I suspect we shall suffer inconvenience from it afterwards, but there is always a chance of a bag. It is like having a few lottery tickets. But it is no substitute for going to work'.[110] He followed this up the next day with an attempt to convert Fisher to his own advanced base scheme as part of the broader Baltic project. The First Lord implored that he was 'wholly with you about the Baltic. But you must close up this side first. You must take an island & block them in à la Wilson; or you must break the canal or the locks, or you must cripple their Fleet in a general action .... No scattering of mines will be any substitute for these alternatives'.[111]

The failure of either party to convince the other of the merits of their version of the Baltic scheme led to both looking for further external support. As has been seen, in late December Churchill outlined his proposals in some detail to Asquith, and the Prime Minister was not unreceptive.[112] Support for Fisher's ideas came from a different quarter, that of the influential Secretary of the War Council and protégé of the old admiral, Maurice Hankey. On the 29 December Hankey reported to Balfour that:

I had twenty minutes talk with Lord Fisher this morning. He is as keen as ever on mining the enemy's coast, but he says that his Chief of Staff and the First Lord are so strongly opposed to it that he can do nothing. He wants me to write something on the subject. But, although I am as strongly convinced as he is of the importance of mining, and can, I believe, make an overwhelming case for it, I find it rather a delicate matter to intervene in so domestic an Admiralty question. Since the war began I have more than once broached the matter to the First Lord, but he has each time brushed it aside as being out of the question. I am trying to hang a memorandum on to some C.I.D. decisions.[113]

Fisher's persuasion clearly worked and he produced a note outlining what he wanted Hankey to say.[114] Two days later Hankey produced the paper the First Sea Lord desired, advocating the adoption of a major minelaying policy in the Heligoland Bight. The reasons he gave, taken directly from Fisher's note, were threefold.[115] Firstly it would inhibit the movement of the German fleet. Secondly it would help protect against excursions by German submarines and minelayers, and thirdly it would prevent trade in neutral ships into German harbours.[116] This last point was particularly pertinent, as trade in cotton from the United States to Germany was increasing sharply. Cotton was a vital war commodity, but for political reasons it had not been declared contraband. Hankey had been convinced of the benefits of mining for some time, but it is obvious that here he was simply acting as a mouthpiece for Fisher.[117] As such the memorandum reinforces the point that the First Sea Lord viewed mining as a solution to a wide range of issues, not simply the precursor to an incursion into the Baltic.[118]

On 4 January, likely with a view to presenting a united front at the War Council meeting three days later, Churchill once again tried to thrash out his differences on strategy with Fisher. He wrote that 'we must agree on certain points'; one of these was that 'Borkum is the key to all Northern possibilities, whether defensive against raid or invasion, or offensive to block the enemy in'. He also suggested that he might be willing to give ground on the mining question, asking the First Sea Lord for 'definite and practical proposals'.[119] Fisher responded later the same day. He agreed that Borkum 'offers great possibilities' but qualified this by saying that 'it is purely a military question if it can be held'. The well-known lack of enthusiasm on the part of the army for such schemes meant this answer was effectively a rejection. Fisher enclosed a memorandum on minelaying, stating with some justification that they were 'opinions I have held since the War began'.[120] The document states clearly that 'there is no option but to adopt an offensive mine-laying policy'. The reasons Fisher gave were virtually identical to those set out in Hankey's paper of the previous week. He stated that by 1 March the navy would have 11,100 mines, but viewed this as 'quite inadequate'. Thus he stated that more mines were to be procured to go with the fast minelayers he was having converted. He therefore accepted that the materiel situation at the time was far from ideal, but steps were being taken to rectify this. In the meantime 'we can only go very slow in mine-laying; but carefully selected positions can be proceeded with'.[121]

Fisher had been strongly promoting a mining strategy ever since his return to the Admiralty, thus it is somewhat ironic that the impetus for the first major British mining operation since October came not from Fisher, but from Wilson. The admiral had been remarkably quiet in the debates between Fisher and Churchill, but in the last days of 1914 he produced a scheme to carefully lay a small minefield on the Amrum Bank, north of Heligoland.[122] The precise intentions behind the scheme were not recorded, but it appears that it was an area believed to be frequented by German submarines. Fisher supported the scheme although he felt it was only a beginning. He wrote to the First Lord: 'myself I think the whole North Sea ought to be clear of everything and a mine blockade of the German ports established beginning with A.K. Wilson's excellent mining plan for the Amrum Light Channel which is just first rate'.[123] The weight of opinion of the two admirals appears to have limited any resistance from Churchill. The mines were laid on the night of 8 January and the operation was considered to have been a success. Fisher noted with glee that 'the mines we laid down off the Amrum Bank have caused the Germans great anxiety'.[124] The success of the operation and the risks run by the old minelayers led Henry Oliver to comment on the arrival of the new fast vessels. He remarked that the '*Princess Irene* will lay the same number of mines with one quarter of the personnel, one quarter of the risk of detection and with 1½ times the chance of escape'.[125] This was, of course, exactly why Fisher had ordered the vessels' conversion. What he required now was for them to be completed and Churchill to come round to his mining scheme.

The prospects of the latter, at least, did not look promising. At the end of December Jellicoe wrote to the Admiralty with a series of proposals regarding mining. These included defensive mining on the British coast, the equipping of destroyers with mines, and the fitting-out of large liners for service as auxiliary minelayers with the fleet. This led to a wider exchange of views regarding mining within the Admiralty. The consensus was largely opposed to Jellicoe's suggestions, with Wilson returning to the old argument that 'the mining policy of the power that aims at keeping the sea open must necessarily be quite different from and much more difficult than the policy of the power whose main object is practically to close it to all comers'. Fisher clearly disagreed with his colleagues and angrily minuted 'I am absolutely in accord with every word written by Sir John Jellicoe'.[126] The same day he wrote to Jellicoe saying he thought the letter was *most excellent*. However he noted that 'A.K. Wilson and Oliver and all the small fry have pulled your letter all to pieces with "*buts*" and "*objections*", of which no doubt the First Lord will take full advantage, as he is dead against a mining policy'.[127] Fisher's remark with regard to Wilson and Oliver was a little wide of the mark. As has been seen, the most recent mining operation had been carried out at Wilson's instigation. Instead, as the Controller, Frederick Tudor, commented, '(t)he question of laying mines off the enemy's ports can only be properly considered in connection with the whole strategy of the war'.[128] Wilson had observed that mines laid 'in waters which we want to use are likely to destroy six of our ships for one of the enemy'.[129] This brought the issue back to the fundamental question of whether the Royal Navy wanted to operate in the Heligoland Bight.

At exactly the same time Fisher himself put forward a proposal to reinforce the minefields that had been laid earlier in the war at the eastern end of the Channel. This was aimed primarily at preventing German submarines from entering the Channel.[130] He pressed hard for the operation to be carried out immediately, but was once again stymied by Wilson and Oliver, questioning both the motivation and operational details of the scheme.[131] Churchill was clearly concerned, but Fisher angrily minuted: 'my view is that these mines should be laid at once. I protest against these delays'.[132] The First Sea Lord's protests clearly worked and Churchill acquiesced to a modified scheme two days later.[133] Fisher was soon bragging to Jellicoe about his success, reporting that '(w)e are laying down over 4000 mines in the Dover Straits'.[134]

Fisher also continued to press home his proposals for an offensive mining campaign. Ten days after the extensive discussions of Jellicoe's proposals Arnold-Forster, at the First Sea Lord's request, drew up two papers justifying a mining policy in the Heligoland Bight, and in the North Sea more generally. These papers sought to undermine the usual arguments that access to the Bight was necessary, suggesting that submarines were not as effective as mines in many conditions, and that it was highly unlikely British heavy ships would enter these waters.[135] Fisher sent the papers to Churchill with a note saying that they were 'two interesting reports on mining, not that it will have any effect as neither Sir A Wilson nor the COS (nor anyone else!) believe anything though one of them rose from the dead!' In a sarcastic reference to what he saw as the negativity and obstructionism of his colleagues he wrote that 'we shall finish the mining experiments desired for perfection when the war is ended'.[136] Churchill had, however, only recently reiterated his objections to offensive mining in a letter to Jellicoe, declaring '(a)s to mines you know my views. We have never laid one we have not afterwards regretted.'[137]

From the beginning of February 1915 discussion of mining faded slightly. There were a number of reasons for this. The most important was that everyone acknowledged that very little could be done until the new fast minelayers were ready, together with sufficient stocks of efficient mines. More broadly the fallout from the Battle of Dogger Bank and the forthcoming campaign in the Dardanelles distracted attention away from the debates about how to prosecute the war in the North Sea, which had framed much of the mining discussion. Between early December and late January the Royal Navy's leaders invested considerable time and effort in debating various mining strategies. There are certain key points that can be drawn from this. The first is that there were multiple drivers of a mining policy. Nicholas Lambert has recently suggested that Fisher was the only officer interested in mining, and that he viewed it solely from the perspective of economic warfare.[138] The evidence does not support this contention. Nor, however, was interest in mining solely derived from the need to close the Kiel Canal as part of a Baltic strategy. Fisher clearly saw a large mine barrage as having multiple purposes and the rationale he put forward changed depending on the audience he was addressing. It should also not be forgotten that whilst others at the Admiralty, notably Churchill and Wilson, did not support Fisher's mining policy, that did not mean they opposed all mining. Indeed the only offensive minefield laid in this period was at Wilson's instigation. Even Churchill continued to see mining as an important part of his broader northern strategy.[139] Finally, interest in mining from a defensive perspective continued to grow. One of the main drivers of interest in mining in the Heligoland Bight, whether that be close inshore supported by the flotilla, as suggested by Churchill and Wilson, or as part of Fisher's wider barrage, was the restrictions it would place on German submarines, minelayers or *in extremis* an invasion fleet. The same rationale lay behind the growing calls from Jellicoe and others in the fleet for mining in British coastal waters and at specific choke points such as the entrance to the Channel. Strategic realities were slowly forcing naval officers to reconsider their peacetime assumptions and one of these was the cultural opposition to mining. This was, however, a very slow process, and many within the navy objected to the concept of using the mine anywhere outside of German coastal waters.

IV

Through the spring of 1915 the materiel Fisher had ordered for his mining operations began to take shape. The small steamer *Paris* was the first to be commissioned in January, and played a role in laying the new minefields in the Dover Straits. The *Princess Margaret, Princess Irene* and *Biarritz* were commissioned in March to complete the new mine-laying squadron and the larger liner *Orvieto* was sent to join the Grand Fleet.[140] Not everything, however, was going to plan. Every time the navy laid a new minefield further technical problems with the mines themselves became apparent. Despite considerable work on the part of Arnold-Forster and Dumas, the mines laid in February in the Dover Straits broke free from their moors on just as great a scale as those in the original field.[141] The modifications made to the firing pistols also proved largely ineffective, with both of the pistols fitted to service mines, the original pendulum-based pistol and the new Heneage pistol, proving liable to fire on laying. The new Vickers Elia mines purchased in large quantities by Dumas proved little better, being very susceptible to wave action.[142] Some of these difficulties had been known for a while, and in January 1915 Fisher appointed a Mining Committee to investigate the issue more thoroughly.[143] This was chaired by Rear-Admiral Robert Ommanney, and consisted of Captain Dudley Pound and Arnold-Forster, with Captain Cobbe of the Minelaying Service, and Captain Field of *Vernon* as associate members.[144] Fisher was furious at the failures of mining materiel, ranting to Jellicoe 'our mines [are] scandalously defective' and that he hoped to 'be "even" with the principle culprits'.[145] However he appears to have been convinced that the committee would solve the problems. Unfortunately the majority of the records of the committee appear not to have survived, but the report produced by Ommanney in May paints a very positive picture of the work that they had been carrying out.[146]

The growing threat posed by German submarines throughout the spring of 1915 saw an increasing recognition that defensive minefields would form part of the solution. In particular Rear-Admiral Horace Hood, commanding the Dover Patrol, pressed for further mining east of the Dover Straits.[147] Although there was considerable discussion about the nature, location and depth of the field, the ideological opposition to mining which had marked out earlier discussions was less obvious. Due to the limited stock of mines only a small field was laid, but it was clear the principle was becoming established.[148] Further fields were laid off the Kentish Knock in May and then in Scottish waters in June.[149] Whilst this evidence suggests that mines were becoming more generally accepted as a defensive weapon it is clear that there were still major disagreements over their use in the offensive sphere. This comes through most clearly when in April Fisher proposed deploying a new type of mine, designed to be laid in the Heligoland Bight and drift on currents towards the German coast. The proposal was rejected by Churchill and Wilson because of the impact it would have on submarine operations.[150] In response Fisher minuted angrily '(h)ere is six months work wasted - and all because it is a sort of Mine!'[151] As an aside it is worth noting that using these unanchored mines would have been a blatant breach of Article 1 of the 1907 Hague Convention on mining, but this appears to have never even been discussed. The opposition to the use of such mines was cultural and operational, not legal.

The early spring of 1915 appears to have been marked by the partial withdrawal of Churchill from the day-to-day running of matters relating to the North Sea. It is notable how his previously ubiquitous red scrawl slowly disappears from the Admiralty dockets. This is likely to have been a result of his increasing preoccupation with events in the eastern Mediterranean. The Dardanelles campaign had initially been envisaged as a relatively straightforward prelude to major naval operations in the North Sea.[152] The initial failures turned this into a much larger project which came to dominate the First Lord's attention. This is not to say that Churchill had given up on his grand plan to seize a German North Sea island. At the beginning of April he instructed Arthur Wilson to '"implement"' a plan he had produced for an attack on Borkum, and the subsequent closure of the exits of the German North Sea rivers.[153] As ever, deciphering Fisher's strategic thought is more difficult, but it is clear that his commitment to mining on a large scale in the Heligoland

Bight remained undimmed. Later in April he wrote to Churchill pressing once again to begin such an operation, concluding that 'I'm quite sick of writing and talking about it'.[154]

It is in this light that one must view Operation Q, the large-scale mining operation carried out in the Heligoland Bight in early May 1915. Operation Q is noteworthy as it is the first major use of the new minelayers in the role they were designed for. It saw a number of what were, by the standards of the time, large minefields being laid deep in enemy waters. There are also, however, clear indications that this operation was originally intended to be something much more significant. The origins of Operation Q remain uncertain, but on 1 May 1915 the Admiralty sent Jellicoe paper M.0096, orders for an operation to be carried out a week later.[155] These orders do not appear to have survived. Indeed, when in 1926 the Historical Section were producing the monograph covering this period they asked Admiralty M Branch if they could trace a copy of the paper.[156] M Branch could not find anything beyond a copy of the covering letter.[157] Although we are lacking a copy of the original orders, some indication of the intended operation can be gleaned from telegrams sent between Jellicoe and the Admiralty over the following days. It appears that Jellicoe had some doubts about the operation and on 3 May the Admiralty telegraphed to say that he was free to modify the plans if he felt it necessary. Crucially the Admiralty requested that he let it know immediately 'in order that transports and movement of troops can be countermanded if necessary'.[158] Further communications make it clear that the intended target was the German island of Sylt off the coast of Schleswig-Holstein.[159] Although the evidence is very patchy it appears reasonable to conclude that, in its original form, Operation Q entailed some form of bombardment, possibly to be followed by an amphibious landing on the island. This was to be supported by the entire Grand Fleet and Harwich Force and take place in combination with a large-scale mining operation.[160] What the Admiralty hoped to achieve through such an attack is far less obvious. Whether this was simply an attempt to draw the German fleet out of harbour, possibly over a newly laid minefield, or a more serious attempt to establish an advanced base may well never be known. Furthermore it is not possible to tell who was the inspiration behind the operation. Elements of the plan appear to fit with Churchill's advanced-base scheme, whilst others suggest Fisher to be the more likely author. Again, unless further information comes to light, these questions will remain unanswered.

In the end Jellicoe's reservations forced the Admiralty to reconsider, and the only aspect of the operation they insisted on carrying out was the proposed minelaying.[161] On 8 May the large, fast minelayers *Princess Margaret* and *Princess Irene* sailed south towards the German coast near the Dutch border and that night laid two parallel fields running north-east from a point to the north of the Borkum Riff Light.[162] It appears that each laid a full complement of 500 mines. Two days later the larger minelayer *Orvieto*, which was attached to the Grand Fleet, laid another minefield at the other end of the Heligoland Bight.[163] This field was laid in a south-westerly direction from the Danish coast near the Horns Reef.[164] The location of these two fields clearly fits with Fisher's mine barrage scheme. These represent obvious starting points at either end of the area to be closed. It should also be noted that these fields are very close to the islands of Borkum and Sylt respectively. These two islands were those that Churchill had been most keen on investigating with regard to his advanced base strategy. It seems likely that the mining aspects of the operation were driven by Fisher as opposed to Churchill, but the context of the wider plan makes it difficult to draw any specific conclusions.

The operations revealed some minor teething problems with the minelayers. *Princess Irene* in particular needed to be docked for work to strengthen her mine rails. Fisher clearly viewed this with considerable frustration, ordering that she be 'put in order forthwith'.[165] Further inspection revealed greater problems and the First Sea Lord angrily questioned whether the other minelayers would suffer the same problems 'after they have had one trip on service'. He desired 'a report definitely fixing the responsibility' for these failing.[166] Although there is no direct evidence it seems reasonable to presume that Fisher's frustration was a result of these problems preventing further mining.

Whilst we have only fragmentary evidence regarding the original intension behind Operation Q, it is clear that the decision to press ahead with the mining aspect of the plan marked the start of the wider mining campaign which Fisher had been promoting since the beginning of the conflict. The Naval Staff history of British minefields produced immediately after the war states that the 'policy laid down in spring of 1915 for Minelaying in the [Heligoland] Bight was to lay a line of minefields approximately between the Frisian Islands and the Danish coast'.[167] This fits into a seam of Fisherite strategic thought dating back to 1905, and was exactly what the First Sea Lord had ordered the conversion of the minelayers for.

Fisher's offensive mining plan in May 1915 was soon overtaken by events. The crisis over the Dardanelles campaign and the doubts over the positions of both the First Lord and the First Sea Lord entirely distracted attention away from operational matters.[168] With regard to mining both the *Princess Margaret* and the *Princess Irene* were taken in hand at Sheerness to fix their defects.[169] At the end of the month the *Princess Irene* would blow up, killing amongst others Mervyn Cobbe. This was believed to be due to the failure of one of the Heneage firing pistols, which ironically Cobbe had helped to develop and fought to retain.[170] This cast a considerable cloud over the mine and mining service in general. Despite this, there are signs that even following Fisher's departure from the Admiralty a major mine barrage in the Heligoland Bight was being considered. In June Henry Oliver noted that the short summer nights made it very difficult to carry out operations aimed at 'satisfactorily mining and sealing up [the] Heligoland Bight'. He noted that 'towards the end of July nights would be more favourable' and that would give more time to improve the materiel.[171] In August further mining operations took place. Operation AZ would have seen the surviving minelayers based out of the Nore lay a field very close to that laid by the *Princess Margaret* and *Princess Irene* in May.[172] Due to enemy activity it was abandoned and replaced by Operation BY, in which the *Princess Margaret* was to lay a field near the Horns Reef, building on the mining conducted by the *Orvieto*.[173] The operation proved something of a disaster, with the minelayer and her escorts being intercepted by German destroyers before they could reach their target.[174]

Offensive minelaying continued with a further operation, CY, in September. Despite this it is clear that the real impetus behind the schemes faded with Fisher's departure from the Admiralty. Over the course of his first months in office Fisher sought to prepare the materiel necessary for a large-scale offensive mining campaign. This became operational in the spring of 1915 and it is clear that he intended to use it for exactly the purpose he outlined, namely to create a mine barrage in the southern North Sea. Following his departure from office Fisher regularly bombarded politicians and naval officers with his views on how the war should be run. He tended to do this by stating what he had done whilst at the Admiralty and how his legacy was being wasted away. Historians have, with good reason, tended to look sceptically on much of what Fisher said following his departure from office. He had a habit of embellishing his own achievements, and unnecessarily denigrating those of others. This was not always the case, and mining appears to be one example where Fisher's actions whilst at the Admiralty support his later rhetoric. In February 1916 he would write to Jellicoe enclosing a memorandum entitled 'Special Causes of Grave Anxiety in the Present Naval Situation', in which he declared:

> The 9th Cause of anxiety results from the lamentable (one might almost say criminal) folly in not steadily pursuing a mining policy and so close the North Sea more effectively than any blockade. Between Nov 1914 and May 1915 most energetic and effective steps were successfully taken to fit very fast ocean-going minelayers and provide mines in very big quantities and certainly had the mining policy been carried out it can be vouched for that on one occasion certainly a most terrible disaster would have over taken the German High Seas Fleet.[175]

He would express similar views, albeit in less forceful terms, to the Prime Minister.[176] Much of Fisher's later writing concerned his Baltic Project, and there is considerable debate over the extent to which this was a realistic scheme, or even one which Fisher himself took seriously. The mining aspects of the scheme have to be treated differently. Fisher entered office intending to implement a large mine barrage off the German North Sea coast, and that was exactly what he started to do.

As in so many other areas, the experience of the first year of the war fundamentally changed the Royal Navy's position with regard to mining. The service entered the war with no mining policy, and an Admiralty convinced that mining had no place in British naval strategy. Ironically the first crack in this position was produced by pressure from politicians and not naval events. The problems Britain faced in mounting an economic warfare campaign in the face of opposition from the United States forced the government to investigate radical options. Mining was one potential solution. It is a matter of considerable irony that American diplomatic pressure drove Britain to abandon a policy based on legal contraband controls and adopt one centred around illegal mining operations. Continued opposition to mining especially from Churchill prevented this policy from being implemented with any vigour, something compounded by materiel failures. Thus it was not until the return of Fisher and Wilson to the Admiralty that mining began to be reconsidered. The former in particular brought a clear vision with him to the Admiralty, and immediately set about implementing it. At the same time as Fisher was seeking to grind Churchill down into accepting his mine barrage scheme, front-line officers slowly began to reconsider their opposition to mining, particularly in the light of German minelaying and submarine activity. Thus by spring 1915 the Royal Navy was beginning to lay a number of defensive minefields in addition to the larger scheme envisaged by Fisher. Had 'Radical Jack' remained at the Admiralty through summer 1915 it is clear that mining would have taken a central role in British naval strategy. This would have been in spite of the continued failures of materiel. As it was the Balfour–Jackson administration took a far more passive attitude to the conduct of the war, and mining never achieved the importance envisaged by Fisher. Mining was, however, now well established as a weapon to be used by both sides in the conflict. This did not mean that the service truly embraced the weapon. Reginald Tyrwhitt summed it up well when he complained to Roger Keyes, '(h) ow I agree with you about submarine & mines. They completely put the hat on all honest fighting.'[177]

NOTES

1. National Maritime Museum (NMM), Phipps Hornby Papers, PHI/210B, 'A History of Mining by Captain P. Dumas'.
2. The National Archives (TNA), ADM 137/1002, Vickers to Admiralty, 27 July 1914, ff. 10–12.
3. No record of this offer can be found in the Vickers archive at Cambridge University Library and the Admiralty record appears incomplete.
4. TNA, ADM 137/843, Arnold-Forster Memoranda, 20 and 23 September 1914, ff. 26–33.
5. TNA, ADM 137/843, Leveson Minute, n.d., f. 34.
6. National Museum of the Royal Navy (NMRN), Submarine Museum (SM), F. D. Arnold–Forster Papers, Family Letters 19, Arnold-Forster to Georgie, 28 September 1914 and Arnold-Forster to Father, 14 September 1914.
7. TNA, ADM 116/1350, 'Suggested Subjects for Discussion: 17th September 1914'.
8. TNA, ADM 137/995, 'Conference on Board Iron Duke 17th September', ff. 103–107.
9. James Goldrick, *Before Jutland: The Naval War in Northern European Waters, August 1914–February 1915* (Annapolis: Naval Institute Press, 2015), pp. 85–86.

10. Michael and Eleanor Brock, eds., *H. H. Asquith: Letters to Venetia Stanley* (Oxford: Oxford University Press, 1985), Asquith to Stanley, 6 August 1914, no. 117, pp. 158–159.
11. Bodleian Library, Oxford (BLO), Harcourt MS. Eng. c. 8269, 7 August 1914.
12. Hobhouse diary, quoted in Edward David, ed., *Inside Asquith's Cabinet: From the Diaries of Charles Hobhouse* (London: John Murray, 1977), p. 179; *Letters to Venetia Stanley*, Asquith to Stanley, 2 August 1914, no. 113, pp. 145–147; BLO, Harcourt MS. Eng. c. 8269, 4 August 1914.
13. BLO, Harcourt MS. Eng. c. 8269, 13 August 1914; TNA, CAB 41/35/29, Asquith to the King, 13 August 1914.
14. BLO, Harcourt MS. Eng. c. 8269, 14 August 1914; British Library (BL), Add Ms 60506, Hobhouse Journal, 14 August 1914.
15. *Foreign Relations of the United States (FRUS)* 1914, Supplement: The World War, Document 708, Bryan to Barclay, 13 August 1914, pp. 455–456.
16. BLO, Harcourt MS. Eng. c. 8269, 17 August 1914; TNA, CAB 41/35/31, Asquith to the King, 17 August 1914.
17. *Letters to Venetia Stanley*, Asquith to Stanley, 17 August 1914, no. 123, pp. 170–172.
18. BLO, Harcourt MS. Eng. c. 8269, 23 September 1914.
19. TNA, ADM 137/843, Churchill Minute, 27 November 1914, f. 71; TNA, ADM. 137/1883, Admiralty to Jellicoe, 1 December 1914, f. 467.
20. BLO, Harcourt MS. Eng. c. 8269, 23 September 1914.
21. TNA, CAB 41/35/47, Asquith to the King, 23 September 1914.
22. BLO, Harcourt MS. Eng. c. 8269, 30 September 1914.
23. *Letters to Venetia Stanley*, Asquith to Stanley, 29 September 1914, no. 168, pp. 255–257.
24. Churchill Archives Centre (CAC), Churchill Papers, CHAR/13/44/83, Asquith to Churchill, 29 September 1914.
25. TNA, ADM 137/843, Churchill Minute, 1 October 1914 f. 37.
26. *Letters to Venetia Stanley*, Asquith to Stanley, 29 September 1914, no. 168, pp. 255–257.
27. TNA, CAB 41/35/48, Asquith to the King, 30 September 1914; BLO, Harcourt MS. Eng. c. 8269, 30 September 1914.
28. Isabel V. Hull, *A Scrap of Paper: Making and Breaking International Law During the Great War* (Ithaca: Cornell University Press, 2014), p. 216.
29. BLO, Harcourt MS. Eng. c. 8269, 14 August 1914.

30. CAC, Churchill Papers, CHAR 13/41/152, Churchill to Jellicoe, 1 October 1914.
31. CAC, Churchill Papers, CHAR 13/41/156, Jellicoe to Churchill, 2 October 1914.
32. TNA, ADM 137/843, Churchill Minute and Admiralty Telegrams 1–3 October 1914, ff. 37–42; Captain Lockhart Leith, *The History of British Minefields: 1914-18*, pp. 94–95.
33. Imperial War Museum (IWM), PP/MCR/96, Dumas Diary, 2 October 1914.
34. NMM, Phipps Hornby Papers, PHI/210B, 'A History of Mining by Captain P. Dumas'; NMM, Oliver Papers, OLV/12, 'Recollections', p. 129.
35. NMM, Ballard Papers, Mss/80/200, Ballard to His Mother, 4 October 1914.
36. IWM, PP/MCR/96, Dumas Diary, 3–5 October 1914; NMM, Phipps Hornby Papers, PHI/210B, 'A History of Mining by Captain P. Dumas'.
37. For details of the licence and arrangements see Cambridge University Library (CUL), MS Vickers Doc 57, Folder 24, f. 15 and Folder 26, f. 110.
38. NMM, Phipps Hornby Papers, PHI/210B, 'A History of Mining by Captain P. Dumas'.
39. IWM, PP/MCR/96, Dumas Diary, 4–5 October 1914.
40. TNA, T 204/1, Naval Expenditure Emergency Standing Committee, 21st Meeting, 6 October 1914.
41. BL, Jellicoe Papers, Add Ms 49006, Fisher to Jellicoe, 11 December 1914, ff. 70–71.
42. BLO, Harcourt MS. Eng. c. 8269, 12 October 1914.
43. BLO, Harcourt MS. Eng. c. 8269, 12 October 1914.
44. TNA, ADM 137/843, Churchill Minute, 14 October 1914, on Marine Bordeaux to Admiralty, 14 October 1914, f. 48.
45. TNA, ADM 137/843, French Naval Attaché to Marine Bordeaux, 21 October 1914 and unsigned note, 2 November 1914, ff. 62, 65.
46. TNA, CAB 41/35/52, Asquith to the King, 12 October 1914.
47. BL, Add Ms 60506, Hobhouse Journal, 14 October 1914, ff. 68–69.
48. BL, Add Ms 60506, Hobhouse Journal, 15 October 1914, ff. 68–69; BLO, Harcourt MS. Eng. c. 8269, 15 October 1914.
49. NMM, RIC/1/10, Richmond Diary, 19 October 1914.
50. TNA, CAB 37/121/126, 'Notes on Mining', 18 October 1914.
51. BLO, Ms Asquith 13, Kitchener to Churchill, 19 October 1914, f. 221.
52. BLO, Ms Asquith 13, Churchill to Kitchener, 19 October 1914, ff. 222–223.

10 THE TEST OF CONFLICT 261

53. TNA, CAB 37/121/126, 'Memorandum on Admiralty Paper "Notes on Mining"', 20 October 1914.
54. *Letters to Venetia Stanley*, Asquith to Stanley, 21 October 1914, no. 186, pp. 280–281.
55. IWM, PP/MCR/96, Dumas Diary, 22 October 1914.
56. IWM, PP/MCR/96, Dumas Diary, 23 October 1914.
57. IWM, PP/MCR/96, Dumas Diary, 27 October 1914.
58. *Letters to Venetia Stanley*, Asquith to Stanley, 2 November 1914, no. 199, pp. 305–306.
59. IWM, PP/MCR/96, Dumas Diary, 30 October 1914; BL, Add Ms 60506, Hobhouse Journal, 6 January 1915.
60. Brian Ranft, *The Beatty Papers: Selections from the Private and Official Correspondence of Admiral of the Fleet Earl Beatty*, vol. 1 (Navy Records Society, 1989), Beatty to Wife, 30 October 1914, no. 78, pp. 148–149.
61. TNA, ADM 116/3412, Churchill to Battenberg, 17 February 1913, f. 192; Christopher M. Bell, *Churchill and Seapower* (Oxford: Oxford University Press, 2012), pp. 38–39.
62. TNA, ADM 116/3096, Churchill to Battenberg, 11 June 1914; Bell, *Churchill and Seapower*, p. 48.
63. NMM, RIC/1/9, Richmond Diary, 9 August 1914.
64. Martin Gilbert, *Winston S. Churchill: Companion*, vol. 3, Part 1 (London: Heinemann), Churchill Memorandum, 19 August 1914, pp. 45–46; BLO, Harcourt MS. Eng. c. 8269, 20 August 1914.
65. TNA, ADM 137/995, 'Conference on Board Iron Duke 17th September', ff. 103–107.
66. TNA, ADM 137/995, 'Conference on Board Iron Duke 17th September', ff. 103–107.
67. Bell, *Churchill and Seapower*, p. 57.
68. Arthur J. Marder, *Fear God and Dread Nought: The Correspondence of Admiral of the Fleet Lord Fisher of Kilverstone*, vol. III (*FGDN III*) (London: Jonathan Cape, 1959), Fisher to Leyland, 15 October 1914, no. 36, p. 63.
69. *Letters to Venetia Stanley*, Asquith to Stanley, 2 November 1914, no. 199, pp. 305–306.
70. Nicholas Lambert, *Planning Armageddon: British Economic Warfare and the First World War* (Cambridge, MA: Harvard University Press, 2012), p. 299.
71. TNA, ADM 137/843, 'Notes on French Minelaying' 2 November 1914, ff. 62–65.
72. It seems highly likely that it was this operation which F. D. Arnold-Forster was helping to plan the previous week, prior to Fisher's return

to the Admiralty. See NMRN, SM, F. D. Arnold–Forster Letters 19, Arnold-Forster to Wife, 27 October 1914.

73. Naval Staff Monographs, vol. 3, no. 8, 'Naval Operations Connected with the Raid on the North East Coast, December 16th 1914', pp. 170–174; Lockhart Leith, *The History of British Minefields: 1914–18*, pp. 96–97.

74. CAC, Churchill Papers, CHAR 13/17B/83–4, Jellicoe to Churchill, 30 October 1914.

75. CAC, Churchill Papers, CHAR 13/42/104–5, Admiralty to Jellicoe, 16 November 1914.

76. TNA, ADM 137/843, Jellicoe to Admiralty, 19 November 1914, ff. 67–68.

77. *FGDN III*, Fisher to Jellicoe, 21 November 1914, no. 51, p. 78.

78. TNA, ADM 137/843, Churchill Minute, 27 November 1914, f. 74.

79. For a detailed study of Wilson's strategic thought see David Morgan-Owen, 'Cooked Up in the Dinner Hour? Sir Arthur Wilson's War Plan, Reconsidered', *English Historical Review*, vol. CXXX, no. 545 (2015).

80. TNA, ADM 137/492, 'The Capture of Heligoland', 10 September 1914, ff. 211–221.

81. TNA, ADM 137/995, 'Conference on Board Iron Duke 17th September', ff. 103–107.

82. CAC, Churchill Papers, CHAR 13/27A/32–7 'Memorandum by Admiral of the Fleet Sir Arthur Wilson, on the Use of Mines for Destroying Submarines', 29 September 1914.

83. A complete account of these events can be found in Christopher M. Bell, *Churchill and the Dardanelles* (Oxford: Oxford University Press, 2017), Chapters 1 and 2.

84. TNA, CAB 42/1/5, 'Meeting of the War Council held 1st December 1914'.

85. BLO, MSS. Asquith 13, Churchill to Asquith and Balfour, 29 December 1914, ff. 242–243.

86. BLO, MSS. Asquith 13, Churchill Memorandum enclosed in Churchill to Asquith, 31 December 1914, ff. 244–253.

87. TNA, ADM 137/452, Churchill Memorandum, 9 August 1914, ff. 208–210.

88. BLO, MSS. Asquith 13, Churchill to Asquith and Balfour, 29 December 1914, ff. 242–243.

89. On Fisher's unwillingness to speak up against Churchill at the War Council see BL, Add Ms 49703, Hankey to Balfour, 21 January 1915, ff. 151–152.

90. *FGDN III*, Fisher to Corbett, 12 December 1914, no. 70, p. 93; Ruddock F. Mackay, *Fisher of Kilverstone* (Oxford: Clarendon Press,

1973), p. 472. Unfortunately Corbett's Diary for 1914 appears to have gone missing since it was consulted by Mackay.

91. TNA, ADM 116/3454, 'On the Possibility of Using Our Command of the Sea to Influence More Drastically the Military Situation'. For Corbett's manuscript version see CAC, FISR 1/17, enclosed in Corbett to Fisher, 19 December 1914.

92. CAC, Fisher Papers, FISR 1/17, Corbett to Fisher, 19 December 1914.

93. Mackay, *Fisher*, pp. 462–465 and *passim*.

94. *Churchill Companion*, vol. 3, Part 1, Fisher to Churchill, 21 December 1914, pp. 322–323.

95. Arthur J. Marder, *Dreadnought to Scapa Flow*, vol. 2 (Barnsley: Seaforth, 2013) pp. 78–79.

96. NMRN, SM, F. D. Arnold-Forster Family Letters 20, Arnold-Forster to Wife, 16 November 1914 and 24 November 1914.

97. NMRN, SM, F. D. Arnold-Forster Family Letters 20, Arnold-Forster to Wife, 13 and 18 November 1914.

98. TNA, MT 23/439/14, 'List of Minelayers', n.d.

99. TNA, MT 23/439/14, List of British steamers with a nominal speed of 19 knots and over, 24 December 1914.

100. NMM, Brass Foundry (BF), Ships Cover 417, Arnold-Forster memorandum, 22 December 1914.

101. TNA, MT 23/439/14, 'List of Minelayers', n.d.

102. TNA, MT 23/339/12, 'Empress of Britain and Orvieto to be taken up as Minelayers', 7 January 1915 and note from Lord Inchcape, 9 January 1915.

103. TNA, MT 23/339/12, Admiralty to Repairs London, 13 January 1914.

104. NMRN, SM, F. D. Arnold–Forster Family Letters 20, Arnold-Forster to Wife, 10 February 1915.

105. NMRN, SM, F. D. Arnold–Forster Family Letters 20, Arnold-Forster to Wife, 30 November 1914, 29 January and 10 February 1915; TNA, ADM 137/843, 'Report from the Mining Committee', 28 May 1915, ff. 152–162.

106. Nicholas Black, *The British Naval Staff in the First World War* (Woodbridge, Suffolk: The Boydell Press, 2009), pp. 116–119.

107. TNA, CAB 17/179, Crease to Hankey, 28 February 1916, ff. 94–99.

108. NMM, Oliver Papers, OLV/12, *Recollections*, p. 122.

109. BL, Jellicoe papers, Add Ms 49006, Fisher to Jellicoe, n.d. (December 1914), ff. 100–105. N. B. Marder dates this letter as circa April 1915, but internal content strongly suggests it was written in late December 1914. See *FGDN III*, no. 155, pp. 181–182.

110. *FGDN III*, Churchill to Fisher, 21 December 1914, no. 79, p. 105.

111. *Churchill Companion*, vol. 3, Part 1, Churchill to Fisher, 22 December 1914, pp. 325–326.
112. *Letters to Venetia Stanley*, Asquith to Stanley, 30 December 1914, no. 241, pp. 345–347.
113. BL, Balfour Papers, Add Ms 49703, Hankey to Balfour, 29 December 1914, f. 126.
114. CAC, Fisher Papers, FISR 5/22, Fisher Note, undated, with 'Minelaying', 31 December 1914.
115. This memorandum is generally, but incorrectly, attributed to Fisher who, although he was the inspiration, did not in fact write it. See Marder, *Dreadnought to Scapa Flow*, vol. 2, pp. 80–81.
116. TNA, CAB 63/2, 'Minelaying', 31 December 1914, ff. 37–40.
117. NMM, RIC/1/9, Richmond Diary, 9 September 1914; IWM, PP/MCR/96, Dumas diary, 1 October 1914.
118. Also see CAC, CHAR 13/56/2–4, Fisher to Churchill, 2 January 1915.
119. *FGDN III*, Churchill to Fisher, 4 January 1915, no. 95, p. 121.
120. *FGDN III*, Fisher to Churchill, 4 January 1915, no. 96, p. 121–123.
121. *FGDN III*, 'Minelaying' enclosed in Fisher to Churchill, 4 January 1915, no. 96, pp. 121–123.
122. TNA, ADM 137/837, 'Laying Mines on the Route from the Lister Deep to the Elbe' n.d., ff. 9–10.
123. *Churchill Companion*, vol. 3, Part 1, Fisher to Churchill, 2 January 1915, pp. 361–362.
124. *FGDN III*, Fisher to Jellicoe, 12 January 1915, no. 102, pp. 128–129.
125. TNA, ADM 137/837, Oliver Minute, 11 January 1915, f. 128.
126. TNA, ADM 137/843, 'British Mining Policy', ff. 79–91.
127. *FGDN III*, Fisher to Jellicoe, 12 January 1915, no. 102, pp. 128–129.
128. TNA, ADM 137/843, Tudor Minute, 11 January 1915, f. 91.
129. TNA, ADM 137/843, Wilson Minute, 8 January 1915, f. 90.
130. TNA, ADM 137/843, Fisher Memorandum, 14 January 1915, f. 92.
131. TNA, ADM 137/843, Oliver and Wilson Minutes, 18 and 20 January 1915, f. 96.
132. TNA, ADM 137/843, Fisher Minute, 21 January 1915, f. 97.
133. TNA, ADM 137/843, Churchill Note, 23 January 1915, f. 112; BL, Add Ms 48990 Churchill to Jellicoe, 25 January 1915, ff. 185–189.
134. BL, Jellicoe Papers, Add Ms 49006, Fisher to Jellicoe, 5 February 1915, ff. 136–137; Lockhart Leith, *British Minefields*, pp. 98–102.
135. TNA, ADM 137/843, 'Notes on Mining in North Sea', 20 January 1915, ff. 100–102.
136. TNA, ADM 137/843, Fisher Note, 21 January 1915, ff. 103.
137. BL, Jellicoe Papers, Add Ms 48990, Churchill to Jellicoe, 18 January 1915, ff. 183–184.

138. Lambert, *Planning Armageddon*, pp. 311–314.
139. BL, Jellicoe Papers, Add Ms 48990, Churchill to Jellicoe, 9 March 1915, ff. 191–193.
140. TNA, ADM 137/1883, Admiralty to Jellicoe, 22 February 1915, f. 473; *FGDN III*, Fisher to Jellicoe, 17 March 1915, no. 141, pp. 166–167.
141. TNA, ADM 137/843, 'Report from the Mining Committee', 28 May 1915, ff. 152–162.
142. TNA, ADM 137/843, 'Report from the Mining Committee', 28 May 1915, ff. 152–162; NMM, Phipps Hornby Papers, PHI/210B, 'A History of Mining by Captain P. Dumas'.
143. IWM, PP/MCR/96, Dumas Diary, 6 December 1914, 15 and 18 January 1915.
144. NMM, Phipps Hornby Papers, PHI/210B, 'A History of Mining by Captain P. Dumas'.
145. *FGDN III*, Fisher to Jellicoe, 21 April 1915, no. 173, pp. 199–200.
146. TNA, ADM 137/843, 'Report from the Mining Committee', 28 May 1915, ff. 152–162.
147. TNA, ADM 137/843, Hood to Admiralty, 28 March and 2 April 1915, ff. 123–124, 128–130.
148. TNA, ADM 137/843, Fisher Minute, 12 April 1915, f. 134.
149. TNA, ADM 137/843, 'Angora, Laying Mines' and 'Offensive Operations Against Submarines in British Waters', 20 May 1915, ff. 141–142, 143–148; TNA, ADM 137/1882, Murray to Smyth, 29 May 1915, ff. 529–532.
150. CAC, FISR 1/19, Churchill and Wilson Minutes, 18 and 21 April 1915.
151. CAC, FISR 1/19, Fisher to the Naval Secretary, 27 April 1915.
152. Bell, *Churchill and the Dardanelles*, p. 69.
153. CAC, CHAR 13/55/1–10, 'Capture of Borkum' enclosed in Churchill to Wilson 1 April 1915.
154. CAC, CHAR 13/57/14–15, Fisher to Churchill, 23 April 1915.
155. TNA, ADM 137/1863, CinC Home Fleet to Admiralty, 3 May 1915, Telegram No. 882.
156. TNA, ADM 137/837, Unknown Minute, 16 November 1926, f. 23.
157. TNA, ADM 137/837, Admiralty to CinC Home Fleet, 1 May 1915, f. 24.
158. CAC, CHAR 13/64/11, Admiralty to Jellicoe, 3 May 1915.
159. TNA, ADM 137/1808, Admiralty to CinC Home Fleet, 3 May 1915, Telegram No. 881.
160. TNA, ADM 137/1863, CinC Home Fleet to Admiralty, 3 May 1915, Telegram No. 893.
161. TNA, ADM 137/1808, Admiralty to CinC Home Fleet, 4 May 1915, Telegram No. 886.

162. TNA, ADM 137/837, Cobbe to Admiralty, 9 May 1915, ff. 138–139.
163. For confirmation that they were viewed as part of the same operation see TNA, ADM 137/113, Admiralty to Jellicoe, 7 May 1915, f. 335.
164. TNA, ADM 137/837, Smyth to Jellicoe, 12 May 1915, ff. 156–157.
165. TNA, ADM 137/837, Fisher Minute, 10 May 1915, f. 142.
166. NMM, BF, Ships Cover 417, Fisher Minute, 14 May 1915.
167. Lockhart Leith, *History of British Minefields*, p. 17.
168. Bell, *Churchill and the Dardanelles*, pp. 164–85; Mackay, *Fisher*, pp. 486–505.
169. TNA, ADM 137/843, 'Report from the Mining Committee', 28 May 1915, ff. 152–162.
170. NMM, Phipps Hornby Papers, PHI/210B, 'A History of Mining by Captain P. Dumas'.
171. TNA, ADM 137/843, Oliver Minute, 6 June 1915, f. 173.
172. TNA, ADM 137/837, 'Orders for Operation AZ', ff. 39–45.
173. Naval Staff Monographs, vol. 14, 'Home Waters—Part V From July to October 1915', pp. 141–142.
174. TNA, ADM 137/837, Litchfield to Admiralty, 20 August 1915, ff. 166–174.
175. *FGDN III*, Fisher to Jellicoe, 14 February 1916, no. 273, pp. 308–310.
176. TNA, CAB 17/179, Fisher to Asquith, 26 February 1916, ff. 69–72.
177. BL, Keyes Papers, Add Ms 82404, Tyrwhitt to Keyes, 14 April 1916.

CHAPTER 11

War, Law and Diplomacy

Questions of international law, and more especially of belligerent and neutral rights at sea, have occupied a prominent place within the historiography of the First World War since before the conflict ended. This has primarily been driven by the debate over the entry of the United States into the conflict, and the role of unrestricted submarine warfare and the Allied blockade in bringing this about.[1] This debate has taken place with little to no reference to the role of mining as a central issue in the legal debates in the first year of the war, and as a result of this, has ignored the crucial context necessary to understand the later crisis over the submarine blockade. The only historian to look at the matter in any detail was James Garner, writing in the immediate postwar period, without access to most of the material.[2] Isabel Hull has recently incorporated some discussion of mining within her analysis of the origins of the first U-boat campaign, but the importance of the issue to contemporary decision-makers remains unrecognised.[3]

The issue of mining came to the fore very early in the conflict. The destruction of the German auxiliary minelayer *Königin Luise* on 5 August and the sinking the following day of the British cruiser *Amphion* caught the attention of a public desperate for war news. On 7 August the First Lord of the Admiralty Winston Churchill gave a statement on the issue to the House of Commons. He declared that 'the indiscriminate scattering of contact mines about the seas' was 'new in warfare' and threatened peaceful non-combatants and neutrals. He went on to state that it:

© The Author(s) 2018   267
R. Dunley, *Britain and the Mine, 1900–1915*,
https://doi.org/10.1007/978-3-319-72820-9_11

deserves, at any rate, to be considered attentively, not only by us, who are, of course, engaged in the war, and who may naturally be prone to hasty judgment in such matters, but deserving also to be attentively considered by the nations of a civilised world.[4]

This attitude resonated clearly with the British public. The loss of the *Amphion* had been one of the first engagements between British and German forces. The German use of mines, a weapon widely viewed as barbaric in Britain, connected with the rhetoric presenting Germany as aggressive and its actions as illegal. The German invasion of Belgium was the pretext widely used to justify British entry into the conflict and the laying of mines appeared, to British observers, to be another instance of Germany showing a complete disregard for morality and international law. It should be recalled that apart from the German invasion of Belgium none of the traditionally cited German breaches of international law had yet taken place. Thus the use of mines was important in confirming German behaviour; all the more so because it took place at sea, in a fundamentally British sphere. *The Times* reflected these views when it condemned the German actions as 'an offence against humanity and civilisation'.[5]

The sincere British belief that the German use of mines in the North Sea represented a serious breach in the accepted practice of war led to it being immediately used in the diplomatic negotiations with neutral powers, most notably the United States. On 7 August the American Ambassador Walter Page called on the British Foreign Secretary, Sir Edward Grey, to ask if Britain intended to adhere to the rules established in the Declaration of London. This agreement, a result of the London Naval Conference, had set out strong maritime and commercial rights for neutral powers in any conflict. The agreement had not been ratified by the British Parliament and so was not legally binding. Its terms were, however, highly favourable to neutral powers, and so the United States was keen to see both sides abide by it.[6] Britain had been a prime mover behind the agreement, but this was largely driven by a desire to protect British trade in the event of the country's being neutral in a conflict. Now that Britain found itself as a belligerent in a major war it was keen to drop the agreement so as to enforce stricter controls on trade to Germany. Diplomatically, however, it was difficult for the Foreign Office to openly disregard an agreement which it had championed, even if it was not legally binding. Grey used German mining in the North Sea as a way out of this particular problem. He told Page that German actions meant that the North Sea 'had become as dangerous to neutral merchantmen as to the warships of the belligerents'. This meant that the area was 'no fit place for merchant vessels' and 'indirectly if not directly, it might make it difficult for us to promise to comply with all the rules of the Declaration of London'.[7] The question of whether or not Britain would adhere to the Declaration of London continued to be discussed in high circles in Whitehall throughout the middle of August.

In the meantime the Admiralty decided to make a statement to foreign governments on the dangers posed by German mines in the North Sea. The precise motives behind this are unclear. It had been recognised within the Admiralty for a number of years that the threat of mines could be used by the British to deter neutral trade to Germany and trade to neutral ports such as Rotterdam. The issuing of a circular to foreign governments highlighting the risk of mines clearly fits within such a policy. At the same time others within the Admiralty appear to have believed that pressure from neutral powers could be exerted on Germany to stop her from laying mines in the open sea. Thus the Admiralty Secretary, Sir W. Graham Greene, noted on 10 August that before any communiqué was sent 'it would be desirable that the object to be attained should be clearly known at the F[oreign]O[ffice]. If the object is to frighten trade away from German ports, the publication abroad is desirable; if on the other hand the object is to endeavour to discontinue such practices the threat of retaliation should be communicated to them through the U.S. Embassy.'[8] Greene does not give any indication as to why the American Embassy should be used, or for that matter why the Americans would be willing to act as a conduit for British communications.

Later that day Churchill sent Sir Edward Grey a note embodying the message the Admiralty desired to be sent. In characteristic style he exclaimed that 'we suffer in our movements by the use the Germans have made of mines in the North Sea. Let them suffer in their food supply!'[9] It is clear that the First Lord at least was primarily focused on the restriction of German trade, but as will be seen the text itself placed a strong emphasis on the possibility of British retaliation. Even after the event the Admiralty appear uncertain as to exactly what their aims were. In a draft letter to the Foreign Office, which was never sent, it was suggested that 'it will be politic that public opinion in neutral countries should be excited against the manner in which Germany has interpreted her rights as a belligerent', something that points to a desire for neutral action against Germany. At the same time the letter continued that 'there are obvious advantages, so far as possible, in frightening trade away from German ports'.[10]

The communiqué was sent on the evening of the 10 August to British representatives at the major neutral trading nations and it stated clearly that the Germans were 'scattering contact mines indiscriminately about the North Sea'. This meant that the southern North Sea was 'perilous in the last degree to merchant shipping of all nations' and it warned neutral ships against entering an 'area of such exceptional danger'. Crucially it also suggested that '(i)n view of the methods adopted by Germany the British Admiralty must hold themselves at liberty to adopt similar measures in self defence'.[11] The telegram was received in Washington the following day, and the British chargé d'affaires Colville Barclay handed it to the Secretary of State, William Bryan. The American response submitted two days later was blunt. Bryan misunderstood the Admiralty's text and believed the British were accusing the Germans of laying unanchored mines, which would have been in breach of Article 1 of the 1907 Hague Convention. He went on to say that he was 'loathed to believe that a signatory... would willfully disregard its treaty obligations'. Furthermore Bryan argued that he did not view German actions as any justification for Britain to lay mines, suggesting that this would simply 'add further dangers to the peaceful navigation of the high seas by vessels of neutral powers'.[12] The Secretary of State's response did not go down well in London. At the Foreign Office George Clerk noted that 'when we are fighting for our lives even the US Gov[ernmen]t should admit that we must defend ourselves against an unscrupulous enemy by all means in our power'.[13] The First Sea Lord, Prince Louis of Battenberg, went further, declaring it to be 'an astonishing document—not to say impertinent'.[14]

Further protests came in, notably from the Dutch Foreign Minister, who told the British chargé d'affaires in The Hague that 'no ships will dare enter or leave Rotterdam, which I gather is what H.M.G. desire'.[15] Ironically, whilst some members of the Cabinet were undoubtedly keen to see mining used to block neutral shipping, the Admiralty was at this stage, far less concerned.[16] Indeed it wrote back to the Foreign Office that it would endeavour 'from time to time and subject to naval exigencies to indicate certain routes and channels by which trade may pass to the Scheldt, and they certainly do not in any degree wish to keep trade away from the English Channel'. It did have to admit that the Rhine was too close to the centre of the war for any British guarantee.[17] This was, at Admiralty request, sent to the governments of all the major neutral powers.[18] Three days later, the Chief of Staff, Vice-Admiral Sir Doveton

Sturdee, wrote a memorandum suggesting that the American government be informed that the British had not laid any mines, and whilst not giving up the right to do so, declaring that it would only be done with 'the greatest reluctance'. He suggested that the United States should work with other neutrals to pressurise Germany and 'endeavour to deny the right of any power to use these unseen dangers to humanity'. Sturdee's opposition to the use of mines by the Royal Navy was well known, but here he appears to have been going further and was undermining the effectiveness of mining on limiting neutral trade in order to get the Americans to exert pressure on Germany.[19] This was a step too far for the Foreign Office and there is no indication that any such message was transmitted to the American government. Instead Sir Edward Grey sent a far more robust message to the Secretary of State, through Colville Barclay. This made it clear that Britain reserved the right to use mines in response to German actions, outlining why the British government could not give up the ability to use a weapon which her enemies were using against her.[20] Indeed Grey told Walter Page that he did not understand why the Americans wished 'to give the Germans license to use mines and bind the English not to use them'.[21] In the light of this it is unsurprising that he did not send Sturdee's highly conciliatory statement.

Later that week the Admiralty cut the Foreign Office out of the loop, releasing a statement through the Press Bureau that embodied much of what Sturdee had suggested.[22] It stated that neutral merchant ships should call on British ports for information on swept channels and other safe routes which the Admiralty would provide. The Admiralty suggested that the German minelaying did 'not conform to the conditions of The Hague Convention' and publicly announced that whilst the British reserved the right to lay mines, they had not so far done so.[23] It could be suggested that this was simply a ploy to try to establish British control over neutral trade, but in fact the statement, like Sturdee's earlier memorandum, appears to have been aimed at mobilising neutral opinion against German mining, and so limiting this threat to the British fleet.

The Admiralty's remarkably open attitude towards neutral trade comes through again at the beginning of September when it issues a further statement, this time through Lloyd's List. This reported that '(t)here appears to be an impression in shipping circles that the Admiralty have prohibited the use of certain trade routes for mercantile shipping. That is quite erroneous. The Admiralty policy is that the sea is free to all'.[24] This policy was taken to its extreme later in September when a despatch from Ernest Maxse, the Consul General in Rotterdam, was forwarded to the Admiralty. Maxse noted that the risk of mines was effectively closing trade through the port of Rotterdam. He went on that representatives of various steamship lines had told him that 'Rotterdam is not considered a safe port and they have been unable to be insured, either under the Government scheme or privately'. Maxse suggested that the government might intervene in order to facilitate British trade and capture that which had previously been done in German ships.[25] Considering that the issue of how to stop trade through Rotterdam had been a known problem within Admiralty planning for a decade, and had been extensively discussed in the Cabinet since the outbreak of war, one would expect the request to have been given short shrift.[26] Instead the head of the Trade Division, Captain Richard Webb, minuted that the issue 'deserved attention' and the idea of the British government insuring vessels trading with Rotterdam 'should be considered'.[27] Webb's suggestion was supported by the Director of Operations Division (DOD), Rear-Admiral Arthur Leveson, and Sturdee, the latter suggesting that 'it is to our advantage to encourage trade'.[28] One can only imagine the reaction of the First Lord, Winston Churchill, when the papers appeared on his desk. His response highlights the gap between the politicians and professional naval officers over the issue of mining and the stoppage of trade more generally.

> There can be no question of relaxing restrictions against the Rhine. Every legal measure, military, commercial, diplomatic, which can restrict the trade of Rotterdam, sh[oul]d be employed. Ships should be discouraged by every possible means from trading with the Rhine. No consideration sh[oul]d be paid to British trade in this direction. No officer at the Adm[iralt]y is to advise any other Dep[artmen]t in a sense contrary to this minute and every measure is to be proposed which will conduce to the main object, namely scarcity in Holland and famine in Germany.[29]

The position adopted by the Admiralty in the wake of the initial German minelaying in early August 1914 gives interesting insight into the organisation. It is apparent that the primary aim of the Admiralty in protesting against German mining was to raise neutral awareness of the issue. This was done in the hope that the United States in particular would use its influence to pressure Germany into discontinuing its mining campaign. Any impact that the Admiralty statements had on neutral trade and trade to neutral ports was a by-product of this main goal. Indeed it is apparent that whilst the political head of the navy was very keen to press for restrictions on trade, some of his professional colleagues were either unaware of this aim, or unsupportive of it. The idea, put forward by Nicholas Lambert, that the Admiralty entered the war with a coherent economic warfare policy appears entirely at odds with the way the organisation dealt with this particular issue.[30]

I

The next phase of the diplomatic and propaganda campaign over mining began in September, but had its origins in minefields laid by the Germans in late August. Up until this point the Admiralty had tended to view German mines as more of an inconvenience than a major threat. Two minefields laid on the night of 25 August began to change that view. These fields were off the mouths of the Tyne and Humber, and although they were discovered within 24 hours, they nearly had a dramatic effect. The battlecruisers *Invincible* and *New Zealand* had been temporarily based out of the Humber to support operations in the Heligoland Bight, and sailed on the morning of 26 August, missing the minefield by only two or three miles.[31] The Admiralty became aware of this later the same day and recriminations began over how the Germans had been allowed to lay mines in these strategically important positions and what could be done about it. Feeding directly into this was the widespread belief that the Germans were using trawlers, some flying neutral colours, to evade British patrols and lay mines.[32]

Days later the Admiralty received what they saw as an unexpected windfall from the engagement in the Heligoland Bight. A number of prisoners were taken from the light cruiser *Mainz*. When questioned they revealed that the vessel had been involved in the mining operations days earlier. The fact that the German minefields had been laid off commercial ports was seen by some in the Admiralty as sufficient evidence of a breach of international law. The idea was therefore floated of putting the prisoners on trial as war criminals.[33] This was soon quashed by both Vice-Admiral Edmond Slade and Sir Graham Greene, with the former noting 'they cannot be shot or hanged without staining our honour and humanity'.[34] Notably, however, both men argued, on questionable grounds, that the German actions were in breach of the Hague Convention. The Admiralty was not willing to let the matter go and therefore decided to follow a less drastic approach, and Greene spoke to Cecil Hurst, Legal Advisor to the Foreign Office, about a protest. At this stage the issue became somewhat unclear, with the Admiralty conflating their two arguments. These were, firstly that minelaying by German warships was in breach of the Hague Convention, and secondly that the Germans were using trawlers under neutral flags to lay mines.[35] In response to the latter the Admiralty was proposing an effective ban on all trawlers operating in the North Sea. Hurst immediately quashed the Admiralty's argument that the minelaying operations carried out by the *Mainz* were illegal, noting that Germany had not accepted Article 2 of the Hague Convention.[36] The Admiralty's proposals with regard to trawlers in the North Sea fared little better. Churchill raised the issue in Cabinet on 3 September and gained considerable support for strong action against any trawlers caught laying mines. Lewis Harcourt noted: 'if we could catch them we should hang every man on board'.[37] The Admiralty realised that catching trawlers in the act was virtually impossible, so Churchill had ordered 'all neutral vessels to be seized or sunk in the North Sea if suspected'. This was a step too far even for the highly belligerent Liberal Cabinet. Charles Hobhouse noted in his diary that 'I told him such a course was a declaration of war on the world, and that though it might be fair to hang people caught laying mines, he himself would deserve to be hung for sinking fishermen or seamen following a peaceful or lawful calling'.[38] Churchill was told to return with some more sensible proposals, which he did the following day. These stated that British ships should have the right to stop and search ships and trawlers flying neutral flags and could fire upon any that resisted. These proposals were approved by the Cabinet.[39]

With this issue settled Graham Greene wrote officially to the Foreign Office requesting a protest be issued, and neutral governments be warned about the new orders issued to British ships.[40] The basic idea was accepted, but the Foreign Office looked to take the matter somewhat further than the Cabinet had explicitly agreed. They wrote back to the Admiralty: 'Sir Edward Grey presumes that the object of the notification will be to endeavour to secure that neutral governments shall discourage their trawlers from coming into the area where it may be necessary for His Majesty's Fleet to take drastic action'.[41] The Admiralty approved this modification and it was decided that neutral trawlers should be effectively excluded from the waters around the east coast of Britain. The orders issued to the fleet stated that '(i)nnocent vessels [are] to be warned off. Those defying the prohibition are to be seized and treated as guilty of unneutral action'.[42] This process largely replicated the demands Churchill had made in Cabinet, and represented the first 'war zone' to be established. The information was sent to the governments of the North Sea neutrals on 28 September.[43]

The broader protest to neutral powers which the Admiralty had first proposed in late August proved easier to agree. Hurst drafted a text which, contrary to his earlier suggestion, accused Germany of breaching the Hague Convention. All of the points raised on this front were contentious. The argument rested on whether the Germans had taken 'every possible precaution' to protect neutrals and whether military exigencies were such as to prevent them from issuing notices to mariners. Hurst was well aware of how weak the precise legal argument was, and so focused on broader principles, declaring that German minelaying was 'in flagrant violation of the accepted principles of international law and contrary to the primary dictates of humanity'.[44] The protest was officially issued on 26 September and was lodged with the governments of all the major neutral powers.[45]

British protests lodged at the end of September 1914 were largely accepted by neutral governments, and there was comparatively little in the way of protest at British actions in closing off the east coast fisheries. The German government lodged a response to the general protest to neutral powers which highlighted the weaknesses in the British arguments regarding the Hague Convention. It also focused attention on the 'continued violation of the freedom of neutral trade by England'. Sir Eyre Crowe minuted dismissively that 'I do not think that we are called upon to enter into a controversy with the German gov[ernmen]t over this'.[46] The Admiralty felt it was worthwhile highlighting what they believed to be the fundamental flaws in the German statement in order to keep neutral attention focused on the matter; however Grey eventually agreed with Crowe and no rebuttal was lodged.[47]

It is difficult to assess the impact of these protests as they were almost immediately overtaken by more drastic action. The motives behind the protests are, however, particularly revealing. The primary focus of both of the protests issued at the end of September was to stop German mining. The general protest issued to all neutral powers looked to channel neutral opinion against Germany in an effort to stop her from laying mines. The communiqué issued to North Sea governments which announced the establishment of the first 'war zone' was also focused on mining, albeit due to the incorrect presumption that neutral trawlers were laying mines. This sheds new light on a number of issues. Firstly it reinforces the point that Admiralty policy with regard to mining in the first two months of the war derived entirely from prewar perceptions of the weapon, largely shaped by the organisation's culture. The aim of the Admiralty's foray into diplomacy regarding mines was to limit, or ideally curtail altogether, the use of mines in the North Sea. For those in the navy who had always wanted mines to be banned, this appeared to be the perfect moment to remove the weapon from the arsenals of civilised powers, something that would also facilitate the service to fight the "right kind of war". The establishment of a large zone where neutral fishing vessels were not permitted to enter was a clear precursor to the later 'war zones'. It has recently been argued that these were a fundamentally new concept pushed through against strong opposition from the Foreign Office by an Admiralty focused on the strangulation of trade to Germany.[48] The precise origins of these later 'war zones' will be discussed below, but it is important to note that the November decisions built directly upon those previously agreed. Graham Greene, when the idea was first proposed, suggested that it was 'a somewhat high handed proceeding', but felt that German mining justified the action.[49] Both the Foreign Office and the Cabinet agreed with this argument. At no stage was the interruption of trade to Germany mentioned; it was the far more traditional preoccupation of the protection of the British navy and merchant marine that drove the decision.

II

The protest against German mining and the declaration of a war zone received little attention due to the fact that the following week the British Cabinet forced the Admiralty to follow the German precedent and adopt a mining strategy. This decision has been discussed in detail in the previous chapter and there is no need to reiterate it here. It is, however, worth recalling that the decision was effectively made by Asquith, as a result of American complaints regarding British modifications to the Declaration of London.[50] The minefield laid by the Royal Navy in early October 1914 was primarily designed to stop neutral trade into Antwerp, Rotterdam and Hamburg. This decision made a complete mockery of the British protest lodged a matter of days before with neutral governments. The British had reasonable grounds to complain that

German minelaying was in breach of the spirit of international law at the time. However, the idea of using mines to stop neutral vessels carrying non-contraband items between two neutral ports was a breach on an entire different scale, and one which no neutral could accept. Thus when it came to writing the statement announcing that Britain was laying mines, no mention of the economic warfare motivation was made. Churchill penned the initial text on 1 October and stated clearly that '(t) he German policy of mining, combined with their submarine activities make it necessary on military grounds for the Adm[iralt]y to adopt countermeasures'.[51] These took the form of declaring a substantial section of the southern North Sea to be dangerous owing to British mines. The message was transmitted to neutral governments the following day.[52] This was treated with remarkable equanimity by the neutral powers. The British justification, which was at least in part truthful, was difficult to argue with; whilst the policy of announcing the dangerous areas was clearly seen as an advance on German actions.

The neutral response to the British decision to mine the eastern end of the Channel and declare the southern North Sea as dangerous was limited. In large part this appears to have been due to continuing efforts by the Admiralty to facilitate neutral trade around the minefields. On 14 October the Trade Division of the War Staff issued new instructions on navigation in the North Sea. These gave details of safe routes by which vessels could avoid the areas known to be dangerous.[53] The routes outlined included one across the North Sea to the Baltic and southern Scandinavian ports. From here there was, of course, nothing to stop the cargo being trans-shipped to Germany, or the vessel itself being rerouted to German ports. It is clear that the Trade Division realised that the information it was giving out was valuable. Richard Webb had indicated with regard to previous notices that the information 'should not, if possible, reach the enemy'.[54] He gave similar instructions for the updated guidance in October.[55] Exactly how he thought this information could be controlled when it was specifically being given to the masters of neutral vessels is unclear. What is apparent is that the Admiralty were continuing to take measures to facilitate neutral trade. Webb had, less than a month previously, been one of the officers supporting the idea of the British government insuring trade into Rotterdam. The information on safe navigation in the North Sea was a similar if less direct intervention. The Cabinet had taken the decision at the end of September to lay mines in the North Sea, primarily to interrupt the flows of neutral trade. The actions of the Admiralty in providing detailed information to facilitate neutral trade was undoubtedly in keeping with common practice, but seems out of step with the far more aggressive line being taken by the politicians, especially Asquith.

At the end of October two events took place which fundamentally changed British policy towards mining and use of the sea more generally. The first of these was the return of Lord Fisher to the Admiralty. It is difficult to overestimate the initial impact which had when replacing Battenberg as First Sea Lord. In part this was due to his energy and focus on high policy, but it was equally important that he rapidly removed key individuals, most notably Sturdee, and replaced them with far more effective officers. The second event was the laying of a comparatively small minefield off the north coast of Ireland by the German converted minelayer *Berlin*. This field claimed a number of casualties, most notably the super dreadnought *Audacious*.[56] The loss of one of the newest and most powerful units of the Grand Fleet was a grievous blow, but it was the message conveyed that was most powerful. The minefield was in an area regularly traversed by the Atlantic trade into Liverpool, including the large liners. The Grand Fleet had retired to these waters precisely because it was considered that they were safe from German mine and submarine attack. The fact that the British could not prevent the Germans from laying mines here emphasised their inability to control the problem. The Admiralty immediately placed the blame on 'vessels flying neutral flags', not willing to believe that a commissioned warship could have penetrated that far undetected.[57] It did, however, send shockwaves through the Admiralty and forced a further reconsideration of the mining problem.

One of Fisher's first actions on his return to the Admiralty was to attend a meeting held on 2 November by Asquith. It was apparent that the discussion was wide-ranging, but the Prime Minister recalled later that day to his confidante Venetia Stanley that '(o)ur main topic was the closing of the North Sea'.[58] Immediately following the meeting the Admiralty issued a statement via the Press Bureau. This announced the declaration of the North Sea as a 'military area'. The justification for this was simple. The minefield laid by the Germans north of Ireland 'wantonly and recklessly endangered the lives of all who travel on the seas, regardless of whether they are friend or foe, civilian or military in character'. Furthermore the Admiralty maintained that the Germans were only achieving this by using ostensibly merchant vessels flying neutral flags. As a result the Admiralty declared that any vessel entering a vast swathe of open sea from the Faroes down to the English Channel 'will be exposed to the gravest danger' and did so 'at their own peril'.[59] It is important to recognise that, whilst the establishment of the 'military area' is often referred to, even by contemporaries, as the closing of the North Sea, it actually did no such thing. Britain sought to use its influence to stop vessels from proceeding into the southern North Sea, but no military measures were taken to ensure this, and neutral ships continued to carry non-contraband items through the area into German ports. It was what John Ferris has described as extra-legal rather than illegal.[60] It used coercive measures backed by the unknown threat of mines to force neutrals to co-operate.[61] John Coogan's claim that Britain had 'replaced the belligerent right of visit and search in the North Sea with a new rule: explode and sink', is partially true. What he missed was that for all the rhetoric Britain laid no fresh minefields in the North Sea in this period. American ships were destroyed 'simply for exercising their basic right to sail the high seas', but by German mines and not British.[62] In fact, in legal terms, the measure itself was far less radical than the closure of large sections of the North Sea to neutral trawlers, which has been entirely ignored by historians, but was in fact backed, at least implicitly, by the threat of force.

The original papers detailing the discussion behind the establishment of the 'military area' do not appear to have survived the war.[63] Recent historians have assumed that the primary motive was to tighten the economic blockade. However the Naval Staff Monograph records that it developed from an idea put forward by Jellicoe on 22 October aimed at controlling the minelaying and spying that it was believed was being carried out by neutral flagged vessels.[64] Churchill persuaded the Cabinet to agree to such a measure for this reason, and Fisher justified the measure to Grey on the grounds of the existence of 'minelaying trawlers'.[65] Thus whilst the 'military area' rapidly developed into an important aspect of British economic warfare, its origins lie in the more straightforward issue of mining. Its purpose was to control neutral vessels. This allowed the British to search a large percentage of ships entering and leaving the Channel and North Sea, both for contraband and for evidence of other unneutral activities such as mining.[66] As Churchill would write to Grey a few days later, the Admiralty viewed the restrictions as 'essential for the safety of the fleet'.[67]

The announcement of the 'war zone' in the North Sea was an extremely rushed affair. The statement was issued in the evening of 2 November following the meeting. It is noteworthy that it was done without reference to the Hydrographer and long before any Notices to

Mariners could be prepared. As late as 6 November the Hydrographer was minuting that 'no official information on these subjects has yet been received in the Hydrographic Department' and that he was keeping abreast of developments by reading *The Times*.[68] The Foreign Office by contrast had received a copy of the statement immediately and it was sent as a circular telegram to British representatives at the major neutrals at 11.15 p.m. on 2 November.[69] As soon as they overcame the shock of the announcement the North Sea neutrals began to complain to the Foreign Office. Initially these protests focused on facilitating specific ships to pass through the area, but soon expanded to broader complaints. The Foreign Office were unsympathetic, with Walter Stewart of the Treaty Department describing these objections as 'the effervescence in Scandinavia and the Neth[erlan]ds'.[70] On 6 November the Danish, Swedish and Norwegian Ministers in London all lodged official protests against the 'military area' in the North Sea. The response drawn up by Sir Eyre Crowe was blistering. It reiterated that British actions were in response to German indiscriminate minelaying and asked rhetorically if the Scandinavian governments had protested against this behaviour. It went on '(i)t would be of interest to learn whether the Danish [Swedish or Norwegian] government would prefer that Great Britain should follow the German example of laying mines in the open sea without notice, and whether, had she adopted this course the Danish Government would have considered it unnecessary to protest or formulate reservations'. It concluded by saying that if the Scandinavians could get Germany to stop mining then Britain would rescind its notice.[71] Following this rebuttal the Scandinavian powers attempted to recruit the United States into a new, more general, protest on infringements of neutral rights at sea, but this was rejected by Bryan.[72] The Scandinavian powers lodged their further protest on 13 November, but by this stage it carried little weight. At the Foreign Office Stewart remarked that 'all these countries, even Sweden seem to be trying to apologise for their protest'. His boss Victor Wellesley concluded that 'we need not take the coming protest too seriously'.[73]

The only protest that the Foreign Office did treat with some respect was that made by the Dutch government. This argued on slightly different lines; firstly, that whilst the British had the right to exclude neutrals from a war zone, this area could only be considered to be the immediate sphere of military operations. British claims extending this to cover the entire North Sea were thus illegal. Secondly, they argued that Britain was failing its obligations under the Hague Convention on mining. The Foreign Office saw merit in these points, Wellesley noting that he found the Dutch argument 'very forcible'. Crowe, in forwarding the letter to the Admiralty, suggested a response subtly avoiding the first point, and addressing the second by pointing out 'as the German Government have already done, that, technically, none of the Hague Conventions are binding upon the belligerents since not all of the latter (notably not Turkey) have ratified them'.[74] This argument, although technically correct, was weak, especially considering the efforts Britain had made to restrict the use of mines. That the Foreign Office was willing to rely upon it highlights firstly the extent to which British actions were unprecedented, and secondly the acceptance within the organisation of the need to push the bounds of international law.

As has been noted above, the late autumn of 1914 saw a considerable strengthening of the Admiralty position on neutral trade and mined areas. Nowhere is this clearer than in the Admiralty's response to the Dutch protest. In the first months of the war the Admiralty went out of their way to assist neutrals in finding safe passage through the minefields. Following the declaration of the war zone some of this still went on, but generally the Admiralty took a much harder line.[75] The Dutch requested that a safe line of passage be established through the minefields into their ports. Richard Webb replied that it was 'impossible to indicate any safe route to Dutch ports'. Whilst neutral traders could proceed east of the Channel, 'they do so at their own risk'.[76] The Foreign Office largely accepted this newfound assertiveness on the part of the Admiralty; however one proposal made at the end of November brought the departments into conflict. As has been seen, the necessity of controlling German mining had occupied the Admiralty since the outbreak of war, and was a key driver in the decision to establish a war zone. Further concerns, combined with a growing fear of submarine activity, led the Admiralty to expand the remit of the restrictions placed on neutral trawlers. They requested that the Foreign Office notify the North Sea powers that neutral fishing craft were now to be banned from all UK ports. They went on to state that any neutrally flagged fishing vessels found in a vast area around the British Isles, including the entire English Channel and Irish Sea, 'will be regarded as under suspicion of assisting the enemy'.[77] As has been noted above, the restrictions previously placed on neutral trawlers were far more problematic in terms of international law than was the more general 'military area'. Thus the Admiralty's unilateral decision to massively expand the region covered by this restriction, the vast majority of which was in international waters, was viewed with suspicion at the Foreign Office. Victor Wellesley described it as a 'somewhat highhanded proceeding', but felt German mining offered 'some justification'.[78] Sir Edward Davidson, the department's Senior Legal Advisor, clearly believed that the action was illegal, but felt that 'we must assume that those directly responsible in such matters consider that it is absolutely necessary for the safety of the state whether they are legally justifiable or not'.[79] As such he was willing to overlook this major encroachment on neutral rights. Crowe and Grey were more sceptical, not of breaking international law, but of the necessity of the step. As such the Foreign Office wrote back to the Admiralty suggesting the issue be discussed further, potentially in Cabinet.[80] In the end the Admiralty decided to settle for merely barring neutral trawlers from all British ports in addition to the existing restrictions off the east coast.[81] These restrictions on neutral trawlers were some of the most direct breaches of international law made by the British state in the first months of the war, far more so than the establishment of the 'military area'. Thus it is important to remember that these steps were not part of the economic warfare campaign; instead they were solely intended to protect the fleet from mining, and to a lesser extent submarines.

The steps taken in November 1914 to restrict neutral use of the seas around Britain were in large part driven by the need to control German mining, and this was the primary justification given for these steps. They were, of course, an important part of the attempts to tighten the economic grip on Germany, but the centrality of mining as a factor in the decision-making should not be underestimated. It should also be kept in mind that the threat from mines provided the key enforcing factor behind British attempts to restrict trade. The Royal Navy had no intention of sinking neutral merchantmen that entered the 'military area'. It was the undefined risk from mines and the impact that had on insurance premiums which forced most neutral trade to comply with British instructions. It has recently been argued by Nicholas Lambert and repeated by Isabel Hull that the establishment of the 'military area' was driven through by the Admiralty, and the Foreign Office did not find out about it for three weeks. As has been seen this was not the case. Nor is there any indication that the Foreign Office objected to the measure or believed it to be a breach of international law.[82] The quotes Lambert uses to justify this claim in fact come from the discussion of the Admiralty's plan to restrict the movements of neutral fishing vessels.

The Admiralty and Foreign Office actually worked closely on the steps taken to restrict neutral use of the seas in November and December 1914. There were remarkably few disagreements between the departments, with both sides feeling that German mining gave Britain scope for novel procedures under international law, but believing that these could not be pushed too far.

III

Over the course of the first six months of the war the British government agreed a series of measures which gradually impeded the ability of neutrals to use northern European waters.[83] These steps, especially the restrictions on trawlers, directly infringed basic rights of neutrals to use the high seas, something that was a core value of international law in the period. Britain justified these actions on the grounds of necessity, arguing that German mining represented such a fundamental break with the accepted rules of war as to allow Britain the right to act outside of the usual bounds. The centrality of mining in these debates derived both from the fact that the weapon posed arguably the greatest threat to British use of the seas, and the fact that mining was the most blatant German breach of accepted practice, and thus was the most persuasive point in discussions with neutrals. From the beginning of 1915 this began to change as the totality of the conflict forced the belligerents to look for novel ways to harm their enemies. The most important of these new developments was the German announcement at the beginning of February of a war zone around the British Isles in which British merchant vessels were liable to destruction without warning.[84] The announcement went on to say that due to British ships frequently flying neutral flags, and other contingencies of war, 'it cannot always be avoided that neutral vessels suffer from attacks intended to strike enemy ships'.[85] The measure was designed to allow U-boats the freedom to destroy British trade without being fettered by the traditional cruiser rules, which had been codified before submarines became a realistic weapon of war. The Germans justified this action on the grounds of reprisal against British measures, particularly the adaptation of the rules around contraband, and the declaration of the North Sea as a military area. The potential impact on neutrals was acknowledged but the explanatory memorandum sought to blame British misuse of neutral flags, and neutral acquiescence with British blockade measures, for forcing Germany to take this step.[86]

In many respects the announcement changed remarkably little. The waters around the British Isles had been a de facto military area since the outbreak of war. German minelaying had already blurred any distinction between military and non-combatant and between neutral and British shipping, with eighteen neutral merchantmen being sunk in the North Sea in the first five months of the war, with the loss of scores of lives.[87] It was only chance that meant that it was the battleship *Audacious* that struck a mine in the Tory Island field, and not the liner *Olympic*, which was passing through the same waters hours later with well over 1000 people on board. This said, it is clear that the new German measure represented a fundamental shift in the attitudes towards war. Mines may have been just as likely to destroy a neutral merchantman as a British warship, but they lacked any agency. Destruction of non-combatant and neutral lives and property could thus be characterised as careless rather than intentional. As Walter Simons, clerk in the German Foreign Office, noted when writing the initial legal appraisal, '(t)he difference between mines and U-boats is that with mines, the merchant ship sinks as the result of its own activity, whereas with U-boats it is done with the conscious activity of our forces'.[88] This may have been a rather academic distinction to the crew of a vessel torpedoed or mined, but represented a step change in the breaches of international law at sea by either side. Outside of Germany it was widely viewed as an extraordinary departure from any form of international law, customary or otherwise. In Britain Asquith declared it to be 'truly absurd', whilst the Foreign Office issued a statement saying that '(t)o destroy ship, non-combatant crew, and cargo, as Germany has announced her intention of doing, is nothing less than an act of piracy on the high seas'.[89] The American government immediately made a protest to Berlin, declaring that were a German submarine to sink a US ship sailing under the US flag it would be 'an indefensible violation of neutral rights which it would be very hard indeed to reconcile with the friendly relations now so happily subsisting between the two Governments'.[90] The Americans refrained from taking any further concrete action, in part, it appears, from an uncertainty which existed in a number of capitals as to whether the Germans would actually act on their threats.[91] The United States objected strongly to the new German measures, but much to the ire of the Foreign Office, also protested against British seizure of food supplies to Germany and the use of neutral flags by British merchantmen.[92] Even the British Ambassador in Washington, Sir Cecil Spring Rice, who many in London thought had "gone native", concluded that it could only be 'fear of the German vote' that forced that State Department into these protests.[93]

The German rejoinder to the US protest placed renewed emphasis on mining. In response to discussion around how to distinguish neutral vessels, the German Ambassador to the United States, Johan von Bernstorff, told Bryan that 'account must be taken of an increased danger from mines, since it is intended to make the most extensive use of mines in all parts of the war area. Neutral vessels must therefore again be most earnestly warned against venturing into this area'. The communiqué concluded with a strong condemnation of the 'murderous character of the English method of naval warfare' and confirmation that Germany would continue its new policy until Britain was 'compelled' to recognise international law.[94] The United States government, understandably worried about the prospect of being placed in an impossible position by the aggressive policies of the two belligerents, sought a compromise. Initially it appeared that there may be some scope for a deal brokered by Washington. On 17 February Grey intimated to Walter Page that Britain might be willing to 'not put food on [the] absolute contraband list if Germany will sow no more mines and will attack no more commercial ships by submarines'.[95] This suggestion is interesting; firstly it is far from clear that Grey had any sanction for making such an offer, or that he could deliver it in the face of his more belligerent colleagues in Cabinet.[96] Secondly, mining comes through as one of the central issues for Britain at this stage, something they were willing to compromise the efficiency of their economic warfare policy to stop. Bryan responded to Page that his telegram offered 'the first ray of hope' and it was on this that the Secretary of State acted.[97]

On 20 February the American Ambassadors in London and Berlin issued identic notes to the respective governments suggesting an agreement for 'reciprocal concessions' to 'relieve neutral ships engaged in peaceful commerce from the great dangers which they will incur in the high seas'.[98] The note suggested that Britain should allow foodstuffs to pass freely into Germany on the proviso that they would be for civilian use only. Britain would also desist from allowing its merchant vessels to use neutral flags. In return Germany would agree that submarines would not attack merchant vessels 'except to enforce the right of visit and search'. The first point on the note, however, was that both Britain and Germany should agree:

> That neither will sow any floating mines, whether upon the high seas or in territorial waters; that neither will plant on the high seas anchored mines except within cannon range of harbors for defensive purposes only; and that all mines shall bear the stamp of the government planting them and be so constructed as to become harmless if separated from their moorings.[99]

The irony that these were almost identical to the proposals put forward by Britain at The Hague, and which the American government did so much to block, appears to have gone unnoticed. What is clear is that mine warfare was, at this stage, still at the very centre of the issues over neutral and belligerent rights at sea that dominated the three-way diplomatic relationship between Britain, the United States and Germany. A resolution of this question was seen as crucial not only because it was a key problem for the British, but also because it was seen as one of the greatest impositions on neutrals, and one which was killing neutral seamen in European waters.

The British reacted badly to the American proposals. Cecil Hurst minuted that 'there is no reason why we should enter into an agreement for relieving Germany of the consequences of her own illegalities'.[100] In Washington Spring-Rice told Bryan of his astonishment that the Secretary of State 'seemed to regard the torpedo and the Prize Court with equal abhorrence'.[101] These views were shared by other influential figures in Whitehall, including Sir Maurice Hankey.[102] This feeling that the proposals were 'greatly in their [the German's] favour' led to many in the Foreign Office believing that 'it would not be safe to count on their declining the arrangement'.[103] The Germanophile American Ambassador in Berlin, James Gerard, also believed the Germans would accept the agreement and suggested that Bryan should then threaten Britain with a ban on US arms exports to force her to comply.[104] In London the frustration was partially lifted when the most junior of the Foreign Office Legal Advisors, William Malkin, suggested that 'we can almost count on Germany refusing the proposed agreement as it would be the loss of all chance of really hurting us'. Malkin suggested delaying any reply to the American note, and waiting to see what response came from Berlin.[105]

At the same time the Foreign Office was desperately looking for how to answer the Americans should Germany agree. Hurst had initially suggested claiming that the British had taken 'no action which is not strictly in accordance with international law', an argument of questionable truth and little validity. As Victor Wellesley noted, 'it will be very difficult to refuse to consider the American proposal in view of the fact that it has always been our view that foodstuffs should not be withheld from the civil population'.[106] If the Germans agreed to the American proposals Britain would struggle to justify continuing its seizure of foodstuffs without being able to rely on the argument of reprisal. It was the former Prime Minister, Arthur Balfour, who suggested a way out, recommending writing 'an elaborate despatch covering the whole ground of German infractions of the law of nations'. Following this it could be pointed out that Germany had been 'party to most if not all of the international laws which she had broken, and that, in the circumstances it seemed folly to make a new set of international arrangements which could be just as easily broken'.[107] This neatly sidestepped awkward questions about British policy and focused attention on Germany. A draft memorandum on these lines was drawn up, and among the accusations levelled at Germany were charges relating to its indiscriminate minelaying.[108]

In accordance with Malkin's suggestion the reply was not sent immediately and the British resorted to stalling tactics whilst awaiting the German response.[109] In the meantime, on 1 March Britain and France jointly presented a declaration to neutrals that they would be reserving the right to intercept all trade going to Germany no matter whether it was contraband or not, as a reprisal for German actions.[110] The implications of this escalation were still being considered in Washington when the State Department received the German response to the American proposals. It is notable that the Germans agreed to the limitations placed on the actions of their submarines, but with regard to mining they were more reticent. They accepted the suggestion that unanchored mines should be banned, and that mines should be stamped to indicate the government that laid them. Crucially however, they did not feel it to be 'feasible for the belligerents wholly to forego the use of anchored mines for offensive purposes'. The Germans accepted the American proposals regarding foodstuffs; however they insisted that this be extended to include all raw materials included on the Declaration of London free list.[111] This last condition effectively removed any chance of agreement; indeed Gerard was forced to admit that this had been included 'so as to make acceptance impossible'.[112] When the Foreign Office in London received a copy of the response they were clearly surprised by its belligerence. An analysis by Walter Stewart went through the response point by point, and with regard to mining he noted that Germany proposed 'not even to make a pretence of abandoning the practice of sowing mines broadcast on the open sea to the great danger of neutral and other peaceful shipping and in execution of no definite military design'.[113] The British memorandum drawn up in response to the American proposals was finally handed to Walter Page on 15 March and noted that the German reply, especially with regard to mines, left little space for negotiation. Instead, as Balfour had suggested, Grey listed German infractions or supposed infractions of international law and used these as a platform to justify the new Allied reprisals.[114]

The refusal of either major belligerent to engage with the American proposals of 20 February effectively represents the end of mining as a central issue in discussion of the laws of war at sea. The German decision to continue with their submarine blockade, and the Allied reprisal which took the form of the 11 March Orders in Council, represented a circular escalation of the issues which saw mining submerged beneath the rising tide of belligerence. From the British and American perspectives the reckless disregard for the lives of neutrals and non-combatants which had been demonstrated by German mining was replaced by the active and calculated decision to destroy the same. Incidents such as the attack on the *Gulflight*, and most especially, the sinking of the *Lusitania*, came to redefine German illegality at sea. Ultimately, as Grey explained to the former President, Theodore Roosevelt, 'with German submarines around our coast, torpedoing merchant vessels and drowning merchant seamen, people here will not stand goods going past our doors to Germany'.[115] The situation had escalated to such an extent that the issue of mining was no longer in people's minds.

At the outbreak of the war German mining had been one of the most important perceived breaches of international law, and it was on this that much of the British diplomacy regarding maritime rights was based. The rising tide of belligerence and the increasing disregard for prewar norms meant that from spring 1915 mining ceased to be one of these key issues. Nowhere is this made clearer than in the report of the Committee of Enquiry into Breaches of the Law of War, established by the British government in late 1918. This little-discussed committee was established to produce evidence for trials of officials and officers from the Central

Powers as war criminals. The first interim report of the committee outlined at some length the perceived German breaches of international law; however the report of the sub-committee on offences at sea focused solely on submarine warfare.[116] The second interim report did include a section on mining, and it concluded that:

> German use of mines during the war was contrary alike to the principles of the laws and usages of Naval Warfare and to the laws of humanity; and they [the sub-committee] think it would be proper that its legitimacy should be challenged by proceedings being instituted in respect of it.[117]

It is clear, however, that this was very much viewed as a secondary issue, to be dealt with after the main question of German submarine warfare had been addressed. In fact, disagreement between the Allies about the concept of individual as opposed to collective responsibility for wartime actions meant that the work of the committee came to nothing. It does, however, highlight how the pressure of total conflict changed attitudes towards law and war.

From the moment mining came to the fore during the Russo-Japanese War it became apparent that questions over its legality would be a major issue in any future European conflict. Within days of the outbreak of war in August 1914 this proved to be the case. In Britain, German minelaying was seen as one of the most significant breaches of international law in the early part of the war. It was this sincere belief that the German actions were not merely in contravention of the Hague Convention, but were fundamentally incompatible with the basic principles underpinning customary international law, that lay behind the British protests. Mining was seen as a major threat to both British naval and commercial activity, something dramatically confirmed by the sinking of the *Audacious*. It was attempts to restrict German mining that drove successive British measures limiting neutral use of northern European waters. These measures may have become a crucial part of the economic warfare strategy, but their origins lay in the defence against minelaying. Similarly these measures were justified to neutrals as being a response to German steps, something that appears to have been reasonably well accepted. As such German minelaying was the genesis of the escalatory spiral in breaches of maritime rights during the First World War; a process which ultimately led to unrestricted submarine warfare, and American entry into the conflict.

NOTES

1. For some of the more recent works on this theme see, Justus D. Doenecke, *Nothing Less than War: A New History of America's Entry into World War I* (Kentucky: University of Kentucky Press, 2011); M. Ryan Floyd, *Abandoning American Neutrality: Woodrow Wilson and the Beginning of the Great War, August 1914–December 1915* (Basingstoke: Palgrave, 2013).

2. James Wilford Garner, *International Law and the World War*, vol. I (London: Longmans & Co., 1920), Chapter 14.

3. Isabel V. Hull, *A Scrap of Paper: Making and Breaking International Law During the Great War* (Ithaca: Cornell University Press, 2014), pp. 215–224, 243–244.

4. Churchill Statement, House of Commons Debate, 7 August 1914, *Hansard*, vol. 65, cc. 2154.

5. 'Law and the War', *The Times*, 11 August 1914, p. 7.

6. *Foreign Relations of the United States (FRUS)* 1914, Supplement: The World War, Document 356, Bryan to Page, 6 August 1914, p. 216.

7. The National Archives (TNA), FO 372/582, Grey to Barclay, 7 August 1914, 37140/711/350.

8. TNA, ADM 137/1002, Greene Minute, 10 August 1914, f. 72.

9. TNA, FO 371/2164, Churchill Memorandum, 10 August 1914, 37812/30342/W39, ff. 79–80.

10. TNA, ADM 137/1002, Admiralty to Foreign Office (Draft) n.d. [August 1914], f. 78.

11. TNA, FO 371/2164, Foreign Office Circular Telegram, 10 August 1914, 37812/30342/W39, f. 77.

12. *FRUS* 1914, Supplement: The World War, Document 708, Bryan to Barclay, 13 August 1914, pp. 455–456.

13. TNA, FO 372/760, Clerk Minute, 17 August 1914, 39810/39810/350.

14. TNA, ADM 137/1002, Battenberg Minute, 1 September 1914, f. 84.

15. TNA, FO 371/2164, Chilton to Grey, 11 August 1914, 38137/30342/W39, f. 208.

16. Bodleian Library, Oxford (BLO), Harcourt MS. Eng. c. 8269, 14 August 1914.

17. TNA, ADM 137/1002, Admiralty to Foreign Office, 11 August 1914, f. 77.

18. TNA, FO 371/2170, Foreign Office Circular Telegram, 14 August 1914, 38814/38551/W39, f. 34.

19. TNA, ADM 137/1002, Sturdee Memorandum, 17 August 1914, ff. 82–83.

11 WAR, LAW AND DIPLOMACY   291

20. TNA, FO 372/633, Barclay Memorandum 19 August 1914, 45455/39810/350.
21. *FRUS* 1914, Supplement: The World War, Document 712, Page to Bryan, 20 August 1914, p. 458.
22. The original draft produced by Churchill can be found at CAC, CHAR 13/27B/20, 'German Mines in the North Sea'.
23. 'German Mines in the North Sea', *The Times*, 23 August 1914, p. 1.
24. TNA, ADM 137/2873, 'Sea is Free to All', 3 September 1914.
25. TNA, ADM 137/1002, Maxse to Grey, 8 September 1914, f. 499.
26. TNA, CAB 41/35/30, Asquith to King, 15 August 1914; BLO, Harcourt MS. Eng. c. 8269, 14 August 1914.
27. TNA, ADM 137/1002, Webb Minute, 16 September 1914, f. 500.
28. TNA, ADM 137/1002, Sturdee Minute, 20 September 1914, f. 500.
29. ADM 137/1002, Churchill Minute, 25 September 1914, f. 502.
30. Nicholas Lambert, *Planning Armageddon: British Economic Warfare and the First World War* (Cambridge, MA: Harvard University Press, 2012).
31. Naval Staff Monographs, vol. 10, 'Home Waters Part I', pp. 100–105.
32. National Maritime Museum (NMM), RIC/1/9, Richmond diary, 28 August 1914; TNA, FO 368/1054, Admiralty to Foreign Office, 29 August 1914, 44386/44152/130.
33. Exactly who suggested this is unclear, but considering his later statements to Cabinet there is a reasonable probability it was Churchill.
34. TNA, ADM 137/1002, Slade Memorandum, 31 August 1914, ff. 100–102.
35. TNA, FO 372/633, Hurst Minute, 1 September 1914, 46042/39810/350.
36. TNA, FO 372/633, Hurst Minute, 2 September 1914, 46042/39810/350.
37. BLO, Harcourt MS. Eng. c. 8269, 3 September 1914.
38. Hobhouse diary, quoted in Edward David, ed., *Inside Asquith's Cabinet: From the Diaries of Charles Hobhouse* (London: John Murray, 1977), p. 188.
39. TNA, ADM 137/1004, Laying of Mines off East Coast, September 1914, ff. 581–584.
40. TNA, FO 372/633, Admiralty to Foreign Office, 8 September 1914, 47574/39810/350.
41. TNA, FO 372/633, Foreign Office to Admiralty, 15 September 1914, 47574/39810/350.
42. TNA, ADM 137/64, Admiralty to All Ships, 27 September 1914, f. 929.
43. TNA, FO 372/633, Foreign Office Draft Telegram, 28 September 1914, 53513/39810/350.
44. TNA, ADM 137/1002, Draft Memorandum, ff. 113–116.

45. TNA, FO 372/633, Grey to HMRR, London, 26 September 1914, 52035/39810/350.
46. TNA, FO 372/634, 'Laying of German Mines in the North Sea', 72595/39810/350.
47. TNA, FO 372/745 'German Answer to British Protest', 1 January 1915, 178/118/350.
48. Lambert, *Planning Armageddon*, pp. 297–300; Hull, *Scrap of Paper*, pp. 183–185.
49. TNA, ADM 137/1002, Graham Greene Minute, 2 September 1914, f. 109.
50. Michael and Eleanor Brock, eds., *H. H. Asquith: Letters to Venetia Stanley* (Oxford, OUP, 1985), Asquith to Stanley, 29 September 1914, no. 168, pp. 255–257.
51. TNA, ADM 137/1003, Churchill Memorandum, 1 October 1914, f. 9.
52. TNA, FO 372/633, Foreign Office Circular Telegram, 2 October 1914, 55558/39810/350.
53. TNA, ADM 137/1003, 'Navigation in the North Sea', 14 October 1914, f. 219–222.
54. TNA, ADM 137/1003, 'Navigation in the North Sea', 11 September 1914, f. 205.
55. TNA, ADM 137/1003, Webb Minute, 13 October 1914, f. 223.
56. James Goldrick, *Before Jutland: The Naval War in Northern European Waters, August 1914–February 1915* (Annapolis: Naval Institute Press, 2015), pp. 156–158.
57. *Letters to Venetia Stanley*, Asquith to Stanley, 28 October 1914, no. 192, pp. 290–291.
58. *Letters to Venetia Stanley*, Asquith to Stanley, 2 November 1914, no. 199, pp. 305–306. For evidence of the other topics addressed see Arthur J. Marder, *Fear God and Dread Nought: The Correspondence of Admiral of the Fleet Lord Fisher of Kilverstone*, vol. III [*FGDN III*] (London: Jonathan Cape, 1959), Fisher to Jellicoe, 3 November 1914, no. 39, p. 65.
59. TNA, ADM 137/977, Draft Statement, 2 November 1914, ff. 12–13.
60. John Ferris, 'Practical Hegemony and British Economic Warfare, 1900–1918: Preparations and Practice', in Greg Kennedy, ed., *Britain's War at Sea, 1914–1918: The War They Thought and the War They Fought* (London: Routledge, 2016), p. 92 and *passim*.
61. Naval Staff Monographs, vol. 12, 'Home Waters Part III', pp. 24–25; TNA, ADM 137/1911, De Chair Memorandum, 17 December 1914, ff. 59–61.
62. John Coogan, *The End of Neutrality: The United States, Britain and Maritime Rights, 1899–1915* (Ithaca: Cornell Univeristy Press, 1981), pp. 196–197, 213–214.

11 WAR, LAW AND DIPLOMACY   293

63. TNA, ADM 137/977, 'Closing of North Sea: Request for Papers', 12 January 1923, ff. 472–477.
64. Naval Staff Monographs, vol. 12, 'Home Waters Part III', p. 18. The papers reference in the Monograph, titled 'Foreign Office 15.9.14' can be found in TNA, ADM 137/1002, but do not contain the communication from Jellicoe.
65. BLO, Harcourt MS. Eng. c. 8269, 22 October 1914; TNA, FO 800/88/76, Fisher to Grey, 7 November 1914, ff. 210–212.
66. TNA, FO 800/909, Minutes of Meeting of 27 February 1915, no. 8.
67. TNA, FO 368/1107, Churchill to Grey, 10 November 1914, 70503/69984/130X.
68. TNA, ADM 137/977, Hydrographer Minute, 6 November 1914, f. 32.
69. TNA, FO 372/633, Foreign Office Circular Telegram, 2 November 1914, 66775/39810/350.
70. TNA, FO 372/633, Stewart Minute, 6 November 1914, 67732/39810/350.
71. TNA, FO 372/633, Draft Memorandum, 8 November 1914, 68633/39810/350.
72. FRUS 1914, Supplement: The World War, Document 712, Bryan to Schemedeman, 10 November 1914, p. 466.
73. TNA, FO 372/634, Stewart and Wellesley Minutes, 15 November 1914, 71232/39810/350. Also see TNA, FO 368/1107, Lowther to Grey, 12 November 1914, 69984/69984/130X and TNA, FO 800/45/23, Grey to Lowther, 24 November 1914, ff. 48–50.
74. TNA, FO 372/634, Foreign Office to Admiralty (Draft), 13 December 1914, 73009/39810/350.
75. For Admiralty concessions for Scandinavian vessels see TNA, FO 368/1107, file 69984.
76. TNA, ADM 137/1003, Webb Minute, 18 December 1914, f. 370.
77. TNA, FO 372/634, Admiralty to Foreign Office, 25 November 1914, 75534/39810/350.
78. TNA, FO 372/634, Wellesley Minute, 27 November 1914, 75534/39810/350.
79. TNA, FO 372/634, Davidson Minute, 30 November 1914, 75534/39810/350.
80. TNA, FO 372/634, Foreign Office to Admiralty, 4 December 1914, 75534/39810/350.
81. TNA, FO 372/634, Admiralty to Foreign Office, 26 December 1914, 87141/39810/350.
82. For discussion on the legality of the British 'military area' see TNA, FO 372/1186, 'Freedom of the Seas', memorandum by Dr J. Pawley Bate, para. 36, 184425/539/350; 'Paper by Dr Peace Higgins on Freedom of the Seas', 198668/539/350 and 'Neutrals Afloat', The Times, 21 October 1914, p. 6.

83. Questions of contraband, although heavily intertwined in these issues, have been intentionally left out in order to focus on the issues arising from mining.

84. Hull, *Scrap of Paper*, pp. 211–224; A. C. Bell, *A History of the Blockade of Germany and of the Countries Associated with Her in the Great War Austria–Hungary, Bulgaria and Turkey: 1914–18* (HMSO, 1961), pp. 198–219.

85. *FRUS* 1915, Supplement: The World War, Document 125, Gerard to Bryan, 4 February 1915, p. 94. For the British translation of the text see TNA, FO 372/760, 15070/13659/350.

86. *FRUS* 1915, Supplement: The World War, Document 130, Bernstorff to Bryan, 7 February 1915, pp. 95–97.

87. TNA, ADM 137/2809, 'Vessels Mined in the North Sea', 30 December 1914.

88. Draft of Memorandum from Undersecretary to Chancellor, 27 October 1914, quoted in Hull, *Scrap of Paper*, p. 218.

89. *Letters to Venetia Stanley*, Asquith to Stanley, 6 February 1915, no. 290, p. 416; *The Times*, 'The Neutral Flag', 8 February 1915, p. 9.

90. *FRUS* 1915, Supplement: The World War, Document 133, Bryan to Gerard, 10 February 1915, pp. 98–100.

91. See for example, TNA, FO 372/760, Langley Minute, n.d., 14908/13659/350.

92. TNA, FO 372/760, Page Memorandum and Spring Rice to Grey, 11 and 15 February 1915, 16937 & 18053/13659/350.

93. TNA, FO 372/760, Spring-Rice to Grey, 11 February 1915, 16698/13659/350.

94. *FRUS* 1915, Supplement: The World War, Document 143, Bernstorff to Bryan, 15 February 1915, pp. 104–105.

95. *FRUS* 1915, Supplement: The World War, Document 154, Page to Bryan, 17 February 1915, p. 111.

96. Asquith was at the lunch when Grey suggested the deal, but did not mention it in his correspondence with Venetia Stanley; *Letters to Venetia Stanley*, Asquith to Stanley, 17 February 1915, no. 310, pp. 434–435. For the Cabinet position see BLO, Harcourt MS. Eng. c. 8270, 18 February 1915.

97. *FRUS* 1915, Supplement: The World War, Document 155, Bryan to Page, 19 February 1915, pp. 111–112.

98. TNA, FO 372/761, 'Telegram Received at the American Embassy', 20 February 1915, 21033/13659/350.

99. TNA, FO 372/761, 'Telegram Received at the American Embassy', 20 February 1915, 21033/13659/350.

100. TNA, FO 372/761, Hurst Minute, 22 February 1915, 21033/13659/350.
101. TNA, FO 800/85/35, Spring-Rice to Grey, 26 February 1915, ff. 107–113.
102. TNA, FO 800/90/60, Hankey to Drummond, 25 February 1915, ff. 176–179.
103. TNA, FO 800/95/7, Nicolson to Grey, 24 February 1915, ff. 23–26; TNA, FO 372/761, Hurst Minute, 22 February 1915, 21033/13659/350.
104. *FRUS* 1915, Supplement: The World War, Documents 170 and 175, Gerard to Bryan, 24 & 27 February 1915, pp. 123, 126.
105. TNA, FO 372/761, Hurst Minute, 22 February 1915, 21033/13659/350.
106. TNA, FO 372/761, Stewart Minute, 22 February 1915, 21033/13659/350.
107. TNA, FO 800/105/29, Balfour to Grey, n.d. [February 1915], ff. 98–104.
108. TNA, FO 372/761, 'Draft of a Possible Reply ...', 21033/13659/350.
109. TNA, FO 372/761, Grey to Spring-Rice, 28 February 1915, 23637/13659/350.
110. TNA, FO 382/185, 'German Blockade and British Reprisals', 23815/22076/1118.
111. *FRUS* 1915, Supplement: The World War, Document 183, Gerard to Bryan, 1 March 1915, pp. 129–130.
112. *FRUS* 1915, Supplement: The World War, Document 185, Gerard to Bryan, 4 March 1915, p. 132.
113. TNA, FO 382/185, Stewart Note, 25327/22076/1118.
114. TNA, FO 372/761, 'Memorandum Handed to Mr Page, 15 March 1915', 21033/13659/350.
115. TNA, FO 800/110/133, Grey to Roosevelt, 13 March 1915, ff. 473–475.
116. TNA, CAB 24/72/51, First Interim Report from the Committee of Enquiry into Breaches of the Laws of War, pp. 90–93.
117. TNA, CAB 24/85/6, Second Interim Report from the Committee of Enquiry into Breaches of the Laws of War, pp. 316–321.

CHAPTER 12

Conclusion

> In so far as the progress of humanity consists in inventing new methods of warfare I would stop it to-morrow if I could, and this Conference cannot set itself better work than to stop it so far as it can be stopped. I believe it can be stopped in the matter of submarines if we all decide to do so.[1]

This book opened with a quote from an address by a British delegate, Charles Ottley, to the Second Hague Peace Conference. The quote above comes from a speech made fifteen years later by Arthur Balfour when at another major gathering, the Washington Naval Conference. The two men effectively made the same argument: that, for the good of humanity, limitations should be placed on the use of military technology at sea. What had changed was the technology; over the course of the fifteen years between the two meetings the mine had been replaced by the submarine as the exemplar of barbarity at sea. The idea of including mines in the discussions at the Washington Conference appears to have never even been considered. The First World War had shifted perspectives on what was acceptable behaviour for belligerents and mines had gone from being infernal machines outside the scope of civilised conflict, to accepted weapons of war.

By the time Balfour made his speech in Washington in 1922 mining had become an acknowledged part of naval warfare. The Royal Navy had a developed mining service and was looking to build a number of new minelayers. This acceptance meant that the subject lost the contested position which made it of such interest in the decade following

© The Author(s) 2018
R. Dunley, *Britain and the Mine, 1900–1915*,
https://doi.org/10.1007/978-3-319-72820-9_12

297

the Russo-Japanese War. It was precisely because mining was not only an extremely effective weapon but also morally, culturally and legally problematic that makes the area so fruitful to explore. Ultimately the subject under consideration is the basic question of what type of war Britain intended to fight in the decade before the First World War, and how this changed over the first year of the conflict. The issue was one which was shaped by the overlapping themes of strategy, culture and international law. Mining was, due to its contested position, located at the centre of this and as such the study of it goes beyond the examination of a technology and sheds light on the people behind the machines.

The Royal Navy had undoubtedly been shocked by the extraordinary success of mining in the first months of the Russo-Japanese War. The initial reaction was extremely negative, but within a short space of time the Admiralty came to embrace the technology as a solution to strategic issues around the blockade. For a period the mine barrage proposed by Charles Ottley appeared to resolve problems in planning for both the military and economic blockade of Germany. The position of mining within British strategy over the following nine years fluctuated and is frequently difficult to assess from the limited archival evidence we have remaining. What does come through very clearly is the extent to which the question of blockade, with which mining was inextricably linked, dominated the strategic debate. The question of how to control the Heligoland debouch lay at the heart of British naval policy. Achieving this was seen as essential to defensive measures from the protection against invasion through to the limitation of the threat from submarines. It was widely accepted to be at the heart of any programme of economic warfare against Germany, and was an essential prerequisite to all forms of offensive campaign on either side of the Jutland peninsula. Mining was rarely the first option considered by British planners in this period; the cultural opposition to the technology was simply too strong. It did, however, constantly recur in British naval planning, for the simple reason that it appeared to offer solutions to otherwise insurmountable problems around the blockade.

For most of this period it is impossible to reconstruct a complete vision of British naval strategy, if one ever existed. It is certainly very difficult to see how many of the pieces of the jigsaw that we do have fit into any coherent scheme of grand strategy for war against Germany. Yet, in spite of this, using mining as a prism through which to look at British naval strategy it is difficult not to be struck by the consistency within it.

In early 1915 there were, within the leadership of the Admiralty, two competing views on how to conduct war with Germany. Both relied upon closing down the Heligoland debouch, one through minefields close into the German coast supported by the action of the flotilla, the other through a larger mine barrage laid further out. The former looked at the possibility of combined operations on the German North Sea coast, and both viewed entrance into the Baltic as the end goal. The above description of Churchill's and Fisher's respective schemes could equally be used to describe the strategic options that were discussed during the Moroccan Crisis of 1905. The mine barrage which Fisher began to lay in May 1915 was slightly further out than that proposed by Ottley a decade earlier, but the rationale remained identical. Considerable focus has been placed within the recent historiography on the economic warfare strategy and mining was seen as having an important role in this throughout the period. It is, however, worth noting that mining was rarely solely viewed through this lens. The tendency of historians to entirely separate strategies for economic warfare from those of littoral operations or sea control was rarely paralleled in the thoughts of contemporary officers. Mining, and other blockade tools, were seen as facilitating multiple strategies which could then be taken forward as circumstances allowed. The extent to which this reflected a flexibility of thought as opposed to a lack of the same, is a matter which may be debated.

These strategic developments ran in parallel to a very different reaction to the emergence of mining as a major naval technology. Public and political response to the widespread use of mines in the Russo-Japanese War drove the concerted British attempt to severely curtail the use of the weapon under international law. This attempt largely failed but the sentiments that drove it continued to dominate wider British reaction to the technology. The situation continued into the war, when German mining immediately bought strong condemnation from British public, politicians and naval officers. The response formed the basis of some of the first British protests about breaches of international law and helped fuel the view that the country was fighting a barbaric enemy. This in turn facilitated the responses, justified in terms of retaliation, that began to close down neutral access to the seas. In doing so mining began the escalatory cycle which saw the belligerents on both sides erode the rights of neutrals at sea. This was a hugely important process in the history of the First World War more generally, and the crucial role played by mining in its early stages has been almost entirely ignored.

More generally this exceptionally strong reaction by the British politicians and public opened up a huge gulf between the publicly stated attitudes towards mines, and the internal position of the British government, driven by strategic necessity. Nowhere does this come out more clearly than in the decision by the Liberal Cabinet in September 1914 to lay a minefield in order to interrupt neutral trade flowing into neutral ports. This step, and the wider context of the gap between the idealistic discussion of arms control and the pragmatic realities of strategy, offers particular insight into British attitudes towards international law. The question of how the British viewed international law, particularly with reference to maritime rights, has become a contested issue within the historiography. Traditional opinion as espoused by John Coogan, and more recently Nicholas Lambert, has suggested that Britain, and particularly the Royal Navy, largely disregarded international law.[2] This has been recently challenged by scholars such as Alan Anderson, and most notably Isabel Hull.[3] Hull in particular uses what she sees as Britain's innate law-abiding nature as a counterpoint to her analysis of Wilhelmine Germany. The picture she paints of Germany is of a society with a black-and-white view of law. Its terms were frequently abided by, but when it was viewed as necessary to breach them this would remove all restrictions on military commanders. It is evident from examining the issue of mining that British attitudes towards the laws of war were more contested than Hull acknowledges. Throughout most of the prewar period Britain secretly planned to use mines in the precise fashion that they objected to so strongly in public. It is apparent that the Royal Navy was happy to break even the very limited agreement reached at The Hague. The rationale behind this is clear. The British officer corps and political elite were willing to exploit the grey areas within international law in order to further their strategic goals, but were unwilling to ever be caught directly breaking it. Mining, partly due to the nature of the weapon, and partly as a result of the failures of the Hague Convention, offered great scope for exploiting these grey areas. To adopt a modern phrase, the use of mines invariably came with an element of "plausible deniability". This is not to say that policymakers were unaware that the schemes they were proposing, and in some cases eventually adopted, were illegal. Instead it provided the grey area in which they could be confident that they would not be caught doing anything that could be proved to be illegal. During the war the perceptions of what was legal or otherwise changed with remarkable speed.

On the outbreak of war the British government sincerely believed the small-scale German minelaying to be entirely outside the bounds of accepted warfare. Within a year Britain was laying numerous much larger fields both off its own coasts, and in the southern North Sea. Initial British mining was publicly justified through the language of reprisal for German action. This rapidly disappeared and by spring 1915 the question of its legality was never even discussed. Ultimately the legal debates responded to and drew from the actions on the battlefield, and in both spheres the submarine began to loom large as the weapon of the moment.

British reaction to mining, both in terms of strategy and international law, was heavily influenced by the society's culture and the organisational culture of the Royal Navy more specifically. British national identity in this period was inextricably connected to the sea. The country's interests were largely perceived to be maritime in nature and the Royal Navy was seen, and saw itself, as the guardian of those interests. Mine warfare struck a particular chord in British society because it was believed to threaten these core interests and do so in a way that could not be responded to in kind. There is no doubt that this reaction was sincere and informed British decision-making throughout the period. Its strength is remarkable, particularly when viewed from the perspective of a twenty-first-century society with virtually no engagement with defence issues. That what appears in many regards to be a relatively insignificant technological development could excite such a response is testament to the importance of these connections between the navy and the nation at the beginning of the twentieth century.

The opprobrium with which mines were held within British society was mirrored by the reaction within the Royal Navy. The service believed that mines represented the antithesis of everything that it stood for. They appeared to be a direct challenge in material form to the navy's organisational culture. Thus it is all the more remarkable that the organisation was willing to see past this deep-seated cultural rejection of mining and embrace the technology. This is testament to the open-minded and pragmatic attitude adopted by the Admiralty in this period. The Edwardian Admiralty has, in the past, been accused by some historians of being technologically reactionary, whilst others have suggested that it was obsessively focused on materiel. The example of mining supports neither contention. The Admiralty under Fisher recognised and looked to exploit the capabilities of the technology to resolve a specific strategic issue. Once mining was institutionalised it then went on to be considered in a more open fashion and it slowly began to be integrated into the fleet.

This is not to suggest that the ideological opposition to mining disappeared. It is apparent that even those who drove the Royal Navy's adoption of mining did so in spite of their dislike of the technology, and this attitude would persist well into the war. Many within the service continued to oppose all use of mines, believing them to be fundamentally antithetical to the navy's aims. In many respects it would take a shift in the very basic concept of what the Royal Navy was designed to achieve before these attitudes began to change. It was only when German minelaying and, in particular, U-boat activity forced the navy to come to terms with the fact that it would never exercise the idealised form of sea control it had once imagined, that attitudes towards the mine could change. If your aim was to control the entire sea up to the enemy's coast, then there was little scope for mining. Once, however, this attitude gave way to a more pragmatic analysis, that the goal should be to facilitate British use of the sea, and deny the same to the Germans, then mining would become culturally accepted. Some officers, most notably Fisher, appear to have embraced this ideology prior to the war, but for most, it was only the development of the U-boat threat that forced this change of mindset.

When Balfour spoke to the Washington Conference in 1922 the question of mining was not up for discussion, and few British naval officers would have wished it to be. The attitude of the service and the country more generally towards mines had changed. The antipathy previously felt gave way to indifference and acceptance. The irony was that it took the mine, and especially the submarine, to fundamentally challenge the Royal Navy in order to shift the very concept of sea power in the minds of those seeking to exercise it. Within this new sense of how to exert power in the maritime sphere the mine ceased to merely represent a challenge, and came to also offer solutions; nowhere more so than in response to the submarine itself. It was not simply that the submarine had replaced the mine as the antithesis of British sea power; it was that the submarine and the mine had themselves shifted those very notions of sea power, leaving the mine as an accepted weapon of war.

NOTES

1. The National Archives (TNA), FO 371/7246, 'Washington Conference on the Limitation of Armaments', p. 18, A447/2/45.
2. John Coogan, *The End of Neutrality: The United States, Britain and Maritime Rights, 1899–1915* (Ithaca: Cornell University Press, 1981); Nicholas Lambert, *Planning Armageddon: British Economic Warfare and the First World War* (Cambridge, MA: Harvard University Press, 2012).
3. Alan M. Anderson, 'The Laws of War and Naval Strategy in Great Britain and the United States: 1899–1909' (Unpublished PhD thesis, King's College, London, 2016); Isabel V. Hull, *A Scrap of Paper: Making and Breaking International Law During the Great War* (Ithaca: Cornell University Press, 2014).

ARCHIVAL SOURCES

PRIMARY SOURCES

Official State Papers

The National Archives (TNA), Kew
Admiralty Papers (ADM)
Cabinet Papers (CAB)
Colonial Office Papers (CO)
Committee of Imperial Defence Papers (CAB)
Foreign Office Papers (FO)
Ministry of Transport Papers (MT)
Ministry of Supply Papers (SUPP)
Treasury Papers (T)
War Office Papers (WO)

The Brass Foundry, National Maritime Museum (NMM BF)
Ships' Covers (Royal Navy Controller's Department Papers) (SC)

The United States National Archives and Records Administration (NARA), Washington DC
General Records of the Department of the Navy (Record Group 80)

United States Naval War College (NWC)
Intelligence and Technical Archives (Record Group 8)

© The Editor(s) (if applicable) and The Author(s) 2018   305
R. Dunley, *Britain and the Mine, 1900–1915*,
https://doi.org/10.1007/978-3-319-72820-9

306 ARCHIVAL SOURCES

United Kingdom Hydrographic Office, Taunton
Admiralty Hydrographic Department Minute Books
Admiralty Hydrographic Department Special Minute Books
Original Documents (OD Series)

Private Papers

Bodleian Library, Oxford
Herbert Asquith Papers
Eyre Crowe Papers
Lewis Harcourt Papers
William Palmer, Second Earl of Selborne Papers

British Library (BL)
Hugh Oakeley Arnold-Forster Papers
Arthur J. Balfour Papers
Henry Campbell-Bannerman Papers
George Sydenham Clarke Papers
John R. Jellicoe Papers
Charles Hobhouse Papers

Cadbury Research Library, University of Birmingham (CRL)
Austen Chamberlain Papers

Churchill College Archives Centre (CAC)
Winston Churchill (Chartwell) Papers
Reginald Brett, Second Viscount Esher Papers
John Fisher Papers

Courtauld Book Library (CBL)
Arthur Lee (Lee of Fareham) Papers

Guildhall Library (GL)
Lloyds of London Papers

Imperial War Museum
Prince Louis of Battenberg Papers
Dudley de Chair Papers
Erskine Childers Papers
Philip Dumas Papers
Liddell-Hart Centre for Military Archives, King's College, London (LHCMA)
Julian Corbett Papers

The National Archives, Kew
Edward Grey Papers (FO 800)

ARCHIVAL SOURCES 307

Frank Lascelles Papers (FO 800)
William Malkin Papers (FO 800)
Ernest Satow Papers (PRO 30/33)

National Maritime Museum (NMM)
George Ballard Papers
Julian Corbett Papers
Bernard Currey Papers
Tristan Dannreuther Papers
William May Papers
Gerard Noel Papers
Henry Oliver Papers
William Pakenham Papers
Herbert Richmond Papers
Edmond Slade Papers

National Museum of the Royal Navy (NMRN)
Thomas Crease Papers
John Fisher Papers
Edward Marjoribanks, Second Baron Tweedmouth Papers

National Museum of the Royal Navy, Submarine Museum (NMRN SM)
Forster Arnold Forster Papers

School of Oriental and African Studies (SOAS)
China Association Papers

United States Library of Congress, Washington DC
Charles S. Sperry Papers

INDEX

A

Amphion, 228, 267–268
Andromache, 177, 179, 198
Angora, 245
Antwerp, 230, 234, 276
Apollo, 177, 179, 198
Arnold-Forster, Commander Forster
  Delafield, 227, 245–246, 250,
  252
Asahi, 54
Asquith, Herbert, 206–207, 228,
  230–233, 236–237, 238, 240,
  243, 247, 276, 277–278, 284
Assistant Director of Torpedoes
  (ADT), 31, 56–57, 74, 113, 119,
  142, 143, 144–145, 213, 217,
  233
Audacious, 2, 241, 278, 284, 289

B

Bacon, Admiral Sir Reginald, 27, 36,
  38–39, 146, 155
Baddeley, Vincent, 181

Balfour, Arthur, 38, 61, 81, 99–104,
  151–154, 157, 174, 243, 247,
  262, 287–288, 297, 302
Ballard committee, 171–174, 176–178
Ballard, Rear-Admiral Sir George,
  135, 155, 170, 173, 202–206,
  208–212, 217, 225, 233–234.
  See also Ballard committee
Baltic, 9, 133, 136–138, 158, 172,
  173, 178, 186, 209, 214,
  239–241, 243–245, 247–248,
  277, 299
Baltic Project (Fisher's, 1914–15),
  241, 244–245, 247–248, 257,
  299
Barclay, Colville, 270–271
Barclay, Sir Thomas, 83, 105
Battenberg, Admiral of the Fleet
  Prince Louis of, 40, 46, 64–65,
  99–101, 109, 183, 208, 209,
  212, 226, 233, 238, 242, 270,
  278
Bayly, Vice-Admiral Sir Lewis, 239
Beatty, Vice-Admiral Sir David, 239

© The Editor(s) (if applicable) and The Author(s) 2018   309
R. Dunley, *Britain and the Mine, 1900–1915*,
https://doi.org/10.1007/978-3-319-72820-9

310 INDEX

Beresford, Admiral Lord Charles, 15, 29, 61, 66, 173, 175–176, 178, 183–186
Berlin, 278
Bernstorff, Johan von, 285
Bethell, Admiral Sir Alexander, 27, 65, 144, 145, 155
Biarritz, 245, 252
Board of Trade, 86, 89–90, 105
Bonham, Captain Thomas, 210, 219
Borkum, 239, 248, 253, 255
Bridge, Admiral Sir Cyprian, 32, 80
Bridgeman, Admiral Sir Francis, 183–184
Briggs, Admiral Charles, 37, 144–145, 155
Brock, Rear-Admiral Osmond de, 185
Bryan, William, 229, 270, 280, 285–286
Bülow, Prince Bernhard von, 133
Butterfield & Swire, 87, 89

C
Cabinet (British), 5, 109, 196–197, 228–233, 235–238, 247, 270–271, 274–275, 276–277, 277–278, 279, 281–282, 285, 300–301
Callaghan, Admiral Sir George, 185–186, 201–202, 204–205, 209–210
Campbell-Bannerman, Sir Henry, 77, 111, 120, 174–175
Campbell, Sir Francis, 86, 118
Captain in Charge of Minelayers, 153–154, 176–177, 187–188, 199, 209–210, 213–214, 217–220
Cawdor, 3rd Earl (Frederick Campbell), 102–103
Chamberlain, Austen, 98, 142–144
Channel Fleet, 134–135, 148, 154–155, 168, 178, 183

Charlton, Rear-Admiral Edward, 198, 237
Chatterton (Orpen), Captain Herbert. *See* Orpen, Captain Herbert
Chief of the (Admiralty) War Staff, 209–210, 213–214, 225–226, 239–240
China Association, 87–90
China Merchants' Steam Navigation Co., 89–90
Chinese Engineering and Mining Co., 86–87
Choate, Joseph, 123
Churchill, Winston, 15, 205, 207, 209, 212, 217, 226–227, 228–229, 230–269, 265, 267–268, 269, 271–272, 274–275, 276–277, 279, 299
Clarke, Sir George, 102, 103–105, 107–108, 137, 139
Clerk, George, 270
Cobbe, Captain Mervyn, 214–215, 218–220, 225–226, 252, 256
Collier's Weekly, 77
Commander, Offensive Mining Service. *See* Captain in Charge of Minelayers
Committee of Enquiry into Breaches of the Law of War, 288
Committee of Imperial Defence (C.I.D.), 65, 98, 101–103, 106, 137, 139, 141–142, 153, 206–207, 247–248
Committee on Designs, 54
Corbett, Sir Julian, 12, 58, 62, 135, 149, 244
Crease, Captain Thomas, 155, 246
Crowe, Sir Eyre, 105–107, 107–108, 111, 119–120, 196, 197, 275, 279–282
Currey, Vice-Admiral Bernard, 176, 185
Custance, Admiral Sir Reginald, 33–34

INDEX 311

D

Daily Chronicle, 75–76, 84
Daily Express, 79, 84
Daily Telegraph, 74, 76–77
Dalny, 97
Dannreuther, Captain Tristan, 199, 213
Davidson, Sir (William) Edward, 98, 105, 107, 282
Davis, Colonel Francis, 105
De Chair, Admiral Dudley, 185
Declaration of London, 231. *See also* London Naval Conference
British adherence to, 114, 268–269
Defiance, 154
Denmark, 149, 167, 209, 243, 245
Desart Committee. *See* Trading with the Enemy (Desart) Sub-Committee
Desart, 5th Earl (Hamilton Cuffe), 105, 120, 206
Director of Intelligence Division (DID), 226
Director of Naval Intelligence (DNI), 1, 32, 35, 40, 46, 64–65, 99, 101–102, 107, 135, 137, 139, 145, 147, 151, 169, 176, 184
Director of Naval Ordnance (DNO), 25, 30, 31, 35, 64, 144–145, 169, 187
Director of Operations Division (DOD), 202–203, 208, 225, 227, 272
Dogger Bank, Battle of, 251
Dogger Bank Incident, 15, 62, 136
Drury, Admiral Sir Charles, 154
Dublin Evening Telegraph, 78
Dumas, Captain Philip, 217, 226, 233–234, 237–238, 245, 252

E

Elbe, 136, 137, 146, 148–150, 172, 178, 227, 243

English Channel, 63, 81, 106, 140, 171, 214, 218, 226, 231, 232–233, 250, 252, 270, 277, 279, 281
Esher, 2nd Viscount (Reginald Brett), 107, 108
Excellent, 154
Eyres, Admiral Cresswell, 46

F

Fauchille, Paul, 195
Findlay, Mansfedlt, 196
Finlay, Sir Robert, 98
Fisher, Admiral of the Fleet, 1st Baron (John), 26, 34, 38–39, 65–66, 98–99, 102–103, 137, 139–142, 144–148, 154, 156–158, 166, 173, 175, 177, 178, 183, 185–188, 212, 219, 234, 238–242, 244, 278, 302
early interest in mining, 26–27, 29, 31
position at First Hague Conference, 34–35
strategic ideas, 1904–1910, 139–142, 151–154, 157–158, 169–171, 187, 198
strategic ideas, 1914–1915, 240–241, 244–245, 246–248, 250–252, 253–258, 278, 279, 299
support for mining, 1914–1915, 241, 244–250, 252–256
views on Second Hague Conference and international law, 98–99, 102–103, 108–109, 123, 174
Foreign Office, 196, 268, 284
attitude towards international law, 107, 280–283
attitude towards War Zones and Military Areas (1914–1915), 276, 279–283

312 INDEX

First Hague Conference, 34
response to German mining (1914–
1915), 268–271, 273–275,
286–288
Russo-Japanese War, 56, 84–86,
88–90, 97
Second Hague Conference, 98,
104–105, 107, 109–110, 118
Third Hague Conference, 196–197
France, 25, 34, 45, 62, 63, 80, 82,
106, 114, 121, 133–135, 145,
146, 148, 149, 155, 157, 158,
165, 167, 170, 172, 182, 207,
230, 287
Fry, Sir Edward, 105, 107, 110–111,
113–115, 117, 119, 121

G
Gamble, Admiral Douglas, 34,
184–185
George, David Lloyd, 90, 207
Gerard, James, 286, 287
German Fleet, 133, 136–137, 148,
178, 179, 181, 182, 201, 204,
235, 239, 243, 247, 254, 257
Germany, 13, 45, 62, 82, 106,
132–137, 139–141, 145–149,
155, 157, 165, 167, 170–172,
178, 179, 181, 182, 200–204,
206–211, 217, 219, 225–230,
239, 243, 244, 248, 253, 254,
257, 269, 272, 275–277, 280,
283–286, 288, 298–300
laying of mines (1914–1915), 229,
230, 233, 244, 268–273,
275–277, 278, 279, 281–289
position at Second Hague
Conference, 110, 112–121,
123, 124, 193
Goeben, 238
Grand Fleet, 227, 230, 237, 243, 245,
252, 254, 278

Greene, Sir Graham, 196, 269, 273,
274, 276
Grey, Sir Edward, 107, 110, 111, 114,
117, 119–121, 196, 229, 268,
269, 271, 274, 275, 279, 282,
285, 288

H
Hague, First Peace Conference
(1899), 3, 33
Hague, Second Peace Conference
(1907), 1, 3, 73, 82, 97, 131,
132, 139, 153, 154, 157, 169,
175–177, 182, 193–195, 197,
203, 206, 209–211, 228, 229,
232, 253, 270, 271, 273, 275,
280, 286, 289, 297, 300
British delegation, 107–108,
110–111
British planning for, 103–111
calling of, 101, 103
discussion of mining at, 112–119
reaction to, 118, 121–124
Hague, Third Peace Conference
(1915), 195–197
Hall, Captain William H., 14, 30–32
Halsbury, 1st Earl (Hardinge Stanley
Giffard), 98
Hamburg, 203, 229, 276
Hankey, Colonel Maurice, 170,
247–248, 286
Harcourt, Lewis, 228, 230, 235, 274
Hardinge, 1st Baron (Charles), 118
Harwich Force, 254
Hatsuse, 51–55, 58, 60, 61, 63,
76–77, 78–79
Heligoland, 242, 249
Heligoland Bight, 137, 147, 152, 167,
174, 178, 179, 205, 226–228,
232, 235–237, 241, 243, 247,
248, 250, 251, 253–256, 273,
298, 299

INDEX 313

Heneage, Captain Algernon, 168, 187, 199–201, 213–215
High Seas Fleet. *See* German Fleet
Hobhouse, Sir Charles, 235 –236, 274
Hogue, 89
Holland, Erskine, 80, 195
Holstein, Friedrich von, 133
Home Fleet, 176, 178, 183, 185, 198, 201, 213–214
Hood, Admiral, 1st Baron (Arthur), 28
Hood, Rear-Admiral Horace, 253
Hopkins, L.C., 87
Horsey, Admiral Algernon de, 79–80
Hoskins, Admiral Sir Anthony, 29–30
House of Commons, 81, 267
Howard, Sir Henry, 107
Howell, W.J., 105
Hozier, Henry, 84
Hsieh-Ho, 90
Hurst, Cecil, 105, 196, 274, 275, 286–287
Hutchison, Rear-Admiral John, 47, 53
Hydrographer, 136, 172–173, 178, 210, 244, 279

I
Inglefield, Admiral Frederick, 155
Inglefield, Captain Edward, 181
Institut de Droit International, 82, 197
  initial discussions on mining, 82–83
  Oxford Manual of Naval War, 195–196
  reaction to the Second Hague Conference, 193–195
Inter-Departmental Committee on the Hague Conference, 105–108, 120–121
International Law Association, 82–83
Invincible, 54, 273
Iphigenia, 168–169, 179, 185

Izvolsky, Alexander, 123

J
Jackson, Admiral Sir Henry, 27, 31, 34–39, 145, 154, 168, 209–210, 217, 225, 258
Jackson, Captain Thomas, 47, 53, 63
Jade, 137, 146
Japan, 40, 45–66, 73–85, 89, 90, 107, 113–114, 137
Japanese Fleet, 45–66, 100, 150
Jardine Matheson & Co., 87
Jellicoe, Admiral Sir John, 169, 187, 227, 230, 232, 238, 240–241, 246, 249–255, 257, 279

K
Kane, Admiral Henry, 31
Kashing, 86
Kebedgy, Michel, 82, 194
Kerr, Admiral of the Fleet Lord Walter, 29, 35, 38, 40, 46, 56, 62, 65, 97–98, 136–137
Keyes, Commodore Roger, 15, 258
Kiel Canal, 133, 136–138, 157, 172–173, 178, 181, 239, 243–244, 247, 251
King
  Edward VII, 62, 109, 123
  George V, 230, 238
King-Hall, Admiral Herbert, 180, 181
Kitchener, Field Marshal, 1st Earl (Horatio), 2, 230, 235–237
Königin Luise, 228, 267

L
Langley, Walter, 86
Lansdowne, 5th Marquess (Henry Petty-Fitzmaurice), 98
Latona, 169, 179, 180

314 INDEX

Lawrence, Reverend Thomas J, 63, 70, 122–123
Lee, Arthur, 109, 183
Leval, Gaston de, 82
Leveson, Rear-Admiral Arthur, 225, 227, 272
Little, Henry, 85
Lloyd-George, David, 90, 207
Lloyds of London, 84–85, 91, 181, 271
Loch Ewe Conference (1914), 227–228, 239, 242
London Naval Conference, 193, 195, 268

M
MacDonald, Sir Claude, 47, 54, 85
Macdonnell, Sir John, 105
Mahan, Admiral Alfred, 77
Maiko Maru, 89
Mainz, 273
Makarov, Vice-Admiral Stepan, 50–51, 75–76
Malkin, William, 286
Manchester Guardian, 78–80, 122
Marschall von Bieberstein, Adolf, 117, 119, 123
Martitz, Professor Ferdinand von, 83
Maxse, Ernest, 272
May, Admiral of the Fleet Sir William, 26, 31–32, 40, 106, 108–109, 178, 198
Maycock, Willoughby, 104, 108
Mediterranean Fleet, 34, 38
Mine
  Carbonit, 216–217, 219, 234
  design of, 36–37, 140–141, 144, 213–220, 252–253
  Elia, 36, 38, 215, 234, 252
  firing pistol, Heneage, 215–220, 252, 256

firing pistol, Hertz horn, 50, 215–216. *See also* Mine, Carbonit
firing pistol, Quicke-Scarff, 140, 214, 215–216
Mine carriers, 167–170, 179–180, 188
Minefields.
See also Operations Q, AZ, BY and CY
  Amrum Bank, 249
  English Channel, 232–233, 250, 253
  Heligoland Bight, 226–228, 232, 235–237, 241, 243, 248, 253–256
Minefields, proposed pre war
  English Channel, 208–209, 218
  Heligoland Bight, 138
Minelayers, 38, 50, 145, 151, 156, 166–169, 171, 175–177, 179–181, 183, 185–188, 198–200, 202, 204, 208–210, 213, 216–217, 220, 228, 235, 245, 246, 248–249, 251, 254–257, 297
  pre-war conversion of, 155–156, 168–170, 176–177
  wartime conversions, 245–246, 251, 255–257
Minelaying
  German, 13, 258, 271, 274, 275, 277, 284, 289, 301, 302
Mines, controlled, 24–26, 32, 52, 144, 194, 212
Mines, countermining, 25–26, 30–31, 37, 65
Mines, cultural objections to, 14–18, 25, 30–33, 59–64, 99–101, 182, 225–228, 231, 233, 235–236, 241, 250–252, 258
Mines, legality of use of, 62–63, 79–82, 84, 97–124, 137–139, 151–153, 167, 173–174,

193–198, 203–204, 210–212, 228–232, 235, 244, 268–289
Mines, morality of, 59–61, 74–76, 78–80, 101–102, 117–119, 121–123, 151–153, 173–174, 228, 267–268
Mines, orders for, 141–144, 146–147, 157, 176–177, 234
Mines, tactical use of, 38–39, 180, 182, 185–188, 199–200
Mining Committee (1908), 185–187
Moore, Rear-Admiral Archibald (A.G.H.W.), 185–186

N
Naval Intelligence Department (NID), 46, 62, 136, 171–172, 173, 181
Naval strategy, blockade, 6, 25, 133–139, 148–150, 154–159, 171–174, 178–179, 198–199, 201–212, 228–232, 239–241, 243–244, 246–252, 279
Naval stratgey, mine barrage, 28–29, 35, 138–139, 146–147, 150–154, 157–159, 167, 173–174, 203–206, 208–212, 226–227, 231–235, 240–241, 244–245, 247–252, 254–257
Neutral trade, 1, 3, 12, 60, 79–87, 90–91, 97–107, 116–118, 120–121, 122, 135, 138–139, 147–149, 152–154, 171–174, 194–195, 203, 206–208, 211–212, 225–226, 228–236, 240–241, 267–289
New York Sun, 77
New Zealand, 273
Nicholson, Captain William, 106
Noel, Admiral of the Fleet Sir Gerard, 32, 46–47, 62, 85, 87–88

North of England Protection and Indemnity Association, 90
North Sea, 133, 135–138, 147–148, 157–158, 171, 173, 178–179, 186, 201–202, 206–210, 214, 225, 227, 229–230, 239–240, 244–245, 246–251, 253–257, 268–270
war zones and military areas, 273–276, 279–285

O
Oliver, Rear-Admiral Sir Henry, 155, 156, 185–186, 226, 238, 246, 249–250, 256
Ommanney, Rear-Admiral Robert, 252
Operation AZ, 256
Operation BY, 256
Operation CY, 256
Operation Q, 254–255
Oppenheimer, Sir Francis, 235
Orpen (Chatterton), Captain Herbert, 154, 166–168, 170, 176, 180, 184, 185, 187, 213
Orpen Committee, 166–167
Orvieto, 245–246, 252, 255, 256
Ottley Committee, 146–148, 157, 167
Ottley, Rear-Admiral Sir Charles, 170–171, 176, 235, 297
attitude towards international law, 108–110
early involvement with mining, 23–24, 26–32
planning as DNI, 101–103, 105, 135, 137–155, 158, 173–174, 298–299
work at the Hague Conference, 1, 106–118

316 INDEX

Oxford Manual of Naval War,
196–197

P

Page, Walter, 268, 271, 285, 288
Pakenham, Admiral Sir William, 47,
49, 51–63
Pall Mall Gazette, 74, 77, 81
Paris, 245, 252
Petropavlovsk, 51–52, 53–55, 58, 60,
63, 74–75, 77, 78–79
Pobyeda, 50, 53
Port Arthur, 45–46, 48–49, 50–52,
56, 58–59, 61, 64, 75, 86, 89,
140, 150, 172, 240, 247
Pound, Captain Dudley, 252
Princess Irene, 245, 249, 252,
255–256
Princess Margaret, 245, 252, 255–256

R

Raids
German, 230, 237, 241, 247, 248
Reay, 11th Lord (Donald James
Mackay), 107, 111, 120, 195
Rhine, 229, 230, 235, 270–271, 272
Ricardo, Rear-Admiral Arthur, 46–47
Richmond, Captain Herbert, 37, 236
Risley, J.S., 105
Rolin, Edouard, 194–195
Rotterdam, 203, 206, 229, 230–231,
235, 269, 270–272, 276–277
Russia, 9, 14, 15, 25–26, 33–35, 38,
40, 45–66, 73–85, 90, 97, 114,
117, 121, 123, 133, 137, 138,
146, 149, 167, 207, 209, 215,
239–240, 243, 247
Russian Baltic Fleet, 48, 51, 62
Russian Pacific Fleet, 46, 48–52

S

Schleswig-Holstein, 243, 254
Scottish Shipmaster's Association, 85
Segrave, Captain John, 107, 118
Selborne, 2nd Earl (William Palmer),
46–47, 63, 97
Shortland, Captain Edward, 89
Siegel, Admiral Rudolf, 110, 114–118,
120
Sir Ernest, Satow, 85, 87, 89, 107,
109, 111, 116–118, 120, 123
Slade, Admiral Sir Edmond, 27, 106,
120, 171, 176, 183–184, 273
Sobralense, 89
Sperry, Rear-Admiral Charles,
112–115, 117, 122
Spithead Confernce (1914), 212, 227
Spring-Rice, Sir Cecil, 284–285, 286
Stanley, Venetia, 228, 230–232, 278
Stead, William Thomas W.T., 109,
117, 122
Stewart, Walter, 280, 288
St James's Gazette, 74, 76, 79
Stockton, Rear-Admiral Charles, 111,
193–194
Sturdee, Vice-Admiral Sir (Frederick)
Doveton, 27, 212, 225–226,
232–233, 236, 238, 270–272,
278
Submarines, 12–13, 16–17, 73, 179,
183, 198, 202, 203, 211, 214,
236
and the Russo-Japanese War, 49,
58, 75
early reaction to, 33–37
German attack on trade, 267,
283–289
threat posed by German, 231, 233,
236, 238, 240–242, 244,
248–253, 258, 277, 278, 282
Sylt, 239, 242–243, 254

T

Thetis, 168, 169, 179, 180, 198
Tientsin, 87
Times, The, 74, 77, 79–81, 109, 117, 118, 121, 122, 268, 280
Tōgō, Admiral Marquis Heihachirō, 50–52, 58, 59, 76, 236, 247
Trading with the Enemy (Desart) Sub-Committee, 206–208
Troubridge, Admiral Sir Ernest, 46, 47, 64
Tryon, Vice Admiral Sir George, 28–30
Tsushima, Battle of, 48, 49, 57, 61
Tudor, Rear-Admiral Frederick, 238, 250
Tweedmouth, 2nd Baron (Edward Marjoribanks), 106, 108, 111, 123
Tyrwhitt, Commodore Reginald, 15, 258

U

U-boats. *See* Submarines
Undaunted, 29
United States, 9, 34, 77, 248, 267
   attitude at the Second Hague Conference, 98, 102, 103, 111–118, 121, 123, 193
   protests at British actions (1914–1915), 230–232, 257, 276
   reaction to mining during the Russo-Japanese War, 79–80, 83, 90, 111
   response to German mining (1914–1915), 268–271, 283–289

V

Vernon, 23, 26–28, 30–32, 35–37, 66, 140, 144, 155, 184, 185, 214–216, 220, 234, 252
Vickers Ltd., 216, 226, 234, 246, 252
Vitgeft, Admiral Wilgelm, 51, 58
Vladivostok, 46, 48, 51, 86

W

Walton Committee. *See* Inter-Departmental Committee on the Hague Conference
Walton, Sir John, 105, 120
War Staff (Admiralty), 202, 205, 209, 218, 227, 239, 246, 277
War zones. *See* war zones and military areas
Warren, Sir Pelham, 87
Washington Naval Conference, 297
Webb, Captain Richard, 272, 277, 281
Wei-Hai-Wei, 86, 88–90
Welch, Joseph, 88
Wellesley, Victor, 280–282, 287
Weser, 137, 146, 150, 181, 227
Whitelock, George, 83
Wilson, Admiral of the Fleet Sir Arthur, 26, 154, 168, 178, 238
   strategic ideas, 1905–1911, 134–135, 148–151, 155–159, 172, 198, 200
   strategic ideas, 1914–1915, 240, 242–243, 247, 249–254, 258

Y

Yashima, 51–55, 58, 60, 61, 63, 76
Yenesei, 56

CPSIA information can be obtained
at www.ICGtesting.com
Printed in the USA
LVOW13*1715090518
576575LV00014B/187/P